We dedicate this book to our parents and
inspirations:

Anne Wright Agnew and Ralph Palmer Agnew and
Esther Weber Minkin and Joseph Louis Minkin,

and to the next generations,

David, Tom, Deborah, Bernardo, Corey, Aviva,
and Daniel who will vigorously create and greatly
enjoy the future of distributed multimedia.

About the Authors

Palmer W. Agnew has provided extensive technical guidance on multimedia, consumer electronics, advanced networking, and other topics, in both industry and academia. Recently a senior technical staff member advising IBM's Multimedia Business Unit, previously he developed design automation software for IBM, designed microcode for terminal controllers, developed microprocessor-based implementations of mainframe architecture, worked with both mainframe and personal computer applications, and is the holder of six patents. Agnew is a graduate of Cornell University with a B.S. in Physics and an M.S. in Applied Mathematics. He is a member of the ACM and the IEEE.

Anne S. Kellerman, a senior manager advising IBM's Multimedia Business Unit, now on leave of absence, has handled special projects focused on multimedia strategies and has managed a large information systems installation. She has also managed several complex technical projects, including the development of architecture for computer and consumer electronics and IBM joint grants to universities, such as UCLA, University of Michigan, Cornell University, and MIT. She has represented IBM in a national K-12 education initiative and has been involved in setting IBM strategies for consumer products and multimedia. She holds five patents. A member of the ACM and the IEEE, Kellerman holds B.S. and M.S. degrees from Georgia Institute of Technology.

As consultants, both authors have worked with college instructors on incorporating multimedia in courses and are coauthors of *Multimedia in the Classroom*, a guide for educators and technologists. Agnew and Kellerman are also adjunct instructors in the graduate school at Binghamton University, part of the State University of New York, and they conduct a distance-learning course given by the New School in New York City. They have traveled widely, learning and teaching about multimedia developments, challenges, social effects, and requirements in business and education.

Preface

'Distributed multimedia has the potential to improve your life by helping you to interact with all media by way of networks and convenient end-user devices that will combine the most useful functions of television sets, telephones, computers, and even game machines. Advances in digital computer technologies are gradually making it practical for you to interact not only with text, graphics, and images, which are traditional computer media, but also with audio and video, which place more severe demands on computers and networks. Advances in digital network technologies, including the Internet and the World Wide Web, allow you to take advantage of all five of these media when communicating with remote users and when interacting with remote data.

In this book we describe the technologies that are making distributed multimedia not only possible but affordable. We describe interactive audio and video applications that will make multimedia attractive and helpful to users. Finally, we outline opportunities, challenges, and risks facing providers of multimedia products and services as today's entertainment, computer, consumer electronics, and telecommunications industries converge into a single digital information industry. We discuss promises that providers are making and clarify how realizing some of these promises can create the reality of a major new industry.

Purpose Why should you read this book? If you are a user who tends to adopt new technologies early, you will see where the industry is going and be able to avoid products that will soon become obsolete. If you are a user who wants to benefit from knowing how things work, you will find out what is inside your boxes and beyond your wall plugs. If you have a technical position in a company that provides particular distributed multimedia products or services, you will see how you and your company fit into the industry, both technically and commercially. If you manage or invest in parts of the information industry, you will gain insights that will help you distinguish reasonable technical proposals from those that amount to perpetual-motion machines and faster-than-light travel. The background knowledge you acquire will help you to recognize proposals for products and services that consumers or businesses will actually want to buy.

Technologies The most important distributed multimedia technologies are inexpensive digital integrated-circuit processor and memory chips fast enough to handle all the media in digital form, inexpensive hard drives with sufficient capacity to store meaningful quantities of all the media, high-capacity fiber-optic cables, and sophisticated circuits that can send media in digital form up and down not only fiber-optic cables but also ordinary television cables, telephones wires, and even power lines.

Applications Users can take advantage of distributed multimedia applications that rely on advanced technologies to ask questions and receive answers more efficiently and effectively than would be possible using merely text, graphics, and images. A user is also likely to find that interactive entertainment is more entertaining than merely receiving audio and video. Distributed multimedia applications allow vigorous competition among providers of telephone service, cable television service, computer networking, and even electric power. They also allow competition among providers of telephones, television sets, computers, and all forms of consumer electronics and entertainment. Individual firms have opportunities to expand into new products and services that are part of the same converged industry, but they risk losing control of existing markets. Governments, as providers of regulations, face conflicting pressures from industries and users to protect existing positions without stifling innovation.

Delivery Networks If differences of opinion make horse races interesting, competing technologies make delivering multimedia fascinating. Local telephone companies have over $300 billion invested in switches and copper twisted-pair local loops designed to carry unique information to and from individual users. However, such telephone lines can carry video only by adding particularly sophisticated circuitry. CATV cable companies have large investments in coaxial cables designed to carry video. Most cable plants, however, have one-way amplifiers that will carry information downstream from a central site to users but will not carry information back upstream. Computer networks are designed for two-way interactivity, but computers and computer networks will require major improvements to send and receive large volumes of isochronous (smooth) audio and video. Both terrestrial broadcasting and satellite broadcasting are in the running as delivery channels for distributed multimedia. Electric power utilities are a dark horse with connections not only to almost every home and business but to almost every room.

Themes   In Chapter 1, we introduce the following unifying themes.

Interacting vigorously with all media is far more effective than passively listening to audio or watching video and the other media.

All media are in the process of converging into a single digital form for storage and transmission, rather than continuing to use different forms, storage, and networks for different media. With distributed multimedia, we will no longer use only audio cassettes, telephone lines, and telephones for audio and only video cassettes, television cables, and television sets for video. Having all media in digital form provides enormous flexibility to combine and distribute the media in creative and effective ways.

Several major industries that deal with separate media are converging into a single industry that deals with all media in digital form. Although this convergence is likely to increase users' choices and decrease users' prices, existing companies within today's industries may not converge or even survive. Another negative aspect of this theme is that distributed multimedia draws inconsistent terminology from many existing industries. In this book , we keep the resulting confusion at bay by continually pointing out ambiguous and conflicting terminology and offering clear definitions.

Results of research into human physiology set numerical limits on acceptable multimedia content. Physiology is as important to distributed multimedia as are computer science and network theory.

The digital forms of text, graphics, image, audio, and video require successively larger storage capacities and speeds in order to be acceptable. For example, you typically read text at 300 bits per second, speak and listen to audio at 64 thousand bits per second, and watch video at more than 1.2 million bits per second. In this book, we provide many sample calculations to tell stories in which the punch lines are such numbers.

Distributed multimedia has genuine potential for improving the quality of lives and the efficiency of businesses because using networks gives more timely access to more interesting and useful information, interacting with information adds significant value, and expressing information in multiple media aids comprehension and enjoyment.

Chapters   After Chapter 1, each chapter discusses one part of distributed multimedia, as the framework figure on the following page shows.

Chapters 2 through 4 discuss technologies that apply to delivery networks, multimedia servers, and end-user devices such as telephones, computers, and television set-top boxes. The figure shows that applications use all three types of technologies and that providers provide applications as well as technologies. Chapter 7 covers trials in which compatible groups of companies provide distributed multimedia technologies and applications to manageable groups of users. The companies use such trials to determine

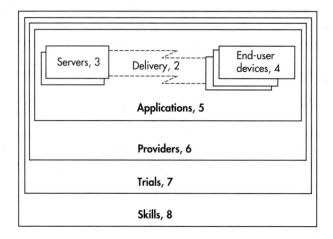

which technologies they can support reliably and which applications they can sell profitably. Chapter 8 discusses skills that you may need in order to participate in distributed multimedia. Like the rest of the book, Chapter 8 provides information that can guide you, whether your primary role is as a user or as a provider of multimedia and whether you are primarily interested in technical or business issues.

Sections   We have organized each chapter around the same set of eight section headings to emphasize the evolutionary nature of distributed multimedia. Better and better functions will become practical for more and more people as prices decrease, as products become easier to use, and as improved infrastructures reach new geographic areas. A chapter's *Background* section gives information that you need in order to understand the chapter's part of distributed multimedia. *Vision for the Next Decade* tells where we expect the chapter's part to be by 2005. *State of the Art* provides a snapshot of where that part happens to be today. *History* illustrates how this state came about and provides cogent examples of past events that you can use to project and comprehend future events. It tells you how fast you can expect the industry to bridge the gap between today's state and the state that we envision existing in 2005. The section called *Differences* provides more details about that gap, and *Trends* looks at what various providers are doing and planning to do in order to bridge the gap. In *Critical Success Factors* and *Summary,* we attempt to distill the major challenges that providers must overcome and the major changes that we expect to take place by 2005. We have used features called *Focus* to set off some details that you may want to skip or scan initially and read in detail later. Focus *interviews* show how real people who work with distributed multimedia feel about what they are doing.

Authors   After designing hardware and software for three decades, we had the opportunity to assemble a large corporation's distributed multimedia strategy. We traveled around the world visiting a wide variety of corporate, governmental, and academic sites in which innovators were inventing, developing, and using distributed multimedia. By employing systematic analyses such as total quality management (TQM), we formed reasonable projections of what such people were likely to develop and use in the next 10 years, attempting to avoid the twin pitfalls of overstating short-term evolutions and understating long-term revolutions. We share the resulting expectations with you in this book. We have accumulated several roomfuls of state-of-the-art multimedia hardware and software and employed them for such practical applications as developing educational materials. We also share the results of this experience, together with decades of experience as early adopters of computers, computer time-sharing terminals, and computer networking. Having taught this book's material in several theoretical and practical courses, we have learned what students and professionals need to know about the subject, and we present it here.

Intended Audience   The following three groups of people will benefit from reading this book.

1. *Knowledgeable people who plan to use or provide distributed multimedia* need more than an introduction to the subject. They need a framework for acquiring future knowledge as the industry progresses. For example, Joe is a retired civil engineer and school teacher who lives in an area slated for a large trial of switched digital video. Joe has been intellectually curious all of his life and wants to know what is behind his local newspaper's headlines about this new technology. As an active financial investor he wonders whether he should invest in multimedia-related stocks. Jeanine is a professor of computer science who knows that most of her students' jobs will depend on developments in the area of distributed multimedia; she wants to give them the best information possible about this field.

2. *People who are actually working in the field of distributed multimedia* need the big picture. Specialists in one area such as content production, Web page creation, or fiber-optic connectors, but who want to gain a general knowledge of the rest of the field, can do so with this book. Among such readers would be the following. Tom sells fiber optic cables and connectors to companies participating in early trials of interactive television. He wants to become knowledgeable about distributed multimedia so he can better serve his customers. Jim is a programmer working as a consultant on a project that involves recommending approaches to multimedia. Bernardo is a doctoral candidate who uses the Internet for his research and who would like to publish electronically his thesis results, which include video. David designs object-oriented systems for telephone companies and others. He needs to know what demands multiple media and interactivity will place on his customers' networks.

3. *College students, primarily in the fields of business and computer science,* can gain valuable exposure to the digital frontier. One example is our former student Mike who writes, "It is really pretty wild to be right in the middle of this multimedia revolution that is happening in downtown New York City." He is applying what he learned in our course to make companies' World Wide Web home pages more dynamic. We encourage students to learn more about distributed multimedia.

Acknowledgments   We want to thank our families, friends, students, and many colleagues around the world who have helped us refine, develop, and test our ideas. We especially want to thank Mike Braun, chairman of the IMA; Lucie Fjeldstad, president of Tektronix Video; and Dr. Frank Moore, Vice President Information Technology at the New School. They were instrumental in making it possible for us to work with and learn about distributed multimedia over many years. We also want to thank our reviewers, particularly Joe Minkin, who both collected massive amounts of information about his local multimedia trial and reviewed many of our drafts, the highly constructive editors, and their reviewers, the more caustic the better. We are also indebted to many colleagues and friends, particularly Tom Kellerman of IBM's Microelectronics Division and Dr. William H. Tetzlaff of IBM Research for their technical expertise and advice.

Owego, N.Y.   P.W.A.
                                                                              A.S.K.
                                                     71621.1506@CompuServe.Com

Contents

Trends 415

Critical Success Factors 430

Summary 431

References 431

CHAPTER 8 Skills 433

Background 433

Vision for the Next Decade 437

State of the Art 437

History 450

List of Tables

List of Figures

List of Focus Sections

Chapter 1

Framework

BACKGROUND

Distributed Multimedia

Multimedia is more than multiple media. As Fig. 1.1 illustrates, multimedia adds interactivity to the combination of text, graphics, images, audio, and video. Adding networks to multimedia produces distributed multimedia, which is the subject of this book.

Distributed multimedia will give you three capabilities that you probably lack today. First, it will enable you to send and receive mail that includes audio and video, as well as text, graphics, and images. Second, it will enable you to communicate with other people by sending and receiving video as well as audio. Third, it will enable you to select from a world of entertainment, educational, and business information that ranges from stored movies and college courses to live sports and news events.

Achieving these three capabilities will amount to adding audio and video media to the functions for which you now use computers, adding video to the functions for which you now use telephones, and adding interactivity to the functions for which you now use television sets. In technical terms, it means you will augment store-and-forward communications (electronic mail, commonly called E-mail) with audio and video, augment real time, streaming communications with bidirectional video (video conference), and augment television reception with interactivity (video on demand or interactive television). Distributed multimedia will thus converge the most desirable capabilities of today's computer, telephone, and television systems.

Today's computer, telephone, and television systems and their networks already perform some distributed multimedia functions. You can use a computer to interact quickly with text and graphics and to interact more slowly with images. That is, you can use a computer to create, store, view, edit, send, and receive these three media sufficiently rapidly to keep your train of thought rolling along reasonably smoothly. You can use a telephone to interact quickly with audio and only a little less quickly with text and images in

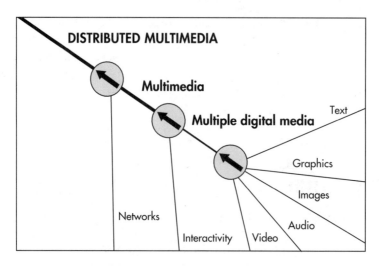

Figure 1.1 Distributed multimedia.

the form of facsimile (fax). You can use television to see video, hear audio, and see incidental text, graphics, and images.

Today's typical computer, telephone, and television systems do not yet have certain functions that are vital for distributed multimedia, however. Most computers do not allow you to record and play back audio or video. Most telephones do not allow you to send and display video. Most televisions provide no more interactivity than merely allowing you to select among a few dozen channels.

Technological improvements are overcoming these deficiencies by converging all five media into a single digital form, storing all media on the same hard drives (hard disks or magnetic disks) and optical storage devices, copying all media without degradation, and transmitting all media on the same networks. As a result, creating distributed multimedia systems by using parts of today's computer, telephone, and television systems is becoming technically and economically practical. As a user, you will be able to create a distributed multimedia system by improving the end-user devices in your home and office, connecting the devices to improved delivery networks, and obtaining access to desirable information content on appropriate servers.

As a provider of distributed multimedia, your most vexing uncertainties concern content. Consumers seem to be more comfortable spending additional money on education and information, but may actually end up paying more for entertainment. Providers can be more confident of profitable sales to businesses. "The most important, most valuable, most sought-after content in the world belongs to corporations and large institutions. It's created and collected every minute, around the world: intellectual property, designs, market intelligence, supply and demand, and customer trends" (Gerstner, 1995). Providers are likely to invest first in multimedia networks for business, where they can be certain of desirable content for networks to carry.

As a user of distributed multimedia, you will have three choices. One choice is to start with a home or office computer, add adapter cards that allow you to record and play back both audio and video, install a high-bandwidth (high-capacity, broadband, or wideband) communications connection that allows you to send and receive these two demanding media as well as the other three media, and subscribe to services that store and retrieve all five media at your command so that you can perform various applications. A second choice is to start with a telephone, replace it with a unit that includes a video camera and a video screen, sign up for a higher-bandwidth connection to improve the video quality, and subscribe to a value-added network service that stores and retrieves video as well as delivers live video to and from other subscribers. The third choice is to start with a television set, equip it to send as well as receive audio and video, connect it to a television cable system equipped with amplifiers that carry information upstream away from you as well as downstream toward you, and sign up for video servers that contain applications and content that you want to see and hear.

The three choices are not mutually exclusive. Eventually, you will be able to provide multimedia capabilities in your home and office by making all three sets of improvements. By the time you can choose to purchase a particular product or service from any of several companies that now think of themselves as being in the computer, telephone, or television industries, these industries will have converged into a single digital information industry. Companies that now consider themselves to be in different industries, such as those in Fig. 1.2, will compete with one another for much of your business.

Devices and companies may not converge, even though media and industries converge. You will be unlikely to converge your end-user devices into one type of device. You will continue to want computer-like devices for concentrated and detailed work such as word processing and spreadsheet applications, telephone-like devices for private conversations and personal viewing, and television-like devices for group and casual use. Moreover, you may not want companies that provide delivery networks, servers, and applications to converge. For example, although costs to providers would surely be lowest if each home or office connects to only a single delivery provider, prices that you pay may be lowest if your home or office connects to several delivery providers that compete with one another. Today, your home proba-

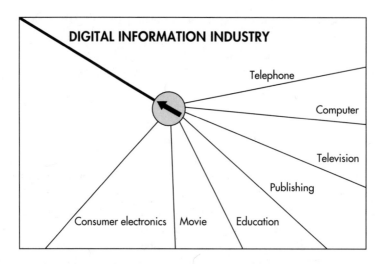

Figure 1.2 Converging digital information industry.

bly has a cable television connection and one or more telephone connections. The companies that provide those connections do not compete, because their services do not overlap. If you had the choice of conversing with friends and computers over the cable connection and requesting video over the telephone connection, the two providers would find that they need to compete to give you the best service at the lowest price. As a user of distributed multimedia, you will be much more interested in whether future services interoperate (work together smoothly) than in whether the companies that own today's services converge or even survive.

If you view yourself as primarily a provider of distributed multimedia, convergence brings you both good news and bad news. The good news is that new products and services are likely to make the converged digital information industry significantly larger than the sum of today's separate industries. Thus, your company will have the opportunity to expand incrementally into new markets as well as expand into existing markets that other companies now dominate. The bad news is that convergence will lower barriers that now prevent other companies from expanding into your company's present markets. A telephone company (telco) may need to compete with a cable (CATV) company to carry a given user's voice conversations, and a CATV company may need to compete with a telco to carry a user's video selections.

The Preface shows the different parts of distributed multimedia that we discuss in subsequent chapters and discusses the common section headings that we employ in all of the chapters of the book. We now continue by discussing interactivity, the five media, and the rest of a framework that will help you understand distributed multimedia as a whole.

Interactivity

Although the name *multimedia* emphasizes using multiple media, the most important feature of multimedia is the ability it affords you to interact with media, both actively controlling what you see and hear and creating your own media. Watching a television program is not an example of using multimedia, even though the program contains all five media, because your degree of interactivity is negligible. Navigating through a large amount of text and a small amount of other media in a CD-ROM encyclopedia is a good example of using stand-alone multimedia. Using a network to interact with vastly larger amounts of remotely located media is a good example of using distributed multimedia. Increasingly important examples of distributed multimedia involve the Internet, which helps millions of computer users interconnect their networks, and the World Wide Web, which helps to extend the Internet beyond text. Creating your own media is more interactive than is using existing content (Auletta and Gilder, 1995), and collaborating with others in the creation of media is still more interactive.

Spectrum of Interactivity   Your degree of interactivity depends on the amount of control you have over what you see and hear, on the speed with which you can exercise that control, and on the extent to which you can send as well as receive information. The following examples illustrate a spectrum of increasing interactivity.

- **Neighbor's radio:** You cannot even turn down the volume.

- **Broadcast television program:** You can change to another channel, mute the sound, or turn the television set off, but you cannot affect the programs on the available channels unless your home is connected to a ratings monitor, in which case your effect is slight and takes years to occur.

- **Movie on a VCR tape:** You can start the videocassette recorder tape whenever you want to see the movie, stop it to get a sandwich, rewind and replay to hear dialog you missed, single step or pause to see details of an interesting scene, or fast forward past boring parts. However, fast forward or rewind can take so long to reach a desired point on the tape that you lose your train of thought, and nothing in the movie helps you to navigate through the content.

■ **Movie on a CD-ROM or suitable laser disc:** You can skip to any desired point in the material in less than one second, without losing your train of thought, but you still get no help in knowing where you want to go.

■ **Hypertext or hypermedia links on a CD-ROM, hard drive, or network:** You can use a mouse to select a button that will link you to what you want to see and hear next. In hypertext, you select one of several *hotwords*, which might be underlined or highlighted, to determine the text that you see next. In hypermedia, you may select any one of several objects on the screen in order to receive information that you want, expressed in media that you prefer. Interactivity is greatest if the entire screen is hot, which means that something useful happens no matter what point you select, if the results of your selection appear in a small fraction of a second, and if you have a wide range of material from which to choose. Variety and speed are often conflicting goals. For example, a hard drive is likely to provide less variety than does a network, but the hard drive is likely to respond significantly more rapidly than the network. A CD-ROM may be intermediate in both variety of content and speed of response.

■ **Virtual reality:** You can change what you see by moving your eyes, turning your head, reaching your hand out into virtual space, or moving some other parts of your body. Sophisticated hardware senses your motions and lets you see and hear the results. Consider the example of an air traffic controller (ATC) talking with the pilot of an airplane flying to the left of the airport. If the ATC looks straight ahead, she hears the pilot more strongly in her left earphone. However, if she turns her head to the left, the pilot's voice becomes stronger in her right earphone. If the ATC points her head directly at the airplane, she hears the pilot equally in both earphones. (Note that devalued definitions of virtual reality refer to anything that appears three-dimensional or even to anything that is interactive in any sense.)

■ **Create media:** You can create and supply your own media as well as select media that other people prepared. In addition to creating media from scratch, you may choose to annotate interesting parts of someone else's media with your own insights. (Right now, using a pencil to jot notes in the margin of pages of this book is more interactive than reading computer-based text that you cannot mark.) This degree of interactivity will gradually blur the line that now divides users from creators, a result that will be one of the most significant effects of distributed multimedia.

■ **Interact with distant people in real time:** Real-time interactivity allows you to affect not only what the other people do and say but also what they think and feel. (You might even convince your neighbor to turn down his radio.) A telephone call is often significantly less productive than conversing face-to-face, especially if the participants do not know each other well; adding video to a call makes the resulting video conference more like a face-to-face conversation. Employing such interaction to collaborate on creating multimedia content, or even to play games with distant partners may be the ultimate degree of remote interactivity. For still greater interactivity, of course, you must be sufficiently close to shake hands or hold hands.

Measuring Interactivity   To some extent, we can measure interactivity in useful numbers. Although it is hard to assign a useful number to the degree of control that you have over what you see and hear, it is easier to measure the speed with which you can exercise that control. Useful measurements include the number of interactions per hour (see Table 1.1 for typical numbers) and the delay between making a selection and seeing or hearing the result.

Delay is a separate concept from the number of interactions per hour, although, at first glance, the two quantities might seem to be reciprocals. Even if you changed television channels only eight times per hour, for instance, you would be highly dissatisfied with a system that incurred a delay of 7.5 minutes before showing you a new channel that you had selected. More seriously, although a participant in a telephone conversation starts talking only about every 6 seconds, a network delay of much more than ¼ second makes conversation almost impossible. Focus 1.1 discusses the origin and consequences of this maximum delay tolerance.

Why can people tolerate interacting over a network that has ¼-second delay, but not tolerate using a network that has ½-second delay? Like many other important questions that relate to multimedia, the answer depends on human physiology rather than on computer science, communications theory, or even physics. Two people standing about 140 feet apart can hold a shouted conversation and ignore the total delay of ¼ second that sound takes to go back and forth between them. (You can tell your calculator that sound travels 1100 feet per second in air.) However, the loudness of our voices and the sensitivity of our ears do not allow us to converse over distances much greater than 140 feet. Thus, we have had no reason to evolve tolerance for round-trip delays much greater than ¼ second.

Why is measuring the delay that people can tolerate so important for distributed multimedia? The key technologies that will allow us to transmit video over affordable connections are digital compression and decompres-

Table 1.1   Typical numbers of interactions per hour.

Interactions per hour	Activity
Over 36,000	Using virtual reality
3600	Playing a video game
1000	Holding a face-to-face conversation
600	Holding a telephone conversation
30	Searching databases for on-line business or academic information
20	Playing chess (counting moves but ignoring body language and aggressive eye-contact)
12	Watching a movie on a VCR tape, using the pause and play controls
8	Watching a broadcast television show and glancing at other channels
0.05	Attending a college lecture series
0.007	Playing chess by exchanging postcards
0.001	Exchanging occasional letters

sion, as we discuss later in this chapter. Compression and decompression require so much processing that they cause significant delay, even with extremely fast processors. In a video conference, the end of a question must pass through a compression and then a decompression, and then the start of an answer must pass through a compression and a decompression, before the person who asked the question starts to see and hear the answer. If each of the four compression or decompression steps requires as much as ⅛ second, people will have considerable trouble interacting with each other over the video conference. Network delays caused by the speed of light in the network will further reduce the allowed maximum delay that compression and decompression can add. Network designs that delay information in buffers, short-term storage areas, reduce the allowed delay still further.

Computer users know from experience that computers sometimes respond less quickly than human conversation partners. When a computer has failed to respond after ½ second, we do not assume that no response will be forthcoming and go on to ask another question. Nevertheless, when we in-

FOCUS 1.1 Telephone delay tolerance.

When long-distance carriers first began to route occasional telephone calls by way of communications satellites, customers began to complain of occasional severe difficulties in communicating by telephone. One party would finish a question, wait for the other party's answer, hear no response, and resume talking just as the other party's answer came over the network. The problem is that the end of the first party's question must travel from an earth station antenna up to a satellite and down to a station near the second party. Next, the start of the second party's answer must travel up to a satellite and down to an antenna near the first party. Only then can the first party start to hear the answer. Each of the four trips to or from a satellite requires approximately ⅛ second, because of the immutable speed of light. The total delay for the four trips is thus just over ½ second.

Long-distance carriers solved the problem. They learned that customers could not tolerate ½ second of delay, but could tolerate ¼ second of delay. Carriers started routing one direction of a call through a satellite and routing the other direction through a land line, such as a chain of microwave towers. A transcontinental land line has only about one-tenth of the delay of a satellite connection, because a satellite height is about 10 continent widths. More recently, carriers have solved the delay problem by routing both directions of most calls through fiber-optic land lines, because fiber connections are now often less expensive than either satellite connections or chains of microwave towers.

If you would like to follow along on your calculator, a communications satellite orbits at a fixed point about 23,500 miles above a point on the equator. (We ignore the fact that the satellite is somewhat farther from an earth station located in the temperate zone.) Light and microwaves travel about 186,300 miles per second. The time a signal takes to go from the ground to the satellite, or back down, is thus

$$23{,}500 \text{ mi} / 186{,}300 \text{ mi per sec} = 126 \text{ milliseconds (ms)},$$

which is about ⅛ second. ∎

teract with computers, even over networks, there is a critical delay time beyond which we become much less effective. That is the delay time after which we stop concentrating on the question we asked and start thinking about something else. Various experiments place the critical delay time between one and four seconds. We can tolerate longer delays, as we do when we play chess by exchanging postcards, but only by diverting our attention.

When a program or network delays much longer than four seconds before responding, the delay seriously interrupts our train of thought. We tend to start thinking about some other subject, such as upgrading to a faster computer or network.

We all have strong opinions about the delays that we will tolerate in other systems. For example, a telephone user seldom considers that picking up a telephone receiver is an implicit request for the network to respond by sending a dial tone. He seldom considers that dialing a number is an implicit request for the network to set up a circuit from his local loop joining his telephone instrument to the nearest telephone central office, one or more microwave relay links and fiber-optic cables, a satellite up link and down link, and the called party's local loop. At least in the United States, if the telephone network takes more than a few seconds to give a dial tone or to set up a circuit, the user thinks the network is malfunctioning and starts wondering how to report the problem without using the telephone. Users expect immediate response even during a calling peak such as during a weather emergency or Mother's Day. Some other countries' telephone networks were designed to handle simultaneous calls from only a small fraction of the users, so users expect to wait ½ hour before the network can give a dial tone or set up a call.

Bidirectional or Symmetrical Networks   Distributed multimedia requires bidirectional networks, but does not necessarily require symmetrical networks. Any interactive system must carry information in both directions, toward you and away from you. E-mail, telephone conversations, and video conferences carry approximately equal amounts of information in both directions; that is, these applications make symmetrical demands on the network.

Other important applications carry far more information *to* the user (outbound or downstream) than *from* a user (inbound or upstream). Consider video on demand (VOD), which allows you to request stored video such as college courses or movies from remote servers, and live video such as sports or news events from remote cameras. The outbound path must carry high-quality video, but the inbound path need carry nothing more than your requests, which may be both infrequent and brief. You typically spend a minute or two interacting rapidly with simple menus, sending only a few dozen bits and receiving a dozen text or image screens. Then you typically receive a few seconds to a few hours of video. Note that even infrequent and brief inbound communications are impossible for a cable network whose circuits amplify only outbound signals. One solution is to send inbound signals over a completely different physical delivery network such as the telephone network or microwaves. The other solution, of course, is to replace today's one-way networks by installations that are bidirectional, although not necessarily symmetrical.

Channels and Interactivity Distributed multimedia cannot rely on the concept of channels, as broadcast stations and television cables use channels. As a user of distributed multimedia, you sometimes require the one unique channel that carries exactly the information that you requested. No reasonable number of channels that carry predetermined content can meet this requirement. In principle, distributed multimedia needs one channel for each active user. In practice, of course, many users will continue to settle for selecting one of a few hundred predetermined channels that carry material intended for a mass audience, mainly because doing so reduces the price. The more people who are paying for a channel, the less each person pays. The transition will be gradual from a dozen channels for all users, to one channel for each user. As channel costs decrease, typical predetermined content will target smaller and smaller audiences. Broadcasting will become narrowcasting.

As an example of this tradeoff consider a form of pay-per-view television sometimes called near video on demand (NVOD), which can use about 150 channels to start transmitting each of 10 currently popular movies every 6 minutes. NVOD gives you some selection of movies and some choice of when to start watching. It even gives you some opportunity to pause, leave the room to get a sandwich, and then pick up the movie about where you left off. This is done by switching to the channel that started the same movie 6 or 12 minutes later than did the channel you were watching originally. Limiting access to going forward or backward in 6-minute intervals makes NVOD significantly less interactive than playing a videotape of a movie in a VCR, but much more interactive than watching a normal television program, and much less expensive than true video on demand.

Media and Terminology

Properties of individual digital media, along with interactivity, form the basis of our discussion of distributed multimedia. Because interacting with media can include creating media yourself, you will need to know how to create and present each medium. You will also need to know approximately how much storage space, processing power, and communications capacity various forms of each medium require. You can expect each medium's expanding requirements to keep up with or outstrip hardware's expanding capacities for the foreseeable future.

In the next five sections, we describe each medium's unique opportunities and challenges. Subsequent sections then relate the media to one another. As you read the next five sections, recall that multimedia relies on storing and transmitting all media in digital form. We begin with text, which is easiest to digitize and least voluminous in digital form, and end with video, which requires significantly more processing power and storage space. For example, one diskette may hold the uncompressed text of an entire book but only a few seconds of even highly compressed video.

Discussing these increasingly demanding media provides the context in which we introduce multimedia concepts that range from hypertext to raster scanning, special multimedia hardware, image resolution, and video quality. These concepts will be important to you, no matter whether your primary interest is in creating salable multimedia content, designing systems that provide multimedia content, or acting as an intelligent consumer of multimedia products and services.

For clarity, we refer to the digital forms of media by the five names that Table 1.2 defines. Occasionally, when we discuss both analog and digital forms, we use terminology such as *analog video* and *digital video*.

Although these names are convenient designations, they are by no means universal standard terms. You will need to recognize the same media by different names. For example, what we call *graphics*, others may call *vector graphics* or *stroke graphics*. What we call *images*, others may call *raster graphics*, *bit-maps*, or even *still video*. What we call *video*, others may call *motion video*.

Table 1.2 Definitions of media.

Medium	Definition
Text	Letters, numbers, punctuation, special characters, and controls, created with a text editor or word processor
Graphics	Lines, circles, boxes, shading, fill colors, and so on, created with a draw program
Images	Still pictures, expressed as the colors of many small individual picture elements (pixels), either captured and digitized from nature or painted using a paint program
Audio	Sound, including voice, music, and special effects, either captured from nature or synthesized
Video	Successive pictures presented sufficiently rapidly to give the appearance of smooth motion, either captured from nature or synthesized, such as by using an animation program

Some authors say that anything you see on a computer display screen is graphics, even if you are seeing moving pictures; others say that anything you see on a computer or television display tube is video, even if you are seeing only letters and numbers. Depending on a manufacturer's whim, the adapter that controls your computer's display may be called a *graphics adapter*, a *video adapter*, or even a *video graphics adapter*, rather than a *display adapter*. Other meanings of the term *media*, itself, range from a diskette to the entire movie or newspaper industry.

As the functions of many technologies and industries that developed independently converge to become distributed multimedia, their terminologies also converge. As a result one term often has several different meanings, and conversely one meaning may correspond to several terms. Even within a single industry, different companies select different names for functionally identical products. Such ambiguities, which exist in all languages, become less confusing as you become more aware of them.

Confusion about names of media often causes significant misunderstandings about multimedia. In particular, when you say "video," many people understand you to mean videotapes of movies that they rent at their neighborhood video rental store. Such people naturally misunderstand *video on demand* to mean nothing more than movies on demand. In fact, video on demand includes interactive access to all sorts of live and stored information expressed in the medium that we call video, including contents of digital libraries. Moreover, because a typical system that can handle video can also handle audio and the other three media (text, graphics, and images), video on demand includes interactive access to live and stored information expressed in all media.

Distinguishing a medium's natural form from its synthetic form is sometimes useful. For example, some sources treat natural images, which you might capture by scanning photographs, as a medium that is separate from synthetic images, which you might paint using a computer. Nevertheless, we discuss both forms together in this chapter's section on images. Because each medium's natural and synthetic forms have many properties in common, we organized our discussion around five media rather than around five synthetic media and five natural media.

Audio and video have particularly important natural and synthetic forms. A book devoted to audio would probably treat natural audio, which you capture from a microphone, as a different medium from synthetic music, which you can create by using the musical instrument digital interface (MIDI). Similarly, some sources treat natural video, which you might capture by converting videotape or movie film from analog form to digital form, as a medium that is separate from synthetic video, which you might create using a three-dimensional (3-D) computer animation program. For example, you might create a 3-D computer model of the inside of a mall that allows you to see how the mall would appear from any viewpoint. Then you could use an animation program to create synthetic video of a walk through the mall by slowly changing your viewpoint along a path that is eye height above the floor. Video that artists in movie studios create by photographing cels (sheets of painted transparent celluloid or acetate) in successive positions on painted backgrounds is a form of analog animation that synthetic digital video is gradually replacing. We now proceed to discuss the five media, in order of increasing demands that they make on digital systems.

Text

(Text represents letters, numbers, special characters, and controls in coded form, such as in the American Standard Code for Information Interchange (ASCII) or American National Standards Institute (ANSI) code) Either code, for example, represents a capital "A" as 01000001, in eight binary bits, which is one Byte. (We capitalize "Byte" but not "bit" to emphasize the importance of distinguishing the two units' respective abbreviations, which are "B" and "b.") If a typical typeset page contains 3000 characters, then the corresponding text occupies 3 kilobytes (KB) of storage. Thus, a 300-page book that contains only text occupies 900 KB or only about two-thirds of a typical diskette.

Such codes allow computers to process and store text far more efficiently than they can process and store any of the other media. For example, a computer can search a digitized museum catalog's text for a vase that has a given name more easily than it can search the catalog's digitized pictures for a vase that looks like a given picture.

Many people are more comfortable obtaining information and even entertainment from text than from any other media. Other people have a strong preference for other media instead of or in addition to text. Moreover, in many applications, other media express information better than does text. For examples, viewing successive images or video of a cut-away internal combustion engine in operation is probably more meaningful than reading a text description of how the engine operates, and hearing a piece of music may be far more desirable than reading about the music.

In our discussion of interactivity, we have noted that(adding hypertext links makes text more <u>interactive</u>) For example, if this book were in hypertext form, you might select the underlined hotword to link you to this chapter's earlier section that defined and discussed interactivity. That is, if you used your mouse to point at the underlined word, and clicked the mouse button, your screen would change to show the start of that section of the book. A button on that screen, perhaps labeled "Return," would allow you to return quickly to the screen that shows this text. For another example, if this were a hypertext book, we might have put only the first sentence of this paragraph in the book's main line and underline both *interactive* and *hypertext* in that sentence. If you wanted to learn more about either of these concepts, you could select the corresponding hotword and see a definition and a detailed description. If, however, you felt comfortable with both concepts, you could continue reading rapidly along the main line until you reached a hotword about which you wanted more information. For a third example of this important concept, hypertext would allow you to concentrate on any one of the themes that we introduced in the Preface. Instead of reading the chapter titled End-User Devices, you might elect to use hypertext links to read the many paragraphs that discuss different effects of human physiology on distributed multimedia.

Hypertext links are good for much more than requesting additional details about an unfamiliar topic. For example, two hypertext links in an article about a news event could show you articles about earlier and later events that relate to the current article. Other links could take you to articles about people who participated in the event. In general, a hypertext link can represent any type of relation between two pieces of information.

The two ends of a hypertext link may be in different documents that different people wrote and stored on computers that happen to be in different cities. For this reason, it is important to have a standard for representing hypertext links. The Hypertext Markup Language (HTML) standard is common on the Internet's World Wide Web, although it is not the only standard, and it does not make creating hypertext easy.

If you have no experience with hypertext, we strongly suggest that you log onto the World Wide Web and see what it is all about. Like hearing music, using hypertext is more desirable than reading about it.

Although amateur and professional authors are now generating a great deal of new text in digital form, only a small fraction of the world's accumulated printed material is available in digital form. Optical character recognition (OCR) and handwriting recognition are approaches to capturing books and other paper documents so that you can read the documents' content over networks. Systems that perform speech-to-text, also known as speech recognition, take another approach to capturing text from the analog world. We discuss these functions in more detail in this chapter's section titled Media Input, Conversion, and Output.

How do multimedia systems display and print text? It is not often useful to show the bits that represent each character. It is not often practical to print entire characters, as typewriter-type or daisy-wheel printers do. It is both useful and practical to encapsulate information about all characters' appearances as a font and to use such a font to convert text for display as either graphics or images, which we discuss in the next two sections. Fonts that convert text to graphics are called *vector fonts, stroke fonts,* or *outline fonts,* whereas fonts that convert text to images are called *bit-map fonts.* The main advantage of vector, stroke, or outline fonts is that they are scalable, meaning that simple computations can determine how to make characters of any desired size, which is not true of a bit-map font. We discuss many other examples of using digital processing to convert one medium to another medium in the section titled Media Input, Conversion, and Output, later in this chapter.

One reasonable view of multimedia systems is that more powerful and affordable digital systems now allow us to augment text, which computers handle most efficiently, by other media, from which people are better able to extract information. Another view is that increasingly many people expect to obtain most of their information from media other than text, now that two generations have grown up with television. In this view, computers that are sufficiently powerful to process the other media have become affordable just in time.

Graphics

Graphics consist of objects, such as the lines and shaded rectangles that make up an organization chart or the lines on the left side of Fig. 1.3. As different ASCII codes distinguish "A" from "b" or "Q" in text, different codes distinguish a circle from a line or rectangle in graphics. Additional graphics codes store information about an object. For a circle, the codes would be likely to store the x and y coordinates of its center, the length of its radius, its thickness, its color, and the color that fills it. If each of the first four codes is two Bytes long, and each of the two color codes is four bits long, then the entire circle requires only about 9 Bytes of storage space. Typical graphics contain text objects that include ASCII codes along with graphics codes that specify the text's position, font, and color. If a page contains a reasonably complex

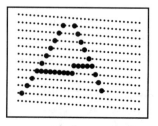

Figure 1.3 Vector and raster display screens.

graphic that has 200 objects such as circles, the page consumes only about 1800 Bytes of storage space, which is less space than a page of typeset text consumes.

It turns out that the practice of using four bits to specify the color of a graphic object is surprisingly important to multimedia. Four bits suffice for specifying one of 16 colors. You can create excellent graphics by using only a few colors. People who designed many computers in the 1980s, including computers that used the IBM standard Video Graphics Array (VGA), probably thought that they were providing more colors than anyone would ever need when they designed computers that could display 16 different colors at one time. Why do we care about that ancient history? First, so many millions of those computers were sold that, even today, we find that well over half of the computers on which we try to create and play multimedia are limited to displaying 16 colors at a time. Second, as we shall note in the next section, acceptable images require at least 256 colors. Trying to show images on a computer that was intended to show only text and graphics is no fun.

Using a computer graphics program, sometimes with "Draw" in its name or description, allows you to create a circle by clicking and dragging the mouse until the circle has the position and size that you want. With a few more clicks, you can specify its thickness and colors. The Draw program shows you the circle, but it stores the corresponding numerical codes. Later, perhaps after you have created many other graphics objects, you can select the circle and change its position, size, or other parameters, or even delete it altogether. Changing a graphics object is thus significantly more convenient than changing a circle that forms part of an image by first deleting each point that makes up the circle and then painting a new circle.

The most direct way to display graphics is to represent each object as a collection of straight lines, also called *vectors* or *strokes*. A rectangle or an "A" requires a few strokes, and a circle requires many short strokes. Some computer displays, mainly those on expensive engineering workstations, actually draw successive individual strokes, each stroke specified by its two end points. The left half of Fig. 1.3 illustrates three strokes on such a vector display screen.

A typical computer display screen, however, similarly to a television set, uses a raster to scan its screen. The raster forms an image by sweeping a beam over the face of the tube repeatedly, brightening and darkening the beam as it goes along to create the desired display. Light dots in the right half of Fig. 1.3 illustrate such a raster, while heavy dots illustrate the points on the raster at which such a screen would brighten its beam in order to show three strokes. Each point where the beam can have a specified color is called a picture element (pixel).

A raster sweeps the beam in a constant ballet that is completely independent of what the display is showing. It sweeps the beam rapidly from left to right, turning the beam on and off to create one horizontal row of the display. The raster then sweeps the beam back from right to left even more rapidly with the beam turned off. This sweep is the horizontal retrace. The raster also gives the beam a slower vertical motion from top to bottom, so that successive horizontal sweeps create successively lower rows of the display. Finally, the raster gives a vertical retrace, moving the beam back from bottom to top to start over.

An actual screen has hundreds of scan lines, rather than the dozen that the right half of Fig. 1.3 illustrates, and also has hundreds of pixels per line. The subsequent section on Images discusses the number of scan lines and pixels per line that a raster display must have in order to make strokes look smooth instead of spotty and jagged. However, even a spotty capital A is easier for human users to read than is 01000001.

The most crucial function that is required for displaying graphics on a raster-scanned screen is vector-to-raster conversion. This function consists of deciding which points of the raster to brighten in order to display a stroke that has given end points. The next most important function is filling a given color throughout a region that is bounded by several lines or arcs. Both functions require significant amounts of processing. Fortunately, most personal computers have main processors that can accomplish vector-to-raster conversion and filling functions reasonably quickly. Inexpensive auxiliary processing hardware, sold as graphics accelerators or Windows accelerators, perform such functions even more quickly.

Like a computer display, a printer controls individual pixels, rather than drawing straight lines. Printing graphics thus also requires conversion from vector form to raster form. A less common way to obtain hard copy of graphics is to use a plotter to draw straight strokes.

Graphics are popular for menus, windows, hypermedia buttons, and similar parts of multimedia content. This is because graphics are convenient to create and modify, occupy relatively little storage space and network capacity, and require reasonable amounts of processing.

Images

An image represents a still picture in digital form by using bits to specify the color of each of many pixels. An image has a given number of pixels across each row from left to right and a given number of rows of pixels from top to bottom. A given pixel's bits often specify its color as amounts of red, green, and blue. In the case of a monochrome image, one bit may specify that a pixel's color is either black or white, whereas several bits may specify that the

Figure 1.4 Images to view from different distances.

pixel is one of a range of grays) Figure 1.4 shows images with two different resolutions in which each pixel has one of 256 different shades of gray.

Consider using a scanner to capture an image by digitizing a photograph. As the scanner slowly moves a narrow horizontal band of light down the photograph, the scanner effectively sweeps three photocells back and forth rapidly, observing the intensities of red, green, and blue light that successive parts of the photograph reflect. The photocells convert these successive amounts of light into three varying voltages. Because more intense light produces a proportionally or analogously larger voltage, the voltages are called analogs of the intensities. The scanner's electronics converts these varying analog voltages to a succession of numbers in digital form, as follows. Electronic circuits sample the voltages at a succession of evenly spaced times, in order to record the intensities of evenly spaced pixels. At each sample time, the scanner feeds the three sample voltages to three electronic circuits, called analog-to-digital converters, that convert the three voltages to three numbers. The scanner then feeds these successions of numbers to a computer that can store them on a hard drive as the colors of successive pixels. Sampling is fundamental to capturing images and, as we shall see in subsequent sections, to capturing audio and video as well.

A scanner's number of pixels per line is equal to its total sweep time divided by the time between successive samples. The number of lines of pixels is equal to the number of times the scanner sweeps across the photograph before reaching the bottom. The analog-to-digital converters determine the number of bits per pixel in the resulting image. The resolution of the image consists of the number of pixels per row, the number of rows, and the number of bits per pixel.

You can capture images in several ways. You can use a handheld scanner or a flatbed scanner, which looks like a photocopier that lost its paper-output hopper. Eastman Kodak supplies photofinishers with equipment with which to scan your color slides or negatives and write images on a Photo-CD disc, which is a particular format of CD-ROM. Some photofinishers offer to put your photographs on a diskette as well as making prints. You can also obtain an image by using a computer to capture a single frame of video from the output of a video camera or VCR. The video capture adapter that performs this function is sometimes called a frame grabber.

If you have artistic talent, you can employ a program to create an image from scratch by applying colors to groups of pixels on a screen as a painter applies oil paints to a canvas. Names or descriptions of programs that you use to create synthetic images thus may include the word "Paint," as opposed to the word "Draw," which applies to creating graphics. Even if you have little artistic talent, but considerable patience, you can use a Paint program to repair minor defects in a captured image. With both talent and patience, you can make major changes to a captured image or combine two captured images to achieve an otherwise impossible result. Converting pictures to digital images makes such changes easier and more convincing but not necessarily more ethical.

A computer presents an image on its display screen by reversing the action of a scanner. Computer software sets up the display by writing bits that specify the color of the image's pixels into a special part of the computer's memory called the frame buffer. Fast dedicated hardware reads the pixels' bits in succession, in the same order as the display screen's raster scans the pixels. The hardware uses each pixel's bits to control the color of the screen at that corresponding pixel by controlling the beam's color at the corresponding time during the display's raster scan.

We have noted that text and graphics seldom strain a computer's processing, storage, display, or communications capabilities. Images, however, can create severe strains. For example, when we log onto Internet from home through the fastest supported modulator-demodulator (modem), we immediately specify that we do not want the network to send any images. Otherwise, the delays are intolerable. The rest of this section uses simple calculations to show how multimedia systems deal with the strains of keeping up their images. The subsequent sections on audio and video show how multimedia systems avoid breaking down completely when faced by those still more demanding media.

On a typical computer display, each pixel's brightness decays rapidly. The computer must therefore read the entire frame buffer repeatedly, typically 60 or 72 times each second, and refresh all the screen's pixels. At a slower refresh rate, a user would see an intolerable amount of flicker. (This is another instance where multimedia depends more on human physiology than on computer science.) A typical computer display screen has 640 pixels across each row and has 480 rows down the screen, for a total resolution of 307,200 pixels. To refresh every pixel 60 times each second, a computer must refresh over 18 million pixels per second, which explains the special frame buffer and special-purpose hardware for reading the frame buffer. This is one of many instances where we will encounter a requirement for special-purpose hardware to perform a job that an end-user device's main processor could not perform sufficiently quickly. Chapter 4 discusses this and other reasons for having special multimedia hardware.

Images come in a wide range of resolutions and formats and may have either more or less resolution than the computer screens that display them. A typical Paint program can convert an image for display at a particular computer's screen resolution, in any size window, and with any of a wide range of magnifications. Displaying an image requires the Paint program to do this preparation only once, rather than 60 times each second. Thus, this function can use the computer's main processor, rather than requiring fast special-purpose hardware. Designers use software that runs on a general-purpose processor wherever possible, to maximize flexibility and minimize cost, and resort to special-purpose hardware only where necessary.

Let's pause for a moment to think about video, which we discuss in detail in a subsequent section. When displaying video, a computer may need to display a new image as often as 30 times each second. You might want special-purpose hardware for preparing each new image, as well as for refreshing the screen. Next, consider virtual reality. Here, a computer must note where your eyes and hands have moved and compute the correct image that it must show you next, about 30 times each second. Much of this computing is too complex for special-purpose hardware, so displaying virtual reality requires a main processor that is orders of magnitude faster than today's personal computers.

Color depth, that is, the number of bits of information that an image contains for each pixel, is as important as the number of pixels in the image. If you have a computer with a VGA display, which we mentioned in the section titled Graphics, you can display graphics and images using a palette of at most 16 colors. With such a display, you cannot show an image that contains a smooth color transition, such as from the brightly lit side of a person's forehead to the shadowed side. Instead, your image is likely to break up the forehead into two or three wide bands of uniform color. If this is deliberate, it is called posterization; otherwise it is called ugly. If you have a computer with a Super-VGA (S-VGA) or Video Electronic Standards Organization (VESA) display, you can use a palette of 256 colors, because your frame buffer contains eight bits or one Byte per pixel, so you can make images that are acceptable for some purposes. However, as Focus 1.2 explains, 256 is actually an extremely small number of colors.

(High-color images, which have either 65,000 colors and 16 bits per pixel or 32,000 colors and 15 bits per pixel, look significantly better than 256-color images. True-color images, which have 16 million colors or 24 bits per pixel, look better yet, because they can have about as many different colors as a normal human eye can distinguish.) This is another important physiological number that few people could guess accurately. Because a photographic slide can show approximately 60 billion different colors, Kodak's Photo-CD format includes archival images that have 36 bits for each pixel. In the section of Chapter 4 on High-Color and True-Color Displays, we discuss why so many of today's personal computers can display palettes of only 16 or 256 different colors and why networks transmit images that use as few colors as possible.

(There is no standard or even typical image resolution. However, to get a feeling for the amount of storage space that an image can occupy, consider an image that uses all the resolution of a 640 by 480 pixel screen and has 3 Bytes that give the color of each pixel. Multiplying these three numbers shows that this image occupies 921 KB of storage. If an average word has 5 letters, so that a word and the blank after the word occupy 6 Bytes, then our image oc-

FOCUS 1.2 Counting colors.

No matter how you look at it, there is something inherently three-dimensional about the color of any one pixel.

Computer Screens: Computer people often think of color's three dimensions as red, green, and blue (RGB). That is, they select a particular red, a particular green, and a particular blue. Then they make up any desired color by adding together an amount of that red, an amount of that green, and an amount of that blue. These dimensions are thus the *additive primary colors.* For example, adding a small amount of red to a small amount of green produces a pixel that appears to be a dim yellow, whereas adding equal, large amounts of all three colors produces a pixel that appears to be a bright white.

Television: Television transmits color as the three dimensions of luminance, hue, and saturation. Luminance tells how bright the color is, ranging from black to highly illuminated, to provide compatibility with black-and-white television sets. Hue tells where the color falls in the spectrum ranging from red to violet. Saturation tells how much the hue dominates white, ranging from a barely tinted gray, which contains mainly white, to a pure color, which contains no excess white. For example, adding more red, green, and blue to a dim yellow pixel gives an unsaturated, washed-out, or impure yellow, that is, a light gray that has only a yellowish tinge.

Printers and Painters: Printers and painters often think of color's three dimensions as cyan, magenta, and yellow (CMY). Instead of adding these colors together, they subtract these colors from the white light that paper or canvas reflects, so these are termed the *subtractive primary colors.* For example, yellow pigment absorbs blue light and reflects red and green light. Applying all three of cyan, magenta, and yellow absorbs all colors, although printers and painters optionally use black pigment for that purpose, yielding CMYK.

In this book, we use the term *color* to mean all three dimensions. You will sometimes see the term used to mean just hue or to mean just hue and saturation. When we need a term that combines hue and saturation, we use the term *chrominance.* Note that black, white, and shades of gray are colors. Occasionally, however, we must use the term *color* with a different meaning, to distinguish a color printer or display from a monochrome version. *(cont.)*

FOCUS 1.2 Counting colors. (*cont.*)

Now, is 256 a small or large number of colors? You can do a good job of filling in a single dimension with 256 different values. For example, you can make a good monochrome image by using pixels that have 256 evenly spaced values of luminance. Any luminance that you need for a given pixel is fairly close to one of these values. However, you cannot do a good job of filling in a three-dimensional cube with only 256 different points. For example, you might try creating a standard palette that contains colors with eight different amounts of red, eight different amounts of green, and four different amounts of blue. Alternatively, you might try using eight different values of hue, eight different values of luminance, and four different values of saturation. In either case, the color you need for a pixel is likely to be unacceptably far from every color that is available in your standard 256-color palette

To show an acceptable image with 256 different colors, you are likely to need to create a customized palette that places most of the palette's 256 colors near the particular colors that your particular image uses heavily. For example, for an image of a red balloon in a blue sky, a custom palette might have 100 blues, 100 reds, and 56 other colors for the basket and its occupants. Even with a 256-color custom palette, you have far fewer colors at your disposal than a human visual system can distinguish so you should not expect superb images. ∎

---

cupies as much space as 153,600 words. If you have a limited amount of space to store information, you may decide to use an image only if the image is worth over 100 times its traditional worth of 1000 words.)

A black-and-white laser printer, ink jet printer, or dot matrix printer does not need to refresh rapidly decaying pixels. It reads a memory that corresponds to the frame buffer just once for each page to determine which pixels it should leave white and which it should make black. However, most printers must either leave a given pixel the color of the paper or make the pixel fully black. Thus, preparing an image for printing usually involves reducing the color depth to a single bit. A typical color printer has the choice of leaving each pixel the color of the paper or applying a full-intensity color, so it must reduce the color depth to a single bit for each of the three or four available colors.

You might think that reducing an image's color depth to one bit or to three or four bits would result in disaster. However, printouts can be surprisingly good, because a typical printer produces about 30 times as many pixels as a typical display screen produces. For comparison to a typical display screen's 307,200 pixels, a printer often produces 300 dots per inch. Over an 8.5 inch by 11 inch page, this gives

$$(8.5 \text{ in.} \times 300 \text{ dots/in.}) \times (11 \text{ in.} \times 300 \text{ dots/in.}) = 8,415,000 \text{ dots.}$$

You can trade off increased resolution against decreased color depth, either for displaying or printing an image. A pointillist painter creates a subtly shaded pastel region by applying many small, separate blobs of brightly colored paints. A newspaper half-tone engraver makes a region appear to have any desired shade of gray by assigning the region an appropriate fraction of tiny black dots. A computer program can take advantage of the fact that an image is in digital form by applying reasonably sophisticated digital processing to reduce color depth by using increased resolution. In this context, the technique is called dithering. Like a person who dithers back and forth between two extreme alternatives, a color depth-reduction program might convert one screen pixel to about 30 printer pixels, of which some are too white and the rest are too black. Through a magnifying glass, you see a meaningless jumble of dots. Similarly, if you look closely at a color printout, you see many tiny marks of a few different excessively strong colors. From sufficiently far away, however, you see an image that seems to have appropriate shades of gray or appropriate colors. Focus 1.3 and Fig. 1.4 quantify and demonstrate this concept.

Just as dithering allows you to trade off increased resolution against decreased color depth, you can go in the opposite direction by using a larger number of colors to make a coarse image look smoother. This technique, which is the opposite of dithering, answers to the improbable name of antialiasing. For example, suppose that the peak of a white capital "A" on a black background should cover only one-third of a pixel and that you are using 256 shades of gray. Without antialiasing, because the letter covers less than half of that pixel, software would make the pixel black. With antialiasing, however, software would make that pixel a gray that is 85/256 of the way from black to white. Like dithering, antialiasing makes an image look better only if you view the image from sufficiently far away that your eye cannot resolve the individual pixels.

You will want to keep the relations among viewing distance, resolution, and color depth clearly in mind when we discuss compressing images and video near the end of this chapter. An important principle of design is to include no more resolution than a viewer will be able to perceive from her actual viewing distance. Making individual pixels much smaller than a two-thousandth of the viewing distance does not make the image appear any sharper; it merely wastes precious storage space and network capacity.

FOCUS 1.3   How close is too close?

Physiology determines how close you should get to an image. Your eye averages individual pixels together into an overall color only if the distance between the image and your eyes is greater than a critical viewing distance. This critical viewing distance is about 2000 times the width (or height) of each individual pixel. Actually, depending on how good your eyes and glasses are and how brightly the subject is illuminated, the number can vary, but 2000 is a good rule of thumb for normal people viewing printouts, computer displays, and television sets (Inglis, 1993). We shall see that this critical viewing distance is important for answering the question of whether digital television should be high-definition television (HDTV) or standard-definition television (SDTV), because the answer depends on how far away from the screen viewers want to sit. For the present discussion of images, we will apply the concept of critical viewing distance to a computer screen and a printout.

Suppose that you are viewing a 14-inch-diagonal S-VGA computer display screen from a distance of 16 inches. The screen is 11 inches wide and has 640 pixels in each row, so each pixel is 0.017 inch wide. Two thousand times the pixel size is about 34 inches. Because your viewing distance is less than this critical distance at which your eyes would perceive the average of several neighboring pixels, a program that uses dithering to increase the screen's color depth produces a grainy mess. To see such an image, you must move back to at least 34 inches from the screen.

Now, suppose that you are viewing a 300 dots-per-inch printout from the same viewing distance. In this situation, 2000 times the pixel size is only about seven inches, so the critical viewing distance is less than half of your actual viewing distance. Your eye, therefore, perceives the average of each block that is two or three pixels wide and two or three pixels high. Dithering works well for printouts.

Figure 1.4 shows two images that use much larger pixels. Although we used Paint Shop Pro's "mosaic" tool to create these images, you can find a similar tool in almost any paint program. We gave the top image a resolution of 133 by 100 pixels and the lower image a resolution of 100 by 75 pixels. Dividing the images' width by their numbers of horizontal pixels gives the sizes of the two images' pixels as

$$4.0 \text{ in.} / 133 \text{ pixels} = 0.030 \text{ in. and } 4.0 \text{ in.} / 100 \text{ pixels} = 0.040 \text{ in.}$$

Multiplying these pixel sizes by 2000 gives the two images' critical viewing distances as

$$0.030 \text{ in.} \times 2000 = 60 \text{ in. and } 0.040 \text{ in.} \times 2000 = 80 \text{ in.}$$

(cont.)

FOCUS 1.3 How close is too close? (*cont.*)

You can easily determine whether you agree with these two numbers. Prop Fig. 1.4 under a good light, step back until the top image barely looks smooth, measure the distance between your eyes and the book, and then do the same for the bottom image. You will probably find that the transition from a grainy image to a smooth image is so sharp that repeating either measurement gives results that agree within a few inches. You can divide your measured viewing distances by the respective pixel widths to see whether 2000 pixel widths is the critical viewing distance for your eyes.

You may find it surprising that you can see an image clearly only when you are sufficiently far away to ignore the image's individual pixels, but you are familiar with the concept that you can see a forest only if you are not distracted by the individual trees. One important consequence is that, if you are sufficiently far back that the bottom image looks smooth, the top image looks almost identical, despite its higher resolution. Images in magazines and newspapers use no more pixels than are necessary for normal viewing. If you look at an image through a magnifying glass, you see meaningless dots rather than seeing more detail. ■

Audio

The medium that we call audio is sound expressed in digital form. Natural sound, including speech, music, and sound effects, consists of a continuously varying air pressure that wiggles your ear drums and causes you to hear the sound. To capture audio, we allow the sound to wiggle a diaphragm inside a microphone and produce a varying voltage that is proportional or analogous to the sound pressure. We then convert this analog voltage to digital form using pulse code modulation (PCM) with the same sort of sampling process that a scanner uses. We sample the voltage at a succession of equally spaced times and pass the successive samples to an analog-to-digital-converter circuit that approximates each sample voltage by a number. We store these numbers on a hard drive as an audio file. Typical hardware for digitizing audio employs a special digital signal processor (DSP) to perform the activity. The DSP frees the computer's main processor for other duties and makes sure that other duties do not produce gaps in the digitized sound.

Audio has a resolution, just as images do. In the case of audio, the selected resolution consists of the number of samples per second and the number of bits per sample. Digitizing two sound channels, such as voltages from

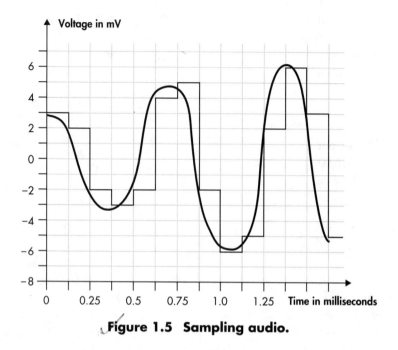

Figure 1.5 Sampling audio.

two separated microphones, produces stereo audio. Selecting monaural or stereo is thus another aspect of selecting audio resolution.

Figure 1.5 illustrates sampling audio 8000 times each second and recording 4 bits for each sample. The interval between two successive samples is 0.125 milliseconds and 4 bits suffice to distinguish 16 different approximations to a sample's voltage, which would produce noisy digital audio. The heavy, wavy curve represents a short portion of analog audio that is increasing in amplitude (loudness) and frequency (pitch). The light, stepped graph represents the digitized form of that audio. The resulting digital audio file would express the figure's portion of an analog audio waveform as 56 bits that are the binary equivalents of

$$3, 2, -2, -3, -2, 4, 5, -2, -6, -5, 2, 6, 3, -5.$$

The stepped graph's vertical and horizontal lines must follow dotted lines that represent sample times and quantized voltages, respectively. Note that recording the exact value of the analog voltage at each sample time would require an infinite number of bits per sample and an infinite data rate.

Physiology and communications theory join forces to tell you what audio resolutions to use for various purposes. Physiology says that human voices produce little energy at frequencies higher than 4000 cycles per second

(4 KHz) and that young people's ears can hear frequencies up to about 22 KHz, especially in instrumental music. Communications theory says that a 4-KHz signal requires at least 8000 samples per second and a 22-KHz signal requires at least 44,000 samples per second. Two of these numbers' most important applications follow:

- Telephone companies sample voice conversations at a rate of 8000 samples per second and use 7 bits per sample for a total audio data rate of 56,000 bps (approximately 56 Kbps). Adding other information about the call raises a line's total data rate to 64 Kbps. This is the fundamental unit of information on digital telephone networks.

- Manufacturers of compact discs (CDs, compact disc-digital audio discs, or CD-DA discs) produce digital audio that is suitable for recording high-quality music by sampling each of two stereo channels 44,100 times per second and using 16 bits per sample. This produces a data rate of 1,411,200 bits per second (approximately 1.4 Mbps). Note that the original single-speed compact disc read-only memories (CD-ROMs) play at the same rate as the ubiquitous CD-DA discs, leaving 1.2 Mbps of data after applying error-correction codes. More recent CD-ROM drives play at two, three, or more times that fundamental rate. Thus, physiology and communications theory determine even the data rates of CD-ROMs.

Multimedia content can use digital audio data rates from well below 56 Kbps to just over 1.4 Mbps, in order to achieve various objectives. Selecting any medium's resolution is always a tradeoff. In the case of audio, increasing the resolution improves sound quality but also increases the medium's requirements for processing power, storage capacity, and network bandwidth. This chapter's section on compressing audio discusses modifications of PCM sampling that you can use to improve digital audio by increasing its signal-to-noise ratio (SNR) and dynamic range while decreasing its data rate. These modifications decrease the number of bits per sample that you need in order to achieve a given audio quality. However, if the rate at which you sample an analog signal is not at least twice that signal's highest important frequency, you will never be happy with the resulting digital audio.

Playing back digitized sound amounts to reversing the digitization process. A playback device reads a succession of numbers from a hard drive, uses a digital-to-analog converter to produce a corresponding succession of voltages such as the stepped graph in Fig. 1.5, smooths out this succession of voltages into a continuously varying voltage, and feeds that voltage through an amplifier to a speaker. The speaker cone wiggles and produces a varying air pressure that you hear as sound. Two identical channels produce stereo sound.

(Audio depends strongly on time, unlike text, graphics, and images) An audio playback device, such as a CD-DA player or a computer's audio adapter, must use samples at almost exactly the same rate at which the audio capture device that recorded the audio created those samples. (More concisely, audio is an isochronous medium.) Human auditory systems are incredibly sensitive to slight errors in playback rate. People who have perfect pitch, often professional musicians, are remarkably sensitive to a playback rate that is slightly wrong, even if that rate is constant. All listeners detect and dislike remarkably tiny variations in the presentation rate of audio. Slow variations are called *wow* and rapid variations are called *flutter*. Human auditory systems are also sensitive to small gaps in playback.

A CD-DA player contains circuitry that avoids leaving a gap when it detects a few erroneous samples. When it reads a single bad sample, it fills the gap with the average of the preceding and succeeding samples. When it reads several successive bad samples, it uses the last correct sample that it read (Clifford, 1987). For example, failing to read four successive samples requires the player to use the last sample for the next 90 millionths of a second. That works fine. You may never hear a CD-DA player produce a gap or a click in thousands of hours of critical listening.

What can a multimedia system, such as a personal computer, do when a hard drive or network fails to deliver the next quarter second of audio? A person might insert "er, ah" into a speech, but there is no natural sound with which a computer can fill such a gap. Applying the ancient maxim that, if you have nothing to say, you can at least shut up, you might suppose that a computer would leave a gap of silence. However, many multimedia designers thoughtlessly decide to emulate a CD-DA player and fill the gap (which is thousands of times longer than the gap that a CD-DA player may need to fill) by replaying the previous quarter second of audio. The resulting stammer can turn the most serious political speech or technical lecture into an unintended comedy skit and can turn music into noise. The only good solution is to ensure that a playback device receives a smooth flow of audio data.

Note that, whereas a computer designed for text and graphics can display at least low-quality images, such a computer cannot play back sounds that are any more articulate than an occasional beep. This is because, although such a computer has three digital-to-analog converters that drive its display, it does not have a digital-to-analog converter that drives its speaker. Such a computer needs an optional card that contains circuitry for playing back audio and circuitry for digitizing audio. For efficient packaging, such a card often also includes a third function, the control circuitry for a CD-ROM drive.

(Electronics for capturing and playing back audio and controlling a CD-ROM drive, together with the CD-ROM drive itself and amplified speakers, are the hallmarks of a multimedia computer. This capability is reasonably well standardized and consumers can afford it. In many product lines, audio and CD-ROM drives are standard features of new computer models) These functions may even be packaged on a computer's main circuit board rather than on optional adapter cards. To provide a snapshot of installed computers, note that the reasonably well-endowed university at which we teach multimedia theory and practice provides one room that contains 20 computers. Five of these computers, including the instructors' station, have audio adapters and CD-ROMs, although not one of the computers can display more than 16 colors at a time. At home, our three main computers have 16 colors and no audio adapter, 256 colors and an audio adapter, and 16 million colors and an audio adapter.

(The Musical Instrument Digital Interface (MIDI) audio standard provides a way to record music without sampling air pressure thousands of times per second. Just as you create text by typing on a computer keyboard, you create MIDI audio by playing a specially equipped musical keyboard instrument that you connect to a computer. Whereas text records only which keys you press, MIDI records the times when you press and release a key, how forcibly you press a key, and how rapidly you release a key. MIDI records any other actions you take as well, such as changing the musical voice from French horn to violin or calling for reverberation to simulate reflections inside a concert hall. Several computer programs dispense with the keyboard instrument and create a MIDI file by marking up a screen that looks like a musical score or by manipulating even more clever screen interfaces. Many digital audio adapters that can capture natural audio can also capture MIDI from a keyboard instrument and play back either natural audio or synthetic MIDI audio files.

Captured audio can severely stress a multimedia system's storage space and network capacity. At data rates of 56 Kbps or 1.4 Mbps, one hour of uncompressed audio occupies 25 MB or 630 MB of storage space, respectively. That probably explains why you buy your music on CDs rather than on diskettes. It also explains why you must compress even low-quality digital audio before you send it over a normal telephone line) This chapter's section on compressing audio describes some compression algorithms.

(MIDI audio stresses a computer's data rate far less than does captured audio. MIDI's data rate depends on how rapidly you play the music, rather than on the audio quality that you capture.) Suppose you are rattling along, striking 3 keys per second with each finger. This amounts to 60 key presses or releases each second. Each record of pressing or releasing a key occupies 3 Bytes, including the voice, note, and volume. A computer can record your playing by storing only 180 Bps. For comparison with captured audio, this is a data rate of only 1.44 Kbps. Storing an hour of such music requires 648 KB, which is only one-thousandth of the space that high-quality captured audio requires. This compactness makes MIDI highly attractive for storing music, leaving captured audio for voices and other sounds to which MIDI does not apply.

Hypermedia links can invoke audio, as well as text and other media, so we need standards for audio information. The American National Standards Institute (ANSI) has a project on music in information-processing systems that refers to a Standard Music Description Language (SMDL) and HyTime, which supports digital audio.)

Video

Video is the digital medium that shows you a rapid sequence of still pictures and gives you the illusion of seeing a picture that moves. This illusion depends on two surprisingly different physiological phenomena called persistence of vision and flicker fusion. Early silent movies pushed both of these phenomena near their tolerable limits. Early cinematic cameras exposed 16 pictures per second. Early film projectors showed approximately 16 pictures per second, subject to the artistic expression and strength of the person cranking the projector. The projector used a rotating shutter to interrupt the light beam twice while showing each picture, before moving the film to show the next picture, so the light beam actually flashed about 48 times per second. Persistence of vision enabled viewers to remember each picture until the next picture appeared, so that the succession of still pictures appeared to be a motion picture. Flicker fusion enabled viewers to ignore the dark intervals, so that the rapidly flashing light appeared to be steady illumination.

It is useful to call each different picture a frame and call each separate flash a field. (In case you find these names hard to remember, note that you would frame only a completed picture.) A silent movie thus provided 16 frames per second and 48 fields per second. For a present-day example, the National Television Standards Committee (NTSC) signal, used in North America and Japan, provides 30 frames per second and 60 fields per second. In Focus 1.6 we explain how interlace allows the field rate to exceed the frame rate and how interlace increases the complexity of multimedia.

(Persistence of vision allows you to track motion with as few as 10 frames per second, but you need 30 frames per second to avoid seeing jerks when a picture changes rapidly. (Thus 30 frames per second goes by the proud name of *full-motion video*.) Flicker fusion allows you to tolerate a dim screen that shows as few as 48 fields per second, but you need at least 72 fields per second to avoid a headache if the screen is large and bright.) These two physiological phenomena thus set rather wide ranges for tolerable video, depending on the subject and the environment, respectively.

(Persistence of vision causes much more trouble for distributed multimedia than does flicker fusion. On the one hand, limited and costly data rates and storage sizes provide strong motivations to reduce the number of complete frames that such systems transmit and store. Much of today's digital video uses only 15 frames per second.) Such video pushes persistence of vision even closer to its tolerable limit than did silent movies 75 years ago. (On the other hand, a computer must refresh its screen at a rate of about 60 to 72 fields per second, even when displaying text, graphics, or images, so flicker fusion provides no new challenge in the case of video. Computer displays have coped with flicker fusion for decades.

Video should be played at almost exactly the same rate at which the video was recorded. That is, like audio, video is an isochronous medium) However, whereas we have noted that ears have almost no tolerance for variations in the rate at which they hear audio, eyes can tolerate slight slow-downs or speed-ups in video. Objects in the real world do not move at such steady rates that we are intolerant of slight variations in video playback. Moreover, whereas using the last available sample value to fill in for missing audio works for mere thousandths of a second, using the last available frame to fill in for missing video can work for as much as a tenth of a second. (Thus, when playing both audio and video, a multimedia system must concentrate on keeping the audio isochronous, even if that leaves the system insufficient capacity to do a perfect job on the video. Moreover, synchronization (called lip-synch) between audio of a speaker's voice and video of the speaker's lips, must be correct to within several milliseconds. Some other pairs of media, such as a narrated slide show of images, may allow synchronization errors up to about one second) Focus 1.4 discusses the relation between two words that appear throughout discussions of multimedia.

(Capturing any digital medium consists of sampling information at specified times or locations and using numbers to represent the values of the samples, so that a multimedia system can store the medium on a hard drive. Thus, neither movie film nor broadcast television is an example of digital video) Movie film samples a scene as a fixed number of frames per second. However, film does not sample an individual frame at regularly spaced

FOCUS 1.4 Isochronous and synchronous.

The term *isochronous* comes from Greek roots meaning "equal" and "time," whereas the more familiar term *synchronous* comes from Greek roots that mean "together" and "time." The terms' meanings are less similar than they might at first appear. Isochronous applies to one medium at a time, whereas synchronous applies to the relationship between two or more media or between two or more instances of the same medium.

We have noted that audio and video are isochronous media, meaning that it is important to play either medium smoothly at a constant rate that is almost exactly *equal* to the rate at which the medium was recorded. If a video clip was recorded at 30 frames per second, an isochronous system delivers the video at a rate equal to 30 frames per second (fps), not 28 fps, not 32 fps, and particularly not dropping back to 28 fps for a while and then compensating by speeding up to 32 fps.

In many cases, to synchronize two or more media is also important—that is, to play media so that they at least begin almost exactly *together*. An important example is synchronizing audio and video, as we just mentioned. However, you may also need to synchronize presentation of two nonisochronous media, such as text and images in a narrated slide show, or synchronize two or more instances of the same medium, such as video of two ends of a conversation or different audio intended for left and right speakers.

One indication of the difference between isochronous and synchronous is that it is possible to have either without having the other. You could present audio and video at the correct rate, isochronously, but have the video appear a second ahead of the audio, out of synchronization. Conversely, you could arrange to interleave digital audio's bits with digital video's bits, so that each tenth of a second has the correct audio and video, synchronously; but you could send the bits over a nonisochronous network, so that the receiver would play each medium at an incorrect, nonisochronous, rate.

Cognitive psychologists quantify the extent to which people can tolerate imperfections in multimedia's isochroneity or synchrony in different situations. For example, a business person who requires a particular piece of information may tolerate imperfections larger than those that a consumer will tolerate in an advertisement or entertainment. Beyond a given point, approaching perfection can become prohibitively expensive. Thus, a multimedia designer must optimize each situation based on the way real people react, rather than blindly applying handbook numbers to all cases.

(cont.)

> **FOCUS 1.4 Isochronous and synchronous. (*cont.*)**
>
> Computer people tend to have some difficulty with the concept that playing an isochronous medium too rapidly is as bad as playing it too slowly. When a user presses a key to get text, graphics, or images, she wants information to fill the screen as quickly as possible. Computer people are more familiar with these three nonisochronous media, for which there is no such thing as being too fast.
>
> You will see the usual wide variety of synonyms for the terms *isochronous* and *synchronous*. Some authors avoid the former term, because it is less familiar, and use the latter term to cover both meanings. Others use even simpler phrases such as *time-dependent* or *real time* to cover both meanings. However, it is more useful to keep the two meanings separate and to reserve *real time* to mean that what a user sees or hears is taking place concurrently. ∎

pixels. Instead, film records light intensities as varying numbers of light-absorbing molecules. NTSC television samples a scene at a fixed 30 frames per second and also samples a frame as about 480 horizontal raster scan lines. (The NTSC standard specifies that about 35 invisible lines occur around the vertical retrace, for a fixed total of 525 lines, which is absolutely independent of the quality of a television set or signal.) However, within a line, television does not sample light intensity as discrete pixels. Rather, television uses continuously varying analog voltages to represent varying colors along a line. Thus, NTSC television is analog video. However, analog video forms a suitable starting point for capturing digital video.

Capturing digital video, that is, converting analog video to digital video, requires three steps. The first step converts the signal that represents analog video's hue, luminance, and saturation into three voltages that represent amounts of red, green, and blue light (see Focus 1.2). The second step samples each of these three continuously varying voltages at regular time intervals, to convert each line into a sequence of pixels. The third step uses three analog-to-digital converters to express each pixel's amounts of red, green, and blue as three numbers. The resulting numbers, stored on a hard drive or transmitted over a network, are uncompressed digital video. Digital video's resolution thus consists of the following:

- Number of pixels per line
- Number of visible lines per frame

- Number of bits per pixel

- Number of frames per second

Multiplying these four numbers together gives digital video's data rate in bits per second. For example, full-screen, true-color, full-motion video requires a data rate of

$$640 \times 480 \times 24 \times 30 = 221 \text{ Mbps},$$

which is equal to 27 MBps or about 100,000 MB per hour (100 GB per hour).

This data rate not only exceeds the carrying capacity of the fastest local area network but also exceeds the capacity of the high-speed bus inside a personal computer. The storage size needed for one hour of such digital video greatly exceeds the storage capacity of a typical computer. This humongous data rate, together with the requirements for isochronous presentation and synchronization with other media, make digital video the most challenging medium.

Most digital video undergoes a fourth step, compression, to reduce its size and data rate before being stored or transmitted. Compressed video then undergoes decompression before being displayed. Compression is a key part of the state of the art of distributed multimedia, so we discuss it in detail in this chapter's State of the Art. Compression typically reduces digital video's data rate and size by about a factor of between 10 and 100. However, in most cases, compression does not reduce a number such as 100 GB per hour to a manageable value.

Designers of multimedia systems further reduce digital video's data rate and size by using fewer frames per second, lower resolution, and less color depth than we used in the last calculation. A rate as low as 10 frames per second is acceptable for some purposes. Broadcast television and home VHS videocassette recorders produce significantly less resolution than a typical computer screen's resolution of 640 by 480 pixels, as we discuss in Focus 1.5 and illustrate in Table 1.3, so resolution provides significant room for reduction, as well.

Table 1.3 shows numbers of lines of horizontal resolution that are often specified for some important sources of analog video, along with their corresponding approximate numbers of pixels.

Focus 1.6 discusses interlace, which is a trick that allows television signals to use only half as much bandwidth as progressive scan (noninterlaced scan) would require. Interlace causes significant troubles when using television sets with computers.

FOCUS 1.5 Analog video resolution.

A lot of digital video starts out as analog video and gets captured. Moreover, a lot of digital video ends up being converted back to analog video and shown on a television set. Your first experience combining computers and television sets shows you that television displays are not as sharp as computer displays. For example, you can read a line of 40 text characters on a television screen as easily as you can read a line of 80 text characters on a computer screen. The concept of sharpness is sufficiently important to deserve a number.

The sharpness of analog video is specified as a number of lines of horizontal resolution. Store displays and catalogs specify this number for television sets, VCRs, laser disc players (also known as video disc players), and other analog video components. This variable number of lines of horizontal resolution is a completely different concept from the fixed number of horizontal scan lines that the NTSC television standard specifies, although the similar names confuse many people. A screen's number of lines of horizontal resolution is defined as the maximum number of vertical alternating black lines and white lines that a viewer can barely distinguish over a width that is equal to the screen's height (Inglis, 1993). This is called *horizontal resolution* because showing many alternating black and white vertical lines requires the display to make rapid changes in the intensity of the beam, as the beam scans horizontally. (Video people and computer people count both black lines and white lines. Photographers count only black lines and ignore the white spaces in between, so you must double a photographic resolution before you compare it to a video resolution.)

Because a television screen is four-thirds as wide as it is high, you must multiply any specified number of lines of horizontal resolution by four-thirds if you want to know how many alternating black and white lines you could barely distinguish over the entire width of the screen. Unfortunately, for comparison to computer displays, that is *not* what you want to know. Instead, you want to know how many alternating fully black and fully white vertical lines the television screen can produce over the entire width of the screen. For all practical purposes, that reduces the number of pixels in a horizontal row back down close to the specified number of lines of horizontal resolution. Moreover, few video systems actually achieve their specified resolutions. As an approximate rule of thumb, just use the number of lines of horizontal resolution as the number of pixels per row.

How many horizontal rows of pixels can a television set show, counting from top to bottom? This turns out to be relatively indepen-

(cont.)

> **FOCUS 1.5   Analog video resolution. (*cont.*)**
>
> dent of the quality of a television set and signal, because the NTSC standard specifies a constant 525 scan lines per frame, of which about 480 are visible on any screen. However, the number of lines of vertical resolution, that is, the number of barely discernible horizontal black lines and white lines, is not equal to the number of visible horizontal scan lines. Instead, this vertical resolution is equal to 480 multiplied by the Kell factor of 0.7, giving 336. The Kell factor is merely an approximation and is one of many peculiar results of interlaced scanning. The number of fully black and fully white horizontal lines that a television set can display clearly and without flicker is still smaller, as we note in Focus 1.6. The number of vertical pixels is about half the number of visible scan lines, or 240. ∎

Digital video illustrates a special advantage of storing media in digital rather than analog form. If you make copies of analog video on successive VCR tapes, accumulated errors will make a third-generation copy (a copy of a copy of a copy) practically unusable. If you make copies of digital video on a computer's hard drive or on a digital videocassette tape, then the third-generation copy or the hundredth-generation copy will be as good as the original.

We have noted that a great deal of digital video comes from capturing natural analog video, whereas synthetic digital video can come from running two-dimensional (2-D) or three-dimensional (3-D) animation programs. An

Table 1.3   Typical analog video resolutions.

Source of video	Lines of horizontal resolution	Approximate equivalent pixels
Laser disc	425	425 × 240
S-VHS VCR or Hi8 VCR	400	400 × 240
Standard broadcast television	350	350 × 240
VHS VCR	240	240 × 240

Abbreviations:
VCR	Videocassette recorder
VHS	Video home system
S-VHS	Super-VHS
Hi8	High-bandwidth 8 mm

FOCUS 1.6 Analog video interlace.
An NTSC video signal could meet requirements of both flicker fusion and persistence of vision by transmitting 60 complete images each second. However, because 30 complete images each second suffice to give the effect of completely smooth motion, transmitting 60 new images each second would waste half of each television channel's precious transmission capacity. Television engineers invented interlaced scanning to enable them to transmit only 30 complete images each second and still provide a flicker-free screen.

A television raster scans all the odd-numbered lines first, providing what is called the odd field, and then goes back and scans all the even-numbered lines, to provide the even field. The two fields form one frame because they contain a complete image. Because the even field's lines interlace between the odd field's lines, one or the other of the fields comes close to any part of the screen 60 times each second. Thus no part of the screen appears to flicker, even though completely new image frames appear only 30 times each second.

A typical computer display does not use an interlaced raster. Instead, it scans all of its lines in their natural order from top to bottom. This progressive scanning makes the field rate equal the frame rate. The difference between interlaced scanning and progressive scanning adds challenges to capturing analog video as digital video and adds other challenges to converting computer displays to analog video.

For example, consider a computer screen that contains a narrow horizontal line that is only one pixel high. After converting the screen to NTSC, that line might happen to match the position of an odd scan line. In this case, the one-pixel line would be scanned during the odd field, but not during the even field, so the television display would brighten the line's pixels only 30 times a second rather than 60 times a second. As a result, the line would flicker violently. The only way to ensure that a horizontal black or white line shows clearly on an interlaced television screen is to make the line at least two scan lines high. This explains television's effective vertical resolution of 240 pixels. ∎

animation program takes some of the drudgery out of preparing thousands of still images in which each image differs slightly from its predecessor. For example, producing six minutes of computer animation for the movie version of *Jurassic Park* took a crew of 100 people only 30 months (McGarvey, 1995). Clearly, computers do not take out *all* the drudgery.

(Three-dimensional animation is a particularly promising approach to combining interactivity with video.) Earlier we discussed how you can make synthetic video of a particular walk through a mall by building a 3-D model of the mall and telling a computer to display what you would see if you followed a particular path along a succession of eye-height viewpoints. To add interactivity, you can allow a user to select the path and perhaps even select choices that alter the 3-D model, such as turning around a bottle of bleach to read the ingredients or turning on a television set that is for sale. This video user interface (VUI) is a promising metaphor for home shopping. Replacing the mall by an office or by the world of information available on the World Wide Web could help such a VUI become the successor to today's ubiquitous graphical user interface (GUI) metaphor. The formidable hardware requirements of 3-D animation now restrict VUIs to high-end engineering workstations. However, as more powerful consumer computers acquire economical 3-D animation capabilities, this form of synthetic video is likely to take its place in the mainstream of distributed multimedia (Gates, 1995). People who want to make this sort of synthetic video sound fancy sometimes call it virtual reality even if you cannot see what is to your side by turning your head.

Another form of synthetic video, or animation, applies to special-purpose game machines and general-purpose computers for which games are important applications. Such machines include fast hardware that can move a few small figures called sprites across a stationary background. Interacting with video by moving sprites requires significantly less computation than does continuously redrawing the entire screen to show a new viewpoint.

Smell, Taste, and Touch

Media that employ the senses of smell and taste are not important to our discussion because there has been relatively little progress in technologies for digitizing these media or playing them back on demand. Nevertheless, requirements for such media do exist. An employee of an automobile manufacturer has stated the requirement to include in E-mail the attractive smells that he develops for new cars. Magazines that include perfume samples show that advertisers will pay to transmit this medium. Storing tastes (along with accompanying smells) for later comparison would make as much sense in a food company as storing blueprints for later retrieval makes in an architectural firm.

Digitizing and playing back smell and taste present unique and challenging problems. The function that is analogous to clearing the display screen is particularly difficult for smell and taste. Just as it is possible to compose any of millions of different colors by mixing appropriate amounts of red, green, and blue light, it may be possible to compose any taste by mixing a few elementary tastes such as sweet, sour, salt, and bitter. However, recent research indicates that one smell may consist of a mixture of any of approximately

1000 elementary smells. Each elementary smell corresponds to a different type of odor receptor that recognizes a particular shape on a molecule that enters a person's nasal passages (Richardson, 1995).

Media that employ the sense of touch can be important in niche markets. A fabric company could benefit from the ability to store and transmit the feel of running a finger across different materials. At least one research laboratory has developed a compelling pilot model in which a user pushes a joystick to move a pointer around a screen that shows regions of sandpaper, velvet, and other materials. Electromagnets shake the joystick with amplitudes and frequencies that cause the user to feel the results of moving a stylus over corresponding textures. Storing and playing back the feel of moving a finger, rather than a stylus, across different materials would require a quite different technology.

Other applications of touch are in the area of virtual reality. One application allows an organic chemist's fingers to feel the computed strengths of chemical bonds. Another trains surgeons by letting them feel the resistance they would feel if they were cutting actual tissue. A robotics application allows an operator to pick up an egg, by providing touch feedback of not only the force the robot's fingers are applying to the egg but also the feel of the egg slipping through the robot's fingers (Amato, 1992). Finally, wearing a flat plastic backpack allows game players to feel some of the sensations of being shot.

Media Input, Conversion, and Output

Distributed multimedia includes a good many subtleties that both providers and serious users need to understand. These subtleties are reasonably comprehensible one at a time, but they tend to blur together as you learn about more and more of them. We find Table 1.4 and Fig. 1.6 help keep track of how to put each medium into digital form, how to get each medium back out in a form that a user can see or hear, and how to convert information from one medium to another medium. The table and figure summarize some of the information that previous sections provided about each medium. More helpfully, they provide mental pigeonholes in which to file many different facts about the media as they appear in the remainder of the book, in the trade press, and even in daily newspapers. Perhaps the most important message is what the table omits. It omits different methods for storing and delivering the different media. The key message is that digital forms of all media can employ the same storage and delivery methods.

Table 1.4 shows several cases where you create one medium by converting information from some other medium, such as capturing an image by grabbing a video frame. It also shows several cases where you convert

Table 1.4   Media input and output.

Media Functions	Text	Graphics	Images	Audio	Video
Input, by creating synthetic form	Keyboard and word processor	Draw program	Paint program	MIDI keyboard Text-to-speech	2-D or 3-D animation
Input, by capturing natural forms	Speech-to-text Optical character recognition	None	Scanner Video frame grabber Digital camera	Microphone and audio adapter	Capture from analog video
Output	Typewriter printer	Vector display Plotter	Raster display Printer	Audio adapter and speakers	Raster display

one medium to another medium that is more convenient to display or print, such as printing text on something other than a typewriter printer. Figure 1.6 illustrates important functions that convert information expressed in one medium to the equivalent information expressed in another medium.

We have already mentioned most of the conversions that Fig. 1.6 shows, as we introduced the individual media. We noted that typewriter printers are uncommon, so most computers display or print text by first converting text to either image or graphics. You may use a bit-map font to convert the text to image form, or you may use a vector, stroke, or outline font to convert the text to graphics form. Moreover, because vector displays and plotters are uncommon, you are likely to display or print graphics by converting graphics to image form. We also discussed vector-to-raster conversion and filling, which convert from graphics to image, frame capture, which converts from video to image, and animation, which converts either or both of graphics and image to synthetic video.

Several other conversions from one medium to another medium are important to multimedia. You can receive text E-mail over a network and store the text on your hard drive. Then you can use the text-to-speech conversion to change the text into a file that contains a string of samples of digital audio. Converting the resulting audio from digital form to analog form and playing the result through speakers allow you to hear your mail read to you.

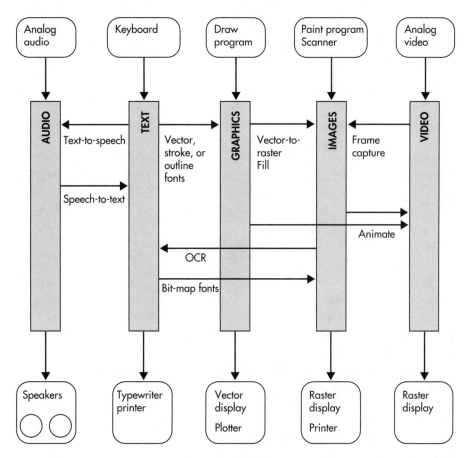

Figure 1.6 Media conversions.

The speech-to-text conversion operates in the opposite direction. It captures a speaker's voice as digital audio and then runs software that attempts to identify the spoken words and store the result as a text string. In general, this attempt is most successful if the speaker pronounces words clearly and separately, uses a tightly constrained vocabulary, or spends several hours accustoming the software to the speaker's voice. You might receive analog audio over a network, convert it to digital form, convert the digital audio to text, and save the information on a hard drive in this extremely compact form.

Optical character recognition (OCR) has been used for decades to convert scanned documents, such as books, to text form. Although the image form is often more meaningful, because it contains particular fonts, figures, and even handwritten annotations, the text form occupies far less storage space and is far more amenable to automated searches, concordances, and summaries. OCR has been used more recently to eliminate keyboards from handheld personal digital assistants (PDAs).

Media Combinations

We discussed each of the media individually because we needed a coherent organization, rather than because typical multimedia content uses the media one at a time. In fact, using several media at once is the rule in multimedia, and using only one medium is the exception. Text is ubiquitous, appearing as an integral part of graphics and images and as titles in video. Audio often appears as voice-overs that explain or enhance graphics, images, and video. Audio also normally accompanies video of speakers and activities that make noise. Graphics appear often in images and video. Images are a natural part of video whenever the picture stops so that the viewer can admire or learn from a scene. Whether you are selecting hardware and software to help you create or play multimedia content, you will need a grasp of the software and hardware involved in combining different media.

Multimedia software products, particularly authoring systems, help creators combine multiple media with interactivity to form multimedia content. Some authoring systems allow you to specify when a user will see and hear particular information by dragging icons that represent various media onto parallel timelines. You might drag a video icon and an audio icon to corresponding points on two adjacent timelines to show that the corresponding video and audio clips should begin simultaneously. You might drag a second video clip onto a third timeline, overlapping the first video clip, to indicate a gradual transition between the clips. Other authoring systems allow you to write scripts that specify the time at which a user will start to see and hear media, such as a spoken narration, and also the duration of nonisochronous media, such as a narrated image. Such software's primary function is synchronization.

Multimedia hardware, too, provides functions for combining multiple media, but here the primary function is multiplexing several visual media onto a single display screen. Figure 1.7 shows hardware that you might find in a television studio, movie special-effects shop, or personal computer equipped to display video. Each of the figure's two frame buffers provides analog voltages that specify the colors of successive pixels. Each frame buffer starts by supplying the color that it thinks should be in the display's upper left corner and proceeds with a repetitive raster scan of all pixels, as we described above, with or without interlace. The multiplexor is simply a rapid

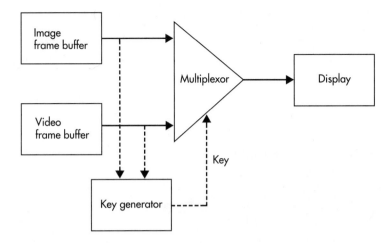

Figure 1.7 Display multiplexor.

switch that, at any given instant, determines which frame buffer's output actually controls the color of the pixel that the display is scanning at that instant.

All the interesting action takes place in the key, which controls the multiplexor. If the key generator supplies a key signal that tells the multiplexor to keep the image frame buffer's output constantly connected to the display, then the display shows only the contents of the image frame buffer. Of course, as we discussed in the previous section on converting information from one medium to another, the image frame buffer may include pixels that represent text and graphics. Similarly, if the key generator supplies the opposite signal, then the display shows only video and no image. However, if the key generator supplies a signal that tells the multiplexor to switch back and forth between the two frame buffers many times during each raster scan, then we get an interesting combination of the contents of the two frame buffers on the single display screen (Jack, 1993).

Figure 1.8 shows the three simplest and most important methods by which the key generator can control the multiplexor, namely, window keying, luminance keying, and chrominance keying. Typical applications of the three methods are to create a video window on top of an image, a text title on top of video, and video of a weather person standing in front of a weather map, respectively. The latter two methods are important enough to have the familiar nicknames of luma keying and chroma keying.

In window keying, the key generator simply uses time to determine whether the pixel that the display is currently scanning is inside or outside some previously specified rectangle, which might be the center ninth of the

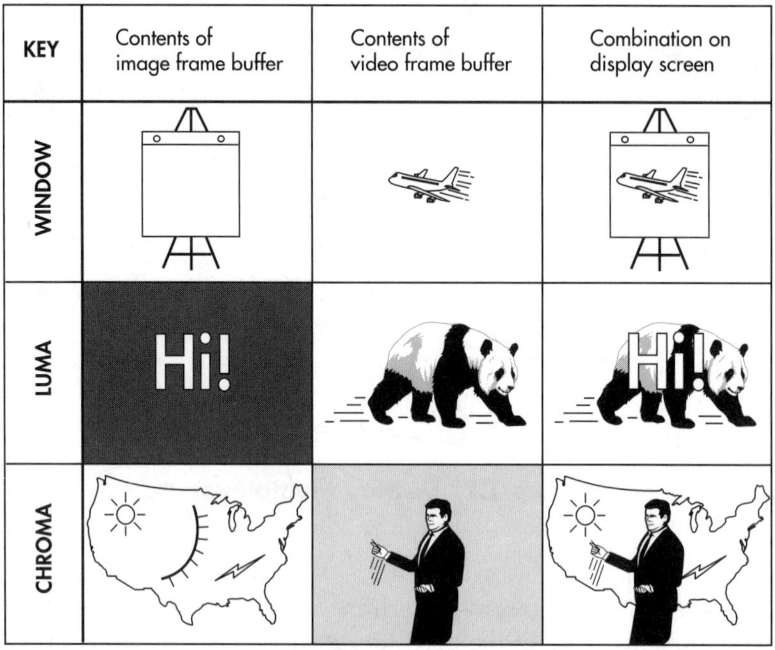

Figure 1.8 Window, luma, and chroma keying.

display screen. (The key generator keeps track of where the beam is by keeping track of the time that has elapsed since the start of the current raster scan. Entire scan lines that are near the top or bottom of the screen are outside the specified rectangle. Pixels on a scan line that is near the middle of the screen may be inside the rectangle, but are actually inside only if they are also near the middle of the scan line.) When the current pixel is inside the rectangle, the key tells the multiplexor to connect the video frame buffer to the display; when the pixel is outside the rectangle, the key tells the multiplexor to connect the image frame buffer to the display. A video-in-a-window adapter uses this type of keying to create a video window. Many multimedia titles use video that fills only a small window and use the rest of the display screen to show an image of a projection screen or television set and other attractive or useful images. This technique avoids video that has excessive storage size or network data rate without wasting the rest of the screen.

In luma keying, the contents of the image frame buffer control the key generator. When the luminance of the current pixel in the image frame buffer is below some previously specified value (indicating that the image at that point is merely black background), then the key generator tells the multiplexor to connect the video frame buffer to the display; otherwise, the key generator tells the multiplexor to connect the image frame buffer. Thus, luma keying overlays any part of the image that is not black background on top of the video; that is, it lets the video appear to show through the image's background. Typically, the image consists of letters that make up a title for the video.

In chroma keying, the contents of the video frame buffer control the key generator. When the chrominance of the current pixel in the video frame buffer is within some specified range, which by convention is often centered on highly saturated blue, then the key generator tells the multiplexor to connect the image frame buffer to the display; otherwise, the key generator tells the multiplexor to connect the video frame buffer. Thus, chroma keying allows the image to show on all parts of the display where the video is blue. In a typical application of chroma keying, a weather person walks around and gesticulates in front of a blue background. A camera pointed at the weather person scans along with a computer that generates the image of a weather map. As thousands of television sets scan along with both the video and the image, viewers see the weather person at each point on their screens where the weather person actually is and see the weather map wherever the weather person is not. If the weather person makes the mistake of wearing a blue tie, chroma keying provides a grisly peek at the weather map through the weather person's chest.

Other methods by which the key generator can control the multiplexor produce special effects (FX) that combine media in more complicated and interesting ways. Some of the most interesting FX involve two sources of video driving the same multiplexor. This allows you to make a gradual transition from showing source A to showing source B in what is called an A-B roll. One A-B roll starts with a small window showing the center portion of source B, in the center of a screen that shows mostly source A, and gradually expands the window until the screen shows only source B. In this roll, as in window keying, the key generator uses time to decide which signal will control each pixel on the display, rather than using either of the input signals. Unlike window keying, however, a roll makes a small increase in the size of the window just before each successive scan begins. By generalizing this discussion, you may be able to guess what the key generator is doing to produce FX that you see in all sorts of contexts that combine media, ranging from multimedia titles to "Monday Night Football."

Software often uses a technique similar to keying in order to form a complete image by showing different parts of different layers. Parts of each layer may be transparent and thus allow other layers to show through. In this context, the information that tells where each layer is transparent is called an *alpha channel* rather than a key.

Media Sizes and Data Rates

We have noted that one of the reasons multimedia makes severe demands on processing power, storage capacity, and network bandwidth is that meaningful amounts of audio and particularly of video tend to be very large. As a result, many of the most important and interesting aspects of distributed multimedia are quantitative. The only way to understand quantitative differences between multimedia systems and earlier systems is to perform back-of-the-envelope calculations based on typical numbers. This book includes many sample calculations. Sample calculations, unlike formulas, show units, such as the simple but vital difference between bits and Bytes, and also provide sample answers that help give you a feeling for the subject. Approximate calculations often enable you to distinguish reasonable possibilities from absurd flights of fancy. However, if you are involved in making design decisions, you should obtain accurate numbers rather than relying on our typical numbers.

Before summarizing previous sections' calculations for each medium, we provide some details that may help you follow our calculations and get correct answers when you perform your own calculations. Focus 1.7 discusses the units that are most likely to cause you to get wrong answers.

Focus 1.8 gives some useful powers of 2 and 10 along with the names of the powers of 10. Focus 1.9 discusses a tradeoff between accuracy and precision. Focus 1.10 discusses why a CD-ROM provides useful units for measuring sizes and data rates and tells what these units are.

After these explanations and hints, Table 1.5 and Table 1.6 quantify the medias' sizes and bandwidths by summarizing the calculations we made in previous sections. The two tables separate nonisochronous media (text, graphics, and images), which have sizes in bits or Bytes, from the isochronous media (audio and video), which have data rates in bits per second or Bytes per second. Except where noted, we give sizes for uncompressed media.

The key message in this section is that each digital medium offers you a wide range of sizes, data rates, and qualities. In many cases, this wide range is independent of a particular server, delivery network, or end-user device. Whether you create multimedia content for personal use or for sale, representing the media in digital form gives you the opportunity to allocate available hard drive space, disc storage space, or network bandwidth among several media in whatever proportion allows you to make your points most effectively.

We have noted that multimedia authoring system software allows you to mix multiple media with interactivity in creative ways. In one memorable ti-

> **FOCUS 1.7 Bytes, bits, and other units.**
>
> A Byte, a group of eight bits, is meaningful for only one medium, text, in which a Byte can represent one character in a typical Western alphabet. For all the other media, and for Kanji text, we would do better to measure everything in bits. However, as in many other highly non-standardized aspects of multimedia, since we cannot change them, we must join them.
>
> In many cases we calculate both in bits and Bytes, because you are likely to have intuitive understanding of network transmission capacities in terms of bits per second and have intuitive understanding of hard drive or diskette sizes in terms of Bytes. On the one hand, you may know that a fast modem can run at 28.8 Kbps, but would not recognize this rate when quoted as 3.6 KBps. On the other hand, you may know that a diskette holds 1.44 M Bytes, but would not recognize this size when quoted as 11.5 M bits.
>
> When we write out the words *bits* and *Bytes*, we capitalize the latter, because the most common single error in calculating sizes of media is to confuse these two units. Many seemingly precise calculations turn out to be highly inaccurate because they err by a factor of eight, which can make the difference between concluding that a function is easy and concluding that the function is impossible.
>
> Capitalizing only the abbreviation for Bytes is not quite universal. For example, an advertisement may use one of "B" and "b" for both units, although usually as a matter of style rather than with any intent to mislead. Capitalizing the word *Bytes* is not common; we do it to help you remember to capitalize its abbreviation and thereby avoid errors. Feel free to curse this convention, until you catch yourself in error by a factor of eight.
>
> Of course, bits and Bytes are not the only units that you should keep track of when writing out calculations. If you write that a network's bandwidth is 9600, you leave open not only whether your unit of information is bits or Bytes, but also whether your unit of time is seconds or minutes. You should always write a number with appropriate units, such as 9600 bits per second, 9600 bits/second, or 9600 bps. ■

tle, a creator showed an image of a beach scene. A button on the scene invited users to invoke video of a narrator. When a user did so, a drop of blue water fell on the sand and splashed to form an irregular outline that occupied approximately one-twentieth of the screen. The narrator climbed into this outline and made a point. The result was more effective than playing the

FOCUS 1.8 Powers of 2 and 10

The abbreviation for each power of 10 is the first letter of its name, except that the abbreviation for 10^{-6} is the Greek letter μ, which every cat pronounces "mu," and the abbreviation for 10^3 is k, at least in km meaning kilometers. Distributed multimedia is making it increasingly important for you to know names for larger exponents.

$2^4 =$ 16	10^3 = Kilo	10^{-3} = milli
$2^8 =$ 256	10^6 = Mega	10^{-6} = micro
$2^{10} =$ 1024	10^9 = Giga	10^{-9} = nano
$2^{16} =$ 32,768	10^{12} = Tera	10^{-12} = pico
$2^{24} =$ 16,777,216	10^{15} = Peta	10^{-15} = femto ∎

FOCUS 1.9 K is 1000 or 1024.

For approximate calculations, you should feel free to assume that $2^{10} = 1024$ is the same as $10^3 = 1000$. That is, you can use "K" for both "1024" and "1000." This makes calculations significantly easier. More important, it eliminates many large errors in placing decimal points. A few 2.4 percent errors are usually harmless, whereas misplacing a decimal point creates havoc. You will find that you spend less time and make fewer blunders if you punch in "000" or some form of "10^3" than if you enter 1024. A calculator that allows you to enter 1000 as "E 3" or "EEX 3" is worth its weight in crumpled wastepaper covered with wrong calculations. Similarly, you can use "1,000,000" for "M." When your results disagree with others', check whether somebody is using 1000 and somebody else is using 1024. Then ask yourself if it matters. If it does matter, go back and make the exact calculation, but always check whether it gives about the same answer as the easy calculation.

Years of experience, including grading graduate students' examinations, indicate that you will get more useful answers if you calculate directly in either bits or Bytes and let your calculator handle all decimal points and exponents, rather than juggling Kb and MB in your head or multiplying and dividing by 1024. Although this advice sounds silly to theoreticians, most practical calculations start with numbers that are uncertain by several percent. If a calculation comes out so close that a proposal will work in theory only if you use the right one of 1024 and 1000, the proposal probably won't work in practice. ∎

FOCUS 1.10 CD-ROM as a unit of measure.

Mailing a CD-ROM is one of the most cost-effective ways of distributing multimedia content. Developers have designed a great deal of multimedia content to play on the original single-speed (or single-spin) CD-ROM drives. Newer drives, such as six-speed drives, play at a specified multiple of the single-speed data rate. Many numbers that are too big to visualize in terms of bits or Bytes are easy to visualize in terms of either the storage capacity of a CD-ROM disc or the data rate of a single-speed CD-ROM drive. The following three numbers, along with their units, are by far the most useful ones to memorize for use in multimedia calculations.

- CD-ROM size is 550 MB.
- Single-speed CD-ROM data rate is 150 KBps.
- Single-speed CD-ROM data rate is 1.2 Mbps.

Let's look at where these numbers come from. A full CD-ROM holds 552,960,000 Bytes. (A disc manufacturer can cram in 23 percent more data by recording on the disc's outermost part, which is susceptible to damage and smudging by fingers.) This number can be written precisely as

$$552{,}960{,}000 \text{ B}/(1024 \times 1024) = 527.34 \text{ MB},$$

but the approximate value of 550 MB is much easier to remember.

A single-speed CD-ROM drive plays a full disc in 60 minutes (or 72 minutes for a crammed disc) so its data rate is given by

$$527.34 \text{ MB} \times 1024/60 \text{ min} = 9000 \text{ KB per min, or}$$
$$9000 \text{ KB}/\text{min})/(60 \text{ sec}/\text{min}) = 150 \text{ KBps}.$$

Looking ahead to our discussion of digital video compression, it is useful to note that this is the data rate that many important video compression schemes produce. Schemes that compress by a larger factor can give higher quality video; but all schemes give the same one hour of video on a full, single-speed CD-ROM disc. Preparing digital video specifically to play on a six-speed drive would have the advantage of allowing either far lower compression or far higher-quality video, but would have the disadvantage of playing the entire disc in only 10 minutes, which would take a lot of the fun out of it.   *(cont.)*

> **FOCUS 1.10 CD-ROM as a unit of measure. (*cont.*)**
> In bits, the speed of a single-speed CD-ROM drive is
>
> $$(150 \text{ KBps} \times 8 \text{ bits per Byte})/1024 = 1.17 \text{ Mbps,}$$
>
> which we suggest you remember as 1.2 Mbps.
>   In connection with telecommunications, it is useful to recall that
> this single-speed CD-ROM data rate is only a little slower than the
> 1.544 Mbps rate of a T1 line. In connection with comparing audio and
> video, it is useful to remember that this is the rate of either uncom-
> pressed, high-quality digital audio or compressed, medium-quality,
> digital video. ∎

Table 1.5 Sizes of nonisochronous media.

Medium and quality or quantity	Calculation and size, in Bytes	Capacity of one CD-ROM
Text, typeset page	3 K characters × 1 Byte per character = 3 K Bytes	183,333 pages
Graphics, with 200 objects	200 objects × 9 Bytes per object = 1800 Bytes	305 K graphics
Image, S-VGA screen resolution	640 pixels per line × 480 lines per frame × 8 bits per pixel = 2.4 M bits = 307 K Bytes	1791 images
Image, copier or laser printer page	300 pixels per horizontal inch × 300 pixels per vertical inch × 8.5 inch x 11 inch × 1 bit per pixel = 8.4 M bits = 1.0 M Bytes	550 pages
Image, Kodak Photo-CD archival resolution	3072 pixels per line × 2048 lines per frame × 36 bits per pixel = 226 M bits = 28 M Bytes	19 images (Note 1)

Note 1: On an actual Photo-CD disc, an image is compressed down to about 5 M Bytes, so that the images of about 100 slides fit onto one disc.

Table 1.6 Data rates and sizes of isochronous media.

Medium and quality	Calculation and data rate (bits per second)	Data rate (Bytes per minute)	Capacity of one CD-ROM
Audio, telephone quality	7 bits per sample × 8000 samples per second = 56 Kbps	420 KBpm	1300 minutes or 22 hours
Audio, compact disc quality	16 bits per sample × 44,100 samples per second × 2 stereo channels = 1.4 Mbps	10.5 MBpm	52 minutes as data (Note1)
Video at full VGA resolution, true color, and full motion	640 pixels per line × 480 lines per frame × 24 bits per pixel × 30 frames per second = 221 Mbps	1658 MBpm	0.33 minutes or 20 seconds (Note 2)
Video on CD-ROM, compressed, with less resolution	150 KBps × 8 bits per Byte = 1.2 Mbps	9 MBpm	60 minutes, by definition
Video, HDTV proposal (Note 3)	1920 pixels per line × 1080 lines per frame × 24 bits per pixel × 30 frames per second = 1492 Mbps	11,000 MBpm	0.05 minutes or 3.0 seconds

Note 1: Single-speed CD-ROM drives and CD-Digital Audio drives read bits off the discs at exactly the same rate. However, a CD-DA drive uses fewer of the bits for error correction, so CD-DA can play 60 minutes as audio, whereas a CD-ROM plays 54 minutes as data.

Note 2: Saying that a CD-ROM can hold 20 seconds of uncompressed digital video does not imply that any conceivable drive could read the entire disc in 20 seconds. Thus, compression is necessary not only to put a useful amount of video on the disc but also to play video from the disc at all.

Note 3: High-definition television signals will undergo extensive compression in order to be broadcast over the same 6-MHz bandwidth channels as NTSC video. The HDTV standard allows other resolutions, including 1280 by 720, 704 by 480, and 640 by 480.

narrator on the full screen would have been. Even more important, this small video window allowed a small size and small rate of digital video to play with a high frame rate, good resolution, and many colors. Digitizing media provides such creative options by decoupling each medium from the details of servers, networks, and display devices.

With this background on interactivity and the five media, we are ready to discuss our vision of where we expect distributed multimedia to go in the next decade.

VISION FOR THE NEXT DECADE

Each subsequent chapter of this book includes a section in which we present our vision for that chapter's particular part of distributed multimedia. In this chapter, we present our vision for distributed multimedia as a whole. We use the word *vision* to denote what we foresee happening by the year 2005 rather than to denote the sense that perceives text, graphics, image, and video.

Establishing a vision is serious business. A prerequisite for devising a corporation's business strategy, it plays a similar role for an individual, educational institution, or government. On rare occasions, establishing a suitable vision can enable you to set a trend and, on even more rare occasions, to profit handsomely thereby. More commonly, establishing a vision helps you avoid losing out by being blind to a trend that is passing you by.

Establishing a vision requires you to consider demographics and economic conditions, which affect what other people will want and be able to afford; technology, which determines what progress is possible; and history, which enables you to judge what progress is likely and how fast it will occur. More subtly, establishing a vision requires you to consider the key providers and regulators involved, so that you can judge what they are likely to promote, invest in, encourage, or prevent.

Our vision comes from several years of experience and a host of excellent sources. A typical published source is *Educom Review—Learning, Communications and Information Technology,* which consistently publishes reports by noted visionaries intended for an audience of faculty and staff at institutions of higher education (see, for example, Auletta and Gilder, 1995). Another source is *Upside Magazine,* which is justified in calling itself "a provocative, insightful magazine that delivers an unflinchingly honest perspective on the people and companies creating the digital revolution." Essentially every issue includes a provocative interview with a major provider's chief executive officer and visionary (see, for example, Bell et al., 1994). Information about what technology will make possible appears first in trade press articles, which constitute the bulk of the references at the end of each chapter, and on networks. Books make up for a publication lag by providing reasoned syntheses of such information (see Gates, 1995, and Negroponte, 1995).

The vision for distributed multimedia is that, within 10 years, anyone should be able to receive, send, and interact with information, using what-

> **FOCUS 1.11 A postchannel universe.**
> A postchannel universe of essentially unlimited choice: virtually everything produced for the medium, past or present, plus a wealth of other information and entertainment options, stored in computer banks and available instantly at the touch of a button. . . . The peacock turns to you and says "What do you want to watch?" and you say "Something funny." The peacock says "Something new or . . . ?" The monthly television bill could ultimately look something like today's telephone bill, with message units reflecting the household's viewing. . . . It will wreak havoc with the television habit. Turning on the set each evening to see what's on becomes meaningless when "What's on?" becomes "essentially anything you want" (*Time*, 1993). ∎

ever media she prefers, independent of where the media may be located. Anybody who has something to communicate should be able to send whatever media are most expressive to the appropriate audience. The metaphor of an information highway is imperfect, but it does emphasize that a highway carries traffic in both directions and that expanding information highways may be as important to the twenty-first century as expanding automotive highways was to the twentieth.

Useful, instructive, and entertaining content is vital to the vision for distributed multimedia. A supporting structure that allows users to find what they want in the mass of available communication partners and accessible information is equally important. We give further details about our vision of information that will flow over a multimedia network in the Vision section of Chapter 5, Applications. The writers of *Time* magazine described their vision of receiving multimedia as in Focus 1.11.

Distributed multimedia is far more than a theoretical possibility because, by 2005, technological and social innovations will make it not only technically possible, but also widely affordable. Like other major parts of our infrastructure, it will be far from free, but a central part of the vision is that users will feel that it is well worth what it costs.

Conspicuously absent from the vision for distributed multimedia is that anyone should be able to receive, send, and interact with all the media from wherever she happens to be. We do not expect sending long streams of video from a wireless unit to become widely affordable to individual consumers by 2005, even if the unit is within range of a cellular transmitting and receiving station. Moreover, wireless reception of a unique video stream that contains exactly what you want to see, when nobody else wants to see the same stream or is willing to help you pay for the stream, will still be too expensive for general use in 2005. However, our vision does encompass sending, receiving, and interacting with all the media other than video, in wireless environments, within 10 years. Focus 1.12 explains wireless video's unique challenges.

As uses of multimedia expanded beyond aerospace simulations and movie special effects, multimedia became subject to the rules of consumer marketing. One of those rules is that consumers are happiest when they can embrace something that is new, but not too new. Consumers prefer evolution to revolution. For this reason, people will view multimedia as enhancing devices with which they are already familiar, such as television sets, computers, and telephones, and as enhancing environments in which they already find themselves, such as education, work, and entertainment. We consider next how our vision for the development of distributed multimedia over the next 10 years will appear when seen from each of these six viewpoints.

Enhancing Television Sets, Computers, and Telephones

Enhancing Television Sets   You may view a distributed multimedia system as providing a new answer to the question "What's on television this evening?" The new answer will be "Anything you want to see!" Whether you want today's general news or a detailed historical background about a news item that particularly interests you, or today's most popular movie or a little-known silent film, you will interact with the network and it will deliver quickly what you request. Similarly, you may be able to turn on your set, get a "video dial tone," and call up a friend or colleague for a conversation that includes not only seeing and hearing the other person, but also cooperatively filling out a spreadsheet. If you call your friend while sitting on your sofa, holding a wireless remote control unit, and watching a large screen, you are likely to feel that you are using a television set.

Multimedia may reduce the total time that you spend watching television. Many people now turn on a set every evening, just to see what is on, and then watch it until bedtime because what is may never be on again. Knowing that you will be able to see whatever you really want to see, whenever you want to see it, will eliminate the now-or-never reason for remaining glued to the tube. Your larger number of more attractive choices every half hour will require companies that provide television entertainment to revise their marketing model, which now relies on a sequence of scheduled programs.

If you envision distributed multimedia as an extension of television, you will not need to know that your television sets or set-top boxes (also known

FOCUS 1.12 Why will wireless video remain expensive?

Meeting multimedia network requirements without using physical connections will take significantly longer than will meeting the requirements using wires and fiber-optic cables. In fact, the lag between wired interactive video and wireless interactive video may be as long as the lag between nationwide wired telephone service, which was essentially complete in the 1940s, and nationwide cellular telephone service, which is still not complete today.

The main problem with wireless video is that video uses a bandwidth that is far higher than that of other media. Even with digital compression, a network that transmits reasonable-quality video requires a bandwidth of approximately 1.5 M bits per second. For example, if a cellular telephone connection could carry an optimistic 64 K bits per second, then sending video would require over 20 times the bandwidth of a cellular telephone. The difficulty of finding room in the electromagnetic spectrum for 20 times today's cellular telephone bandwidth is one major problem with wireless operation. Space in the radio frequency spectrum will remain scarce, and thus expensive, even as fiber-optic cables increase the capacity and decrease the price of wired connections.

Power consumption is another major problem, because a transmitter's power consumption is roughly proportional to the transmitted signal's bandwidth. Extending the distributed multimedia vision beyond the reach of wires and fibers, which carry both signal and power, will require improvements in battery technology sufficient to make 20 cellular telephone batteries easily portable.

For the foreseeable future, users who are beyond the reach of wires and fibers will have to make do with receiving video broadcasts intended for more than one user. Such users will have to limit their interactions to the other media, which require far less bandwidth than does video.

As an example of the nontrivial nature of wireless transmission, a state-of-the-art satellite telephone link that operates beyond the reach of telephone wires or cellular telephone transmitters and receivers is the size of a suitcase, weighs 27 pounds, and costs $17,880. An equivalent unit that can transmit video is much larger, heavier, and more expensive. Such a unit is a familiar sight at a news scene or sports event, but it occupies a truck rather than a suitcase (*Discover*, 1994). ∎

as television converter boxes or cable converter boxes) will hide extremely powerful computers. After all, many people are already accustomed to setting a new television's brightness by interacting with a three-layer menu structure, rather than by turning a knob. The extension to using a remote control to navigate the World Wide Web is a quantitative rather than a qualitative change from using today's television sets.

Enhancing Computers   You may view distributed multimedia as adding video and audio to your already highly interactive computers. Just as your computer interactions now produce a new text or graphics screen every few seconds, you will be able to invoke a new video and audio data stream as frequently as once every few seconds. This capability will enhance communicating with friends, co-workers, and educators, retrieving and supplying information, and playing games against remote friends, strangers, or computers. Many people who would never consider writing and mailing letters regularly to friends, family members, or colleagues have embraced E-mail and spend hours every week exchanging electronic mail. Multimedia will allow you to employ video and audio in situations where those media are more expressive than is unadorned text.

Computer-oriented people will thus gain an increasing ability to view entertaining or educational television programs and to communicate with other people without leaving their computers to turn on a television set or to pick up a telephone. As a user, you will employ a database to dial a telephone just as you now use a database to address an envelope. You will record or forward an incoming video signal for later use, just as you now record or forward an incoming piece of text E-mail.

Enhancing Telephones   You may feel that a multimedia system's most important effects will amount to augmenting telephones with video display screens and with either alphanumeric keyboards or touch screens. The screens not only will allow you to see other people, but also will help you to avoid the growing number of voice-response units. We expect reading a menu on a telephone's screen to be a huge improvement over listening to a recorded voice that reels off a collection of choices. One reason is that most people can read more words per minute than anyone can speak. A more important reason is that, when you are selecting among several alternatives, it is quicker to flick your eyes back to a previous alternative than to request a repetition of the entire list.

You will find a multimedia-capable computer wherever you now find a telephone, including in airports, in libraries, on street corners, and in places of business. Entering your password or scanning your charge card will not only establish your ability to pay, but will also personalize the device's interface for you. Dialing a friend by entering "Jim" will work as well from a gas station telephone booth as from a home telephone, except for the problem of hearing Jim over the traffic noise.

As an extreme case, video communications might become so familiar that we would refer to plain old video service (POVS) in the same casually respectful way in which we talk about today's plain old telephone service (POTS). Suppose that you could use POVS to do everything with video that POTS can do with audio and images. You could use POVS to establish a two-way, full-motion, full-screen, full-color connection with anybody else in the country or the world. You would almost never find that all lines are busy so you must try your call again later. You could dial up the Weather Channel just as you now dial up a recorded local weather forecast. You could use POVS to dial the equivalent of a 900 number in order to access any movie, television drama, news broadcast, sports broadcast, or any other new or old video that anybody had ever recorded. You could use equivalents of talking telephone books and information operators to locate any desired person, live broadcast, or recorded video, within a couple of minutes. You could use POVS to exchange digital media with people and databases at a rate several hundred times higher than you now attain by using POTS. You could have one or more end-user devices with the desirable attributes of a television set for group and casual use, a telephone for private use, and a computer for extensive and intensive use.

Several telephone companies are gearing up for POVS under names such as video dial tone (VDT) or switched digital video (SDV). We describe some early efforts in Chapter 7 on Trials.

Enhancing Education, Work, and Entertainment

Enhancing Education   Distributed multimedia holds the promise of greatly improving all forms of remote education and training. For example, interactivity makes multimedia especially effective for just-in-time training, ranging from a three-hour minicourse at your desk to a five-second bout with an application program's help feature.

If you have been taking courses by passively watching lectures on television, you will gain the ability to interact with course materials and with distant instructors. If you have been using computers and modems for text-only distance learning, you will gain the ability to get more meaningful information in the form of image, audio, and video. If you tend to wait to telephone a guru as you find that you need each piece of information, you will gain the ability to access a wider universe of sources of instant information.

Enhancing Work   Most workers' routine interactions with distant co-workers and distant sources of information now use primarily audio, by way of telephones, and text, by way of paper documents, E-mail, and fax. Use of images and video has been far less common and less well supported. A technician sends a distant colleague written or oral explanations of how a machine malfunctions, because she has no good way to send an image or video of the misbehavior. Adding image and video capabilities to traditional voice capabilities will make a business communications network more useful and will make employees more productive.

Video conferences have met with only limited approval and success, even where they are available. Expensive business travel remains necessary because successful collaborations and negotiations depend on building relationships and earning trust. Like E-mail, video conferences now work best after participants have met and worked together face-to-face. The extent to which improved video conferences can replace face-to-face interaction is the subject of ongoing debate, dispute, and research. It should be possible for a video conference to provide a better sense of presence by reducing delays, allowing eye contact, providing full duplex audio that allows both parties to speak at one time, and accommodating multisite participation.

Enhancing Entertainment   Distributed multimedia will blur the boundaries among television shows, video games, and telephone conversations with friends. For example, a conversation with a distant friend may include not only seeing real-time video of the friend, but also playing a board game such as checkers or backgammon or playing a computer game. Multimedia entertainment is often thought of as increasing people's interactions with computers. Instead, we envision that multimedia entertainment will increase people's interactions with other people and decrease their reliance on entertainment programs produced for mass audiences.

Convergence of Views

It is perfectly valid to view a distributed multimedia system from any of the six viewpoints we have just discussed. A user should not care whether her end-user device receives and sends all the media over one or more networks that are descendants of today's telephone networks, television cable networks, or computer local area networks. As we discuss in Chapter 4, each of her end-user devices probably will look like a descendent of a television set, telephone, or computer, while having the capabilities of all three types of devices. For example, a computer's system unit may appear as a television set-top box; its keyboard may appear as a handheld infrared remote control unit; and its display may be a high-definition television (HDTV) set. A telephone instrument may hide an alphanumeric keyboard behind a hinged lid and, if it performs sophisticated video compression and decompression, it may have more processing power than any of today's personal computers.

The roles that you play throughout a typical day, such as employee, student, businessperson, and consumer of entertainment, will converge significantly during the next decade. A few years ago, you might have spent every business day in an office; communicated with distant co-workers by way of your employer's leased tieline telephone, fax, E-mail, and video conference networks; and had no television cable connection for access to even job-related news coverage. Then, in your role of student, you might have taken an evening class in a room that contained an educational television CATV connection but no telephone jack. Finally, you might have gone home and had only the options of mail or telephone for conducting personal business or communicating with distant friends and a television cable for news or entertainment. In the next decade, you will be increasingly likely to get just-in-time education during the workday, rather than in the evening. You will be increasingly likely to spend workdays at home or on the road, rather than in an employer's office building. When you go to an educational institution, you will not tolerate isolation from job and personal communications. You will be more likely to use a network to update the value of your stock portfolio, rather than keying in numbers from a newspaper.

As a result, it will no longer suffice for you to access separate and unrelated networks from office, campus, and home. The vision of converging all media into digital forms that are compatible with all networks and providing you with access to all stored information and all communication partners from wherever you happen to be, as Fig. 1.9 indicates, will be crucial for converging the roles that you play during a day. You probably will not care whether you access one physical network or whether one company owns the networks you access, but you will care whether you can access business, educational, and personal information and communication partners from home, work, campus, and other locations.

STATE OF THE ART

We will not reiterate what you already know about the separate systems that provide highly interactive computing (with text, graphics, and some images), interactive telephony (with audio and some fax images), and nonin-

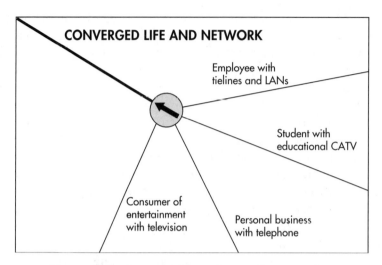

Figure 1.9 Converging roles and networks.

teractive television (with video and other media). Instead, we begin our presentation of today's state of the art of distributed multimedia by discussing forces that are encouraging more video that has interactivity and more computing that has audio and video. Next we mention some examples of convergence that these driving forces have already brought about. Finally, we discuss the state of the art of compression, which is highly relevant to all parts of a multimedia system. For the state of the art of an individual part of distributed multimedia, we refer you to the State of the Art section of the corresponding chapter.

Driving Forces

Technological Improvements Technological improvements are the strongest driving forces behind distributed multimedia. The most important technologies are silicon large-scale integration chips and glass and plastic fiber-optic cables. Other important technologies are denser and faster hard drives and circuitry that can transmit high-bandwidth digital video signals over wires designed for low-bandwidth analog audio signals. Still other technologies such as improved displays and batteries may turn out to be revolutionary. Much of this book is devoted to describing capabilities that such technologies are likely to make economical before about 2005.

We emphasize technological improvements that make capabilities economical, rather than merely making capabilities possible. For example, as a potential consumer product, interactive digital video is important only because chips that can compress and decompress digital video already cost only a few hundred dollars and will cost only a few dollars by the late 1990s. Existence of million-dollar supercomputers that could perform similar functions in the 1980s interested movie studios and the military, but did not imply that consumers or even businesses could ever afford the same functions.

Corporate Revenues Perhaps surprisingly, the next strongest driving force behind multimedia is the negative effect of technological improvements on corporate revenues and profits. The effect of improved personal computer technology on the mainframe business is too well known to require more than a mention. Continuing improvements require personal computer manufacturers themselves to run furiously in order to keep up with technological progress. If computer manufacturers produce machines with constant performance, then continuing technical improvements will make it possible for them to build those computers more and more cheaply. Competitive pressures will then drive the average price of their products lower and lower, causing their revenues and profits to drop unacceptably. Computer companies need applications that will encourage increasing numbers of customers to purchase increasingly powerful products, thus preserving or improving the companies' revenues and profits. Multimedia applications promise to make use of all foreseeable improvements in computer performance.

Somewhat less well known than the effects of improved digital electronics on the computer business are the effects of improved fiber-optic cables on the network business. For many years, AT&T provided good returns for its stockholders and meaningful work for its employees largely by installing, operating, and maintaining a lucrative network of long lines, which ran between central offices, as well as a network of short local loops, which ran from central offices to individual homes and businesses. Long lines were enormously expensive when they were composed of coaxial cables with many repeater amplifiers, chains of microwave relay towers exposed to winds and birds, and communications satellites. However, long lines composed of fiber-optic cables now cost much less to install and maintain and, as a result, have rapidly replaced the other types of connections. Even for local loops, which do not need the enormous bandwidths of long fibers, fiber optics may now be slightly less expensive than copper twisted pairs, partly because fiber's higher reliability reduces the lifetime cost of running a few fibers to each neighborhood relative to the cost of running and maintaining traditional bundles of many copper twisted-pair wires. Network companies are not enthusiastic about using technological improvements to provide the same service for lower and lower prices, thereby decreasing their revenues and profits. They need applications that require customers to transmit more and more high-bandwidth content, so that the companies can charge customers the same or higher tariffs for more and more service, which companies can provide for approximately constant costs. Multimedia applications promise to make use of all foreseeable increases in network capacity.

As a solution to computer companies' excess performance and network companies' unused capacity, multimedia is almost too much of a good thing. Although a Pentium or a Power PC has much more performance than simple text editing requires, such computers have far less performance than decompressing and displaying television-quality digital video requires. Even with special co-processors, available performance limits typical personal computers to smaller screens, fewer colors, and fewer frames per second than you see on a television set. Although intercity long lines have much more capacity than is required for traditional voice telephone calls, few businesses and essentially no homes have access to high-speed communications lines that can carry digital video. Even if a customer had access to a line that can transmit 24 times as much information as a voice-grade line, he could not afford to use it, because the network company prices (tariffs) the high-speed line at about 24 times the price of a voice-grade line. Multimedia replaces companies' problem of how to charge for more performance and capacity by the problem of how to make near-term products and demonstrations look good enough to whet consumers' appetites for capabilities that will become affordable over the next decade. To the extent that multimedia products and services move into the realm of high-volume consumer items, these products and services will attract providers other than traditional computer and networking companies.

Customer Demand   Customer demand is a third, far weaker, force driving distributed multimedia. Some demands exist. One is the demand for educating students and training employees in classrooms that are remote from teachers. There is demand for accessing a wide variety of movies, sports, news, and other video programming at times that users select. There is demand for business video conferences. However, in essentially all such cases, the real demand is for a function such as improving education, expanding entertainment options, or reducing travel and traffic. Users can meet such demands in many ways that do not involve multimedia. Customers will use and pay for multimedia only if it provides better solutions at lower costs than available alternatives. Relatively few multimedia solutions now have higher quality and lower cost than alternative solutions. A few potential customers have seen impressive demonstrations of high-quality functions that are already technically possible but that the customers will not be able to afford for 5 to 10 years. Other potential customers have great difficulty demanding functions that they cannot even imagine.

Government Pressures   Finally, government officials at all levels want
to take actions that visibly benefit their constituencies. A new national information infrastructure (NII) would be as appropriate for an information society as the interstate highway system was for an industrial society. Vice
President Albert Gore invoked this analogy by using the name "information
superhighway." Paying for the NII with federal taxes could reduce problems
analogous to those of highways that require drivers to stop every few miles
to pay tolls or highways that are too expensive for some segments of society
to use at all. Emphasizing media other than text would help equalize opportunities for less literate portions of the society and save time for more literate
portions. Governments could even look back on the success of their subsidies
of ARPANET, NSFNET, and then Internet. Another motivation, in an era
when costs of most government services are increasing, is the opportunity to
be associated with technologies that might allow governments to reduce
costs even while increasing functions. At the very least, government officials
see the opportunity to act as cheerleaders and to insist on standards. Standards can encourage universal access to the multimedia network as well as
encouraging competition; both tend to reduce prices.

   In summary, distributed multimedia gives companies opportunities for
new products and services to replace or supplement old products and services that, as a result of technological improvements, can no longer maintain
their revenues and profits. Distributed multimedia gives customers the option of buying those products and services. Multimedia can solve companies'
problems only if customers turn out to be willing to pay for the products and
services. Daily news reports of alliances, investments, and trial installations
testify to the seriousness with which companies in all related industries and
governments take this prospect. Other news reports of delays, plan changes,
and breakdowns of alliances testify to the difficulties that all parties face.

Beginnings of Convergence

Technological advances have made it possible to transmit all the different
media in digital form on one network. Although a network requires more
bandwidth to carry a digitized video signal than a digitized audio signal,
both kinds of information can travel on the same digital network along with
other media. Converting information to digital form thus lowers barriers
among networks that carry different types of media, leaving a set of network
requirements such as for bandwidth, reliability, billing, and security. There is
reason to believe that a converged network would be more valuable than the
sum of the preexisting networks. However, the fact that a converged network
is possible and the opinion that the result would be beneficial do not imply

that total convergence will occur. Such a convergence would strongly affect several very important industries and would have significant regulatory ramifications.

Television, movies, telephones, publishing, computers, education, and consumer electronics are now separate industries that use very different approaches and technologies to supply their respective forms of information and entertainment. Most significantly, these industries rely on separate and incompatible delivery mechanisms. We easily recognize a television set, a telephone instrument, a personal computer, a book, a diskette, or some other product associated with one of these industries. Moreover, we readily recognize whether one of these products is likely to use a television cable, a telephone network, a local area network, the U.S. Postal Service, or some other delivery mechanism.

Each of these incompatible delivery mechanisms is associated with particular media. The television network is associated with video and audio, the telephone network with audio, computer networks primarily with text, publishing with text and some images, and so on. As we discuss in detail in Chapter 2, Delivery, these networks keep different signals separate by using very different multiplexing methods such as frequency-, space-, and time-division.

Each of the delivery mechanisms is also associated with particular degrees and types of interaction. The television network is almost exclusively one-way and thus not at all interactive. The telephone network is two-way and is interactive. However, it is much more commonly used to bridge space by interacting in real time than to bridge time by interacting with previously stored media. Computer networks are usually two-way and interactive. Moreover, they allow bridging both space and time. The U.S. Postal Service's physical network is very effective at distributing previously stored media, such as video games, on CD-ROMs with which recipients interact.

The barriers separating these industries and their products are already beginning to blur. Some examples of barrier crossings follow, arranged roughly in order from those that are ubiquitous to those that are merely subjects of pilot tests or discussions.

- Many telephone connections carry images, in the form of facsimile.

- Many answering machines, information numbers, and talking ads allow telephone users to interact with stored media, in order to bridge time, although seriously constrained by keypad entry and voice response.

- Some pay telephones have screens that display instructions as text.

- Many television sets require a user to go through several layers of computerlike menus to set brightness or contrast.

- Some mailed automobile advertisements are switching from magazines or brochures to interactive content on diskettes or networks.

- Products as unsophisticated as those that hold hair in place come with instructions on VCR tapes.

- Some books take the form of miniature CD-ROM discs that play on book-sized computers.

- Some Internet transmissions provide radio programs such as talk shows.

- Some telephone local loops carry digital information, so that a computer no longer needs a modem to convert its bits to and from audio on the wires.

- Some telephone local loops carry video signals.

- Some computer local area networks carry a few voice channels or a very few video channels.

- A few television cable networks carry voice conversations among subscribers.

- A few television cable networks allow subscribers to interact with television programs more or less as computer users interact with application programs.

- A few theaters receive movies over networks, rather than by way of messenger services.

Compressing Images and Video

Table 1.6 shows that uncompressed video at VGA resolution, with true color and full motion, has the enormous data rate of 221 Mbps, or 27.6 MBps. Note that this is high-quality video, significantly better than the quality that a laser disc produces, although not nearly as good as HDTV. Following the suggestion in Focus 1.10, note that this data rate is 184 times greater than the 150 KBps data rate of a single-speed CD-ROM player. Some other useful comparisons to typical data rates are as follows. Uncompressed video's 27.6-MBps is

- 1.7 times the approximately 16-MBps peak memory-to-memory data rate of the industry standard architecture (ISA) bus

- 13 times the roughly 2-MBps rate at which today's typical personal computers read or write their hard drives

- 26 times the roughly 8-Mbps rate at which computers communicate over local area networks

- 130 times the 1.544 Mbps nominal rate of an industrial-strength T1 telecommunications line

- 1726 times the 128 Kbps nominal rate of an ISDN telecommunications line.

Not to put too fine an edge on it, there is nothing that economical computers or networks can do with uncompressed, high-quality, digital video. Using digital video with economical multimedia systems depends on settling for lower-quality video in order to obtain a more reasonable uncompressed data rate, and also compressing that lower data rate to obtain a still-lower compressed data rate.

It is often perfectly acceptable to reduce digital video's data rate by using smaller numbers of pixels per line, lines per frame, bits per pixel, and frames per second. For example, settling for a video window that is one-third as wide as a VGA screen and one-third as high as the screen, using 16 bits per pixel instead of 24, and using 13 frames per second instead of 30, together combine to reduce video's data rate by a factor of 31. The resulting data rate is only six times the single-speed CD-ROM data rate. So why not just get a six-speed CD-ROM player and use CD-ROM discs recorded at that rate? The reason is that at this high rate, a full CD-ROM disc would play for only 10 minutes! You would probably prefer to get an hour of this none-too-spiffy video on a CD-ROM, by compressing the video by a factor of six. For most purposes, you would be still better off with more sophisticated compression and a higher compression factor, which allows higher-quality video.

The tradeoff among compression ratio, data rate, and video quality is arguably the most important type of decision in the entire field of distributed multimedia. Higher compression factors and higher data rates increase costs to both users and producers. For example, we shall see that a high compression factor requires special-purpose hardware for decompression during

Table 1.7 Examples of video compression.

Parameters Case	Pixels per line	Lines per frame	bits per pixel	Frames per sec	Compression ratio	Bytes per sec	Special decompression hardware?
Example	640	480	24	30	1	27 M	No
JPEG	720	480	24	30	30	1 M	Yes
MPEG-1	352	240	15	15	16	150 K	Yes
MPEG-2	720	480	24	30	100	300 K	Yes
Indeo	320	240	24	15	23	150 K	No
Indeo	640	480	24	30	184	150 K	Yes
Cinepak	240	180	24	10	8.6	150 K	No
Fractal	320	200	15	15	45	40 K	No
H.261 or Px64	176	144	8	15	24	2 x 8 K = 16 K	Yes

playback, as well as for compression during preparation. We have already seen that a high data rate reduces the number of minutes of video that a given type of disc can store.

This tradeoff applies to sending and receiving video over telecommunications lines, even more strongly than it applies to playing video from discs. An expensive T1 line corresponds roughly to a single-speed CD-ROM drive. However, an ISDN line corresponds to only a 1/10-speed drive, so video over even this moderately sophisticated line must have both lower quality and higher compression than are possible on T1 lines or CD-ROMs. To send and receive video over a standard telephone line with a 28.8 Kbps modem, which together correspond to a 1/44-speed drive, you must be prepared not only to settle for low video quality but also to pay for expensive compression and decompression hardware. Even doting grandparents have had no trouble at all resisting this sort of VideoPhone service for decades.

Table 1.7 shows some important cases of this tradeoff. Many of the names in the first column are in fact families of compression and decompression algorithms or products that allow wide ranges of parameters, so each row shows typical parameters. The first case is the uncompressed example with which we began this section. Each other case employs compression and decompression that provide sufficiently high quality and sufficiently low data rate to be useful for some purposes.

The cases in Table 1.7 differ widely with regard to the sophistication and cost of their compression and decompression methods. Perhaps most significantly, although all cases require special hardware for converting video from analog to digital, and almost all cases use special hardware for compressing video, some cases require no special hardware for decompression, that is, for playing video. Cases that require no special decompression hardware employ software decompression. That is, they decompress video by executing special-purpose software on a personal computer's general-purpose main processor hardware. In general, users are more willing to purchase a fast main processor, which makes all applications run faster, than to purchase special-purpose video decompression hardware that may be difficult to install and may become obsolete within a year. Producers are more willing to create multimedia content that uses software decompression than content that only a few users who have purchased special decompression hardware can view. One compromise solution is to integrate on a computer's main circuit board, or on an adapter that accelerates other display functions, some hardware that assists video decompression. You may hear this compromise called hardware decompression, to emphasize that it improves video quality, and also called software decompression, to emphasize that it is not very expensive.

An algorithm for compression and decompression may be symmetric or asymmetric. A symmetric algorithm uses compression hardware and decompression hardware that have approximately equal processing powers and costs. An asymmetric algorithm uses much more processing for compression than it uses for decompression. Investing more computational resources in compression, to reduce the computational resources required for decompression, makes good sense in many situations, such as when a professional author creates a CD-ROM title and sells the title to thousands of users, so that video is compressed once but decompressed many thousands of times. Symmetric algorithms make sense for video conferences and electronic mail, in which a given piece of video is decompressed only once or a few times.

Asymmetric compression covers a wide range of asymmetry. The most asymmetric algorithms achieve high compression ratios by using expensive highly parallel supercomputers that run several minutes to compress each second of video (off-line compression) and use merely a computer's normal processor to decompress the video. Less asymmetric algorithms achieve lower compression ratios by using a workstation or a moderately expensive personal computer adapter card that compresses video as fast as the video comes to the computer (real-time or on-line compression) and may use inexpensive special hardware for decompression. In any case, of course, decompression occurs in real time.

We next explore several of the more popular and important cases of compression and decompression. Note that compression and decompression are sometimes called *coding* and *decoding*. Related algorithms and products are therefore sometimes called *coder-decoders* or *codecs*. Although it is common to speak of only compression, every compression has its corresponding decompression.

JPEG Compression   The Joint Photographic Experts Group (JPEG) devised a popular standard for compressing an individual image. Because video consists of a rapid succession of such images, JPEG is useful for compressing video as well. This use of JPEG is sometimes called *motion JPEG* (MJPEG).

JPEG's definition allows a designer to select different video qualities and data rates. The numbers for JPEG in Table 1.7 are merely a representative example of its use that happens to employ particularly fancy decompression hardware. Software decompression using only a fast personal computer's main processor can sometimes give adequate results.

Like many other compression algorithms, JPEG performs a forward discrete cosine transform (DCT) of which the details are beyond our scope (Steinmetz, 1994). DCT compression is lossy; that is, compressing an image and then decompressing the result produces an image that has lost some of the detail of the original. All lossy compression algorithms rely on a physiological quirk. The human visual system seems to fill missing colors in parts of a picture where colors change quickly (Jayant et al., 1993). The JPEG standard provides for lossless compression, at low compression ratios that range from three to five, for special applications that require perfect playback.

MPEG Compression   The Motion Pictures Experts Group (MPEG) provides standards that apply to video rather than to images. MPEG compression achieves some of its reduction in data rate and storage size by using DCT to compress individual frames, as does JPEG. However, MPEG gains most of its reduction by using the fact that a typical frame is closely related to preceding and succeeding frames. That is, MPEG performs not only intraframe compression but also interframe compression.

The simplest form of interframe compression would record the color of every pixel in an index frame (I-frame), then record only each pixel's changes in colors for several successive frames, then record another I-frame, and so on. However, because the whole idea of video is that objects move around on successive video frames, there are far more sophisticated approaches to interframe compression. A better approach would use the previous frame to predict where a block of several pixels will be next, then compute differences between the colors of the actual pixels and the predicted pixels, and write the result as a predicted frame (P-frame). MPEG uses a better approach that positions blocks of pixels in following frames, as well as in previous frames. The results are bidirectionally predicted frames (B-frames). An MPEG data stream might have an I-frame, several B-frames, a P-frame, several more B-frames, a P-frame, more B-frames, and then start over with another I-frame.

MPEG compression makes good use of the perhaps surprising physiological fact that the human visual system has about twice as high resolution for transitions between regions that have different values of luminance than for transitions between regions that have the same value of luminance but have different values of hue and saturation. MPEG uses 1 Byte per sample for each of three dimensions. However, whereas it samples the luminance dimension for each pixel, it samples the other two dimensions for each square of 4 pixels. Thus it records 6 Bytes of information for each such square, rather than the 12 Bytes that it would record if it sampled 1 Byte for each of three dimensions at each of 4 pixels. Expressing color as television people do rather than as computer people do gives an immediate compression ratio of 2 (see Focus 1.2). This is, of course, why television people express color as hue, luminance, and saturation rather than as red, green, and blue.

The processing required to compress MPEG by applying intraframe compression to the I-frames and also computing the P-frames and B-frames is remarkably sophisticated. As Focus 1.13 indicates in the interview, developing MPEG decompression and compression chips is about as challenging as developing a series of IBM mainframe computers, which were the same group's previous projects.

MPEG products allow you to vary several parameters when you set up a sampling and compression job. For example, you can specify the number of B-frames between P-frames and the number of P-frames between I-frames in order to achieve the quality and data rate appropriate for a particular type of subject. A sports program includes far more motion than does a dramatic production, so those subjects require significantly different parameters.

Most applications of MPEG employ asymmetric compression and decompression. Today's MPEG compression hardware costs approximately $5000 and decompression hardware costs approximately $250, although both are dropping quite rapidly.

The MPEG group has supplied two standards for somewhat different applications and is working on a third standard. The group developed MPEG-1 primarily for compressing content intended for CD-ROM discs at the original single-speed data rate. They developed MPEG-2 primarily for digital television, usually over cables. MPEG-2 not only allows significantly higher-quality video at higher data rates, it also takes into account peculiarities of delivery networks, which we discuss in Chapter 2. For example, MPEG-2 carefully minimizes the effect of losing an entire cell of Asynchronous Transfer Mode (ATM) data. Because of intraframe compression, one lost cell could otherwise destroy a large number of succeeding frames. MPEG-2 also takes advantage of ATM's ability to give each of many different signals only the bandwidth that the individual signal needs at any instant. That is, MPEG-2 can achieve a constant quality by using high bandwidth when a scene includes a lot of movement and by leaving most of the bandwidth available for other signals when a scene is nearly constant (*Multimedia Systems*, 1994).

MPEG standards go beyond compressing video. They include specifications that we discuss in the section titled Compressing Audio. They also include plans for an MPEG-4 standard that encompasses MPEG-1 and MPEG-2 and also extends them to lower bit rates and higher degrees of interactivity. The MPEG-4 Syntactic Descriptive Language allows a data stream to specify an object that retains its identity as it moves, which greatly decreases the data rate that synthetic video requires (Yoshida, 1995).

Indeo   The compression and decompression algorithm that we happen to use in our personal projects and in our university classes is Intel Corporation's Indeo, as embodied in Microsoft's Video for Windows software and Intel's Smart Video Recorder Pro adapter card hardware. We like these products' ability to capture students' quarter-screen video, that is, 320 by 240 pixels, 24 bits per pixel, and about 15 frames per second, running on our most powerful personal computer.

We like even more these products' ability to produce video that our students can play back on campus and at home using personal computers that have no special video hardware whatsoever, although they do need digital audio hardware. That is, the video uses software decompression. It plays video at whatever rate the main processor on a student's computer can support. Students can tell the playback software to make sure that audio plays isochronously. If the computer's processor, hard drive, and bus are sufficiently fast, the software plays all the captured video frames. Otherwise, the software drops video frames, but the video remains recognizable, if somewhat jerky. The number of frames per second that we quote in Table 1.7 requires a fairly fast computer.

Indeo is becoming a de facto standard. So many people have purchased its hardware and software that it has become an attractive format for which

FOCUS 1.13 Interview with:

David A. Daniels

**Digital Video Products
Business Planner at IBM**

When we were members of IBM's Development Laboratory in Endicott, New York, we developed IBM mainframe computers. What digital video products is the group developing these days?

We designed and built an economical, single-chip MPEG-2 decoder (digital video decompression) chip and announced it in July 1994. We designed a set-top box that IBM deployed in the Hong Kong trial of video on demand. That box used the OS-9 operating system from Microware Systems in Des Moines, Iowa, although a decoder chip can use any operating system that has a device driver written for the chip. We then designed an enhanced follow-on MPEG-2 decoder chip. At a price of less than $35 in large quantities, this chip is suitable for use in set-top boxes, personal computers, adapter cards, and custom systems. This decoder is sufficiently complex to match perfectly with our system skills and chip technology skills. However, these chip designs cannot take two or three years to complete, as mainframe designs used to do. The enhanced chip uses IBM's most advanced and densest CMOS (complementary metal oxide semiconductor) technology and contains over 250,000 circuits. The technology's smallest features are ½ micron wide, which allows the chip to be relatively small and to consume less than 1 watt of power, whereas some MPEG-2 chips use over 2 watts. Although most of the chip's functions are hard-coded, high-speed digital logic, the chip contains a RISC (reduced instruction set computer) microprocessor and comes with a diskette containing microcode. A manufacturer loads microcode into the chip to control the decoder's operation, such as selecting NTSC or PAL video and converting movies compressed at 24 frames per second to video displayed at 30 frames per second.

What are some of your future directions?

All chip manufacturers need to go to higher levels of integration, putting more functions on fewer chips, to decrease the costs of set-top boxes. It would be nice to integrate audio decompression together with video decompression on the same chip, along with the demultiplexer for

to produce content, even though no formal standards body created it or blessed it. Generally speaking, you would prefer to have a formal standard and also have commercial success, but if you can have only one, opt for commercial success.

The same Indeo algorithms can give full-motion, true-color, full-screen video playback, if a user happens to have appropriate decompression audio and video and a graphics accelerator. We plan to develop a continuing family of chips, including the encoding (MPEG-2 digital video compression) chip that we announced in March of 1995. It is an I-frame-only encoder, meaning that it provides complete compressed video information for each frame, rather than compressing between frames. At $700 per chip in quantities below 50, it is not suitable for consumer use, such as in desktop video conference applications. The encoder chip is 10.9 mm square, whereas the decoder is only 7.2 mm square.

Do you perform functions other than chip design?

Yes, we work very closely with customers—that is, with consumer product manufacturers. We explain the capabilities of the chip to them and then work with them throughout their design and debug phases, which can require from four months to one year. This sort of marketplace requires total dedication to working with customers to ensure that they will be successful. We also train marketing representatives who sell the chip and then assist their customer support efforts. We have also been deeply involved in the MPEG international standards committees.

If you were hiring an employee, what skills would you look for?

A new hire needs far more than digital circuit skills. Several of our people are extremely proficient in NTSC, others know a great deal about graphics, and the team leaders are skilled in both. Our people must also know operating systems and device drivers, because you don't sell just chips. Customers need a reference design for a typical product so that they can create unique designs quickly.

What do you find is most exciting about digital video development?

We are leading some aspects of this technical revolution. For example, our I-frame-only encoder was the first that fit on a single chip. Moreover, it still remains the only such economical chip that is available.

What have your main frustrations been?

This is a very new technology in which all participants are learning together. For quite a long time, we were unsure that MPEG would turn out to be the selected standard. We went ahead with development on this assumption. We are glad that our assumption turned out to be correct. ∎
Printed with permission.

adapter hardware. However, that point is definitely not academic; few universities of which we are aware can afford to provide students with the necessary decompression hardware.

Wavelet Compression The most recent version of Indeo uses wavelet technology to provide better quality video for a given data rate, or a lower data rate for a given quality of video. It also provides other enhancements, such as offering a user the opportunity to adjust contrast and brightness or display a small video window within a larger video window, which justify its new name of Intel video interactive (IVI) (Reveaux, 1995). Wavelet compression replaces JPEG's DCT by a discrete wavelet transform (DWT) that decomposes a signal into separate, for low-, medium-, and high-frequency bands. Other companies are using wavelet algorithms to achieve symmetric compression, with a $50 chip performing both compression and decompression, and to achieve compression ratios as large as 480 (Chinnock, 1995).

Fractal Compression   If you are compressing video that you expect millions of paying customers to decompress, you could be willing to spend a lot of money to give the customers high-quality video without requiring the customers to buy special decompression hardware or even to buy particularly fast computers. Fractal compression service bureaus give you the opportunity to do just that. Fractal compression vies with Duck Corporation's True Motion-S for the honor of being the most asymmetric compression and decompression algorithm that gives the highest compression ratio while giving good results with the lowest playback performance.

Fractal compression is scalable; that is, because it considers patterns rather than pixels, it can double the size of an image mathematically by scaling the size of the pattern while maintaining constant quality. Scaling the results of other decompression algorithms degrades video quality because it interpolates extra pixels in between decompressed pixels. One advantage of scaling is that you can show the video on a screen that has any available resolution. Another advantage is that you may be able to zoom in on video to see details that you would miss at full-screen resolution.

H.261 Compression   The Consultative Committee for International Telephony and Telegraphy (CCITT), which changed its name to the International Telecommunications Union (ITU), ratified an international standard for video conferences in the spring of 1991. This standard is sometimes called P×64 because replacing P by a small integer describes a particular use of the standard. For example, 2×64 refers to using two 64-Kbps channels, such as the data channels that a basic rate integrated services digital network (ISDN) line provides. Using 4×64 compression gives significantly better results by using twice as much communications bandwidth. Like MPEG, H.261 uses interframe predictive compression, which turns out to be very effective for typical video conferences in which relatively little motion takes place.

The ITU has included H.261 as part of its H.320 umbrella standard. This standard outlines all phases of the procedure for establishing a video conference call among disparate systems, recommends standards for interoperability, and defines protocols and procedures. The same standards group is working on standards for screen and document sharing and for video transmission over packet-switched networks.

Compressing Audio

Hard drives and networks can store and carry uncompressed audio with less strain than handling uncompressed video would cause. For example, a CD-DA disc can contain an hour of high-quality digital audio, even though CD-DA audio is not compressed. However, audio compression is becoming more common as digital processing circuits become less expensive, as low-bandwidth network transmission becomes more important, and as creators desire to put several hours of audio, along with other media, on a CD-ROM disc.

Mu-law Compression　Even the earliest digital telephone lines used a simple form of compression. Long-distance telephone companies passed analog audio through an inexpensive nonlinear circuit that amplified quiet sounds more than it amplified loud sounds, before they converted the analog audio to digital form. The telephone-quality audio rate in Table 1.6 is for digital audio that circuitry has compressed in this way. The particular nonlinear sampling technique known as Mu-Law-255 allows telephone networks to use 7 bits per sample and get results that sound about as good as using 14 bits per sample would sound without a nonlinear amplifier. It is thus reasonable to say that nonlinear sampling effectively provides a compression ratio of two.

Nonlinear sampling reduces noise on weak signals, such as you produce when you speak softly into a telephone. If Fig. 1.5 had illustrated Mu-law sampling, its dashed horizontal lines would have been concentrated near the middle of the figure, near zero volts, with fewer lines near the top and bottom of the figure. The size of the steps between successive samples determines the absolute magnitude of the quantization noise that digitization adds to a digital audio signal. Providing equal-sized steps adds equal absolute amounts of noise (measured in volts) to both small and large signals. This means that weak signals receive smaller signal-to-noise ratios (SNRs, measured in volts of signal divided by volts of noise) than do strong signals. Providing small steps near zero volts, for digitizing weak signals, adds smaller absolute amounts of noise to weaker signals and larger absolute amounts of noise to strong signals, which makes audio sound far less scratchy. Nonlinear sampling thus increases the dynamic range of digital audio, which is the ratio of the strongest and weakest signals that digital audio can reproduce with acceptably large SNRs. Note, however, that frequency response depends mainly on the number of samples per second.

ADPCM Compression   Further compression is possible by replacing pulse code modulation (PCM), which we illustrated in Fig. 1.5, by the significantly more complex method called adaptive differential pulse code modulation (ADPCM). ADPCM attempts to predict the value of the analog signal at the next sample time, using an algorithm that adapts intelligently to the signals it has processed recently. At each sample time, it stores a quantized approximation of the difference between its prediction and the actual value of the sample. Because the predictions tend to be good, these differences tend to be small, so a very small number of bits per sample suffice to record an excellent approximation to the analog waveform. ADPCM can reduce a 56 Kbps signal to 16 Kbps without significantly reducing quality.

MPEG Audio Compression   A typical digital video compression product includes compression for audio, which usually accompanies video. Although we usually think of MPEG-1 and MPEG-2 as video compression standards, they also include standards for audio compression. Audio compression is one of several arenas in which algorithms fight to the death to become either formal standards or de facto standards. One gladiator that duels with MPEG audio compression is Dolby Laboratories' Dolby AC-3 compression. A particular product might implement MPEG video compression and AC-3 audio compression.

MPEG audio compression standards allow a wide range of analog audio sampling rates and digital audio data rates, although all use 16 bits per sample. The original standard allowed sampling rates from 32 KHz (meaning 32,000 samples per second) to 48 KHz and bit rates from 32 Kbps to 448 Kbps. Recent extensions allow sampling rates as slow as 8 KHz and bit rates as low as 28.8 Kbps or 14.4 Kbps. These data rates are particularly important because they allow typical modems to receive streaming audio from the Internet. A rate of 28.8 Kbps produces audio quality approximately equal to that of an amplitude modulation radio broadcast (Amdur, 1995). In general, streaming audio is more appealing than waiting to download a file slowly and then playing back the file at the isochronous rate.

MPEG audio compression uses a close relative of the DCT algorithm, which JPEG image compression and MPEG video intraframe compression use. The principal difference is that audio compression operates on a voltage that varies in the single dimension of time, whereas image and intraframe compression operate on three color dimensions that vary in the two spatial dimensions of width and height. Like DCT compression, MPEG audio compression is lossy and relies on a physiological quirk to ensure that people will never miss information that it throws away. The MPEG audio compression algorithm divides the frequency spectrum that humans can hear (roughly 20 Hz to 24 KHz) into 32 bands and saves only the strongest signal in each band. The physiological quirk is that the human auditory system ignores weaker signals in each band.

We now move from discussing today's state of the art of distributed multimedia to considering some historical events that resulted in this state. As we noted in the Preface, our purpose is to use the timing of past progress to give you a feeling for the rate at which you should expect future progress. Subsequent sections then provide more details about changes that must occur in order to convert today's state to the state that we envision for 2005 and then discuss trends that constitute changes already in progress. History sections of subsequent chapters, which discuss individual parts of distributed multimedia, similarly invite you to use past events to help you predict future events that relate to those parts.

HISTORY

We often read that the human species started out hunting and gathering. Then, about 10,000 years ago, came a wave in which our ancestors domesticated plants and animals and became farmers. A couple of hundred years ago came a wave in which many people became factory workers. Finally, a few decades ago, came a wave in which exchanging information first became important and we entered the information age. Right? No, not even close! In fact, exchanging information was an absolutely essential part of being human all along and of successful hunting and gathering, agriculture, and industry.

Success of humans, relative to animals that had greater strength and sharper teeth, depended on humans' ability to communicate information about hunting and gathering. In fact, humans' primary distinguishing feature is that we communicate qualitatively better than any other species. A group of hunters and gatherers could feed more people, and leave more surviving offspring, because members of the group could exchange and preserve more information about where and how to gather plants and where and how to hunt animals. Preserving and distributing information about the technology and culture of hunting and gathering required the technology of speaking and gesturing, but did not require the technology of writing and reading (literacy). Word of mouth and gesture of hand, along with memory, were all we had available for a large fraction of human history. It was supremely effective and it made us what we are.

Transmitting information across time and space was no less important to farmers than to hunters and gatherers. Learning what to plant, when to plant, when to harvest, and how to protect food from rats had greatest benefit if the people who originated such information preserved it for use by later generations and distributed it to distant people.

Homer did not write *The Odyssey*; Homer *spoke The Odyssey*. Others memorized it, traveled to distant regions, and recited it to still other listeners. Some of the listeners memorized it and spread it farther. Young people memorized it and preserved it for future generations, thus transmitting it across time as well as space. Using sharp sticks to draw graphics in dirt or sand could have accompanied many such recitations.

The earth-shaking new technologies of writing on papyrus scrolls or clay tablets allowed scribes who could read to pass *The Odyssey* on to others, without the labor of memorizing it and without introducing errors. However, literacy was merely a quantitative improvement over memorization, which had preserved *The Odyssey* and all other information about culture and technology for many generations. Moreover, whereas a master storyteller had included meaningful intonations, given personal insights based on how and from whom she memorized the material, and answered listeners' questions, a scribe with no feeling for the material he read aloud surely gave inferior presentations. Mass distribution entailed some loss of quality from the very outset.

The industrial age required more people to have access to more information than had the agricultural age. Printing with movable type was as important to the industrial revolution as were steam engines, iron refining, and coal mining. Printing books allowed successive generations to accumulate and disseminate information about technologies, as well as about religion and culture, more effectively, rapidly, and widely than word of mouth or handwritten books could have done, although the few people who were accustomed to illuminated handwritten books probably missed the images. Reading about James Watt's steam engine was less educational than visiting the master and asking him to explain parts of his engine, but far more people had the opportunity to read than to visit.

Information technologies that supplement innate human capabilities have thus become increasingly important throughout some of the agricultural age and all of the industrial age. They are becoming even more important as more of us become information workers rather than either wheat growers or lathe operators.

The history of each medium, including both its analog and digital forms, consists of highly episodic advances in several directions, such as the abilities to make one permanent copy of the medium, make many copies, create content sufficiently easily that amateurs can participate, distribute copies to many people over a large region, and access different parts quickly. As examples of the latter, consider the advantage of flipping through a bound book's pages to find desired text rather than rolling through a scroll, moving radially across the surface of a CD-DA disc to find a desired music cut rather than winding forward or back through an audio cassette tape, or using the World Wide Web (WWW) for worldwide hypertext and hypermedia access, as we discuss in Chapter 4. By now, you will surely recognize advances in all these directions as examples of increasing your degree of interactivity.

Rather than attempting to tell the stories of all such advances in each medium's technologies, we present in Table 1.8 a small sample of illustrative technologies. Moving down the table represents increasing your ability to interact with media. Moving to the right represents using increasingly demanding media. In general, moving down and to the right is equivalent to moving later in time, although the entries near the top right came before the entries near the top left. You might want to think of a few more examples for each of the table's boxes. You might also highlight the technologies that are older than you are and note that the highlighted technologies cluster in the upper left corner.

Much as we would like to give you a single meaningful date for each entry in Table 1.8 and be done with it, each major technology presents us with a sequence of dates as successively larger portions of the population adopt the technology. For example, the table's three entries on photography merely hint at the succession of advances that Table 1.9 summarizes.

It clearly makes no sense to assign a single date to photography. After professionals, who were willing to devote their lives to photography, could achieve consistently good results, there was a gap of about 50 years before technology advanced to the point where photography was at all practical for amateurs, who spent most of their lives on other activities. Moreover, the 1888 date does not do justice to the history of amateur photography. Few doting grandmothers had the advantage of seeing amateur photographs of their grandchildren enjoying holiday seasons in 1889. Rather, like any new consumer product, amateur photography required decades to become common.

As Moore (1995) wrote in *Crossing the Chasm*, first a few pioneers are eager to adopt any new technology just for the love of technology, then a somewhat larger number of early adopters are willing to put up with monumental difficulties and expense, and only after a significant delay (the chasm) do early mass market customers adopt the technology. Pioneers might account

Table 1.8 Media and interactivity.

Medium / Interactivity	Text	Graphics	Images	Audio	Video
Unrecorded transient	Black-board	Black-board	Sand painting	Live speech	Impromptu live theater
Professional, record one copy	Cuneiform on clay Ink on scroll	Pen and ink drawing Etching	Oil painting Water color Early photograph	Wax cylinder Tin-foil cylinder Wire recorder	Early video tape
Professional, record and distribute many copies	Movable type Book Magazine Newspaper	Etching	Lithography Mimeograph Printing press	Vinyl record Audio-cassette tape CD-DA disc	Movie film VCR Laser disc CD-ROM
Amateur, record one copy	Ball-point pen Word processor	Draw program	Photograph Paint program	Audio-cassette tape	Video camera and VCR Video capture adapter CD-R
Amateur, record many copies	Carbon paper	—	Photocopier	—	CD-R
Rapid access	Bound book (vs. scroll) Hypertext	Hyper-media	Hypermedia	CD-DA Hyper-media	Laser-disc CD-ROM Hyper-media
Rapid long-distance transmission	Telegraph Early computer networks	Some early computer networks	Recent computer networks Fax	Radio Telephone	Television
Rapid long-distance transmission and rapid access	Prodigy America Online WWW	Prodigy America Online WWW	Prodigy America Online WWW	Talking telephone book Prodigy WWW	Video on demand WWW (limited use)

Table 1.9 Some history of photography.

Date	Event
1519	Leonardo da Vinci died some time after describing a camera obscura (dark chamber) in which a pinhole projected an image that helped him make accurate sketches.
1727	J. H. Schulze noted that light turned silver nitrate dark.
1826	J. N. Niepce exposed a chemical-coated metal plate through a lens for eight hours to make the first photograph.
1830s	Louis Daguerre and William Fox Talbot made permanent photographs on coated paper.
1888	George Eastman introduced the Kodak box camera loaded with roll film and labeled "You push the button and we do the rest."
1907	Autochrome was the first commercially successful color photography process.
1924	Leica introduced high quality cameras that were sufficiently compact to carry around, just in case a photographic opportunity turned up.
1947	E. Land introduced Polaroid instant photography, shortening the delay between taking a photograph and seeing the result.
1989	Digital press cameras allowed reporters to file stories with images over networks.

for roughly 0.5 million households in the United States, early adopters for 5 million, the early mass market for 40 million, and the late mass market for 43 million. Laggards make up the remaining 5 million households. Many established technologies go through a decline as newer technologies supplant them. Other established technologies redefine themselves to coexist with newer technologies. We encourage you to think about some particular part of today's state of the art in this context. Is it in the process of replacing earlier technologies in the mass market or is it being itself replaced by newer technologies?

Table 1.10 gives approximate dates when individuals and industries could begin wide-scale adoption of commercial versions of some key technologies. For context, it mentions other key dates for telephones. Table 1.15 provides the context for television (*Business Week*, 1994; Messadie, 1991; Bowers, 1995).

Table 1.11 shows some milestones in the history of computers. A key message is that it is at least as important to make computers more available to in-

Table 1.10 Commercialization dates for some technologies.

Date	Technology
1800	Telegraph
1900	Telephone (invented in 1876; in 40 percent of U.S. households by 1940)
1903	Movies capable of telling a story
1920	Radio
1945	Fax
1950	Television
1956	Videotape recorder
1960	Communication satellite
1963	Touch-tone telephone
1965	Geostationary communications satellite for telephone and television communications
1970s	Cable television and analog set-top box
1977	Video games
1981	Coaxial cable, first transcontinental U.S. television transmission
1995	Digital set-top box

dividual people and to reduce the price for a given amount of processing, as to increase the amount of processing power in a single box.

Table 1.12 notes some dates when important multimedia technologies became reasonably common.

Table 1.13 summarizes video's progress from film to analog video to digital video. Early films were brief, jerky, and black and white and had low resolution. Progress gradually overcame each of these defects, but it required a half-century rather than a few years or decades. The next major step was to television. Early television's analog video was, again, black and white and had significantly lower resolution. Television represented progress because television gave higher interactivity, that is, more convenient access to a wider choice of content. Television progressed to color and to larger screens, but the requirement that new signals play on old television sets prevented major improvements in resolution. The next major step was to digital video. In many cases, early digital video had the same defects that had plagued films a cen-

Table 1.11   Some computer history.

Date	Event
3000 BC	Babylonians invented the abacus.
1617	John Napier invented an analog device for multiplying numbers by adding distances that represent the numbers' logarithms, the precursor of the slide rule.
1823	Charles Babbage began his Difference Engine.
1890	Herman Hollerith used punch cards in the U.S. census.
1943	IBM and Harvard completed the Mark-I relay computer.
1945	Electronic Numerator, Integrator, Analyzer, and Computer (ENIAC) went into operation with 18,000 vacuum tubes.
1957	One of the authors constructed his first digital computer for personal use, as a change from using analog computers.
1958	Jack Kilby at Texas Instruments and Robert Noyce at Fairchild separately invented the integrated circuit.
1960s	Typewriter terminals and high-function vector graphics displays made it possible to access mainframes remotely.
1971	Intel invented the microprocessor.
1975	IBM 370 mainframes produced 10 million instructions per second (MIPS) for $10 million.
1977	Steve Jobs and Steve Wozniak introduced the Apple II.
Late 1970s	DEC VAX provided 1 MIPS for $200,000.
1981	IBM Personal Computers provided 0.25 MIPS for $3000.
1983	Lotus 1-2-3 became the first personal computer killer application.
1984	Apple announced the Macintosh with a graphical user interface and the first killer suite of personal computer applications, MacWrite, MacDraw, and MacPaint.
1993	Sales of computers surpassed sales of color television sets.
1993	Sales of encyclopedias on computer-readable CD-ROM discs surpassed sales of encyclopedias on paper.
1995	Pentium-based multimedia computers provided 66 MIPS for less than $3000.

Table 1.12 Some history of multimedia technologies.

Date	Multimedia technology
1979	CD-DA (Compact Disc-Digital Audio) discs
1984	Audio on digital data files
1984	Text and numbers on CD-ROMs
1984	CD-ROM application (McGraw-Hill's Science and Reference Set)
1987	Still images on CD-ROMs
1989	Audio synchronized with text or data and images on CD-ROMs
1990	Remote multimedia visual communications
1991	Video on consumer CD-ROMs at five frames per second and partial screen size (*Mammals*)
1991	*Compton's Multimedia Encyclopedia* on CD-ROM
1992	Full-motion, partial-screen video on CD-ROMs
1994	Playback of games on affordable personal computers
1994	Shared video archives for LAN-attached users
1994	CD-ROM titles in discount stores and retail stores
1995	Recordable CD-ROM (CD-R) writers priced below $1200
1996	Full-motion, full-screen video using MPEG decompression hardware and large, fast hard drives

tury before, but digital video was progress because it provided even more interactivity than did analog video. The future of digital video should include HDTV, with resolution almost as good as late films. However, amateurs are likely to continue creating digital video that has less resolution than broadcast television has. The next half-century is sure to improve digital video enormously.

Companies in the movie and television industries have made many changes to increase their products' interactivity. A theater with 10 small auditoriums gives a customer more choice of films than would a single large auditorium. A movie producer is happy to get revenue from VCR rental stores as well as from theater box offices. Cable television and direct broadcast satellites give customers more choices of programs than does terrestrial broadcasting. Survival depends on accommodation and redefinition.

Table 1.13 Some video history.

Date	Event
1824	Research into video's underlying phenomenon, persistence of vision, began.
1877	Eadweard Muybridge met Leland Stanford's challenge to prove that a galloping horse sometimes has all four hooves off the ground at once, by triggering many cameras in quick succession.
1895	Edison installed on Broadway peep shows that displayed 15 seconds of action, such as his assistant's sneeze.
1896	Edison and others projected almost one minute of film.
1903	A director in the Edison company told a story, *The Great Train Robbery*, in eight minutes of film.
1912	*Quo Vadis?* ran two hours.
1915	*The Birth of a Nation* marked the emergence of motion pictures as a significant new medium.
1927	Synchronized sound of Al Jolson in *The Jazz Singer* made silent films obsolete.
1928	Walt Disney's *Steamboat Willie* synchronized sound with animation.
1936	The British Broadcasting Corporation inaugurated partly mechanical television broadcasting.
1939	*Gone with the Wind* made color a major box office draw.
1940	The National Television Standards Committee (NTSC) defined a black-and-white electronic broadcast standard.
1954	NTSC extended that standard to include color that was compatible with the tens of millions of black-and-white sets already in use.
1956	The first previously recorded program was broadcast from videotape.
1978	Two competing types of laser discs became parts of a single universally adopted standard.
Early 1980s	Home VCRs became sufficiently inexpensive and common that rental movies began to supplement movie theater attendance.
Late 1980s	Consumer video cameras merged with videocassette recorders and the resulting camcorders improved sufficiently in price, size, and weight to completely replace film-based home movies.

Table 1.14   Interactive full-motion video history and projection.

Date	Interactive full-motion video availability
Early 1990s	On stand-alone personal computers
Mid-1990s	On one local area network (LAN) within a building
Late 1990s	On enterprise-wide networks
Later 1990s	On inter-enterprise networks
Later yet	On consumer networks

Table 1.14 presents some past and future history relating to wide availability of multimedia's most challenging medium, namely, full-motion interactive video.

Terrestrial broadcasters (as opposed to satellite broadcasters) must increase their services' interactivity, in order to extend the history that we summarize in Table 1.15. Many radio stations have switched from music and news to the far more interactive talk radio format, in which their customers are talkers as well as listeners. Television has made a similar jump, although on a smaller scale, by airing customers' voices and funny or interesting home videos. Customers enjoy being producers of content as well as watchers.

Distributed multimedia presents companies in the publishing industry, including newspaper publishing, with the interesting challenge of maintaining revenues and profits as distribution costs decrease rapidly. Both professional publishers and amateur authors have the opportunity to publish large volumes of current information increasingly cheaply, by placing information on either CD-ROM discs or network servers. This is a major change from the events in Table 1.16 and Table 1.17, which apply to relatively large professional publishing companies. Successful futures will depend on publishers' maintaining the value that they add by selecting and editing content and by suitably modifying the balance between the parts of their mission, namely, content and delivery.

Newspaper readership has been declining for the past 30 years. Most large cities have dropped from several competing newspapers to one. On-line newspapers constitute competition for paper newspapers' remaining readership. However, such on-line information appeals most strongly to 18–35 college-educated people, many of whom are not potential customers for paper newspapers. Paper newspapers are likely to define offerings that are synergistic with on-line information, as they redefine themselves to coexist with the newer technology. Table 1.17 summarizes newspapers' history.

The key message of this section on history is that past events have not led up to today's state of the art as a carefully crafted story's events lead to its in-

Table 1.15 Some broadcast history.

Date	Event
1920s	Commercial radio began with no precedents for what sort of content people wanted or whether listeners would tolerate advertising.
1920	KDKA, the first radio station in the United States, announced that Warren G. Harding had been elected president.
1922	WEAF, which became WNBC, broadcast the first commercial radio advertisement.
1926	RCA established NBC, the first commercial radio network.
1928	"The Queen's Messenger," an experimental television show, was broadcast in Schenectady, New York.
1938	RCA announced television sets to the public.
1941	First commercial television broadcasting.
1939	RCA introduced television to the 1939 World's Fair.
1953	In the Golden Age of television, viewers perceived television as radio with pictures or as a live play in their living rooms. Television had far less uncertainty about content than prevailed when radio was first introduced.
Late 1950s	Game shows came to prominence.
1960s	The Nixon–Kennedy debates attracted millions of viewers.
1960–1965	Viewers found that situation comedies were habit forming.
1971	Television programming began to reflect social mores.
1979	Television sets were in 90 percent of U.S. households.
1980	Live shows, other than sports and news, became uncommon.
1985	The Fox Broadcasting Company, owned by Rupert Murdoch, and the Public Broadcasting Service (PBS) started to take significant audiences away from CBS, NBC, and ABC.
Late 1980s to 1990s	Major networks' audiences declined as audiences spread across many cable networks such as Ted Turner's CNN and TNT.
1990	The United States contained approximately 1500 television stations, including both the VHF and UHF bands.
1991	Operation Desert Storm brought a war to the world, live.
Mid-1990s	Talk radio and television shows allowed more interactivity with people calling on telephones and sending faxes and E-mail. Home video programs allowed some viewers to become creators.

Table 1.16 Some publishing history.

Date	Event
15th century	Johann Gutenberg invented printing with movable type.
18th and 19th centuries	Publishing industry began to emerge and grow in the United States.
1920s	Book clubs and mail distribution began.
1936	Paperbacks began in England and moved quickly to the United States.
1980s	Number of new hardbacks and paperbacks exceeded 50,000 per year.
1990s	Publishing emphasized best-sellers, superstores, subsidiary rights (film or television), mail order, audiocassette books, multimedia CD ROMs, and college custom publishing.

evitable climax. The present state is more like a collection of incomplete drafts by many different authors, most of whom have only recently met and begun to discuss their work. Because distributed multimedia is the convergence of many separate development activities, we have a right to be surprised whenever anything that we need happens to be available. Only the flexibility of digital representations of media, along with digital storage and transmission, enables creative providers to produce acceptable results today and projects better conditions for the future. In making such projections, it is

Table 1.17 Some newspaper history.

Date	Event
1609	Newspapers were first published in northern Germany.
1690	Newspapers were first printed in the American colonies.
1783	Daily newspapers were first printed in the United States.
1789	The First Amendment to the U.S. Constitution was adopted, ensuring freedom of speech and press.
1980s and 1990s	The number of daily newspapers declined and consolidations among newspaper publishers became common.
1990s	About 1700 daily newspapers printed over 60 million copies.
1994	Several major daily newspapers and magazines tried on-line editions.

important to consider the different rates at which involved industries have progressed. In general, major changes such as the shift from mainframe computers to personal computers have required decades.

DIFFERENCES

We now proceed to a discussion of the differences between the state of the art and the state that we envision for 2005. In a nutshell, distributed multimedia will add video to telephone and computer systems that are already interactive, including store-and-forward E-mail and real-time communication, and will significantly increase the degree of interactivity of systems that create and distribute video, including television. Starting from today's distinct systems and approaching a system that allows users to interact with all media will amount to converging not only today's networks but also today's information industries.

Overcoming the differences between the state of the art and the vision will be as difficult in practice as the differences are simple in concept. Making the changes will be as time-consuming as the major changes listed in the History section. Audio and video are highly demanding media. We have seen that processing and transmitting these media require significantly more computing power and capacity than does handling data, text, graphics, and even images. Interacting with these media, such as selecting unique video streams and sending as well as receiving video, requires a far more robust network than does merely viewing a movie or television program from beginning to end.

A fully developed distributed multimedia system can allow each active user to select and receive a unique incoming video data stream and also allow a significant fraction of the users to create and transmit their own video streams. Multimedia has more to do with providing each user with a unique bidirectional channel than providing millions of users with merely a choice among a common set of 500 channels. Because different people will use multimedia to widely different extents, billing will probably be like today's telephone network, billed by minutes of use for each service, rather than like today's base rate cable service, billed by a flat monthly fee. Multimedia promises to help people interact more efficiently, effectively, and entertainingly with other people and with computers. It promises to eliminate reliance on television program packagers by allowing an end user to select from all the programs that were ever created. One of this book's goals is to clarify how realizing these promises can create the reality of a major new industry.

Interactive audio and video make severe demands on processors and networks because these two media are voluminous, isochronous, and synchronous. Audio and especially video are voluminous because meaningful amounts of these media occupy vastly more digital storage or bandwidth than do meaningful amounts of data, text, graphics, and images. Audio and video are isochronous because it is important to present either of these media at exactly the intended rate, rather than too fast, too slow, at a varying rate, or with gaps. Audio and video are synchronous because, in most important applications, it is also important to present these media in the correct time relationship to each other and to the other media. For example, video of a speaker's lips must match audio of the speaker's voice. Adding interactivity to audio and video makes them vastly more demanding, as well as more promising, than noninteractive audio and video.

The most significant differences between state of the art and vision, however, are not in the networks and processors. Although the new networks will be expensive, they may be quite similar to the networks that telephone companies and cable television companies have been busily installing for the past several years, as they replace old parts of networks and build new parts to serve new regions. Fiber-optic cable technology promises to provide necessary and even excess bandwidth. Chapter 2 discusses this topic in detail. Although processor speeds will continue to limit the practical degrees of video compression and related functions, special-purpose processors are already capable of producing acceptable video, and general-purpose processors will soon be sufficiently powerful to take over many such functions. Rapid improvements in the cost and performance of large-scale integrated digital integrated-circuit chips are almost certain.

The most significant differences will be in the content that the more robust networks will carry and the more powerful chips will process. Relatively few amateurs have the skills required to create publishable video. Even fewer professional videographers have experience in creating interactive video content. Some content is straightforward. A video conference's basic content is a talking head. A reference document is a natural extension of today's paper, disc, and on-line encyclopedias. However, these simple examples of straightforward content may be the exception, rather than the rule.

Nobody knows what will constitute optimal interactive content for the purposes of education, persuasion, and entertainment. Educators preach educating by means of a Socratic dialog or Mark Hopkins on one end of a log and the student on the other. However, educators and authors practice crafting linear presentations that define terms and then use the terms to explain what they think students must understand. Politicians and others who want to convince you of something want you to proceed linearly through their arguments and reasoning; they do not want you to skip over their arguments to reach material that interests you. Authors who tell stories in books and movies know how to create interest and tension, build suspense, reveal information gradually, and achieve an interesting and satisfying climax; they do not know how to allow you to guide the story line or influence the characters without destroying the story.

Even if storytellers knew how to weave together dozens of interesting stories so that whatever selections you make will lead to an interesting resolution of conflicts, they would not relish the prospect of doing dozens of times more work than they would have to do when creating a single story. It is not enough to mimic a video game in which you spend weeks trying to find the one satisfying solution while all other solutions lead to the same shattered windshield or blood-splattered arena. An actress who played a part in the video game *Psychic Detective* noted that its script contained more than 500 pages, whereas a normal drama's script contains about 120 pages. The script for the CD-ROM had 10 to 20 different variations of each scene (Haring, 1995).

History indicates that any new delivery vehicle begins by replicating existing content and then moves on to content that is more suited to the new vehicle. Early users of the printing press replicated the huge hand-inscribed books that monks read on monastery tables. Only after printers realized that they could reduce the sizes of books to fit into saddle bags did books spread out over the countryside. Producers of televised dramas began by buying a front-row-center theater ticket for a single television camera. Only after producers discovered that they could make a far more interesting presentation by varying the camera angle and using close-ups did television dramas become popular. It is entirely possible that we cannot yet imagine the differences from today's state of the art that will make distributed multimedia popular in 2005.

Interacting with other people, using appropriate media and networks, may bridge space or time. Interaction over a network may occur between a user and one or more remote users in real time. This simulates face-to-face conversation, so it bridges spatial separation. Interaction may also occur between a user and media previously stored by other people, thus bridging temporal separation. Interacting with media stored by other people may simulate interacting with the other people themselves, with imaginary people, or neither. As a simple example, consider using a word processor program. This activity not only simulates interacting with a typewriter, such as when setting tabs, but also simulates interacting with a person who knows how to use the typewriter, such as when invoking a help system that explains how to set tabs. As a less simple example, it may become possible to use on-line information access agents to replace interacting with an intimidating worldwide library by interacting with a stored model of a helpful research librarian. As a still less simple example, consider whether the ideal form of interactive education is a simulated interaction with a superb teacher, a simulated interaction with a piece of laboratory apparatus, or something entirely different. Is the ideal form of interactive entertainment a simulated interaction with a fascinating storyteller, a simulated interaction with a group of fictional characters, or something entirely different?

Another significant unknown difference between today's content and the forms of content that distributed multimedia will make successful is the question of what interactivity will mean to a group of users. How can several people in a living room, a full elementary school classroom, or an audience in a theater interact with content? If you yourself have no control over what you are seeing and hearing, then you are not interacting with the media. To you, the media are as linear as today's television programs. Moreover, the experience is likely to be as unpleasant as trying to watch one program while someone else is using a remote control unit to watch five programs. Answering this question is vital, to avoid producing content that decreases communication among people who are together, while increasing interactions among people who are far apart in time and space.

Thus the difference between today's state of the art and the state that we envision for 2005 is a combination of reasonably well-understood but enormously expensive changes to networks and processors and largely unknown changes to the skills that people will need to prepare suitable interactive content. Chapter 8 discusses the latter in detail.

TRENDS

Alexander Graham Bell is said to have invented telephones for the purpose of delivering concerts to mass audiences. He considered telephones unsuitable for business communications because, unlike telegrams, telephone conversations left no written records. People who are inventing and investing in distributed multimedia may be no more prescient than was Bell. The new systems may turn out to be completely unsuitable for the purposes that the systems' creators have in mind and, conversely, the systems' major uses may include some that the networks' creators rejected out of hand. The only way to predict the extent to which people will use a specific application with a specific price structure is to make the application available to a representative sample of people and measure usage. Perhaps the most important single trend in distributed multimedia is thus the trend toward conducting experiments, or trials, to determine what functions will appeal to real users. See Chapter 7 for more on trials. Some trials involve the following functions, most of which we define and discuss further in Chapter 5:

- Video on demand, where a user can select any of a few hundred movies or television programs and any desired starting time and can pause, rewind, fast forward, and perform any other function of a VCR

- Home shopping, based on on-line hypermedia catalogs arranged as virtual stores in a virtual shopping mall, containing video of products in use and with the option of conveniently completing a purchase

- Banking at home, including full access to information about accounts as well as the ability to initiate and complete financial transactions

- Video games, including downloading a game and playing it locally for hours or playing against remote players and conversing with other players during and after the games

- Interactive live entertainment television, with selection of camera angles and access to selected statistics and background information of the sort that users now obtain from sports magazines

- Digital libraries, increasing the quality and variety of materials to which each individual has access, including rare and historical documents from around the world, as well as current periodicals. They will also accept materials from users and support both hypermedia navigation and browsing serendipitously.

- Conversations among users of personal computers that include shared control of word processors, spreadsheets, or other application programs as well as forums and E-mail

- Similar conversations among users of televisions that include shared viewing of live video as a subject of or catalyst for discussion

- Video conferences, in which each technical improvement or cost reduction may reduce business travel, daily commuting, and even personal travel to visit distant friends and relatives

- On-line interactive transaction services, such as selecting and purchasing airline and resort reservations based on video and other media that describe the offerings

- Educational multimedia, at best making each student's study hours more productive and at least motivating a student to spend more time on task

- Remote education to allow several communities to combine students to fill an advanced class

- Remote training, to help workers adapt to increasingly demanding and transitory job assignments by studying at their desks rather than traveling to specific education centers

- Hypermedia navigation through books, periodicals, and data bases to find required information, along with scanning materials that might or might not turn out to be relevant

- Video alternatives to literacy, empowering people who have limited reading skills

- Personalized multimedia newspapers, based on interest profiles, with various attempts to retain the serendipity that results from scanning printed materials

Some other trends are as follows:

- Large variations in capital spending among cable television companies, local telephone companies, and long-distance telephone companies, based on wide differences of opinion about the extent to which installed hardware would repay the investments

- A tendency to promote small changes in capital spending plans as a large commitment to constructing the information superhighway

- Continuing installation of local fiber-optic cables, increasingly close to users, at a cost of between $1000 and $2000 per household

- Decline in price and increase in performance of digital hardware, with increases in sales of multimedia equipped personal computers to businesses and individuals

- Rapid growth of the Internet and of on-line services such as Prodigy, America Online, and CompuServe

- Improvements in end-user devices, including better video decompression and compression hardware and multimedia authoring tools

- Increasing popularity of hybrid applications, which distribute voluminous media by mailing CD-ROMs and interchange small amounts of up-to-date information over wires

- Mergers, buyouts, alliances, and partnerships among companies seeking synergism, control over a complete range of distributed multimedia products and services, or simply more profit

- Positive but slow progress in standards with the goal of achieving interoperability among different suppliers' networks, processors, and content

- Computer industry wars over dominance in operating systems, platforms, and even basic chip architectures

CRITICAL SUCCESS FACTORS

For an individual who uses distributed multimedia, critical success factors are as follows:

Ease of Use: Products and services should be easy to buy, install, learn, use, and maintain.

Affordability: Users should perceive products and services as affordable, both in cost per hour of use and cost relative to reasonable alternatives.

Accessibility: A critical mass of compelling, interesting, time-saving, and useful content and services should be available.

Skills: Users should acquire new skills to appreciate and operate the products and services.

For a provider, critical success factors are as follows:

Customers: Producers of goods and services must determine who potential customers are and what they want and will buy and then move beyond business users and early adopters to mass market customers. They must manage public relations to create customer interest without creating unrealistic hopes.

Sales Force: Firms must determine who will do the selling and how they can sell effectively. They must expand against the inroads made by new competitors from industries that were previously separate.

Content: Companies must provide compelling content in contexts of services for which end users will pay.

Profitability: Providers must maintain revenue and profit streams while developing, testing, and rolling out new and interim products and services.

New Business Opportunities: Firms will have to work with partners from what were previously different industries, with significantly different corporate cultures, over a sufficiently long time to achieve economic success. They will have to transform existing businesses to work well with digital distribution (networks and discs) that have different cost structures.

For providers who are creators of content, critical success factors are as follows:

Software: Learning to produce suitable software despite today's hardware limitations is crucial.

Standards: Selecting standards, formats, and platforms that ensure sufficient numbers of potential customers who have equipment with which to play the content is important.

Content: Hiring or developing skills to create new kinds of content, particularly highly interactive education and entertainment content, economically and quickly is critical. Providers must develop an understanding of winning content to avoid wasting investment in resources and time on profit-losing proposals.

Confidence: Profitability requires gaining confidence that the public will pay for feasible design points.

Referrals: Satisfied end users will buy products and services based on brand names and act as reference sells for future buyers.

Distribution: Establishing effective and remunerative distribution channels for content is vital.

SUMMARY

Let's return to the themes that we introduced in the Preface. First, we have noted that interactivity is as much a part of multimedia as is having several media. At least as many of multimedia's benefits result from interacting with media (and thus interacting with people across time and space) as result from using five different media. Exercising rapid and effective control over a wide choice of information is at least as important as expressing each piece of information in the most effective medium or media. Second, we have seen that converging all media into a single digital form for storage and transmission is key to interacting effectively with all five media. For example, although there are excellent reasons for transmitting analog telephone and television signals over different networks today, these reasons evaporate when we convert both audio and video to digital forms that differ only in data rate. Third, converging several industries into a single industry, in which companies must compete for customers' business, promises to give customers better functions at lower prices. This convergence also promises to make companies' lives more interesting, in the sense of the ancient curse, "May you live in interesting times." Fourth, we have noted several situations in which simple but useful calculations depend on numbers that come from the study of human physiology. Fifth, we have seen that today's state of the art for processing and networks is quite sufficient for text and graphics, requires some patience for images, may or may not suffice for audio, and usually requires significant compromises with quality in order to support video. Each of these themes reappears at unpredictable intervals throughout the following chapters that describe particular parts of a distributed multimedia system.

REFERENCES

Amato, Ivan. 1992. "In Search of the Human Touch." *Science*, November 27, p. 1436.

Amdur, Dan. 1995. "The Scene Is Set for Multimedia on the Web." *NewMedia*, November, p. 42.

Auletta, Ken, and Gilder, George. 1995. "Focal Point on Convergence." *Educom Review*. (Washington, DC: Educom Interuniversity Communications Council), vol. 30, no. 2, March/April.

Bell, Gordon; Lucky, Robert; Myhrvold, Nathan; Raskin, Jef; and Warnock, John. 1994. "On the Future." *Upside Magazine*, October (San Mateo, CA: Upside Publishing Company).

Bowers, Richard. 1995. "The Resource Directory: The History of Media and Media Technology." *CD-ROM Professional*, July, p. 109.

Business Week. 1994. *The Information Revolution*—special edition. New York: McGraw-Hill.

Chinnock, Chris. 1995. "Wavelets Challenge MPEG, Fractals." *Byte*, December, p. 34.

Clifford, Martin. 1987. *The Complete Compact Disc Player.* Englewood Cliffs, NJ; Prentice-Hall, p. 267.

Discover, 1994. "Noises Off." October, p. 84.

Gates, William H. III. 1995. "3-D Graphics to Change Computing." *Asbury Park Press*, June 5.

Gates, William H. III, with Myhrvold, Nathan, and Rinearson, Peter. 1995. *The Road Ahead*. New York: Viking.

Gerstner, Louis V., Jr. 1995. COMDEX keynote address, November 13.

Haring, Bruce. 1995. "Multimedia Projects Offer Actors a New Stage." *USA Today*, August 7, p. 3D.

Inglis, Andrew F. 1993. *Video Engineering*. New York: McGraw-Hill, p. 26.

Jack, Keith. 1993. *Video Demystified, A Handbook for the Digital Engineer*. Solana Beach, CA: HighText Publications, p. 344

Jayant, Nikil, et al. 1993. "Signal Compression Based on Models of Human Perception." *Proceedings of the IEEE*, October, p. 1385.

McGarvey, Joe. 1995. "SGI Merger Creates Digital Data Shop." *Inter@ctive Week*, February 13.

Messadie, Gerald. 1991. *Great Modern Inventions*. New York: Chambers.

Moore, Geoffrey. 1995. *Crossing the Chasm*. New York: Harper Business.

Multimedia Systems. 1994. ACM and Springer International, vol. 1, no. 5.

Negroponte, Nicholas. 1995. *Being Digital*. New York: Alfred A. Knopf.

Reveaux. 1995. "Intel Makes Wavelets as It Demos Indeo Video Interactive." *Computer Video*, November, p. 1.

Richardson, Sarah. 1995. "The Smell Files." *Discover*, August, p. 30.

Steinmetz, Ralf. 1994. "Data Compression in Multimedia Computing—Standards and Systems." *Multimedia Systems*, vol. 1, no. 5, p. 187.

Time, April 12, 1993, pp. 48–58.

Yoshida, Junko. 1995. "MPEG-4 Spec Targets Broader Spectrum." *Electronic Engineering Times*, July 17, p. 16.

Chapter 2

Delivery

BACKGROUND

In this chapter we discuss the vision of delivering nearly universal access to interactive media, the state of the art of delivery, and the changes needed in order to apply today's major networks to this end. We focus on multimedia delivery, that is, on the networks themselves, as shown in the center of Fig. 2.1. The endpoints of multimedia networks, that is, the servers and end-user devices, are the topics of Chapters 3 and 4, and the applications that make use of the entire distributed multimedia system are the focus of Chapter 5.

Multimedia is revolutionizing the way we think about and use three separate types of networks. For many years, computer networks have transmitted immense volumes of interactive text but little graphics, images, or audio. The telephone network has a long history of transmitting highly interactive audio, with a rapidly growing amount of other media, including image transmission in the form of fax. Television networks, both broadcast and cable, have long supplied video to noncomputer receivers, but it is not interactive.

Advances in digital electronics and fiber-optic cables are enabling the convergence of these separate networks into a single multimedia network, as Fig. 2.2 indicates. Although different companies are likely to own different parts of the network, the parts will operate together sufficiently smoothly that the companies will be able to compete to serve customers' needs. A converged multimedia network can have the best properties of each of today's three networks; it can be as interactive as are today's computer and telephone networks and as capable of carrying video as are today's cable and broadcast television networks.

VISION FOR THE NEXT DECADE

Delivery networks will someday make accessing remote media and communicating with people at a distance almost as easy, quick, and economical as accessing local media and communicating within a room. This vision entails

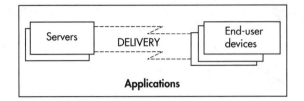

Figure 2.1   Context of delivery.

network users' being able to receive, send, and interact with full-motion, true-color, full-screen video that is synchronized with high-quality audio, wherever the source of the media may be located. The other media—text, graphics, and images—are also important to end users, but they pose less significant challenges. To meet the multimedia vision, networks must support interaction with video and audio.

Understanding the content that flows over a multimedia network is key to grasping the scope of the vision for the network. In general, the network itself does no more than deliver multimedia content from the content's source to where it is wanted, although a company that owns and operates a network may add value to the network by adding other services. In applications such as video E-mail and video conferences, an individual user creates content and sends it to one person or to a few people. In other applications, such as video on demand, professionals create content for much larger audi-

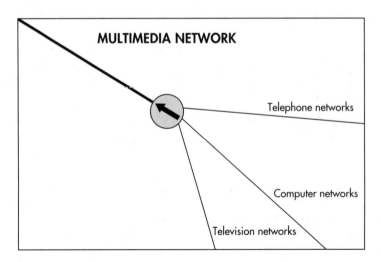

Figure 2.2   Network convergence.

ences. The vision for multimedia delivery is to provide rapid, interactive access to a significant fraction of all the entertainment and educational programs recorded in the past, as well as to live programs on weather, news, financial matters, and emergency procedures. One reasonable conjecture is that the most significant and profitable applications that will flow over multimedia networks may not yet have been invented.

Distributed multimedia will change the ways we live and work by enormously increasing our individual access to people and information, when and how we want it. None of today's networks, however, is suitable for meeting the requirements imposed by the vision for distributed multimedia. In particular, no existing network is capable of economically delivering interactive video to homes and businesses over wide areas. It is likely that many of the next decade's technical innovations, business investments, and regulatory changes will be directed at rectifying this situation.

To participate in these improvements, or even to understand newspaper reports about them, we must understand the requirements that multimedia places on networks. To transmit multimedia, networks must have high capacity that is affordable, must be interactive, and must handle audio and video. We next discuss these important requirements in detail.

Affordable High Capacity

Meaningful amounts of images, audio, and video consume far more storage space than do meaningful amounts of text and graphics. To transmit images, audio, and video in reasonable times, therefore, multimedia networks require high bandwidths—that is, large information-carrying capacities (see Focus 2.1). For example, a 9600-bits-per-second (bps) modem and a voice-grade telephone line are perfectly suitable for sending or receiving text. They can write 1000 text characters on a screen in about one second, which is fast enough to keep the user's train of thought rolling along smoothly. However, sending even a low-quality image is a different story. Chapter 1 notes that an image may occupy about 2.3 M bits or 300 K Bytes. Sending such an image through a 9600-bps modem and a telephone line requires

$$(2.3 \text{ M bits}) / (9600 \text{ bps}) = 251 \text{ sec} = 4.2 \text{ min},$$

which is a delay that will derail almost any train of thought. Sending the same image over the type of high-speed digital telephone line called T1 requires only

$$(2.3 \text{ M bits}) / (1.544 \text{ M bps}) = 1.5 \text{ sec}.$$

FOCUS 2.1 Bandwidth.

Although a digital network's information-carrying capacity is measured in bits per second, this capacity is often referred to as bandwidth. The term *bandwidth* comes from analog networks, where true bandwidth is measured in cycles per second or Hertz (Hz). In television, each channel occupies a band of frequencies 6 MHz wide. For example, television Channel 3 occupies frequencies between 60 MHz and 66 MHz. Other channels occupy different 6-MHz-wide bands of the frequency spectrum. A Channel 3 television signal transmits the brightness of successive parts of a picture by rapidly modulating the carrier amplitude (making the amplitude smaller and larger). This modulation causes the channel's carrier frequency to swing through most of the band from 60 MHz to 66 MHz. The rest of the band is occupied by audio information frequency modulated onto a separate carrier (directly making the frequency higher and lower) and by guard bands that separate the channel from adjacent channels. The 6-MHz width is what limits the amount of information in the channel and thus limits the quality of the television signal. By analogy, it makes sense to use the term *bandwidth* for the information-carrying capacity of a digital channel, as well. Besides, it is much easier to say "bandwidth."

Note that saying a network is "fast" usually means that it has a high bandwidth. Bandwidth affects the time between when a receiver receives the start of a transmission and when the receiver receives the end of the transmission. *Fast* also may mean that the network has a short delay or latency, measured between the time when a sender starts sending a transmission and the time when a receiver starts receiving the transmission. ∎

Unfortunately, T1 lines are so expensive that almost no homes and relatively few offices can afford them. A casual survey of T1 line prices shows that a 10-minute transcontinental T1 connection costs from $21.50 to $53.28 for the global portion only, and a leased T1 line costs about $13,200 per month (*PC Magazine*, 1993). Other sources quote prices 2 to 10 times lower, but nevertheless far too high for consumers to afford on a routine basis. In general, different companies own the local and global portions of such a line. The companies tariff (price) these portions separately, and both portions may have high prices.

Users will consider a multimedia system to be affordable if it provides desired information, contact with people, or entertainment less expensively than do other methods. For example, a $1000 business video conference may be eminently affordable if it obviates an intercontinental air ticket, a hotel room, and meals. Distributed multimedia is becoming more attractive as the costs of installation and operation decrease. Whereas in previous decades, only movie studios, television networks, and the military could afford to use multimedia networks, in the next decade businesses, consumers, and educational institutions will be able to afford to do so.

Besides cost, content determines whether users perceive a distributed multimedia system (including the delivery network, servers, and end-user devices) as affordable. To be considered affordable, the system must give access to a critical mass of potential communication partners and sources of information. For example, a mother may decide that she can afford to buy a video telephone, but that she cannot afford to buy one for each of her grown children to turn them into video-communication partners. Similarly, video on demand may languish unless the choice of television shows and educational programs it offers is very large, and its selection of movies is larger than the local video rental stores' selection.

Governments have played an important role in establishing a critical mass of potential communication partners by subsidizing early users of networks. For example, ARPANET, NSFNET, and then the Internet provided academic researchers with over a decade of free electronic mail, remote log-in, and file transfer. Now that most researchers are on-line as communication partners, most of them see that sending text over the network is worth what it costs, although they hope that the subsidies will continue. A proposed gigabit network would have the capacity to transmit a great deal of video as well as other media. Researchers and others may need a similar subsidy to convince them that they can afford the higher cost of the gigabit network.

Interactivity

An interactive network must deliver information in both directions with only a short delay. With a two-way network, a user can create and distribute media, and can transmit requests for media, as well as receiving media. With a short-delay network, a user can receive requested media in real time, without losing his train of thought, or can hold a live conversation with someone at a distance, without experiencing disruptive pauses. Remember that telephone networks and computer networks are adequately interactive, but handle little video, whereas television networks handle analog video, but are not interactive because, with few exceptions, they are one-way networks.

Introducing a moderate delay is acceptable in some cases, as long as that added delay is constant. For example, a movie-on-demand application can tolerate a constant delay of several seconds between the time when you demand a particular piece of video and the time when you start to see it. In video games, however, the delay must be no more than a fraction of a second. In conversations between people, even a perfectly constant delay of much more than ¼ second is intolerable (see Chapter 1). Delays result not only from transmission but also from digital processing, such as compressing a signal before transmitting it and decompressing the signal after receiving it.

Audio and Video Capability

The vision for multimedia networks includes presenting each of audio and video to users at the correct rate and presenting media in correct time relationships to one another. However, this requirement that a distributed multimedia system must be isochronous and synchronous does not necessarily mean that the network part of the system must be isochronous and synchronous. It is possible to achieve this vision by dividing responsibility among a server, a network, and an end-user device in several different ways. Only one of these ways requires the network itself to be fully isochronous and synchronous. Because the other ways place more responsibility on the server, we discuss this matter in the background section of the next chapter, which describes servers. The important result for this chapter is that if a multimedia system is to handle not only audio and video but also be highly interactive with short overall delay, then the network part of the system must be essentially perfectly isochronous and synchronous.

STATE OF THE ART

Today's networks represent some of the largest investments society has ever made. Ranging from billions to hundreds of billions of dollars, these investments are on a par with investments in highways and other infrastructure. These huge investments make building a new multimedia network from scratch infeasible economically and provide a strong motivation to use as much as possible of what is already installed as a base for implementing the envisioned multimedia network. For this reason, before discussing approaches to building a converged multimedia network, we must analyze today's networks. Although today's networks are suitable for delivering the media for which they were designed, none of them meets all the requirements for delivering multimedia. Their main weaknesses relate to interactive video. Some handle video but are not interactive; some are interactive but do not handle video.

Table 2.1 summarizes the media and the networks that carry them. This table extends Table 1.4 by concentrating on delivering media over networks, rather than on getting media in and out of computers. In this table we com-

Table 2.1 Media and networks that carry them.

Media Networks	Text and Graphics	Audio	Images	Analog video	Digital video
Broadcast	Data in retrace[++] Home shopping[++]	Radio[+++]	—	Television[+++]	—
Direct broadcast satellite	—	—	—	—	Pay-per-view movies[++]
Cellular-telephone PCS	Cellular modems[++] Home shopping[+]	Cellular telephone[+++]	Fax to car[++]	—	—
CATV	Data in retrace[++] Home shopping[+]	European telephone over cable[++]	—	Cable television[+++] Pay-per-view movies[+++]	ATM[+]
Telephone	Fax[+++] E-mail[++] Bulletin boards[++]	Plain old telephone service[+++]	Fax[+++]	—	ADSL[+] Video-conference[++] Picture-phone[+]
Computer networks	Token ring Ethernet[++] FDDI,[++] FCS[++]	Isochronous LAN[+]	CD-ROM server outputs[++]	F-coupler[++]	ATM compression[++]
Mail Auto-mobile Hand-carry	Newspaper[+++] Book[+++] Letter[+++] Diskette[+++] CD-ROM[+++]	CD-DA[+++] Audio tape[+++]	Diskette[+++] CD-ROM[++] Maga-zine[+++]	VCR tape (video rental)[+++] Laser disc[++]	CD-ROM[+++]

+++	= Ubiquitous
++	= In limited use
+	= A reasonable possibility
—	= No significant application
F-coupler	= Frequency coupler
ADSL	= Asymmetric digital subscriber loop
ATM	= Asynchronous transfer mode
PCS	= Personal communications services
FDDI	= Fiber distributed data interface
CATV	= Community antenna television
FCS	= Fiber channel standard

bine text and graphics, because networks treat these media similarly, and we separate analog video from digital video, because networks treat these media differently.

Converged Global Portion

The global portions of different networks are already converged. In fact, the long lines connecting cities and countries never diverged. End users see only the last mile, the short part of a network that connects customers' homes and offices to a CATV cable company's head-end unit or to a telephone company's central office. End users thus see only the large differences among television cables, telephone local loops, and local area network (LAN) wires, which connect to corresponding end-user devices. It is as if travelers on a superhighway could see only the narrow and confusingly different access ramps. In fact, unified intercity information superhighways are already in place, and some even have excess capacity. Network users do not see that there is an interoperable long-lines network that carries video, voice, and text.

The first long lines were telephone wires strung between poles; later they were cables on poles and in trenches. Next came microwave beams between relay towers on hilltops, subsequently joined by microwave beams to and from satellites at fixed points high above the equator. Now more and more long lines are fiber-optic cables. Figure 2.3 shows two microwave towers, one

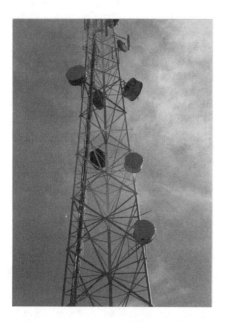 

Figure 2.3 Microwave towers.

with dish antennas and one with horn antennas. Such towers are spaced at roughly 26-mile intervals in long chains that join cities.

A network of long lines carries video, audio, and data among cities and continents. Since the late 1920s, live radio programs have traveled from centrally located studios to individual broadcast stations over telephone company long lines. It was the high cost of using AT&T's long lines that first forced radio networks such as NBC and CBS to begin soliciting paid advertising. The necessity of attracting sufficiently large advertising revenues, in turn, led these networks to centralize their programming (Smulyan, 1994). Live television programs have followed the same route since the 1950s, when AT&T installed a coaxial-cable system that connected the Atlantic seaboard with the Midwest. Television programs often reach cable companies via the same long lines, although cable companies also operate private satellites and microwave links. Similarly, most connections among LANs in different cities use the same long-line network as telephone and television signals.

Before 1984, AT&T operated the long-lines network, along with local loops that made up the remainder of the public switched-telephone network (PSTN), throughout the United States. It was, in effect, a natural monopoly. This monopoly would not have allowed emerging radio and television networks, despite the word *network* in their names, to install their own network connections, even if they had wanted to do so. The 1984 breakup of AT&T resulting from deregulation by Congress allowed other companies such as MCI and Sprint to compete by installing their own long lines or by reselling portions of AT&T's lines. Thereafter, competition kept prices low enough to discourage many others from installing and maintaining additional long lines. Most of the 500-odd other companies that interrupt your dinner to try to sell you long-distance telephone service merely resell capacity that AT&T, MCI, and Sprint install and maintain. Interoperability standards ensure that we continue to have the benefits of a single global network, despite multiple owners.

We next discuss the different local portions of familiar networks and some unfamiliar uses of these networks, as a foundation for grasping how today's installations will need to change to handle multimedia.

Familiar Networks

Each of the familiar networks listed in the left column of Table 2.1 is a complex hybrid including a local portion near customers, a global or long-lines portion, and switches to interconnect the local and global portions, all highly optimized for delivering the network's particular medium.

Broadcast Networks   These networks deliver analog audio and analog video as radio or television signals. The local portion of this network is wireless. Electromagnetic waves in assigned frequency bands propogate from a station's transmitting tower in all directions, as the name *broadcast* indicates. A consumer's receiving antenna intercepts a tiny fraction of these electromagnetic waves' energy, amplifies that fraction, and extracts analog audio or video information. The global network brings program material from worldwide sources, including companies such as ABC, NBC, CBS, and CNN, which also own some broadcast stations. Television and radio stations form the connections between the network's global and local portions and also generate their own programs. Note that these radio and television networks, which place their transmitting towers on the ground, are called terrestrial broadcast networks as opposed to satellite networks, which we discuss next.

DBS Networks   Direct broadcast satellite (DBS) networks mainly provide premium-priced channels and pay-per-view access to a selection of current movies and sports events. The local portion of this network, too, is wireless. A broadcaster maintains an uplink station, which transmits a narrow beam of electromagnetic waves up to a geostationary satellite high over a fixed point on the equator. The satellite contains several transponders. Each transponder receives a television signal on one frequency, amplifies that signal, and rebroadcasts the same information in a wide beam on another frequency back down toward the earth. A user selects a particular satellite by pointing her small dish-shaped antenna in its direction. She also selects the frequency and polarization on which one of that satellite's transponder channels broadcasts. Circuitry attached to the user's antenna extracts digital video information. In some cases, a user also arranges to pay to have a password sent to her set-top box over a telephone line, so that the box can decrypt the received signal.

You can think of a DBS network as a terrestrial broadcast network that uses a 23,500-mile-high transmitter tower. The satellite network's advantage is that the top of its transmitting tower, the satellite, is within the direct line of sight of a large number of potential customers who are willing to pay for its channels. As the name implies, a DBS network broadcasts directly to many end users, rather than to a few CATV companies that redistribute its signals. It employs expensive satellites that broadcast high-frequency, high-power, digital signals in order to reduce the size and therefore the total cost of the many customers' antennas.

Some details on one example of DBS, the Digital Satellite System (DSS), are in order, not because DSS has the potential to be the ultimate network that gives each user her own unique downstream and upstream video signals, but rather because DSS is one of the first networks to supply compressed digital video signals directly to customers' homes. Focus 2.2 provides some of these details. This option is attractive to consumers who live too far from television broadcast stations to receive signals clearly, who live in areas not served by cable, or who simply want more channels.

FOCUS 2.2 Digital Satellite System.

DirecTV and United States Satellite Broadcasting (USSB) send digital video and audio from Castle Rock, Colorado, and Oakdale, Minnesota, to several satellites that orbit above the equator at 101 degrees west longitude, near the Galapagos Islands. These uplinks use carrier frequencies assigned in the band from 17.3 GHz to 17.8 GHz. Each of 16 transponders on each satellite receives a signal, amplifies it, and rebroadcasts it with a power of 125 watts on a downlink carrier frequency assigned in the Ku-band from 12.2 GHz to 12.7 GHz. Because rain interferes with these frequencies, the satellites beam more power toward the rainy southeastern states than toward other regions of the United States.

A customer purchases an RCA or Sony 18-inch-diameter dish antenna and integrated receiver decoder (IRD) set-top box for approximately $600. The customer or an installer mounts and connects these two units and swings the antenna around until a light illuminates in response to a signal from the satellites. The customer selects a program by using a handheld, infrared remote control unit to interact with a graphical user-interface program running on the 32-bit microprocessor in the IRD. A decryption microprocessor, which verifies that the customer has paid for the selected channel or program, is packaged on a card in the IRD so that the system can change passwords and decryption algorithms either by sending a new algorithm along with the video and audio or by mailing out a new card.

DSS's relatively high bandwidth and MPEG-1 compression produce video that usually has higher resolution than users get from terrestrial broadcasters or CATV companies. However, when a scene contains rapid motion, DSS backs off to lower resolution. Users see motion tiling, that is, large squares of constant color. The providers are in the process of changing over to MPEG-2 compression to eliminate this digital artifact. Compressed digital audio already gives DSS broadcasts excellent sound quality, comparable to what users get from CD-DA discs. ∎

Cellular Telephone Networks   These networks carry audio and, less frequently, text and fax images. The local portion is wireless for a mile or so between a customer's cellular telephone and the nearest cellular base station. A key function of the cellular network is to reestablish a connection after a brief interruption of service as the customer's car moves out of range of one cellular base station and into a neighboring cell. To transmit text, a modem connected to a cellular telephone must preserve a connection during such interruptions. The modem must also deal with a relatively high error rate, as the cellular radio signal undergoes fading and reflection.

CATV Networks   Poor reception of distant television broadcast stations motivated many communities to set up large antennas and run cables from the antennas to homes. These two parts of the network gave rise to its formal name, community antenna television (CATV), and its informal name, cable television. Locating an antenna on a hill or a high tower, so that the antenna was within the line of sight of a station's transmitting tower, improved reception. Although many CATV networks continue to operate antennas, many tap directly into the same global network that broadcast networks and DBS networks use.

The units that connect the global network and the antennas to the local portions of CATV networks are called head-ends. Like television stations, cable company head-ends often inject some of their own programming, particularly community-service channels that announce cultural events and weather forecasts.

The local portion of a CATV network employs large coaxial cables in trunk lines that branch off into feeder lines, and also employs smaller and more flexible coaxial cables that tap off the feeders and run for a few dozen yards into homes and offices. Feeder and trunk lines require repeater amplifiers to restore the signal strength about every quarter-mile. Thus, even the local portion of a CATV network is a hybrid network.

CATV is a $22 billion annual business. Approximately 11,000 CATV head-ends and networks that contain about one million miles of cable serve about 60 percent of homes in the United States that contain television sets. The cable networks pass within a few hundred feet of about 90 percent of such homes. The two largest multiple system operators (MSOs) serve over 20 million subscribers.

Telephone Networks   The public switched telephone network (PSTN) originally carried plain old telephone service (POTS). It now carries large amounts of text and fax images as well. Your local loop, also called a *subscriber loop* or *subscriber line*, runs between your home or business and the local exchange carrier's (LEC's) central office. A typical local loop consists of an unshielded twisted pair (UTP) of two copper wires up to 18,000 feet long. A central office's switch connects your local loop directly to a second local loop when you happen to telephone another subscriber whom the same central office serves, that is, when you call a seven-digit number of which the first three digits match your own. Otherwise, the central office's switch connects your local loop to a trunk line that leads to some other central office or to long lines. A long-distance carrier or interexchange carrier (IEC) owns and operates the long lines, which form the global portion of the PSTN.

In the United States, the LECs operate about 140 million local loops, consisting of more than one billion miles of twisted-pair wires. The LECs have a total investment of approximately $300 billion, or about $2000 per local loop. The seven Regional Bell Operating Companies (RBOCs) provide about 76 percent of the local loops in the United States. The local telephone business is about three times as large as the CATV business (Yokell, 1995).

The most important thing to remember about the telephone network is that it has a superb infrastructure for finding out what signal you want, connecting exactly that signal to you, and billing you for it. Telephone companies have always made their living connecting you to your Aunt Susie when you dial her number. They do not wait until you and thousands of other people want to hear Aunt Susie, then package her voice (along with commercials) on a channel that anybody can tune in. Telephone companies thus represent the essence of interactive communications.

Computer Networks Computer networks are optimized for carrying text, graphics, and images. Making them suitable for the isochronous media (video and audio) will require more than further increasing their bandwidth. The local portions of computer networks are aptly named local area networks (LANs). The global portion is sometimes subdivided into metropolitan area networks (MANs), which encompass about a dozen miles, and wide area networks (WANs), which encompass the world. The various connectors between the local and global portions are called *bridges, routers, gateways,* and *packet switches.*

Mail and Other Physical Transport The type of network that involves physical transport of physical disks, discs, newspapers, and so on is not an electronic (or optical) network and is not a real-time network. Nevertheless, it is by far the best way to transmit media in cases where low cost is more important than short delay. This network's local portion, say, a drive to the video store to bring home a tape, competes very successfully with the local portions of the broadcast, DBS, and CATV networks. Physical transport is an important part of the global portions of the broadcast, DBS, CATV, and computer networks themselves. Whenever there is enough lead time to mail or express ship a program on tape to a broadcast station, DBS station, or CATV head-end, then doing so makes sense because it costs far less than using an electronic network. Mailing diskettes is arguably the highest capacity, as well as the most economical, part of the global portion of computer networks.

For one of the most illuminating calculations in the field of multimedia, suppose that you have a CD-ROM that contains 550 MB of video and other media that you want to transmit from New York to a friend in California. You suspect that mailing the CD-ROM might save money, but you are in a hurry and you have heard that an electronic network carries information at the speed of light. You find out that the U.S. Postal Service's Express Mail will get the disc to your friend in 24 hours at a cost of $9.00. You note that your computer has a 28.8 Kbps modem, and you find that a transcontinental telephone call at night costs you $0.15 per minute. Which method is faster and which method is cheaper? Assuming that the network actually transmits 28.8 Kbps (ignoring start bits, stop bits, parity bits, and line errors), and that you can finish in one night, you compute

$$(550 \text{ MB} \times 8 \text{ b/B})/(28.8 \text{ Kbps}) = 152{,}777 \text{ sec} = 2546 \text{ min} = 42.4 \text{ hr,}$$
$$2546 \text{ min} \times \$0.15 \text{ per min} = \$381.94.$$

Thus, transmitting your information over the electronic network would take almost twice as long as using the mail and cost almost 50 times as much!

Less Familiar Uses of Networks

Table 2.1 lists several uses of networks that may not be as familiar to you as POTS and broadcast television. These less familiar uses form part of the conceptual base for a multimedia network, because they illustrate how today's networks are gradually handling additional media and becoming more interactive.

Data in Retrace   This method is for sending information, such as stock market quotations or sports scores, to a limited audience over the same channels that send television to a mass audience. Recall from Chapter 1 that a television channel, either as broadcast over the air or carried on a cable, scans each field quickly from left to right while also scanning more slowly from top to bottom. The time that is required for the beam to move back from the bottom to the top, called the *vertical retrace interval* or *blanking interval,* occupies about 10 percent of the total time. Because a television set must turn off (blank) the beam to ignore whatever a station broadcasts during the vertical retrace interval and to avoid showing garbage on the screen, a television station can encode high-bandwidth data during that interval. Special devices that receive the signal can ignore the picture content and can display whatever is broadcast during the retrace intervals. Many of these devices connect to CATV networks. Some others that receive broadcast signals are packaged to look like pocket pagers or even wristwatches. Today, every television set sold in the United States must be capable of decoding closed captions, which stations broadcast during the vertical retrace interval to aid the hearing impaired.

Home Shopping   One home shopping service called Eon, proposed by a company formerly called TV Answer, combines two of today's networks. It sends out video advertisements describing what it has to sell over a normal television channel. It provides special set-top boxes that allow customers to send back orders over cellular telephone links to local hubs, from which the requests travel over the normal telephone network. Using a cellular telephone avoids tying up the customer's telephone line. Placing an order may involve interacting with several graphic screens and making selections with a handheld wireless remote control, but using it is far less intimidating than doing the same interaction with a computer. Because Eon does not involve selecting an individual video stream, it is not an example of interactive video or of video on demand.

PCS   Personal communications service extends the popular concept of the cordless telephone. PCS eliminates the wires between telephone poles and homes by placing what amounts to a cordless telephone base station on top of every telephone pole. Each customer gets a wallet-sized telephone that can communicate with the closest base station. In addition to giving everybody the advantages of a cordless telephone, PCS's major advantage is that a given customer's telephone always responds to the same telephone number, no matter what pole the telephone happens to be near. The same advantage applies to exchanging text and fax images with a palm-top computer that is equipped with PCS. However, PCS telephones have insufficient bandwidth for exchanging video. Focus 1.12, in Chapter 1, discusses the problems of transmitting wireless video. Note that PCS will not replace the local networks that cellular telephones use, because PCS lacks sophisticated mechanisms necessary to reestablish a connection after a user drives out of one cell and into another cell.

Network Connections

Figure 2.4 summarizes the state of the art of today's networks. It emphasizes that each network is a hybrid consisting of at least two parts, the global portion at the left and the local portion at the top right. Note that even the global

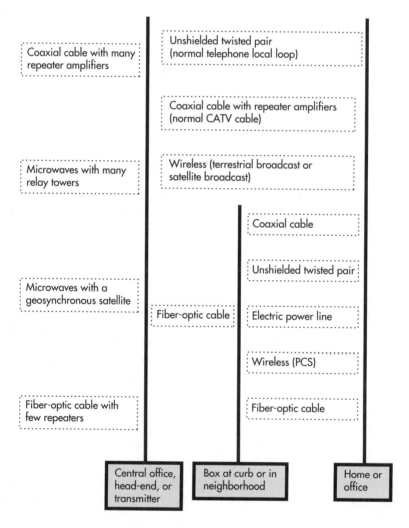

Figure 2.4 Some important networks.

portion is often a hybrid; a signal may travel part way to its destination over coaxial cables, then continue over microwaves or fiber-optic cables. The lower right corner of the figure is a preview of the trend to turn the local portion of a network into a hybrid, too, by driving fiber deeper into the network, closer to homes and offices. Although the state of the art now includes some usage of the connections in the figure's lower right corner, this is such an important trend that we defer discussing it until this chapter's section titled Trends.

Figure 2.4 also emphasizes that the local portions of today's networks are completely different. Whereas the long lines apply equally to all networks, different networks make contact with the long lines at different installations. A local telephone company makes contact at a central office, a CATV company makes contact at a head-end unit, and a broadcaster (terrestrial or satellite) may make contact at a studio or transmitter. To reach customers, a telephone company uses unshielded twisted pairs, a CATV company uses coaxial cables, and a broadcaster uses wireless transmission. The lower right corner hints that, as all networks drive fiber-optic cables closer to customers' homes and offices, there is a trend for networks' differences to disappear. Many telephone and CATV companies already use variations of the lower right corner, either to reduce costs or to enhance service.

HISTORY

A capsule history of some delivery networks is offered in Table 2.2. Two of the most important events for distributed multimedia were development of techniques that allowed the parts of cable networks nearest customers' homes to carry audio and video upstream as well as downstream and allowed telephone local loops to carry video as well as audio. These developments made it possible for both the CATV and telephone industries to consider deploying multimedia networks in an incremental fashion, without replacing their entire existing installations.

DIFFERENCES

We next contrast the vision for distributed multimedia in the year 2005 with the state of the art of today's networks. We discuss the extent to which each of the networks shown in Table 2.1 does and does not meet the requirements of a multimedia network. Recall that interactive video places the most challenging requirements on networks, requiring them to have high affordable capacity and be interactive, isochronous, and synchronous. Today's state of

Table 2.2 Some history of delivery systems.

Date	Event
1844	A telegraph wire sent text in Morse code between Washington, D.C., and Baltimore, Maryland.
1885	A telephone wire sent audio between Boston and New York.
1920s	Regulated telephone companies provided voice telephony service and carried radio network programs from studios to affiliated stations.
1944	An RCA laboratory director foresaw chains of microwave relay towers, 20 to 50 miles apart, carrying voice and television.
1948	A television station experimented with broadcasting World Series games from a B-29 Superfortress flying 30,000 feet over Pittsburgh, Pennsylvania.
1950s	AT&T long lines transmitted television network programs from centralized studios to remote affiliated stations.
1962	The first geosynchronous communications satellite, Telstar, was launched.
1973	Typical CATV networks redistributed 3 to 15 local channels.
1982	Alameda, California, got the world's first CATV over fiber-optic cables.
1984	Antitrust action broke the AT&T Bell system into seven regional Bell operating companies (RBOCs) and the AT&T long-lines interexchange carrier.
	New alternative interexchange carriers such as MCI and Sprint emerged.
	Alternative local carriers emerged.
1985–1994	Fierce competition became fiercer.
	Cellular telephones became popular.
	Telephone companies bought positions in CATV operations.
	Long-distance carrier telephone companies upgraded transport networks to fiber-optic cables.
	Cable laboratories developed circuits that allowed the last ¼ mile of cable to carry video both downstream and upstream.
	AT&T developed ADSL that allowed telephone local loops to carry compressed digital video into customers' homes.

(cont.)

Table 2.2   Some history of delivery systems. *(cont.)*

Date	Event
1995	CATV companies upgraded their networks.
	Wireless network providers upgraded their facilities.
	New high-bandwidth networks appeared but remained far from ubiquitous.
	Consolidations and mergers increased.
	The long-term cost trend in transporting high-bandwidth digital signals between fixed points strongly favored fiber-optic networks over satellite and copper networks.
	Cellular systems became more common for mobile workers.
	Greatly expanded public switched telephone network and high-bandwidth networks became available to the public in many countries.
	CATV companies started thinking about becoming interactive.
	Wireless networks achieved expanded coverage.
	Electrical utility companies became aware of the possibility of delivering audio and video service, along with controlling the times when appliances use electric power.
	Internet grew enormously in numbers of users and in visibility.
	Global networks expanded.
	Corporate networks expanded and a few became available to outsiders.
	Although a great deal of dark fiber (unused fiber-optic cable) was in the ground, the cost of the optoelectronics that were required to use it remained high.
	State regulators strongly encouraged competition with the goal of lowering telephone rates.
	Customers wanted one-stop-shopping for cable and telephone service, along with lower rates.
	More cable channels and satellite broadcast became available in many locations.

the art does not come close to allowing the ideal situation in which each user has dedicated, unique, downstream and upstream video channels.

Broadcast and DBS Networks   These networks are inherently isochronous and have high bandwidth, so their video does have acceptable quality and they do synchronize sound with video. They have enough capacity to carry a few hundred video channels in each region. Each terrestrial broadcast channel requires 6 MHz out of a geographic region's available electromagnetic spectrum and must be 6 MHz away from any nearby station's channel to prevent interference. In a given region, therefore, there may be up to 6 of the 12 very-high-frequency (VHF) channels, which are the channels numbered 2 through 13. There may also be many of the 69 possible ultra-high-frequency (UHF) channels, which are numbered 14 through 82. However, UHF frequencies die out in a shorter distance than do VHF frequencies, so different stations on the same frequency can be closer together in the UHF band than those in the VHF band.

In addition, there are a few hundred DBS channels at still higher frequencies. The number of different DBS satellites that can be within sight of customers is limited because a dish antenna must be able to select a desired channel from a desired satellite without receiving interference from another satellite that is transmitting on the same frequency band from almost the same direction. A DBS customer's antenna, which is 18 inches in diameter, is not as directional as is a CATV company's head-end antenna, which is 10 feet in diameter. Moreover, it is unreasonable to expect that a customer will point an antenna as accurately as does a professional. Thus, just as there is a minimum distance between terrestrial broadcast towers that transmit the same channel frequency, there is a minimum angular separation between DBS satellites that transmit the same channel frequency. A mount that allows rotating the antenna to point at any of several widely separated satellites in order to select from all available channels costs significantly more than does a fixed antenna mount.

The limitation to several hundred channels, even with rotatable antenna mounts, means that terrestrial broadcast and satellite broadcast networks are not particularly interactive. Their transmitters send out streams of video. A customer's only choice is to select one of the streams or none. The reason that such networks are not interactive is the simple and implacable economics of supply and demand. Channels are scarce, because the electromagnetic spectrum has only so many usable frequencies and there are only so many transmitting tower regions or geostationary satellite locations. Transmitters and satellites are expensive to install and operate. For example, a company that needs sole use of a satellite transponder channel must be willing to pay between $300 and $1000 per hour to use it (Wexler, 1994). Therefore, these broad-cast networks are economical only when thousands, and preferably millions, of viewers, can share the cost of each channel. The number of available and affordable channels is vastly smaller than the number of active users.

A typical consumer cannot afford to pay for a long-distance full-motion video channel that contains a stream of video that only she wants to receive or send. Even when she selects a pay-per-view DBS movie, her interaction is limited to requesting an available movie at an available start time and re-ceiving a password that will allow her set-top box to decipher the corre-sponding satellite signal. She does not actually request a unique video stream that only she wants to see, as would be the case for true video on de-mand.

Nevertheless, satellite broadcast networks have a role to play in fully interactive networks. Where economy is not a requirement, and where no alternative is available, such as when covering a news event in a remote lo-cation that has neither wires nor cellular telephone sites, satellites provide the only available delivery network. Similarly, satellites are the only rea-sonable solution for economical networks that need send video only down-stream to sites out of reach of both wires and terrestrial broadcasting stations.

Several interesting proposals get around the small number of positions that are available for geosynchronous satellites by using a large number of low-orbit satellites, which need not stay above the equator. These proposals have the disadvantage that their satellites appear to move across the sky. Thus a user's antenna requires not only the ability to point toward different satellites but also the ability to track a rapidly moving satellite. Russia has used such constellations of low-orbit satellites for decades to solve the prob-lem that, from high northern or southern latitudes, geosynchronous satellites appear to be excessively close to the horizon.

Using compressed digital video could increase the number of channels in a broadcaster's serving areas by about a factor of ten, as we discuss in the HDTV section of Chapter 4. (DBS broadcasts are already digital and com-pressed.) Increasing the degree of digital video compression, however, will not allow terrestrial and satellite broadcasters to keep up with the demand for individual multimedia channels.

CATV Networks   CATV networks have capacity sufficient to carry dozens or hundreds of channels to a community, and they are both isochro-nous and synchronous, but only a few of today's CATV networks are inter-active. Most use repeater amplifiers that are one-way devices that amplify only downstream signals, outbound from a head-end to customers. We shall see later that there are ways around this problem that preserve some of the investment in CATV networks by deploying two-way amplifiers and breaking up a community into smaller neighborhoods in which different customers can use the same channels to receive and send different signals.

Telephone and Cellular Networks Highly interactive, these networks allow each receiver to be a transmitter as well, and they let one party dial any other party to initiate a communication. Moreover, these networks are isochronous, so that speech has the cadences and frequencies upon which we all rely for comprehension, and they have acceptable delays. However, these networks employ local loops or radio links that have insufficient capacity to deliver video with reasonable quality using inexpensive electronics. With a traditional modem, a normal telephone local loop can carry only about 28.8 K bits per second. We have noted that even compressed VCR-quality video requires about 1.2 M bits per second, so video is about 40 times too fast for a normal telephone line. It is important to note that a local loop's information carrying capacity depends not only on the line itself but also on the electronic circuits that drive signals onto the line and receive the signals that the line delivers. Telephone companies can use ISDN and ADSL electronics to send high-bandwidth digital video signals over normal unshielded twisted-pair copper wire local loops, as we discuss later.

Computer Networks From their inception, computer networks have been highly interactive. However, most of them have sufficient bandwidth for at most a few video signals, even using sophisticated compression, and they tend to be not at all isochronous. The reason for this is the way computer networks multiplex different signals on the same wire or fiber. Nevertheless, techniques drawn from computer networks have much to contribute to building the envisioned multimedia network. We will discuss ways of taking the good without the bad later in this chapter.

Mail and Other Physical Transport With enormous affordable capacity, this network can transmit all the media, including video on CD-ROMs or laser discs. However, even using sneaker-net within a home (walking to an adjacent room and bringing back a CD-ROM) tends to take long enough to derail a train of thought. In this respect, this network is far down the spectrum of interactivity. Nevertheless, once a disc is in your computer, you can interact rapidly with the contents, individual media are isochronous, and groups of media are synchronized.

TRENDS

We next discuss how network providers are attempting to close the gap between today's state of the art and the distributed multimedia that we envision for 2005. The trends are for providers to use as much of their existing networks as they can, switch from analog transmission to digital transmission, install higher-bandwidth connections such as fiber-optic cables, and change the ways in which they keep different customers' signals separate on a single connection.

Remember that today's delivery systems represent enormous investments. As a result, there is a strong trend to use as much as possible of existing networks and invest in new capabilities only where absolutely necessary. We have seen that none of the existing types of networks meets the requirements of a multimedia network, either because they lack interactivity or because they cannot support video. Thus, we must analyze the networks to see which of their parts can be used as a base for a multimedia network and which parts must change. The global portion of the networks comes relatively close to meeting all the requirements for delivering multimedia, although it does not have sufficient affordable capacity. The global portion is already converged, in the sense that portions that different companies own and operate nevertheless work well with one another and with the local portions of different networks. Moreover, the global portion is already mostly digital. This portion uses effective techniques such as synchronous transfer mode (STM) that allow isochronous signals to share a given link's bandwidth with other signals. Existing global capacity meets the demand for intercity and transcontinental telephone calls, including voice, text, and fax. It also can supply video to the local portions of broadcast networks, DBS, and CATV. Long-line companies such as AT&T, MCI, and Sprint invest continuously to increase the global network's supply as demand rises. Individuals are willing to pay today's rates to transmit voice conversations, and companies are willing to pay today's rates to transmit video and audio of sports and news events and other programs. However, a typical individual consumer cannot afford a unique video stream on the global network.

The following three trends will increase the global network's capacity and gradually lower network tariffs sufficiently that a typical consumer will be able to afford either to transmit a video stream or to request that a unique video stream be sent to her or him.

1. Advances in digital electronics are making it more economical to compress video by larger factors and thus send video over less bandwidth.

2. Increasing the number and capacity of fiber-optic cables is decreasing the cost of sending a given bandwidth a given distance.

3. Improved protocols such as Asynchronous Transfer Mode (ATM) are gradually integrating the global part of the network with digital local networks. This will eliminate today's sharp boundaries where global and local networks meet and will reduce the cost of equipment that is now required whenever information crosses these boundaries. This will improve efficiency and allow incremental increases in capacity.

Figure 2.4 showed that, whereas telephone, television, and computer networks use the same global portion, these three networks have different local portions. A multimedia network will combine the strong points of the three networks' local portions:

- Telephone network's ubiquitous local loops and flexible switches

- CATV network's high-bandwidth connections and sources of video

- Computer network's digital multiplexing approaches

Determining the most economical way to get from today's networks to a network capable of carrying multimedia is serious business. Companies involved are deciding how to invest hundreds of millions or even billions of dollars over the next few years. The rest of this chapter concentrates on the technical differences among types of networks. Chapter 6 discusses corresponding nontechnical differences.

When we analyze the local portions of telephone, television, and computer networks, we find that each is unique in whether it transmits information in analog or digital form, in its type of connection, and in the way it keeps different users' streams of information separate. That is, designers of each network long ago selected one choice from each row of the following menu:

- Analog or digital representation of information

- Twisted-pair wiring, coaxial cable, or fiber-optic cable connections

- Circuit-switch multiplexing, frequency-division multiplexing, or time-division multiplexing, to separate different users' signals

Table 2.3 Network characteristics.

Multiplexing	Connection	Analog	Digital
Circuit-switch multiplexing	Twisted pair	Telephone	ISDN; ADSL[+]; Switched Ethernet
	Coaxial cable	—	Switched Ethernet
	Fiber-optic cable	—	FCS[+]
Frequency-division multiplexing	Twisted pair	F-Coupler	—
	Coaxial cable	CATV	Digital CATV [+]
	Fiber-optic cable	—	—
Time-division multiplexing	Twisted pair	—	Token ring; Ethernet; CDDI
	Coaxial cable	—	Ethernet
	Fiber-optic cable	—	FDDI; ATM[+]

[+] Potentially suitable for large-scale interactive video.

Because the items on this menu allow three, three, and two choices, respectively, there are eighteen possible combinations, as Table 2.3 shows. In the next sections, we discuss the three items on the menu. Thereafter, we discuss all the entries in the table.

Each of today's telephone, cable, and local area networks, which we introduced as a row in Table 2.1, appears as an entry in Table 2.3. The local telephone network is circuit-switched, copper twisted pair, and analog. Common CATV cable networks are frequency-division multiplexed, copper coaxial cable, and analog. Local area networks are time-division multiplexed, digital, and use various types of connections. Electric power wiring, not shown in Table 2.3, can carry digital information throughout a home by using both frequency-division multiplexing to separate digital signals from the 60-Hz power line and time-division multiplexing to separate several digital signals from one another.

Next, we discuss trends that apply to each of analog or digital representation, the types of connections, and the ways networks keep different signals separate. Along the way, we pick up the other entries in Table 2.3.

Digital Transmission

The current trend is to transmit all media over networks in digital form. The global portion of the network has carried significant amounts of information in digital form for years, such as over copper cables between central offices up to 50 miles apart, starting in the 1960s, and over fiber-optic cables. When a digital computer cost millions of dollars, the cost of the necessary digital electronics limited digital transmission to the global portion of networks.

Now that the price of digital electronics has dropped into the consumer range, there is a trend to drive digital transmission deeper into the network, that is, closer to offices and homes.

What advantages make digital transmission so attractive? In Chapter 1, we described sampling of images, audio, and video in order to convert these media from analog form to digital form. Having all media in digital form allows you to compress them, store them on the same disk or disc, copy them without degradation, and transmit them on the same network. For network delivery, the important advantage of having all media in digital form is that a single network can transmit all media in compressed form without degradation.

Any signal that passes along a copper wire, microwave beam, optical fiber, or other connection becomes weaker and accumulates noise (random fluctuations that degrade the signal) in the process. When you receive the signal, you must restore its original strength. You may be using the signal yourself or you may be acting as a repeater that transmits the signal over another connection. A long network path may require a large number of successive repeaters and connections to pass the signal along.

Receivers work completely differently in analog networks and digital networks. In an analog network, a receiver amplifies both the desired signal and the undesired noise. After passing through many analog repeaters and connections, a signal can completely disappear into the noise. In a digital network, however, a receiver determines whether each incoming bit is a one or a zero and supplies the corresponding perfect one or perfect zero. That is, unless the signal has degraded so badly that a one becomes a zero, or the reverse, a digital receiver restores the received signal to an exact replica of the transmitted signal. Sending information through a long succession of digital repeaters and connections often delivers the information with no noise whatsoever.

Later, in Focus 2.6, we note that a network may have sufficiently low noise to allow a digital receiver to determine which one of 1024 different symbols it receives at each sample time, in order to receive 10 bits at once. The important attribute of a digital network is that, at each sample time, it carries one of a finite number of symbols, rather than carrying an infinitely variable analog signal. A digital receiver need only determine which symbol it receives at each time, which allows it to eliminate a great deal of noise.

Transmitting media over a network in digital form has the further advantage that, even when a connection adds enough noise to turn a few ones into zeroes and the reverse, the receiver can still reconstruct an exact copy of the original signal. To allow the receiver to do this, the transmitter calculates an error-correcting code and transmits that code over the connection along with the data. The receiver checks the code and data, determines when the network has sent a few wrong bits, and uses the code's redundant information to compute what the data should have been.

Sending digital information over an increasingly noisy connection exhibits the behavior that Oliver Wendell Holmes attributed to the Deacon's wonderful one-hoss shay, which ran a hundred years to the day. A digital signal remains completely intact up to the point at which it goes all to pieces. In many (although by no means all) circumstances, this behavior is preferable to an analog signal's tendency to vanish quite slowly into the noise, more like the Cheshire cat in Lewis Carroll's Wonderland.

Higher-Bandwidth Connections

Figure 2.5 illustrates some types of connections used in important networks. The figure shows each type's width approximately life size although, of course, the connections may be miles long. Connections include not only copper and aluminum wires that carry information as electronic signals but also glass and plastic fiber-optic cables that carry information as photons of light.

There is enough to be said about such types of connections to fill many textbooks with concepts and fill many catalogs with available wires and fibers. We shall limit our discussion to the important trend toward using connections that will carry more information for less cost. It is this trend that makes it reasonable to envision two-way digital video connections to homes and businesses within the next ten years. Without this trend, the large data volumes that characterize multimedia would prevent wide deployment of multimedia networks and would limit the foreseeable future of multimedia distribution to mailing CD-ROMs and increasing the number of professionally packaged CATV channels.

Information-Carrying Capacity   Before we can discuss the trend toward using connections that can carry more information, we must consider how to measure the amount of information a connection can carry. You might think that this is a simple matter of stating that, for example, a piece of CATV coaxial cable will carry 600 MHz. You might reach this conclusion by looking

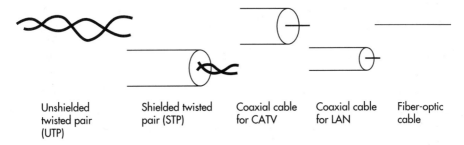

| Unshielded twisted pair (UTP) | Shielded twisted pair (STP) | Coaxial cable for CATV | Coaxial cable for LAN | Fiber-optic cable |

Figure 2.5 Types of connections.

at the point where a CATV cable enters your home and noting that the components' labels say that the components are usable to 600 MHz. Alternatively, you might figure that about 100 channels, each of which occupies 6 MHz of bandwidth, together require a cable that can carry about 600 MHz.

Then you might start to doubt that a piece of CATV cable could carry 600 MHz for 3500 miles across the Atlantic Ocean. You might estimate that your home is 5 miles from the cable company's head-end and conclude that CATV coaxial cable can carry 600 MHz for at least 5 miles. However, this estimate fails to allow for the fact that the cable company that serves your home installed and maintains a repeater amplifier about every ¼ mile between the company's headend, where the signals originate, and your home. A repeater amplifier is necessary approximately every ¼ mile because, in fact, coaxial cable will carry 600 MHz for only about ¼ mile, not for 3500 miles and not even for 5 miles.

A connection's figure of merit (FOM) is defined as the number we get when we multiply the connection's bandwidth by the maximum distance that the connection will carry that bandwidth. For example, performing this multiplication for our CATV cable gives

$$\text{FOM} = 600 \text{ MHz} \times \tfrac{1}{4} \text{ mi} = 150 \text{ MHz-mi.}$$

A connection's FOM tells how bandwidth relates to distance for all connections of the same type. If you multiply the bandwidth by seven, the distance the same type of connection will carry that higher bandwidth drops by a factor of about seven, leaving the product of the bandwidth and distance nearly unchanged. (Like all linear approximations of highly complex reality, FOM applies only to a reasonable range of values.)

Armed with an FOM, we can answer questions such as "How far could the same type of CATV cable carry one 6-MHz-wide video channel?" The answer is

$$\text{Distance} = 150 \text{ MHz-mi} / 6 \text{ MHz} = 25 \text{ mi.}$$

The answer to "How much bandwidth could CATV cable carry for five miles?" is

$$\text{Bandwidth} = 150 \text{ MHz-mi} / 5 \text{ mi} = 30 \text{ MHz.}$$

Clearly, two ways to achieve higher-bandwidth connections are to convince people to live closer together, so that we can use shorter connections, or to put repeater amplifiers closer together. Equally clearly, these ways are unattractive and we need a third way to achieve higher-bandwidth connections. That way is to use types of connections that have larger FOMs.

To compare the FOMs of different types of connections, it is necessary to use identical units. We will use kilometers as our unit for distance, so the CATV cable used in the preceding example has FOM of

$$150 \text{ MHz-mi} \times 1.6 \text{ km /mi} = 240 \text{ MHz-km}.$$

FOM always has units that are given by bandwidth multiplied by length, such as MHz-kilometer (MHz-km). It is sometimes hard to resist "correcting" the units to MHz/km, which may seem to look more meaningful, but which is nonsense. To understand that the correct units involve multiplication rather than division, note that either increasing the bandwidth or increasing the length must give a higher FOM. For digital networks, bandwidth is expressed in bits per second rather than in Hertz, so a digital network's connection has a FOM with units such as Mbps-km.

Table 2.4 gives approximate FOMs for some important types of connections, ordered according to decreasing FOM within the separate categories of analog and digital networks.

The approximate numbers are meant to give you a feeling for the subject and numerical examples for the rest of this book. These numbers indicate why some proposals will cost less or work better than others, but you should not use these numbers to design networks.

For examples of actual bandwidths and distances for important types of connections, in addition to the FOMs in Table 2.4, you can read Focus 2.3 and Focus 2.4, which illustrate typical values for copper and fiber-optic connections, respectively.

Prices of Connections   Affordability, rather than mere technical feasibility, will determine whether distributed multimedia becomes an everyday reality in our private lives and jobs. The fact that different types of connections have different FOMs has important economic consequences. For example, the small, flexible, black, inexpensive, and easily handled coaxial cables that CATV networks typically run from telephone poles into homes have a significantly smaller FOM than do the large silvery coaxial cables that run between poles. Nevertheless, because the small coax is used for much shorter distances, using the small coax preserves the network's overall bandwidth. Hybrid networks that connect long runs of high-FOM fiber-optic cables to short runs of low-FOM twisted pair or coaxial cable are a similar case. Distributed multimedia involves many such tradeoffs between bandwidth and

Table 2.4   Important figures of merit.

Type of connection	Analog FOM (MHz-km)	Digital FOM (Mbps-km)
CATV coaxial cable	240	
F-Coupler video over token ring STP	38	
Audio over telephone local loop UTP	0.022	
Best optical fibers available in labs		5,500,000
AT&T long-lines fiber		411,000
FDDI over multimode fiber-optic cable		200
CDDI over shielded twisted pair		10
ADSL over telephone local loop UTP		8.47
Ethernet over thick coaxial cable		5
T1 over telephone local loop UTP		2.8
Ethernet over thin coaxial cable		1.8
Token ring over STP		1.5
ISDN over telephone local loop UTP		0.790
9600 bps modem over telephone local loop UTP		0.052

distance. In fact, essentially any practical network is a hybrid of long connections that have high FOMs and shorter connections that have lower FOMs.

A completely different sort of hybrid network sometimes makes economic sense. Video on demand, surfing the Internet, and some other popular applications require significantly more bandwidth downstream, toward users, than they require upstream, toward servers. In areas where CATV networks can carry information only downstream, it may be reasonable to supplement such connections with upstream connections over telephone local loops.

A network's affordability includes its costs of installation and maintenance, which vary widely for different types of connections. For example, in addition to high FOMs, which allow long runs between repeater amplifiers,

FOCUS 2.3 FOMs for copper connections.

Token Ring Typical token ring LANs run at 16 Mbps over shielded twisted-pair (STP) wiring. The signal can go about 300 feet between adjacent stations, each of which acts as a repeater amplifier for the signal. This gives an FOM of

$$16 \text{ Mbps} \times 300 \text{ ft} = 4800 \text{ Mbps-ft} = 1.5 \text{ Mbps-km}.$$

Frequency Coupler A frequency-coupler (F-Coupler) can run up to 70 television channels over a short run of the same STP that token-ring signals are also using. The FOM of this same wiring, as an analog network, is thus

$$70 \times 6 \text{ MHz} \times 300 \text{ ft} = 126,000 \text{ MHz-ft} = 38 \text{ MHz-km}.$$

Ethernet An Ethernet LAN runs at 10 Mbps over various types of connections. With no repeater amplifiers, it can run up to 500 m over thick coax or 185 m over thin coax, giving respective FOMs of

$$10 \text{ Mbps} \times 500 \text{ m} = 5000 \text{ Mbps-m} = 5 \text{ Mbps-km}$$
$$\text{and}$$
$$10 \text{ Mbps} \times 185 \text{ m} = 1850 \text{ Mbps-m} = 1.8 \text{ Mbps-km}.$$

POTS Typical telephone local loops are unshielded twisted pairs (UTPs) up to about 18,000 feet long. In normal use, they deliver analog voice signals that include frequencies up to about 4 KHz. In this use, the type of connection in telephone local loops has an FOM of

$$4 \text{ KHz} \times 18,000 \text{ ft} = 72 \text{ MHz-ft} = 22 \text{ KHz-km}.$$

ISDN Integrated Services Digital Network, ISDN, transmits two 64-Kbps signals and one 16-Kbps signal over the same sort of UTP local loop, so its FOM as a digital network is

$$(2 \times 64 + 16) \text{ Kbps} \times 18,000 \text{ ft} = 2.6 \text{ Gbps-ft} = 790 \text{ Kbps-km}.$$

One of these two 64-Kbps signals can deliver a digitized but uncompressed voice signal, leaving the other signal free for a computer's data.

(cont.)

FOCUS 2.3   FOMs for copper connections. (*cont.*)

T1 A physical T1 line carries the digital form of 24 voice-grade (POTS) signals over two pairs of copper wires, one pair to carry information in each direction. Each voice-grade signal consists of 64 Kbps, so T1's total rate is 1.544 Mbps. At this bit rate, telephone local loop UTP requires a repeater amplifier every 6000 feet, so it has an FOM of

$$1.544 \text{ Mbps} \times 6000 \text{ ft} = 9.264 \text{ Mbps-ft} = 2.8 \text{ Mbps-km.}$$

Since the early 1960s, it has been common to send T1 over UTP for a distance up to about 50 miles, either in a local loop between a customer and a telephone central office or in a trunk between one central office and another. A longer-distance T1 line uses a portion of the bandwidths of fiber, microwave, or satellite links, in addition to using UTP at each end (Bell Laboratories, 1977).

ADSL The FOM for a given type of connection depends on how it is driven and received. Asymmetric digital subscriber loop service can send about 1.544 Mbps from a central office to a home or business over a single ordinary UTP local loop connection that is up to 18,000 feet long, with no repeaters. ADSL achieves this high bandwidth by using sophisticated digital signal processing on both ends of the connection and, in particular, by providing the high bandwidth in only one direction. The corresponding FOM is

$$1.544 \text{ Mbps} \times 18,000 \text{ ft} = 27 \times 109 \text{ bps-ft} = 8.47 \text{ Mbps-km.}$$

To compare ADSL against using the same local loop with a 9600-Kbps modem, note that driving and receiving the line with such a modem gives an FOM of only

$$9.6 \text{ Kbps} \times 18,000 \text{ ft} = 172 \text{ Mbps-ft} = 52 \text{ Kbps-km.}$$

CDDI A proposed LAN standard called CDDI, Copper FDDI, or C-FDDI runs at 100 Mbps over shielded twisted pairs for lengths up to 100 meters. This gives an FOM for the shielded twisted pair of

$$100 \text{ Mbps} \times 100 \text{ m} = 10,000 \text{ Mbps-m} = 10 \text{ Mbps-km.}$$

Recent extensions to 500 meters make CDDI genuinely competitive with fiber, because this length suffices for many applications. ■

FOCUS 2.4 FOMs for fiber-optic connections.

FDDI A fiber distributed data interface (FDDI) local area network runs at 100 million bits per second over fiber-optic cables that can be up to two kilometers long. That type of fiber-optic cable thus has an FOM of

$$100 \text{ Mbps} \times 2 \text{ km} = 200 \text{ Mbps-km}.$$

Comparing FDDI to CDDI illustrates that a particular fiber-optic cable will carry a given information rate about 20 times as far as a good shielded twisted pair.

AT&T Long-Lines Fibers Many AT&T long lines use fibers that carry about 3.4 Gbps and can have repeaters as far apart as 75 miles. The fiber's FOM is thus

$$3.4 \text{ Gbps} \times 121 \text{ km} = 411 \text{ Gbps-km} = 411{,}000 \text{ Mbps-km}.$$

By 1997, Nynex Network Systems Company and five partners plan to complete humanity's longest structure, an underwater fiber-optic cable from Great Britain to Japan. Relative to AT&T's long-lines fibers, each submarine fiber will carry more information for a shorter distance, yielding a similar FOM of

$$5.3 \text{ Gbps} \times 85 \text{ km} = 450 \text{ Gbps-km}.$$

Research Fibers The FOM for the best optical fibers available in research laboratories is about 5.5 Tbps-km. As shown in Focus 1.8, the "T" in Tbps means "Tera," or 10^{12}, so this FOM can also be written as 5.5×10^{12} bps-km. The best optical fiber's FOM dwarfs that of the best twisted pair or coaxial cable.

The maximum practical FOM for fiber-optic cables has doubled every year for 15 years. Moreover, the best FOM is expected to continue to increase as improved manufacturing methods produce purer glass and tighter tolerances. Optical fiber's rate of improvement is outstripping even the phenomenal improvement rate of integrated digital electronic circuits (Metz 1992). An AT&T spokesman foresees achieving an FOM of approximately 20 Tbps-km by the year 2000 and eventually achieving 100 Tbps-km (Brinkman, 1995). ■

fiber-optic cables tend to have low maintenance costs and are immune to electromagnetic interference from other connections and from lightning. Unfortunately, fibers have no more immunity to a carelessly wielded backhoe or anchor than do copper cables.

The two basic types of optical fibers, named for the number of modes (paths) in which light can travel from one end of a fiber to the other, have significantly different costs. A multimode fiber is large and easy to handle, so it is inexpensive to install. However, its large size allows light to bounce from one end to the other along many different modes. These modes have slightly different lengths, so a narrow pulse of light spreads out and gets lost if it travels a long distance in the fiber, resulting in a relatively low FOM. A single-mode fiber is so tiny, 5 to 10 microns in diameter, that light has no choice other than to travel straight along the fiber. This single mode results in a higher FOM, but the small size makes a single-mode fiber more expensive to install or repair. (In this chapter's section on Fiber to the Home, we discuss graded-index multimode plastic fibers, which combine high FOM with good economy.)

Improvement in fiber-optic cables' FOM does not necessarily imply a corresponding reduction of communication prices for end users. Just as the price of a transcontinental telephone call has not dropped by a factor of a thousand in the past decade, we cannot assume that the price of a transcontinental full-motion uncompressed video connection will drop by a factor of a thousand in the next decade. One reason for this is that installing networks of fibers with successively larger FOMs all over the country will require enormous investments. Another is that, whereas prices of fibers with successively higher FOMs may remain approximately constant, the prices of the associated optoelectronics (the laser or light-emitting diode that generates the light that goes into the fiber, the detector that senses the light coming out of the fiber, and the associated electronics) will increase significantly as they are called upon to handle higher and higher bandwidths. For example, the optoelectronics for one end of a 1-Gbps fiber cable cost over $1000, whereas optoelectronics that handle only one-half of the bandwidth cost about one-half as much. Fortunately, optoelectronics will become more economical as time passes and production quantities increase. Installation costs, which include paying for labor, are more likely to increase than decrease. As we discuss in Chapter 7, still other reasons why prices consumers pay for communications will not drop as rapidly as costs companies pay for fiber-optic cables and optoelectronics drop involve supply and demand as well as government regulations.

Twisted pairs, coaxial cables, and optical fiber connections have significantly different prices. Some approximate (1996) prices for 1 meter, on a reel rather than installed, in quantities of approximately 1000 meters, are as follows:

- $1.45 for glass fiber

- $1.17 for thin coax

- $0.45 for plastic fiber

- $0.26 for unshielded twisted pair

In correspondingly configured LANs that interconnect 50 computers, these connections themselves accounted for only one or two percent of the total prices. The total prices included attachment cards in the personal computers, but not the computers themselves. Attachment cards for one or two computers cost as much as the connections for all 50 computers (*LAN Magazine*, 1991).

On the other hand, the wires, cables, and fibers that make up local loops and long lines do contribute a significant part of their total prices. Because of regulations, including who is allowed to own a connection that crosses a public street, individuals and most businesses must rent rather than own local loops and long lines. Table 2.5 shows some typical monthly rentals. Note that the prices vary widely with supplier. The last two happen to be for lines between New York City and Foster City, California, and their prices are in addition to prices for corresponding local loops at each end.

For all these reasons, communications bandwidth will most definitely not become too cheap to meter. An hour-long transcontinental telephone conversation is a significant expense for most individuals. A full-motion video conference covering the same time and space is prohibitively expensive for most individuals. The price of a transcontinental video connection is now so high that there is no contradiction in saying both that the costs of

Table 2.5 Communication line prices.

Price	Service
$10–$40	Voice-grade local loop and local calls
$68	ISDN local loop carrying 144 Kbps (Maddox, 1995)
$474–$763	Local loop carrying 1.544 Mbps, T1 (*Communications Week*, 1993)
$1900	Leased line, New York to California, 56 Kbps
$13,200	Leased line, New York to California, 1.544 Mbps, T1 with wide variations (*PC Magazine*, 1993)

bandwidth are declining rapidly and that video bandwidth will remain costly for many more years.

Although there is a trend toward using higher-bandwidth connections, and even a trend toward reducing the costs of a given bandwidth, these are slow trends. Rather than waiting for a distant and unlikely day when bandwidth is too cheap to meter, we must give careful consideration to the FOMs of different types of connections and use these connections wisely. We must use increasingly sophisticated digital electronics to make interactive video more affordable by compressing video into smaller and smaller bandwidths. Moreover, we must take advantage of the fact that many applications do not need video with quality as high as that of normal broadcast television.

In the next three sections we discuss today's most important types of networks in detail. We emphasize how each type keeps signals separate and discuss the trend toward using the most suitable parts of each network to interchange a two-way video signal with each active user. We then note that several of the entries in Table 2.3 are good for delivering multimedia, but that all of those good entries differ from today's networks, and that the entries' advantages will appear in different circumstances and at different times. Fortunately, it is possible to implement some of the good entries by using major portions of today's networks, which would be enormously expensive to scrap and replace.

Circuit-Switch Multiplexing

Figure 2.6 shows that telephone local loops keep different signals separate by means of circuit-switching. That is, the switch in the central office shown at the left side of the figure connects different analog signals to different twisted pairs that run to homes and businesses shown at the right. Because a telephone network puts different signals in different physical locations, thus dividing up space among the signals, circuit-switching is also called *space-division multiplexing*.

Figure 2.6 is highly schematic. Almost all modern local loops are bundled into cables, rather than being connected to different insulators on telephone pole arms, and many run underground. The important point about circuit-switching is that different signals run on different twisted pairs.

Circuit-switching or space-division multiplexing is clearly ideal for interchanging a different stream of information with each active user. The extremely flexible switch in each central office makes its living by doing just that. Telephone companies have an infrastructure that determines what signal you want, controls one or more switches so that they connect that signal to you, and bills you for it. Another of its advantages is that the telephone

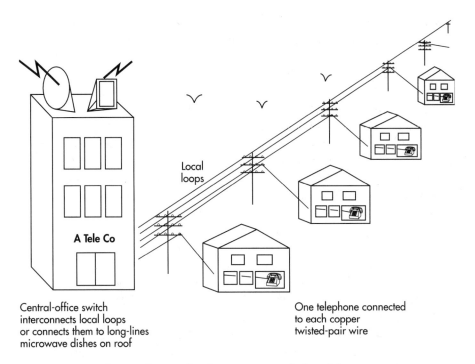

Central-office switch
interconnects local loops
or connects them to long-lines
microwave dishes on roof

One telephone connected
to each copper
twisted-pair wire

Figure 2.6 Telephone network local loops.

network reaches into the largest number of homes and offices and is the most reliable of all communication networks. One of the most important trends in multimedia delivery is applying digital transmission to circuit-switched local loops. We next describe an old and a new example of this trend.

ISDN   Integrated Services Digital Network is a local loop service category that illustrates the trend toward bringing digital service closer to customers' homes and offices. ISDN allows some businesses and a few homes to exchange computer data with central offices directly in digital form. Without ISDN, your telephone connects directly to your local loop, but your computer needs a modem to convert bits to and from analog form. If you had ISDN, your computer would connect directly to your local loop (through a terminal adapter), but your telephone would need a coder-decoder (CODEC, which does *not* mean compression and decompression in this context) to convert your voice to and from digital form.

The ISDN basic rate interface (BRI) provides two 64-Kbps bearer channels (B-channels) for voice or data and a third 16-Kbps delta channel (D-channel) for setting up calls. There are also a primary rate interface (PRI) that provides up to 23 B-channels and one D-channel and, later, an even faster Broadband-ISDN (B-ISDN) that flows over ATM and SONET.

Telephone companies have made ISDN service available in annoyingly small portions of the United States. People who enjoy conspiracy theories accuse telephone companies of deliberately keeping ISDN unavailable, expensive, or at least practically impossible to install. Such people say that the telephone companies want to avoid letting customers find out the extent to which an inexpensive 144-Kbps digital connection meets their needs, because that would reduce sales of the more profitable higher-bandwidth connections. They point out that a monopoly allows a company to sell only what is most profitable, whereas competition forces a company to sell what customers want. Early in 1995, the Federal Communications Commission (FCC) seemed to be trying to help keep ISDN expensive by ruling that its mandatory monthly subscriber line charge (SLC) applies separately to each of the 3 or 24 channels that compose one ISDN connection (Loudermilk, 1995). Even without a conspiracy, buying pieces from several different suppliers makes ISDN difficult to install. A senior editor reported on the effort and frustration involved in getting an ISDN line operating. After three months, suppliers of her local loop, terminal adapter, and Internet service got her ISDN line working, but at only 56 Kbps (Maddox, 1995).

Focus 2.5 discusses the advantage of sending digital information over an ISDN connection, which a telephone company knows to be digital, rather than sending digital information over a connection that the company must assume to be carrying an analog voice signal.

ADSL   The asymmetric digital subscriber loop (or line) technology allows most existing copper twisted-pair local loops to deliver compressed digital video from a central office to a home or business, as well as supplying POTS service. The first version of ADSL allows a local loop to carry 1.544 Mbps over any good-quality local loop that is up to about 18,000 feet in length, so it applies to about 70 percent of the local loops in the United States. Longer local loops are unsuitable for ADSL, because they must contain loading coils, which improve their ability to transmit voice frequencies but destroy their ability to carry higher frequencies. Other local loops are unsuitable, because they contain splices or use several different wire sizes. As we have seen, a data rate of 1.544 Mbps suffices to deliver digital video that has been compressed down to the 150 KBps rate that single-speed CD-ROM discs use. It is also the data rate of a T1 link.

A more recent version of ADSL can transmit 6.1 Mbps downstream and 124 Kbps upstream over local loops that are up to 12,000 feet long. That increase in bandwidth, coupled with a reduction in the longest applicable distance, should come as no surprise after this chapter's discussion of figure of merit (Wingfield, 1995; Goldberg, 1995; Baines, 1995).

FOCUS 2.5 What puts the "D" in ISDN?

ISDN transmits digital information over the same type of twisted-pair local loop that was originally designed and installed for the purpose of delivering analog voice signals. This illustrates the important fact that it is not the physical connection, but rather the electronic circuits on both ends of the connection, that determine whether a network is analog or digital. Even when a network is transmitting digital information, a reasonably close look at the actual physical connections shows that the signals are analog. In fact, unless you look unreasonably closely and see individual electrons and photons, any quantity in the real world is analog, meaning that it varies continuously.

We talk about a digital signal as if it jumps instantaneously back and forth between zero and one. However, in fact, zero and one are merely two particular ranges of some analog value at a particular instant. An electrical network delivers a continuously varying value of voltage and a fiber-optic network delivers a continuously varying value of light intensity. Transmitting instantaneous jumps is impossible because doing so would require infinite bandwidth.

An ISDN terminal adapter sends a computer's information by simply changing the voltage on the line to successive values at successive sample times. It uses the values of -3, -1, 1, or 3 volts to represent the symbols of 00, 01, 11, or 10, respectively, so each symbol that it sends carries two bits. An ISDN terminal adapter receives information for a second computer by sampling the voltages that it receives and determining, for each sample, which of -3, -1, 1, or 3 volts the sample most closely matches. It then delivers the corresponding two bits to the second computer. The data rate is limited by how quickly a terminal adapter can change the voltage on the line from one value to the next and by the degree with which the line carries these changes without smearing them out or adding noise to them.

Instead of imposing voltages on a line to represent successive bits, which is called *baseband transmission*, it is often useful to modulate digital information onto a carrier signal by changing the carrier signal's amplitude, frequency, or phase to represent successive bits or groups of bits. (We discuss modulation in more detail in the next section, which describes ADSL, and discuss frequency-division multiplexing in its own section later in this chapter.) Modulating a carrier is called *broadband transmission*. This terminology is sometimes misleading, because broadband transmission does not necessarily transmit a broader bandwidth of information than does baseband transmission. The data rate of broadband transmission is limited by how quickly the modem can change the carrier from one modulation state to the next and by the accuracy with which the line transmits the modulated carrier.   *(cont.)*

FOCUS 2.5 What puts the "D" in ISDN? *(cont.)*

Without ISDN, you can use broadband transmission over the public switched-telephone network (PSTN) to establish a digital connection between your computer and a second computer that is thousands of miles away. Your computer sends a stream of bits to your modem, perhaps at 14.4 Kbps. Your modem uses those bits to modulate a carrier, creating a broadband analog signal, and sends that signal over your local loop to the nearby telephone company central office. Circuitry in the central office samples your modem's signal, just as if the signal represented your voice, using the technique that we discussed in the section on Audio in Chapter 1, and sends the resulting 64-Kbps bit stream along with vast numbers of other bits over a succession of fiber-optic cables to the central office that is near the second computer. There, the telephone company's circuitry converts the bits back into an analog signal and sends that signal over a local loop to the second computer's modem. That modem receives the analog signal, converts it back to the bits that your computer originally sent to your modem, and sends those bits to the second computer.

Using a 64-Kbps long-line channel to send 14.4 Kbps of data is horribly inefficient. However, this method of operation became ubiquitous when few PSTN connections were digital. It allows the PSTN to handle all connections as if they carried analog voice. Now that many connections are digital, however, a better method is sorely needed.

Consider establishing an ISDN connection to a computer that is thousands of miles away. Your computer sends a stream of bits to your ISDN terminal adapter, perhaps at 64 Kbps. Your terminal adapter sends those bits as a baseband analog signal over your local loop to the nearby telephone central office. Circuitry in the central office recognizes the successive voltages as representing successive pairs of bits that make up a 64-Kbps bit stream, rather than as representing a voice signal, and sends that bit stream over the succession of fiber-optic cables that lead to the central office near the second computer. There, the telephone company's circuitry converts the bits back into a baseband analog signal and sends that signal over the second computer's local loop. The second computer's ISDN terminal adapter interprets the analog signal as the bits that your computer originally sent your terminal adapter, and sends those bits to the second computer.

The "D" in ISDN means that circuitry in your telephone company's central office knows that you want to establish a digital connection, rather than an analog voice connection. As a result, the circuitry can recognize and transmit the bits that you want to send, rather than creating bits by sampling your analog signal. This eliminates unnecessary conversions and increases the data rate without changing the long-lines network.   *(cont.)*

FOCUS 2.5 What puts the "D" in ISDN? (*cont.*)

By allocating just over twice as much bandwidth on the fiber-optic cables, the network can send two B channels and one D channel to a second computer. As we shall see in the next section, the local loop's twisted pair is not necessarily the bottleneck that limits how much data you can send and receive over the PSTN, and connections that the telephone company recognizes as digital need not use baseband transmission. ∎

AT&T developed ADSL to deliver digital video or other high-bandwidth services without causing the obsolescence of telephone companies' enormous investments in existing copper twisted-pair local loops, and without sacrificing reliability of service to customers. A single local loop can deliver compressed digital video simultaneously with analog audio telephony. Thus ADSL not only uses the same sort of wire as today's installed local loops, but it actually uses today's installed local loops without preventing them from fulfilling their present function. For reliability, when a customer loses power, ADSL allows POTS to continue operating, powered from the central office.

Despite these advantages, the first version of ADSL has three problems with meeting the requirements for a multimedia network. First, as the *asymmetric* in its name emphasizes, it carries video or other high-bandwidth digital information in only one direction, downstream from a central office to a customer. Second, to transmit video with VCR quality, which is somewhat below broadcast quality, ADSL requires a degree of digital video compression that is difficult to perform in real time. For example, creating one second of compressed video for a CD-ROM has until recently required a powerful computer to work for several seconds. For real-time video, it has been necessary to use a compression method that produces lower resolution and a lower frame rate. Third, the electronics that ADSL requires on each end of each customer's local loop have been relatively expensive. Each line now requires approximately $500 worth of electronics at each end, in addition to the customer's electronics that decompresses video (Yokell, 1995).

Nevertheless, ADSL may have a bright future as it overcomes the preceding problems. First, one-way video and non-real-time compression suffice for a customer to select and receive movies and other preexisting and precompressed programs. An early trial of ADSL by Bell Atlantic therefore concentrated on the video-on-demand application, particularly movies on demand. Moreover, for many applications of the Internet, downstream bandwidth can be much higher than upstream bandwidth. Second, improvements in compression technology, along with the more recent version's higher bit rate, are increasing the availability of high-quality real-time video. Third, even with expensive electronics, in a large region in which only a few customers want digital video, ADSL may deliver video to a home more economically than other approaches, which rely on sharing the cost of a single optical fiber among many customers. Moreover, as you would expect, prospects of large sales volumes have encouraged several companies to integrate ADSL's electronics onto a few chips that cost a total of less than $100.

Supplying video by way of ADSL requires a very significant investment. To be sure, ADSL allows telephone companies to use their existing local loops, and highly integrated chips will reduce the cost of the electronics they must add in their central offices and in customers' homes. However, the central offices require access to all the video content from which customers select, such as live sports and news feeds and a large library of compressed movies, television programs, and educational materials. Accessing such content represents a major expense, whether a central office stores content on a local server or obtains content from remote locations. Subsequent chapters explore methods for reducing costs of video on demand and other applications and costs of video servers. However, accessing remote content will remain expensive. Although ADSL's sophisticated modulation techniques increase the effective digital bandwidth of a local loop by a factor of a couple hundred, they do nothing for the global portion of the network, which is already modulated to the hilt.

Any sufficiently advanced technology is well known to be indistinguishable from magic. If you would like to relate to ADSL as the advanced technology that combines quadrature amplitude modulation with discrete multitone modulation, rather than as the magic that sends video over a wire designed to carry audio, then Focus 2.6 is for you.

Frequency-Division Multiplexing

Figure 2.7 shows that, unlike telephone networks, CATV (cable television) networks keep different signals separate on a single copper coaxial cable by using each analog signal to modulate a different carrier frequency. This is frequency-division multiplexing (FDM). Note that FDM is the method that separates ADSL's many separate bands, which flow on one twisted pair of wires. The cable company runs a single common cable that connects their head-end to all the homes in a neighborhood. The switch at the head-end dedicates an entire analog channel, that is, about 6 MHz of bandwidth, to each of about 40 television programs. Each user has a television set with a tuner, which selects the desired signal by tuning to the frequency that the selected signal modulates.

FOCUS 2.6 The technology of ADSL.

ADSL relies on quadrature amplitude modulation (QAM) to send an average of about 24 Kbps of digital information over about 4.3-KHz of analog bandwidth. ADSL also relies on discrete multitone (DMT) modulation to cram about 250 such 4.3-KHz bands onto a single unshielded twisted-pair local loop. The combination sends a remarkable total of more than 6 Mbps over the local loop. Let's look at QAM and DMT separately.

You may have started using QAM recently. Suppose that you just upgraded your computer to a 14.4-Kbps modem. Circuitry in a telephone company's central office limits voices and modems to sending a maximum frequency of 4 KHz over a normal local loop. This frequency range or bandwidth suffices to carry your voice intelligibly, as you speak into a telephone. However, to send 14.4 Kbps, one bit at a time, a modem would need to generate frequencies significantly higher than 4 KHz. Circuits at your nearby central office would filter out and ignore those higher frequencies. These circuits, which sample a signal 8000 times per second, must filter out any frequency above 4 KHz to avoid a problem called *aliasing*, which makes any higher frequency seem to go by the alias of some erroneous lower frequency. To send 14.4 Kbits per second over an ordinary local loop, therefore, a modem must send more than one bit at a time.

In fact, your new 14.4-Kbps modem sends six bits at a time. Each group of 6 bits forms one symbol. To send a particular six-bit symbol, the modem modulates both the amplitude and the phase of a carrier to send the corresponding one of 64 possible valid combinations. This more or less explains the general name, quadrature amplitude modulation, and the specific designation, QAM-64. The modem can switch from one to another of the 64 valid combinations 2400 times each second without generating any important frequencies that exceed 4 KHz. The available network bandwidth thus allows your modem to send 2400 symbols per second, which is defined as a rate of 2400 baud. (The unit *baud* honors Emile Baudot, a pioneer in printing telegraphy.) Multiplying 2400 symbols per second by 6 bits per symbol gives your new QAM modem's data rate of 14.4 Kbps. (Note that anyone who calls this a 14.4-Kbaud modem is attempting to show technical competence by using a fancy word, but is instead showing ignorance by using the word incorrectly.)

Now let's turn to discrete multitone modulation, which is the other technology behind ADSL's magic. DMT uses 255 different carriers at 255 different frequencies, all on one local loop, to send different parts of a single bit stream. One enlightening way to consider ADSL's elec-

(cont.)

FOCUS 2.6 The technology of ADSL. (*cont.*)

tronics is to visualize a stack of 255 sophisticated modems at each end of a single local loop. To transmit a total of about 6 Mbps, each pair of modems must exchange an average of about 24 Kbps. Thus, on average, each of these modems is somewhat more sophisticated than a 14.4-Kbps modem. Given that it has been barely a decade since a 1.2-Kbps modem cost $100, a similarly priced modem that averages 20 times faster on each of 255 channels is a suitably impressive representative of today's very-large-scale integration digital chip technology.

Why did the last paragraph continually refer to an average over all 255 modems? The answer involves the fact that, although a local loop can carry frequencies as high as 1 MHz, it cannot carry all frequencies equally well. It attenuates (cuts down) high frequencies much more than it attenuates low frequencies. As a result, it adds relatively more noise to a higher-frequency carrier than it adds to a lower-frequency carrier. A network's signal-to-noise ratio (SNR) is about as important as its bandwidth. The amount of noise that the network adds to the carrier's signal limits the number of bits per symbol that a network can deliver reliably, just as the network's bandwidth limits the number of symbols per second the network can deliver. For example, a low SNR might make it impossible to be sure which one of 1024 different symbols came over the network, whereas it might be easy to tell which of four different symbols arrived.

Because the 255 different carriers on one ADSL local loop use different frequency bands and thus have different SNRs, different carriers can carry different numbers of bits per symbol. Each carrier has a symbol rate of 4 Kbaud. (The carriers' center frequencies are spaced 4 KHz apart. Each carrier has a bandwidth of about 4.3 KHz, because the carriers do overlap to some extent. This bandwidth is measured between frequencies where the power drops to half of its center value, whereas a normal local loop's 4-KHz bandwidth refers to frequencies at which power drops to zero.) A low-frequency carrier, such as the one that occupies the band between 0 Hz and 4.3 KHz, can send 10 bits per symbol, whereas a high-frequency carrier, occupying a band that is near 1 MHz, can send only 2 bits per symbol. Note that a 10-bit symbol can have 1024 different values among which the receiver must distinguish reliably. It is the average over all the carriers that allows ADSL electronics to send more than 6 Mbps over a single local loop. ∎

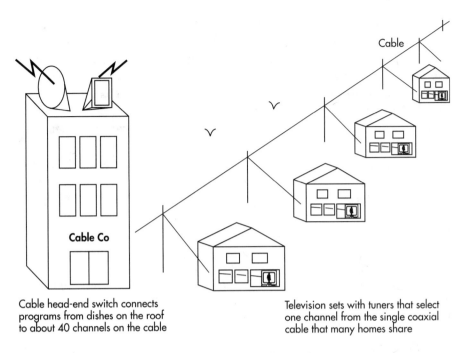

Cable head-end switch connects programs from dishes on the roof to about 40 channels on the cable

Television sets with tuners that select one channel from the single coaxial cable that many homes share

Figure 2.7   CATV network.

The head-end's switch and each user's tuner comprise a distributed switch that corresponds roughly to a telephone central office's switch. Being part of a distributed switch greatly reduces the size and cost of the cable company's head-end switch. More important, however, the head-end switch must handle only about 30 to 150 different channels. Contrast a head-end's switch to a telephone central office's switch, which must handle thousands of different signals. In principle, the central office may need to handle one conversation for each of its subscribers. In practice, of course, it can get by with far fewer signals, even during a regional disaster or on Mother's Day. Nevertheless, telephone central office switches handle far more different signals than CATV head-end switches.

CATV networks differ from telephone networks in more than their multiplexing method. The other major difference is that the cable network's switches and wires can handle the large bandwidth of analog video. The fact that the cable has enough bandwidth to carry dozens or hundreds of uncompressed channels does not matter to a user of a multimedia network. If one of the channels on the cable has exactly what a user just requested from the cable company, then she does not care whether or not there are dozens or hundreds of additional channels on the cable. However, the ability to carry many channels on one cable could matter a great deal to cable companies because frequency multiplexing 40 uncompressed analog video signals onto one coaxial cable is one way to send 40 different one-way signals to 40 active users or to exchange 20 two-way signals with 20 active users.

CATV networks pay a considerable price for their high bandwidth. First, their coaxial cables cost more per foot, and cost more to install, than do telephone local loop twisted-pair wires. Second, as we have seen, their high bandwidths force them to place a repeater amplifier about every quarter-mile along every cable run. Just as local loops are a major part of the investment in a telephone network, cable and repeater amplifiers are major parts of the investment in a CATV network. Just as the bandwidth of local loops limits telephone networks to one-way interactive video, repeater amplifiers limit most of today's cable networks to one-way video. Either raising the bandwidth to get more channels or going to two-way video requires a cable company to replace its expensive repeater amplifiers.

Thus, cable companies have neither switches nor network topologies that are suitable for exchanging a different two-way signal between each user and their head-end units. What they do have are:

- Wires with high and affordable bandwidth that enter approximately 60 percent of the homes in the United States and pass near about 90 percent of those homes

- Familiarity with video

- Arrangements for getting video from many different sources to the head-end units

- Cash flows with which to finance improvements (although less than telephone companies)

- A strong desire to recapture customers who go to video rental stores to get wider selections of titles and start times.

CATV cable companies have several more or less attractive options for making the most of their advantages and eliminating their disadvantages. We next discuss the two options that continue to employ copper coaxial cables. We defer to the end of this section our discussion of the option to drive fiber deeper into the network.

Two-Way Analog Copper   A cable company could elect to rewire its network with copper coaxial cable that has a sufficiently high FOM to carry 150 analog channels and, at the same time, replace one-way repeater amplifiers with two-way versions. Each group of a few hundred homes (which might have a total of 150 active one-way users or 75 active two-way users) would then need its own expensive cable and repeaters, all the way to the cable's head-end. The head-end would need a switch capable of handling a separate communication with each active user. The number of potential users connected to each cable could be made to exceed the number of active users, because the head-end would assign a free channel to each user as she becomes active and would return that channel to the free pool whenever she ceases active use. Billing could be by the minute, which is familiar to telephone companies but not to cable companies. Charges could depend on whether the video connection is one-way or two-way.

Digital Copper Alternatively, cable companies could send information in digital form and use video compression to increase the number of channels by a factor that could range roughly from 10 to 100. Note that real-time compression and decompression by such factors will be priced suitably for television set-top boxes by the late 1990s. Improvements in size and cleverness of electronic circuits will continually increase the compression ratio and decrease its cost. Nevertheless, this option requires more cable runs from the head-end unit to neighborhoods of several hundred homes, all new repeater amplifiers that are both digital and two-way, and all new set-top boxes.

Time-Division Multiplexing

Figure 2.8 indicates that, unlike cable television networks, computer networks keep different signals separate on a single connection by breaking up each signal into packets and sending packets for different signals over the same connection at different times. This is time-division multiplexing (TDM). At one time a packet goes to one user, such as the second house, as the top half of the figure shows. A short time later, a packet on the same shared connection goes to another user, such as the fourth house, as the bottom half shows. Each station that wants to send a packet contends for the privilege of doing so. Each user's station receives all packets, rather than only packets addressed to it, but is expected to be sufficiently polite to ignore packets that are addressed to other stations. When politeness fails, enciphering ensures that only a packet's intended recipient can decipher it.

Figure 2.8 is only schematic. The connection does not really run to one user at one instant, as shown at the top, and to another user a short time later, as shown at the bottom, although that is the effect of TDM. The connection itself may be a twisted pair of wires, a coaxial cable, or an optical fiber. It may be wired as a bus that goes to all stations, a ring made up of

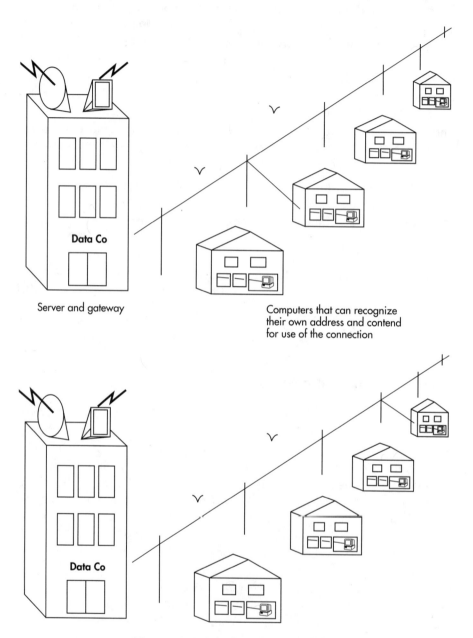

Server and gateway

Computers that can recognize
their own address and contend
for use of the connection

Figure 2.8 Computer network.

separate portions that run between pairs of stations, or a pair of such rings. In general, Fig. 2.8 notwithstanding, the connection may be restricted to a single building.

TDM often combines with other multiplexing methods, particularly with circuit-switch multiplexing. For example, it is TDM that separates one ISDN connection's D and B channels from each other, while circuit-switch multiplexing separates one ISDN connection from another ISDN connection. When a telephone company uses T1 to combine up to 24 different voice signals, in digital form, on one twisted pair running in each direction, it uses TDM to keep the signals separate. Because adding T1 electronics allows two twisted pairs to do the work of 24 twisted pairs, this practice goes by the interesting name of *pair gain*.

A computer network's TDM is completely distributed. No sort of central office switch or head-end unit determines what flows over the connections at each instant. The hypothetical Data Company that Fig. 2.8 shows merely represents one of many possible server, router, and gateway stations that might supply data to individual users' stations and connect a local area network to one or more wide area network links. Both local area networks and wide area networks use TDM on each connection. The Data Company might be a data switching exchange (DSE), a full-blown packet switch that recognizes when a packet is addressed to a station outside the particular local area network, receives the packet, decides which of several long lines leads toward the addressed station, and retransmits the packet over that line. Space-division multiplexing, or circuit-switching, separates signals on different long lines from each other, and from signals on local area networks, just as in a telephone network.

Different types of computer networks differ greatly in the ways in which they use TDM to allocate one connection's resource among stations that want to transmit packets. We will summarize some common ways because they strongly affect a computer network's ability to deliver multimedia.

Token Ring A token-ring LAN allocates its resource among all of its stations by using a uniquely identifiable bit pattern, called the *token*. As its name also implies, it is wired as a closed loop, or ring. A section of wire runs out of the first station and into the second station, and so on until a section of wire runs from the last station's output back to the first station's input. A token pattern that is inserted at an arbitrary point during initialization will circulate around and around the ring, passing through all the stations in turn. Each station that has no packet to transmit just receives the token from its incoming section of the ring and transmits the token on its outgoing section of the ring. When a station has a packet ready to transmit, the station must first wait for the token to reach it. When it receives the token from the incoming section, the station transmits the bits of its packet onto the outgoing section of the ring, instead of transmitting the token. While it is transmitting, there is no token at all on the ring, so no other station can start transmitting. After it has finished transmitting the packet and has seen that the destination has received the packet, it again transmits the unique bit pattern that is the token. Then the next station along the ring that has a packet ready to transmit transmits its packet. If all stations happen to be ready to transmit, then each of the other stations gets a chance to do so before the first station gets a chance to transmit its next packet. If no other station is ready to transmit, then the first station can transmit its next packet as soon as the token makes one complete circuit around the ring.

The token-passing algorithm divides a token ring's bandwidth reasonably fairly among all the stations that want to transmit. If only a few stations want to transmit compressed video at 1.5 Mbps, they can all do so with quite good results on a 16-Mbps token ring. Waiting variable lengths of time to get the token does tend to introduce jitter, but on a lightly loaded ring, long waits are uncommon. However, if 20 stations all are ready to transmit compressed video, the algorithm allows all of them to start, even though one-twentieth of the total bit rate is insufficient to allow any of them to succeed. Similarly, if more than 10 stations are in the midst of transmitting long files that fill the ring's available bit rate, the algorithm will allow a station to start transmitting compressed video, even though the results will not look acceptable to the recipient. If one station has been transmitting video over an unloaded ring, nothing prevents each of 20 other stations from beginning to use their "fair" shares of the bit rate and incidentally destroying the video transmission. In essence, a token ring's principal problem with isochronous data is that its allocation algorithm does not know how to say no to an additional station that wants to use the network's resource. Special setup can alleviate this problem to some extent by allowing individual stations to reserve fixed bandwidths. However, a subtler problem is that one token ring can serve scores or even hundreds of users who will settle for text, so there may well be an economic problem with allocating an entire token ring to just a few video streams (Feeney and Day, 1991).

Ethernet   An Ethernet allocates transmission time on its one continuous cable among all of its stations by the algorithm known as Carrier Sense Multiple Access with Collision Detection (CSMA-CD). When any station is in the process of transmitting a packet, other stations sense the first station's bits and refrain from transmitting. (There is no actual carrier wave for the stations to sense. Ethernet inherited the term *carrier* from its ancestor, AlohaNet, in which a group of Hawaiian data radio broadcast stations using the same frequency agreed not to start transmitting when they could detect another station's carrier.) Any station is free to start transmitting the bits of a packet at any time when no other station is transmitting. However, the station does not necessarily continue to the end of the packet. If the station detects that some other station started transmitting at about the same time, which is called *detecting a collision*, then the station stops sending its packet, waits a random amount of time, and tries again. Similarly, a station that has lots of packets to transmit waits a while between packets to give other stations a chance to use the cable.

On a lightly loaded Ethernet, collisions are very infrequent. One station can send long packets quite close together, starting almost as soon as it gets the packets ready. As a result, CSMA-CD allocates a cable's resource adequately using inexpensive adapter cards, which accounts for Ethernet's popularity. However, if more than two or three stations try to send continuous compressed video streams over an Ethernet, each station falls behind the required bit rate and the network ceases to be adequately isochronous. Whenever a station that is sending an isochronous data stream has to wait for another station to finish a transmission, or starts transmitting and encounters a collision, the resulting variable delay shows up as jitter in the received signal. Isochronous Ethernet and Switched Ethernet are two solutions to this problem, which we discuss later in this chapter.

FDDI   A fiber distributed data interface network allocates use of the fiber-optic connection among many users by means of the token passing algorithm that we just described. Refinements in this algorithm allow an FDDI ring to use almost 80 percent of its rated 100-Mbps capacity. Some protocols allow two tokens on the ring at one time, so that different parts of the ring can transmit different data streams simultaneously. If an FDDI network carried 100 Mbps of compressed video, the network could carry 53 streams.

The FDDI standard also provides for a "synchronous mode" service, which assigns high priority to a few stations. Other stations may get the ring's token only when no high-priority station has anything to transmit. Note that the term *synchronous* is used here to mean "isochronous" (Wallace, 1993). A proposed extension to FDDI called FDDI-II goes further and allows a station to reserve a fixed amount of bandwidth in order to send isochronous media, particularly voice. This extension allocates the 100-Mbps bandwidth among one 0.75-Mbps packet channel and sixteen 6.144-Mbps isochronous channels. It also includes increasing the bit rate to 139 or 154 Mbps and using single-mode optical fibers to extend the maximum distance between nodes to 40 km from multimode fiber's 2 km (*Computer Design*, 1990). Significantly, the retail price of a FDDI connection is estimated to be $1000. Although this price is dropping, it has some distance to fall before reaching the consumer price range (Magel, 1993).

Wide Area Computer (WAN) Network Protocols   Typical WANs use protocols such as X.25 or the International Standards Organization's Open Systems Interconnect (ISO-OSI) to carry critical data over noisy and unreliable connections. These protocols enable WANs to cope with noise that destroys a significant fraction of their packets and also cope with equipment failures and line failures that make particular links unavailable for quite long intervals. Despite this failure-prone environment, WANs carry automatic teller machine (a different use of the abbreviation ATM) transactions and interbank transfers extremely reliably. ATMs are almost always available and essentially never deduct money from one account without also adding the money to another appropriate account.

These time-division multiplexing protocols are also very economical for sending the bursts of traffic that are characteristic of ATMs and other sources of data communications. Operators of networks that use packet-oriented time-division multiplexing may elect to charge each user for only the bits that user actually transmits. For contrast, the operator of a network that uses either circuit-switch multiplexing or frequency-division multiplexing would probably charge each user for a fixed bandwidth that would handle that user's maximum requirements, even if the user actually needs that bandwidth only during infrequent bursts.

The protocols that make WANs so effective and economical for delivering ATM transactions make them remarkably unsuitable for delivering multimedia. A typical WAN protocol sends a message to its destination by breaking the message up into packets and using one or more physical links to send the packets. The protocol retransmits any packet that fails to reach its destination because the network corrupted the packet, lost it, or threw it away as part of flow control. The protocol may use Data Switching Exchange nodes to reroute some packets over other paths, to bypass links that failed or became congested part way through transmitting a message. Thus a network may use several different sequences of links to send the packets that make up one single message. Rerouting and retransmission tend to cause the packets that make up a given message to arrive at their destination out of order, so that the destination machine must reassemble them in the correct order to recreate the original message. Every time a packet is stored and forwarded, and every time it waits for service at a bridge, gateway, or router, the packet gets a variable delay that appears as jitter. All in all, one would be hard pressed to imagine a less isochronous network protocol. Frame relay takes one step away from the X.25 protocol by dropping the error-correction capability, but several such steps are necessary in order to transmit multimedia.

A typical WAN protocol is far too processor-intensive to meet multimedia's capacity requirements. One reason is that it handles variable-length packets. This requires a processor to parse some of each packet, to read the length, and then execute complex buffer-allocation and garbage-collection algorithms. A second reason is that the protocol also expends considerable processing power deciding on the optimal routing for each packet.

A third reason WAN protocols are processor-intensive is that a protocol typically copies data from one part of memory to another, to allow buffer reuse, each time it changes between successive layers of the protocol. Even a very fast processor may take as long to copy a packet as a fast network takes to carry the packet to a distant destination. For example, suppose that a processor capable of 50 million instructions per second is executing a seven-layer network protocol and driving a 1-Gbps network. If the processor can execute 50 million load-and-store instructions per second, then it can make 25 million 32-bit moves per second. Thus it could move only 800 Mbps, even if it did not have anything else to do. If the processor must copy each piece of information seven times as it goes from layer to layer, then its net throughput of different bits is 114 Mbps. These processor copy operations alone would limit the 1-Gbps network to an effective throughput of little more than 100 Mbps. Reducing the protocol's processor requirements is a better approach than increasing processing power.

A typical WAN protocol is also memory intensive. It must store packets after transmitting them, in case the receiver asks for them to be retransmitted. For example, storing the last two seconds of information sent over a 1-Gbps link requires 250 MB of very fast random access memory. The data rate is far too high for disks.

All the properties of WAN protocols we have described are splendid for carrying automatic teller machine data transactions, but are terrible for carrying interactive video. When a network finds that it has corrupted or lost a video frame, so that a viewer has seen some "snow" or jitter on the screen, the worst thing the network can do is retransmit the frame so that it interferes with some later part of the viewer's video stream. Since there is no benefit in correcting a video stream, even detecting such errors just wastes processing power and causes unnecessary delay. Another reason to change protocols is that the gradual changeover to fiber-optic links has greatly reduced the incidence of line noise and outages.

The assumption that every wrong bit must be retransmitted is not the only assumption that is correct for ATM transactions and incorrect for multimedia. Many of today's WAN protocols were designed for 56-Kbps links. As a result, they could assume that processing speeds and memory-to-memory copying speeds were far faster than network speeds. Also, today's protocols are optimized for routing successive small packets to different destinations.

Sending a movie's 6 billion bits to a single destination makes it far more desirable to decide on one route and stick with it.

Thus we see that today's local area networks and wide area networks fail to meet the requirement for multimedia networks, particularly the requirements that they must have high capacity and be isochronous. We next discuss a half-dozen approaches to solving this problem.

Clever Software   One approach to the problems inherent in using today's LANs to deliver interactive video is to use existing hardware without change and add software that allocates to a few stations sufficient bandwidth for sending isochronous media. For example, ProtoComm's VideoComm product performs this function for a token ring. This approach may dedicate to a few users of video an entire LAN that could serve many users of text and data. Its major advantage is that it preserves all of a user's hardware installation (Magel, 1993).

Switched Hubs   The second approach is to convert a LAN from time-division multiplexing to circuit-switched multiplexing by adding a switched hub. This converts each portion of the LAN into a two-point connection that runs only between the hub and a single user. As a result, there are no other users contending for the portion's bandwidth resource, and therefore no conflicts. This may seem to be a brute-force approach, because it wastes the cable's ability to carry anything other than one user's signals, and it wastes the contention-resolution hardware in the user's LAN adapter card. However, it does work with existing wires and adapter cards and it gives good results. This approach goes by the names *switched hub, two-point Ethernet, switched Ethernet,* and *dedicated Ethernet.* One example of this approach is Starlight Networks' StarWorks, which we discuss in Chapter 3.

FCS   The proposed Fibre Channel Standard is another use of circuit-switching. It operates at the high data rate of 100 MBps. Note that this is eight times the speed of FDDI, which runs at 100 Mbps. Note also that the spelling of *fibre* is British. An FCS switch, called a fabric, sets up fixed-bandwidth connections among stations that last as long as the stations want to exchange information. A given connection may use a channel's entire bandwith of 100 MBps. Alternatively, one connection may use some fixed fraction of the channel's bandwidth and allow other stations to make connections over the same physical channel. This uses a special sort of time-division multiplexing to create several virtual channels over one physical channel. In principle, if one virtual channel needs one-third of the bandwidth and another channel needs two-thirds, then the channel could carry a stream of data in which every third bit belongs to the first channel and the other bits belong to the second channel. This form of time-division multiplexing is also used in Synchronous Transfer Mode in the global portion of television and CATV networks. If a virtual channel does not need some of its allocated bits, this synchronous form of time-division multiplexing wastes the bits, rather than allocating them to some other virtual channel (Wallace, 1993).

F-Coupler   Another approach employs frequency-division multiplexing to add analog isochronous channels in order to carry audio and video on the same cable that token ring uses for time-division multiplexing of non-isochronous digital data. IBM's F-Coupler adds an inexpensive passive (unpowered) filter at each end of a short run of normal shielded twisted-pair wire. The filter separates low frequencies and high frequencies onto separate connectors. Normal data traffic uses the low-frequency connector. Up to 70 analog video signals use the high-frequency connector. These channels are modulated on normal television carrier frequencies, exactly as on CATV cable. However, the twisted pair's relatively low FOM limits the run length to considerably shorter distances than is possible with CATV coaxial cable. Typical token ring wiring runs from a wiring closet to a station and back, then out to the next station, and so on. One F-Coupler in the wiring closet puts video on the wire that leads out to one station. A corresponding F-Coupler at the station takes the video off the wire. Supplying video to many stations requires many such pairs of F-Couplers, all driven by a video distribution amplifier.

Isochronous Time-Division Multiplexing   This approach uses special hardware that provides isochronous digital capability in parallel with existing nonisochronous data traffic on existing wires. IBM and National Semiconductor are working on an isochronous extension to Ethernet called IsoEthernet or IsoEnet. This proposal retains today's 10-Mbps bandwidth for media that are not isochronous. It adds 6.11 Mbps of bandwidth, on the same wire, for isochronous media, in the form of 96 channels that have a fixed bandwidth of 64 Kbps each (*Electronic Engineering Times*, 1993).

ATM   Asynchronous transmission mode replaces a network's inherently nonisochronous time-division multiplexing protocol by a protocol that is effective for delivering isochronous audio and video and also is efficient for delivering bursty data (transmitted in bursts) such as text, graphics, and images. This approach deserves a close look because it is not a brute-force approach, but rather is an approach that uses connections effectively and efficiently. It applies to both local area networks and wide area networks. It also scales well; that is, it applies to many different types of connections that have a wide range of bandwidths, at least from 25 Mbps to several Gbps. This is a huge advantage over most other protocols, which require algorithm changes to accommodate different transmission speeds. It carries voice and video as isochronously as today's synchronous networks, which use synchronous transfer mode (STM) to allocate fixed time slots to each of many different audio or video signals, thus assuring each signal a fixed fraction of a connection's bandwidth. ATM also carries the nonisochronous media efficiently, because it allows many different bursty streams to share a fixed amount of bandwidth, as packet-switched networks do.

ATM is also a lightweight protocol, meaning that it makes light demands on a computer's processing and storage resources. The three main reasons for this are that it does not have variable-length packets, it does not individually route the separate packets that make up a given stream, and it does no error detection or correction on data.

The ATM specification uses the term *cells* for the fixed-length entities that ATM transports, in order to distinguish them from variable-length packets. The specification also uses octet for Byte, although having an abbreviation "O" that is easily mistaken for "zero" is about as bad as having an abbreviation "B" that is easily mistaken for the abbreviation for "bits." Each ATM cell is 53 octets long and consists of 5 octets of header and 48 octets of payload. Having fixed-length cells means that a computer need not read and understand one cell in order to know where the next cell starts. Having a short, fixed length means that relatively few bits are wasted when a given message needs only part of a cell. Critics point out that each of the short cells wastes one-tenth of its bits on the header; however, a short cell helps reduce jitter and improve smoothness, which is especially important for audio. Critics also point out that today's implementations of ATM do not transmit voice as efficiently as the ATM protocols allow (Csenger, 1994).

Most of a cell's header is used for 24 bits that define the stream of which the cell is a part. Any switch that gets the cell uses these bits to decide on which outgoing connection to put the cell. All cells that are part of the same stream contain the same 24 bits. Before the stream starts, a unique 24-bit code is assigned and that code is inserted into a routing table in each switch that the cells must traverse. That is, ATM preroutes all the cells in one stream over a virtual circuit, so each computer along the route that receives a cell need only look up in a routing table where to send the cell. This takes far less processing than other protocols, in which each computer that receives a packet must read the packet's destination address and compute an optimal routing toward that destination. From a network protocol viewpoint, ATM's most interesting characteristic is the fact that ATM preroutes a virtual circuit and places in each cell's header the identity of its circuit, rather than the address of its destination.

The header includes an error-check octet with which the computer makes sure that it read the header correctly. However, ATM calls for no error detection on the payload. In particular, it does not require a computer to store cells that it has already sent, in case it must retransmit them for error correction. This is the third reason why ATM requires far less processing and storage than other protocols.

ATM was originally designed to be carried by Broadband Integrated Services Digital Network (B-ISDN) at 155 Mbps or 620 Mbps and by Synchronous Optical Network (SONET) at 51.84 Mbps (STS-1) up to at least 2.488 Gbps (STS-48). Recent proposals include running Low-Speed ATM over existing LAN wiring at 25 Mbps or 52 Mbps. These proposals, championed by IBM and Chipcom and by AT&T and HP, respectively, do not greatly increase today's LAN speeds, so they can be implemented quickly and sold cheaply. Their main advantage is that they make the LANs isochronous.

High-bandwidth ATM installations will be quite expensive for the foreseeable future. One ATM connection costs roughly $4000 (*Information Week*, 1993). A 155 Mbps ATM optical fiber interface adds $9500 or $11,500 to the price of a Cisco Systems Inc. router (Raynovich, 1995). Whereas ATM has obvious advantages as the protocol of choice for carrying many streams of many media, it is clear that transmitting a high-bandwidth ATM connection all the way into each home or office is prohibitively expensive. The economic requirement to share such an ATM connection among roughly 100 homes or offices limits the degree to which it is economical to drive fiber deeper into the network, as we discuss next.

Fiber Deeper in the Network

The lower right corner of Fig. 2.4 illustrates what is arguably the most important and interesting trend in multimedia networks. This trend is subtler than providing local connections that can carry two-way video and other media by converting to digital transmission, installing higher-bandwidth connections, or changing the network's multiplexing method. This trend involves converting the local portion of a network into a hybrid subnetwork. That is, a network provider starts at a central office or head-end, runs a high-FOM fiber-optic cable to a distribution point that is near a reasonable number of homes or offices, and runs some lower-FOM connection, such as coaxial cable, the rest of the way from that distribution point to the end users.

There is vigorous disagreement about the type of connection that should run from the distribution point to the end users, the number of end users that one distribution point should serve, and whether signals on the fiber should be analog or digital. However, most of the disagreements concern timing.

There is general agreement that, as time goes by, fiber will push deeper into the network as distribution points move closer to homes and offices; connections into homes and offices will increase in bandwidth; and a larger fraction of the signals will be digital.

Several designs for local hybrid networks appeal to CATV companies and telephone companies. However, even when the two sorts of companies deploy identical networks, they use different words to describe what they are doing. Because CATV companies operate trunk and feeder lines, they talk about "fiber trunk (FT) networks" and "fiber trunk and feeder (FTF) networks." Because telephone companies operate local loops, they talk about "fiber in the loop (FITL)." When a telephone company offers to connect you to any of a wide range of sources of video, the company says it is giving you a "video dial tone (VDT)." When a telephone company is proud of going digital and still switching signals for you, they say they are deploying "switched digital video (SDV) service." Individual companies also devise more customer-friendly names such as "full-service networks (FSN)" and invent an endless variety of names for their distribution points.

Both CATV companies and telephone companies agree on some terminology that will help you understand newspaper articles describing multimedia system trials. They agree that a neighborhood contains roughly 200 to 2000 homes, so when they run fiber to a distribution point that serves 200 to 2000 homes they say they are deploying "fiber to the neighborhood (FTTN)." When they run fiber closer to homes, so that a distribution point serves only about 20 customers, they say they are deploying "fiber to the curb (FTTC)." We next discuss these two designs in some detail and then wrap up this Trends section with a discussion of running fiber all the way to the home (FTTH).

Fiber to the Neighborhood   An FTTN network uses a fiber-optic cable to carry about 100 channels of analog video to a neighborhood distribution point. It then runs one or more coaxial cables from the distribution point to between 200 and 2000 subscribers' homes. This design is, therefore, also called hybrid fiber coax (HFC). It does not run fiber particularly deeply into the network and it does not use the fiber to carry digital information, so it is the weakest example of the trend we are discussing. Nevertheless, for several years, FTTN has been the most economical way for CATV companies to use fiber to replace trunk and feeder cables and their expensive and unreliable repeater amplifiers. In fact, where population density exceeds 500 homes within a 1.5-kilometer diameter, as is typical in Japan, this design can completely eliminate coaxial repeater amplifiers. In that case, called a *passive coaxial design,* it is a particularly economical and reliable solution.

Many CATV companies have deployed FTTN networks when they needed to replace worn-out installations or expand to cover new regions. As much as 10 percent of the CATV installations in the United States include some fiber. Telephone companies have planned and deployed the same design to a lesser extent. Even Bell Atlantic, which has installed about 1.5 million miles of fiber, has installed fiber in less than 1 percent of its local loops. We consider FTTN to be a trend for the future, rather than being part of today's state of the art. Many of today's installations merely provide unchanged CATV or telephone service at a lower cost to the service provider. The interesting and important trend is toward using such installations to provide additional services for customers.

In a typical FTTN installation in the United States, analog video flows over the fiber as amplitude-modulated information with a total bandwidth of 750 MHz, while 550 MHz of bandwidth is more common in Japan. Separate fibers carry voice, data, and video. Optoelectronic circuits at the distribution point convert a fiber's optical signals to electronic signals. The optoelectronics' cost, roughly $6000, is affordable when shared among even 200 customers. Electronic circuits at the distribution point merge voice, data, and video onto one coaxial cable that runs to homes. At each home, a box on the outside wall splits the signals onto existing thin coaxial cable that runs to each television set and existing unshielded twisted-pair modular telephone cables that run to each telephone or computer modem.

FTTN is an excellent technology for making a gradual transition from analog to digital transmission. It uses fiber to carry about 125 analog television channels, each of which has 6 MHz of bandwidth. Relatively simple circuits in a distribution node can convert many of those channels directly from optical signals on the fiber to electrical signals on the cable that runs to homes. More sophisticated circuits in a head-end or central office can modulate digital information, including digital video, onto the remaining analog channels. Corresponding circuits at a distribution point or home can demodulate the signal to recover this downstream digital information. The upstream direction works similarly.

As more customers want to send and receive digital video, FTTN allows the supplier to change more channels from analog to digital without disturbing the connections. Quadrature amplitude modulation, which we discussed in Focus 2.6, makes it possible to send as much as 36 Mbps of digital information over one 6 MHz analog channel (Lawton, 1995). This digital bandwidth suffices for sending 10 high-quality digital video signals over a single analog video channel. The supplier can make a gradual transition to a network that is capable of transmitting about 10 times as many channels by using more and more analog channels to send 10 digital video signals each.

Fiber to the Curb   An FTTC network uses fiber to carry all media in digital form to a distribution point that serves only about 20 customers. At the distribution point, optoelectronics separate video from audio and may separate different customers' signals from one another. In a typical installation, the distribution point connects each customer's audio signal to a copper twisted pair that runs only to that customer and puts all video signals on a single coaxial cable that runs to all customers. Other designs are possible, as more customers want their own unique video channels, as well as their own telephone conversations. In the variant called switched digital video (SDV), the distribution point puts a customer's digital video on a copper twisted pair that runs only to that customer's home or office. FTTC is probably the most economical method for transporting multimedia to and from homes and is thus today's strongest trend (Jones, 1994).

Clearly, many possible designs are intermediate between FTTN and FTTC. For example, there is no reason that a distribution point could not serve a number of customers that is between 20 and 200. Moreover, there is no reason why a distribution point that serves over 200 customers could not use digital transmission. The more interesting variants, however, use different connections from the distribution point to homes and offices. In one variant, this last hundred yards is wireless, as in the case of PCS. Another variant of FTTC, which we discuss next, employs existing wires that not only run into the home, but already run to every electric power outlet in the home.

Fiber to the Transformer   In the mode called FTTT, each fiber-optic cable distribution point would be near a utility company's transformer that supplies electric power to a small group of homes. Optoelectronics at the distribution point would convert between optical signals on the fiber and electrical signals on the wires that carry power into and throughout the homes.

A New Orleans electric utility executive, Jack King, says that utilities can save enough money by using fiber-optic cables to control use of home energy to pay for the fiber network. The network creates smart homes that can buy electricity based on real-time pricing. King also points out that only 4 percent of homes in the United States fail to connect to power lines, whereas 6 percent do not connect to the telephone network and 34 percent do not connect to CATV cable. Sears, Roebuck is considering using signals on power lines to monitor and troubleshoot home appliances from remote locations. A microprocessor in a new washing machine, water heater, air conditioner, coffee maker, motion-sensing alarm unit, or any other appliance could send and receive digital information over the same plug that supplies it with power. An existing appliance could plug into a new box that plugs into the power line. A microprocessor in that box could send and receive enough information to turn a water heater on when power is cheap and off when peak load makes power expensive, for example.

Novell is working with utility companies on power-line modems and NetWare protocols that can exchange between 2 Mbps and 3 Mbps of information with new appliances and with new boxes attached to existing appliances. Note that this high bandwidth results from sophisticated digital processing and uses frequency-division multiplexing to separate information from the 60 Hz power-line signal. It works, not because a power line has a particularly high FOM, but rather because the power line from the pole or curb to all parts of your home is relatively short.

Most of the microprocessors in your home are probably embedded in appliances, so power-line connections would give most of your processors useful two-way communication with the rest of the world. These connections could produce savings that would pay for the network. But doesn't it seem that we have forgotten something? Oh, yes, there would be plenty of bandwidth left over for computers, telephones, and television sets. The 2-Mbps to 3-Mbps bandwidth could carry one or two digital video streams, several digital audio streams for voice and high-fidelity music, and orders of magnitude more data than today's telephone line modems (Fogarty, 1995).

Technical and economic factors are not decisive in deciding what companies and what industries will build the national information infrastructure. If the notion of buying telephone service from your friendly local CATV company or getting video from your telephone company seems odd, you'll find even odder the idea of buying both types of services from your electric power utility. If culture clashes result from telephone companies' experience with billing by the minute and CATV companies' billing by the hour, think of the change that would be required in a power utility's billing by total kilowatt-hours. Then consider whether the agencies that regulate telephone companies and broadcasters would enjoy turning over their jobs to the Electric Power Commission. Finally, note that no company would benefit from eliminating the rat's nest of telephone wires, CATV cables, and speaker wires that clutter our homes, but carrying all these signals on existing power wires would benefit us significantly.

Fiber to the Home (FTTH)   There is general agreement that, in the next decade, we will not see the trend of driving fiber deeper into the network carried to its logical completion. We do not expect to see fiber-optic cables running into every home or office, let alone running to every telephone, television set, and personal computer. Running fiber-optic cable all the way from a central office to an end-user device might seem to be ideal for delivering interactive video because it would have both optical fiber's characteristic of huge bandwidth and the telephone network's characteristic of individually switching one signal to each active user over a separate connection.

However, fiber into the home is not necessary, economical, or even particularly desirable. It is not necessary because one end-user device needs only one video stream, or perhaps several streams if a user asks to see a few video windows while sending out video showing herself and showing her environment. A fiber-optic cable could carry far more streams than even a house full of such devices could use. This design is not economical because optoelectronics (the combination of optical components with electronics that convey information between the optical form that the fiber-optic cable carries and the electrical form that the end users' devices employ) are too expensive to place even one set in each home. The advantage of a distribution point that serves many end users is that all the users can share the several-thousand-dollar cost of one set of optoelectronics. Fiber into the home is not desirable because there is no good way to deliver a home telephone instrument's operating power over an all-fiber local loop. Powering telephones from a utility company's power lines reduces the reliability of telephone service. Customers expect their telephones to continue operating, even after a falling limb or carelessly operated backhoe cuts a power line, if only so that they can report the outage to the utility company. Focus 2.7 uses the concept of FOM to illustrate two extreme options for running fiber all the way from a central office into a home.

FOCUS 2.7 Two cases for fiber to the home.

We have seen that changing from copper telephone local loops as used by ISDN to the optical fiber used by FDDI would increase the connection's FOM from 790 Kbps-km to 200 Mbps-km, which is a factor of about 250. Telephone companies could use this change to increase bandwidth and distance in many different combinations. For example, optical fiber could carry the same information for a distance 250 times greater than the 18,000 feet that is typical for local loops, namely, about 850 miles. As another example, over the same distance as today's local loops, this fiber could carry 250 times as much information, namely, about 36 Mbps or 23 compressed video streams.

Neither example is particularly attractive for an individual home. Local loops that can run 850 miles would make it technically easy for a single central telephone office in Columbus, Ohio, to connect a separate fiber local loop capable of carrying ISDN to each home east of the Mississippi, but it would be economically absurd to do so. Local loops that can carry 23 video streams would make it technically possible for today's many central offices to send each home its unique choice of 23 different signals, but only 23 individuals who share a home but share no common tastes would consider paying for such service. ∎

Envisioning distributed multimedia without fiber into the home may turn out to be like envisioning space flight without computers. Predicting that multimedia networks will run coaxial cables into homes may be like predicting that astronauts will use slide rules to compute orbits. Three articles from *Science*, well outside the mainstream multimedia trade press, foreshadow the sorts of breakthroughs that futurists often miss.

One article describes research at Pennsylvania State University that might completely eliminate the expensive optoelectronics that convert information from varying amounts of light to varying amounts of electric current or voltage (Service, 1995a). A change in the amount of light leaving a fiber-optic cable can cause a piece of photostrictive ceramic to change shape rapidly. The piece of ceramic could move a diaphragm to produce sound or move a mirror to change the fraction of a bright light source that reaches a screen.

A second article describes a photonic amplifier or optical amplifier, which amplifies a light signal directly, without first converting the signal to electrical form (Brinkman, 1995). Such an amplifier might make light leaving a fiber sufficiently strong to illuminate successive parts of a screen and thereby display video. The possibilities that these two articles raise are highly attractive, because optoelectronics typically cost 20 times as much as the corresponding electronics that drive or sense a cable that carries electrical signals, but they do not solve the entire problem.

The last article describes research at Keio University in Yokohama, Japan, on optical fibers that could be run into homes far more economically than could today's fibers. Today's single-mode glass fibers are thinner than a human hair, so connecting them requires careful technicians and expensive equipment. The researchers are developing plastic graded-index multimode fibers that are large enough to install easily and cheaply in homes and that can carry 2.5 Gbps of information for about 100 meters (Service, 1995b). Because it often requires more than a decade to move promising ideas from research laboratories to customers' homes, it is probably safe to conjecture that the trend to push fiber deeper into the network will not reach all the way into homes before 2005.

CRITICAL SUCCESS FACTORS

The factors that are critical for successfully achieving the vision we have described for the delivery part of a distributed multimedia system include:

Greater Capacity at Lower Cost: Projected increases in information-carrying capacities and decreases in costs must occur for fiber-optic cables, optoelectronics, electronics for driving higher bandwidths over fiber and other connections, and electronics for compressing and decompressing video.

Standardization: Standardization is needed not only so that a customer can switch easily among interoperable networks that different companies own but also to encourage competition.

Applications: Well-understood applications, multimedia content, and communication partners are necessary to drive revenues that will motivate companies to invest in suitable networks (see Chapter 5).

Deregulation: Deregulation is necessary to encourage network suppliers to compete by offering increased functions at decreased prices (see details in Chapter 6).

Systems Integration: Systems integration companies must provide individuals and companies with one-stop shopping for multimedia networks as an alternative to developing a high degree of competence.

Trials: Successful trials must test theories and justify widespread deployment of multimedia networks (see Chapter 7).

SUMMARY

In this chapter, we have discussed important characteristics of the delivery network part of a distributed multimedia system, the requirements that such a network must meet, the corresponding characteristics of today's important networks, and many of the ways that companies may decide to change today's networks to meet the requirements. Companies' actual investment decisions will depend on business and regulatory developments, as well as the outcomes of many technology trials. Perhaps most of all, their decisions will depend on predicting the products and services consumers will want and be willing to pay for—an always difficult business task.

Although technical innovations that would make parts of the network better or cheaper would be welcome, deploying known techniques could achieve the vision for delivering multimedia. Two widely differing techniques, either of which could preserve large portions of today's networks while achieving the vision of universal interactive video, are asymmetric digital subscriber loop (ADSL) and fiber to the neighborhood (FTTN). For the global portion of the network, both use optical fibers and other existing types of connections. For the local portion of the network, ADSL uses twisted-pair local loops that exist in the telephone network and replaces existing electronics by expensive new electronics to achieve video's required high bandwidth. FTTN replaces by fiber much of the coaxial cables that exist in CATV networks and retains cable for only the last run into customers' homes and offices. These and other techniques may coexist for years, with ADSL serving areas where homes and businesses are far apart and FTTN serving more densely populated regions.

REFERENCES

Andrews, Edmund L. 1993. "A Baby Bell Primed for the Big Fight." *New York Times*, February 21, Section 3.

Baines, Rupert. 1995. "Getting Information to Everyone's Home." *Electronic Engineering Times*, October 2, p. 48.

Bell Laboratories. 1977. *Engineering and Operations in the Bell System*. Western Electric Co., Inc., Indianapolis, IN.

Brinkman, William. 1995. "A Revolution Is Occurring in Telecommunications." *Science*, March 17, p. 1613.

Communications Week. 1993. "Local Loop Waves." July 5, p. 40.

Computer Design. 1990. "Realization of FDDI II Stalled by Unsettled Standards." June 1, p. 52.

Csenger, Michael. 1994. "ATM Hums, but Can It Sing?" *Network World*, October 3, p. 92.

Electronic Engineering Times. 1993. "PC Designers Are Hungry for Bandwidth." July 19, p. 45.

Feeney, Mary, and Shirley Day, eds. 1991. *Multimedia Information*. London: Browker Saur.

Fogarty, Kevin. 1995. "Zap! NetWare Users Get Really Wired—Over Electric Power Lines." *Network World*, July 3, p. 1.

Goldberg, Lee. 1995. "Broadband to the Home: Challenges on the Last Mile." *Electronic Design*, October 2.

Information Week. 1993. "Breaking Down the Walls." April 19, p. 22.

Jones, J. Richard. 1994. "Baseband and Passband [fiber to the curb] Transport Systems for Interactive Video Services." *IEEE Communications*, May, p. 90.

LAN Magazine. 1991. "Is Plastic Fantastic?" June, p. 44.

Lawton, George. 1995. "Telco to Network Homes Using Cable-TV Techniques." *Lightwave*, February, p. 1.

Loudermilk, Stephen. 1995. "ISDN Allies Lobby FCC." *LAN Times*, May 8, p. 1.

Maddox, Kate. 1995. "ISDN—A Consumer Nightmare." *Interactive Age*, August 14, p. 22.

Magel, M. 1993. "Building Better Information Highways: Networked Multimedia." *AVideo* May, pp. 100, 103.

Metz, K. H. 1992. "Next Generation CATV." SPIE vol. 1786, Fiber-optics for Voice, Video, and Multimedia Services, p. 185.

PC Magazine. 1993. "Pricing the WAN." March 16, p. 204.

Raynovich, R. Scott. 1995. "Cisco Targets IBM Shops with APPN." *LAN Technologies*, June 5, p. 20.

Service, Robert. 1994. "Capturing Sound, Light, and Strength with New Materials." *Science*, December 16, p. 1807.

Service, Robert. 1995. "Paving the Information Highway with Plastic." *Science*, March 31, p. 1922.

Smulyan, Susan. 1994. *Selling Radio*. Washington, DC: Smithsonian Institution Press.

Wallace, R. B. 1993. "FDDI vs. Fibre Channel." IBM technical report, April 20.

Wexler, Joanie. 1994. "Video over Cellular Makes TV News." *Network World*, November 7, p. 32.

Wingfield, Nicholas. 1995. "AT&T Paradyne Chip Set Speeds Modem Links." *Infoworld*, July 31, p. 16.

Yokell, Larry. 1995. "New Services on Your Old Network." *Convergence*, June, p. 34.

Chapter 3

Servers

BACKGROUND

This chapter discusses multimedia servers, which are the sources of some media delivered along multimedia networks to end users (see the left side of Fig. 3.1). As an end user, you may be familiar with the concept of a file server. A file server makes the files on one or more hard drives available to a large number of end users by way of a network. In principle, digital video, digital audio, and the other media are just files, storable on a file server until called forth for presentation on a suitably equipped end-user device, such as a computer. Whereas a file server merely sends files to and receives files from applications, a multimedia server may be much more involved in details of individual applications. The unique properties of digital video and audio usually require a multimedia server to be quantitatively and qualitatively different from a typical file server.

Quantitative Difference

A multimedia server's quantitative difference from a file server results from the fact that video files are much larger than traditional text files and programs, for which typical file servers are designed. For example, consider only movies and ignore the television programs, college courses, and other content that should occupy most of the space on a multimedia server. Converting a 90-minute movie from analog video to digital video and compressing it to achieve a low data rate of 150 K Bytes per second produce a digital file that occupies

$$90 \text{ min} \times 60 \text{ sec/min} \times 150 \text{ K Bytes/sec} = 810 \text{ M Bytes}.$$

A library of 5000 such digitized movies requires about 4 T Bytes. This is not a huge movie library—a typical movie catalog lists between 13,000 and 20,000 titles—but 4 T Bytes is a vast amount of hard drive space. A large airline reser-

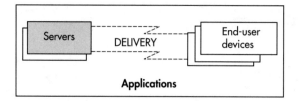

Figure 3.1 Framework.

vations system uses about 0.1 T Bytes to store information about flights and bookings (*Business Week*, 1994), and Boeing used just under 3 T Bytes to store the computerized designs for their 777 jet transport (Norris, 1995).

For contrast, consider the number of characters in a typical paperback book,

$$56 \text{ characters/line} \times 39 \text{ lines/page} \times 322 \text{ pages} =$$
$$703{,}248 \text{ Bytes per book.}$$

The number of such books that would occupy the same space as one movie is

$$810 \text{ M Bytes}/703{,}248 \text{ Bytes per book} = 1151 \text{ books,}$$

which amounts to a sizable personal library.

Qualitative Difference

A multimedia server's qualitative difference from a file server results from the fact that video and audio are isochronous media. That is, users are sensitive to small errors in the rate at which they see and hear these media. Moreover, these media often need to be synchronized with each other and with other media. Synchronizing audio with video and other media is particularly important when video shows a speaker's lips and audio carries the speaker's voice, but it also applies to composite multimedia documents in which a voice narrates rapidly changing images or graphics. One way to achieve synchronization is to interleave the media that must be synchronized. For example, CD-ROM-XA is a disc format that interleaves small fractions of a second of each of several audio channels with small fractions of a second of a single video channel. The same approach works over networks.

There is a wide range of methods by which a server, a network, and an end-user device can share responsibility for ensuring that a user receives media isochronously and synchronously. All but one of these methods require a multimedia server, unlike a file server, to become intimately involved with the data it stores. We complete our background on servers by discussing these methods for sharing a system's responsibilities.

In the first method, the server supplies media to a network at a smooth and correct rate and with all media correctly synchronized, the network then transmits the media with a short and constant delay, and the end-user device presents the media to the user with a short and constant delay. In this method, which television and telephone networks employ today, the server, network, and end-user device share responsibility equally. This method applies well to video on demand and live video of news or sports and even better to video conferences. We have noted that participants in a video conference find more than about ¼ second of delay intolerable. When you see and hear a network or a local hard file supplying audio and video that has occasional breaks, pauses, or repetitions, you are seeing a not-quite-successful application of this method.

In the second method a server and network supply media at the most economical and convenient speed, the end-user device receives and stores all the media on a local hard file, and subsequently the end-user device presents the media to the user isochronously and synchronously. In this method, which computer networks employ extensively under names such as *file transfer* or *file download*, the end-user device bears all the responsibility for presenting acceptable media, whereas the server and network perform on a best-effort basis. This method applies well to multimedia E-mail. If you send a piece of video and audio E-mail that you expect someone else to view several hours later, you will not care whether the network transmits your information in a burst at once, waits to send it in a burst an hour later, or dribbles the information slowly over several hours.

Unfortunately, the first method places severe timing constraints on the server, network, and end-user device, and the second method introduces a long delay before the user begins to see and hear any media. A more complicated method is sometimes required to allow a server and network to supply and transmit media at somewhat variable rates without requiring a user to wait until a transmission is complete. At this point in the game, computer scientists take the ball away from physiologists, because this method relies on real-time operation and deadline scheduling.

In the third method, for the server to share responsibility with the network and end-user device, the server breaks up a media clip into packets and applies a time stamp to each packet. A packet's time stamp tells the end-user device when to present the packet to the user, relative to the time when the clip starts. (If all packets occupy the same amount of time, then actual time stamps are unnecessary. Talking about timestamps clarifies the description and allows for variable-time packets.) In this method, the server may put individual packets on the network earlier or later than desired, using periods of light load to get ahead in order to live through subsequent periods of higher load. The network, similarly, may deliver individual packets to the end-user device with different delays, shorter when the network is almost idle and longer when the network is heavily loaded.

The end-user device attempts to present each packet to the user at the time that the packet's time stamp specifies. It compensates for receiving a packet too early by buffering the packet (temporarily storing the packet, often in random access memory rather than a hard file) until the time stamp becomes current, unless so many packets come so early that stored packets overflow its buffer capacity. It compensates for receiving packets too late by deferring the clip's start time enough to accommodate any expected delays. In order to do that, the end-user device must know how long to defer starting the clip. If, for example, the server and the network tell the end-user device to expect that some packets may arrive as much as 20 seconds later than desired, then the end-user device can defer starting the clip until slightly more than 20 seconds after it receives the clip's first packet. Then, if the packet that has a time stamp of 1 minute arrives 1 minute and 15 seconds after the arrival of the clip's first packet, the end-user device still has 5 seconds to show that packet to the user. However, if the same packet arrives 1 minute and 25 seconds after the arrival of the first packet, it is already too late for the end-user device to present that packet isochronously, because the server and network did not stay within the maximum delay that they committed to the end-user device.

This third method for sharing responsibility spans the entire range between the other two methods. At one extreme, if the third method adds no intentional buffering delay and simply counts on the server and network to get each packet to the end-user device just before the user needs to see or hear the packet's contents, then this amounts to the first method. This provides the shortest possible delay but places the most severe demands on the server and the network. At the opposite extreme, if the server and network insist on the freedom to delay parts of the clip for a time that is longer than the entire clip, then this third method amounts to downloading the clip as a file, before playing any of the clip, as in the second method. This involves the longest delay, but gives the server and the network the most flexibility in scheduling when they will perform their functions. It also places the most severe demands on the end-user device's buffer space, perhaps requiring a hard drive.

The essence of a real-time system is committing to meeting deadlines, such as delivering each packet within a given maximum delay time relative to the packet's desired time. In some applications, the maximum delay can be quite long and is easy for a server and network to achieve. If a user is willing to wait for a selected movie to start in 10 minutes, the server may begin immediately delivering the movie's packets, and the end-user device may start buffering packets. The user will see isochronous delivery of the movie as long as the server and network never exceed a combined maximum delay of just under 10 minutes. However, in other applications, the maximum delay must be quite short and is difficult for a server and network to achieve. If a user selects the next video clip in a fast-paced training video or video game, the user expects the clip to start in less than a second. In this application, the server and network must commit to deliver packets with no more than about ½ second of maximum delay.

Whether easy or difficult, reserving enough resource in advance to ensure that a system can meet a succession of deadlines is a different way of doing business from just adding load to each part of a system until customers start to complain and then upgrading the hardware. Real-time computer operating systems handle isochronous media efficiently and effectively, whereas batch and transaction oriented operating systems are inefficient and are effective only if supported by enough brute-force hardware performance.

Remember that a multimedia server has unique requirements because two of the media are large, isochronous, and synchronous and the other three media may require synchronization. A multimedia server that meets the requirements for isochrony and synchrony of media economically may not be a single processor with a single hard drive but a hierarchy of processors and associated storage devices distributed over a wide geographic area. Parts of the distribution network may be within the server system, rather than between the server system and the end-user devices. A server implementation may use different processors for interpreting user requests, which are non-isochronous and small, than for delivering streams of data, which are isochronous and often large. It may also use different types of storage for frequently requested content than for content that no user has requested for weeks or years.

Operations

A multimedia server must mesh smoothly with the environment of the company that owns or operates it. A server's physical environment may consist of a small closet or a large raised floor. A server's operational environment may include specific procedures for general functions such as installation, failure detection, repair, and billing, as well as specific functions including making additional copies to satisfy many simultaneous demands for a popular movie, and deleting all copies of an unpopular movie. A server's operating system's functions may provide the ability to automatically manage the quality of service that the customer signs up for and agrees to pay for. For example, some customers may pay enough to get whatever they want when they want it; others may pay enough to get what they want but not as fast as they request it. This entire aspect of management, service, and operations, or backroom operations as it is sometimes called, is discussed in more detail in Chapter 6. From the point of view of this chapter, however, servers must come with enough hooks or programming interfaces in the operating system for applications to be written to permit and facilitate the server's successful operation in a reasonable physical environment by average people, not rocket scientists.

Multimedia servers will be extremely important to companies that provide computers and software. Dataquest predicts that revenues from video server sales will more than double each year, growing from $296 million in 1995 to $5.2 billion in 1997 (Ryon, 1994). This chapter applies to an even larger portion of the overall digital information industry. Many of the discussions throughout the rest of this chapter apply not only to a server that many users share, but also to the storage part of an end-user device that is dedicated to a single user. In either the multiuser or single-user environment, multimedia creates enormous increases in the required amount and sophistication of storage.

VISION FOR THE NEXT DECADE

For content providers, ranging from movie makers to government printing offices, the vision is to have a server on which to put their content so that all end-users who want to access it can do so easily and economically. For end users, the vision is to be able to access all the content that they want, about as quickly, easily, and reliably as if all the content resided locally on their own end-user devices, at an acceptable cost. For server providers, the vision entails being able to bill server operators enough to pay for the total cost of developing and supporting the servers with a decent profit margin. Server operators want to bill end users or content providers enough to pay for the total cost of installing and operating or supporting the servers, again with a profit.

STATE OF THE ART

We illustrate today's state of the art in multimedia servers with two systems. Optimized for video, the first allows little interactivity. The second system is highly interactive but suitable for only small amounts of video. The subsequent section discusses ways of creating systems that can provide highly interactive access to large amounts of video and other media.

Manual Analog System

Our first example of a state-of-the art multimedia server is a manual analog system that a large hotel might install so guests can select movies to watch in their rooms. The system we describe is hypothetical and does not mirror any real setup but rather shows some characteristics needed to fulfill the vision of an automatic digital system. Note labor costs would make a manual analog system too expensive for large-scale deployment.

Suppose that a hotel's management wants to be able to show up to 100 movies at a time, perhaps including showing several copies of a popular title at different starting times. The management could wire the hotel with a 100-channel cable network driven by 100 videocassette recorders, where each VCR sends its video output signal to all the guest rooms on one of the 100 channels using frequency-division multiplexing. The hotel could purchase or rent 500 videotapes, not all of different titles, and arrange them in convenient racks near the VCRs. They could hire several people to act as the manual part of the server, receiving a guest's telephoned request for a movie, placing the selected tape in any unused VCR, telling the guest to tune to the channel which that VCR drives, and charging the movie to the guest's room.

This system could include laser disc players or laser disc jukeboxes in place of some of the VCRs. It could also include some CD-ROM players, each with MPEG video decompression hardware that converts the CD-ROM player's digital output to an analog video signal. Like a VCR, a laser disc player or CD-ROM drive has the important property that it produces only a single stream of video at any one time.

The hotel's manual analog system is near the low end of the interactivity spectrum. It is more interactive than television, because a guest can request a particular movie. It is less interactive than a home VCR, however, because the guest would have to make a telephone call in order to pause so she can go out for a snack or to rewind so she can see an interesting scene a second time. Allowing much of this sort of interactivity would require the hotel to hire an unacceptably large staff of people to perform the server function. Providing high interactivity, such as allowing a guest to select a new video stream several times per minute, is out of the question with this system.

LAN Server System

Our second state-of-the-art multimedia server is an ordinary LAN's file server on which some of the files happen to contain digital video. When an end user invokes a part of an application program that includes video, her computer reads the corresponding file, uses software or hardware to apply a corresponding video decompression algorithm, and displays the resulting video on the display screen. If the server and network are about as fast as a local hard drive, then the computer may play the video directly from the server. In other cases, it is natural for the computer to download a file from the server to its own hard drive or memory in advance of need and to play the video from there. For example, the help system of a graphics program may include video clips of a person explaining how to create a presentation. The end user's computer loads this video from the server, along with the rest of the graphics program, and subsequently plays the clips at appropriate times.

Although highly interactive, this system is limited to small amounts of video. For example, a typical token ring LAN has a maximum bit rate of 16 million bits per second, or 16 Mbps. Assuming that a video stream requires 150 K Bytes per second, the theoretical maximum number of users to whom such a network could supply video at one time is given by

$$16 \text{ Mbps}/(150 \text{ K Bytes}/\text{sec} \times 8 \text{ bits}/\text{Byte}) = 13.3.$$

Queuing theory shows that users must wait significantly longer as a network's load increases toward its maximum data rate. By downloading files a network can allow several users to play video at any one time. This might easily suffice to support 100 users on the LAN as long as their use of video-based help systems or other video is only occasional.

Of course, as we pointed out in Chapter 2, using such a network for more than about five video streams may cause so much interference among the streams that isochronous playback is impossible. Downloading the files and then playing them as a separate step eliminates this problem. The network must meet only the less demanding requirement of maintaining a sufficiently high data rate to satisfy the users' average requirements for video along with other data.

Downloading a complete file and playing it as a separate step is attractive in some applications. For example, downloading a 90-minute compressed movie by dedicating the full theoretical bandwidth of a 16 M bits per second network to a single user would require

$$(810 \text{ M Bytes} \times 8 \text{ bits}/\text{Byte})/16 \text{ Mbps} = 405 \text{ sec}$$

or about 7 minutes. Of course, the end-user's device would need 810 M Bytes of free hard drive space to contain the downloaded movie. Is that a lot of free space? A couple of years ago, that was more total hard drive capacity than on all of our personal computers put together. Today, our computers have a total of about that much free storage. In a couple of years, each of our computers may have that much space free. In a few more years, every television set may have that much free storage.

Neither of the state-of-the-art servers we have used as examples comes close to achieving the vision of supplying highly interactive access to large amounts of video and other media. The manual analog server is uneconomical and seriously deficient in interactivity; the digital file server cannot handle much video. In general, the most promising way to approach the vision involves sending video over the network as users need it, like the former, but storing and transmitting the video in digital form, like the latter.

HISTORY

Table 3.1 shows that servers evolved from a long history of using computers to share information. The costs and prices of computer system components have dropped greatly since the 1970s although the cost reduction has been greater for some components than others. An optimal system design uses more of the inexpensive components, of course. Cost changes have thus caused fundamentally different system designs to be optimal at different times. The unique requirements of serving interactive video, along with continuing cost reductions, will change the optimal system design in the

Table 3.1 History of mainframes and servers.

Date	Event
1964	IBM announced the System/360 mainframe line, beginning its dominance of the mainframe market.
1972	IBM announced the 3270 series of remote terminals for IBM mainframes.
1970s	Minicomputers made their presence felt but mainframes remained dominant.
1980s	Personal computers and LANs became important.
1993	Sales of mainframes dropped 9 percent and sales of minicomputers priced above $1 million dropped 20 percent (McWilliams, 1994).
1995	Compaq announced plans for a home server priced under $2000 to handle multiple personal computers and perform household automation functions.
1995	IBM reorganized its major hardware platform development into a server division, recognizing their new role serving clients.

future. Before we discuss future changes, we need to see how we got where we are today.

Starting in the late 1960s, many users stored their shared information on remote central host computers, either mainframes or large minicomputers, and accessed this information from dumb terminals (terminals incapable of running application programs) that were based successively on teletype machines, electric typewriters, and cathode ray tube displays. The host computers not only stored shared information but also ran application programs. A typical application sent the terminal a full screen, such as a form for an accident report. After the user filled in all the form's blank fields and hit Enter, the application received and processed the fields and then eventually sent another screen. This was only minimally interactive computing, with about one interaction per minute. For example, a user could not learn about a mistake near the top of the form before completing the entire form. An application program had no chance to process one field that the user entered and supply a corresponding list of reasonable choices for the next field. Users tried to become accustomed to waiting half a minute or more for the computer to respond. They learned that the response might come in 10 seconds or 10 minutes, depending on how many other people were using the same system.

This dumb terminal system design was not a bad design; it was rather a good design optimized for the relative costs of components that existed in the 1970s. This design allowed many users to share a single processing unit. Sharing was then an economic necessity, because computation was most economical if performed on the largest available computer. In accordance with Grosch's law, the price of a computer did not rise linearly with the computer's price but rather rose much more slowly, as the square root of the price. In the 1970s, processing was therefore characterized by huge economy of scale. Moreover, the dumb terminal design minimized the load on a slow and expensive telecommunications network, which typically provided one 56-Kbps link between a host computer and an office full of dumb terminals.

Technological improvements in the early 1980s reversed processing's economy of scale, resulting in diseconomy of scale. With personal computers, computing became most economical on the smallest computer that could complete a job in an acceptable time. During the early 1980s, many users acquired personal computers to make their nonshared work quicker, easier, more effective, and more economical. Increasingly powerful and economical large-scale integration microprocessor chips not only repealed Grosch's law but replaced it by a law saying that computation was now most economical on a one-chip computer.

Giving each user an individual computer allowed applications to be far more interactive, moreover, typically involving several interactions per second. A typical personal computer application program can completely rewrite the screen's contents each time the user presses a key or moves a mouse. For example, the application can relabel the function keys to show how their functions change when a user presses the Alt key, and the application can change the shape of the mouse cursor to tell a user that he has moved that cursor over a hot region, where clicking the mouse would invoke a hypermedia link. Such interactivity had been unthinkable over a mainframe's shared 56-Kbps telecommunications link but is very reasonable over the high-bandwidth cable between a personal computer's processor and the screen only a foot or two away. Unfortunately, although using individual computers made interactivity much better, it made sharing information significantly more difficult. In the early 1980s the typical method for exchanging programs and text among computers was sneakernet—hand carrying or mailing diskettes. This method corresponded to today's uses of CD-ROMs as the primary method for exchanging digital audio and video.

As the value of sharing became clearer in the mid-1980s, groups of users connected their personal computers to networks. Some groups employed existing dumb terminal networks by equipping their personal computers with attachment cards and application programs that emulated the functions of dumb terminals. They ran minimally interactive host applications as well as highly interactive personal computer applications and exchanged data between such applications by explicitly uploading and downloading files. They got a lot of practice keeping track of whether their most recent data were located on a personal computer or a host and could not miss the difference between one interaction per minute with mainframe applications and one interaction per second with personal computer programs.

In the late 1980s, more and more groups equipped their personal computers with LAN programs and attachment cards and invested in LAN wiring and servers. They ran application programs on their personal computers and used the servers only to share files, printers, and low-bandwidth communications facilities such as modems. Some of these shared servers were centralized minicomputers or mainframes, but most were simply high-end personal computers.

Data sharing has strong locality of reference, meaning that people who work together in a group tend to share more information with one another than with people outside the group. In the early 1990s, locality of reference drove a trend toward hierarchies of servers and networks, in which groups containing a few dozen users had their own servers interconnected by low-bandwidth backbone networks. Members of such groups could exchange large amounts of text with other members of their own groups and could exchange much smaller amounts of text with members of remotely located groups. Today, although increasingly many corporate departments have LANs that will carry several streams of digital video, relatively few such departments can exchange digital video streams with remotely located groups.

Thus, the history of servers has involved major changes in the partitioning of functions among different parts of the system. Most of the changes have been in the direction of moving both data and processing power away from central sites and toward individual users and groups. In general, these changes made computing more economical and interactive but made sharing data more complicated.

DIFFERENCES

A multimedia server will be significantly different from earlier text-oriented file servers with respect to both of its most important resources, processing and hard drive space. Because of a multimedia network's very high bandwidth, a multimedia server can locate its processing resource either near each user or at a remote central site, without sacrificing interactivity. However, because of video's very high data rate, a multimedia server must read very large blocks of data in order to use its hard drive resource in an optimal fashion.

More Options for Function Splits

A multimedia network will remove the requirement to put a processor near a display screen in order to deliver full interaction between an application running on the processor and a user sitting in front of the screen. Whereas the typical connection between a mainframe and several dumb terminals was a shared 56-Kbps teleprocessing line, a multimedia network could provide each user with a dedicated connection that runs at least 150 K Bytes per second or 1.2 M bits per second. Such a connection can carry an individual stream of compressed video continuously to each active user and also continuously monitor each user's input from keyboard or infrared controller and pointing device such as a mouse. If the connection can carry a video data stream, with 30 high-resolution images every second, then the connection can most assuredly carry a new screen that the application program selects every time the user presses a key or moves a pointing device.

Running an end-user interface program far from the end user may have significant advantages. Consider a typical on-line specialty retailing application. This retailer, which we shall name Acme to protect confidentiality, accepts orders and tells manufacturers to ship direct to customers. Acme has no showroom and no stock. Acme's assets include its manufacturer relationships, customer list, record of what each customer has purchased in the past, and algorithms for using all this information to decide which clips to show each customer, at each time of year, and each time of day, to elicit maximum orders. Acme uses all this information in the end-user-interface program that they run each time a potential customer invokes Acme's service and selects a product area. The retailer is adamant that its end-user interface must run on a computer that the retailer controls, rather than downloading the valuable program and its valuable data to run on an end user's computer.

Figure 3.2 shows three fundamental methods for splitting a system's functions between a server and an end-user device. In each method, a network connects the end-user device to the server. The top of the figure shows a function split in which the user's application program runs in the end-user device and uses the network to read and write files that the server stores. The middle of the figure shows a split in which the part of the application that is most concerned with the display (and other media that the user sees, hears, and creates) runs in the end-user device but most of the application runs in the server. The two parts of the application communicate as peers over the network. The bottom of the figure shows a split in which the entire application runs in the server and uses the network to send screens to the end-user device and receive back information about the user's actions, including key presses and pointing device movements. (In many cases, the end-user device

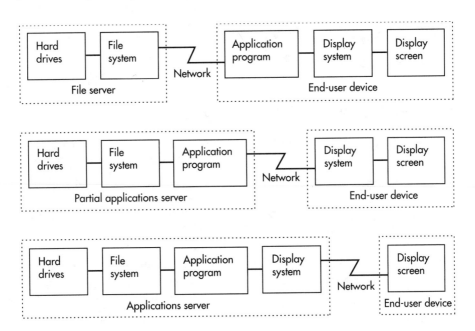

Figure 3.2 Three function splits.

is called a *client*. However, UNIX and the X-Window system reverse the terminology. They call the applications server the *client* and call the end-user device the *server*, presumably because the display merely obeys orders in this function split.) We discuss these methods further in Chapter 4's section titled Less Self-Sufficient Devices.

A variant of the top function split takes advantage of the fact that an end-user device can have its own local file system and hard drives and also can have access to one or more remote file servers. One way to employ this split is to keep all shared data on remote storage and keep only personal data on local storage. Another way to employ this split is to keep all permanent data on remote storage and use local storage as only a temporary cache. Of course, the extreme case of this variant is a stand-alone end-user device that has access to no electronic network.

Another variant of the top function split takes advantage of two or more networks. Consider a situation in which the electronic network's bandwidth limits it to sending text, although an application requires images, audio, and video. One solution to this problem involves periodically mailing a CD-ROM that contains images, audio, and video, which special signals from remote servers can call up at appropriate points. The opposite solution involves periodically mailing a CD-ROM that contains not only images, audio, and video, but also a program that requests text from remote servers at appropriate points. In either case, the creators use a CD-ROM to hold material that the creators expect to be useful for weeks or months and use a network to transmit changes that have occurred since they mailed the CD-ROM. We discuss this further in Chapter 5's section titled Hybrid Applications.

More Options for Processors

Processing is now so economical that it is no longer necessary to use whatever form of computing is most economical. The reason is that microprocessor and memory chips not only changed the shape of the curve that relates performance to price, but they also shifted that curve's position toward vastly lower costs. We have seen that chips reversed the economy of scale that Grosch's law embodied, so that a one-chip computer now performs a given computation more economically than a large, shared host computer. The chips also vastly increased the performance available for a given cost and, conversely, decreased the cost of a given amount of processing power and memory, for all sizes of processors.

As a dramatic example of the reduction in the cost of processors, consider the mainframes, designed in the 1960s, that are still handling the Federal Aviation Administration's terminal radar-approach control (TRACON). A total of about 64 mainframes are installed in the eight largest cities in the United States. These mainframes' combined main memory capacities would barely suffice to run one copy of the personal computer game Flight Simulator (Stix, 1994).

Shifting the cost curve that relates processors' performance to their cost has significantly reduced processors' fraction of the cost of a multimedia server system. There may be no reason to minimize this small fraction, if using a somewhat more expensive processor can cause other parts of the system to cost less or work better. Even if processing in an end-user device is more economical than processing in a remote applications server, both may be too inexpensive for the difference to matter.

It is fortunate that it is no longer absolutely necessary to run an end-user-interface program near each end user, because it may not be reasonable for a typical user's computer to store enough information to run an end-user interface. Such an interface could include a total of 90 minutes of alternative short video clips (such as views of people wearing different clothing) that would require 810 MB of hard drive space in the end-user device and would require 90 minutes to download to the end-user device, even over a network that is capable of carrying high-quality video. Because any given user is likely to request only a few of these short clips, there is no reason to download all the clips first, in order to play a few later. It may work better to send video and other information from the server to the end-user device just when the user demands the information.

Let's return to the example of the specialty retailer. As Acme makes more use of video to display its products to better advantage, the end-user-interface program becomes enormous. In particular, the library of hours of video, from which the program selects small clips to show to a given customer, will be far larger than Acme could download to each end user's device, even if they wanted to do so, which they do not. For this application, running the end-user interface at a central site and sending out only the screen displays is clearly the best solution, in terms of both economical operation and protection of proprietary information.

Multimedia servers need not return to a function partition in which applications run on centralized processors that are remote from all end users, but centralized processing may again be a viable option for applications in which it turns out to be advantageous.

More Demands on Hard Drives

The other major difference between previous servers and a multimedia server affects how a server must use its hard drive resource. The data rate of video data streams has almost caught up with the rate at which a large hard drive can read data. Whereas such a hard drive can support many text data streams, it can support only a few video data streams (Huynh and Khoshgoftaar, 1994; Keeton and Katz, 1995; Gemmell and Han, 1994).

In a text application, a hard drive's data rate is essentially infinite. A human reader can read a page of a paperback book that contains 2184 characters in about 52 seconds. To deliver continuous text to one user at that rate, a server would need to deliver a data rate of

$$2184 \text{ Bytes} / 52 \text{ sec} = 42 \text{ Bytes} / \text{sec.}$$

(This corresponds to 336 bps, so early 300-bps modems delivered text about as fast as people could read it.) A large, fast hard drive can deliver approximately 2 M Bytes per second, averaged over a few minutes, including the times when it is reading data as well as the times when it is finding the next data that it must read. The number of streams that such a hard drive can handle is

$$(2 \text{ M Bytes} / \text{sec}) / (42 \text{ Bytes} / \text{sec}) = 47{,}619 \text{ text data streams.}$$

Thus the hard drive's data rate is not likely to limit the number of text users that a server can serve. However, the same is not true of video users.

We have already seen that one user's video stream completely monopolizes a video tape player, a laser disc player, or a normal CD-ROM disc drive. This is a major reason why a multimedia server is likely to store its video on hard drives. However, even a large and well-managed hard drive can support only about a dozen video streams. If we again assume that the hard drive can deliver 2 M Bytes per second, and that each video data stream requires 150 K Bytes per second, then the maximum number of streams that this hard drive can deliver is

$$(2 \text{ M Bytes} / \text{sec}) / (150 \text{ K Bytes} / \text{sec}) = 13.3 \text{ video data streams.}$$

Restriction to a small number of video data streams can have a large influence on the design of a server for the movies-on-demand application. Suppose that 100 different users want to see the same popular movie, each wanting a slightly different starting time and each wanting to occasionally rewind and see a scene over again or pause to go get a sandwich. If each hard drive can support 13.3 video data streams, the server must have at least eight copies of the movie, all on different hard drives, because

$$100 / 13.3 = 7.5.$$

Moreover, any other movies stored on these eight hard drives are unavailable whenever 100 users are watching this one popular movie.

Whereas having a fast multimedia network makes it possible to run a highly interactive end-user interface on a processor located at a remote central site, the small number of video data streams per hard drive means that it is not possible to have just one copy of each movie at a central site and use it to serve the entire country, or even an entire state. If each metropolitan area has enough users so that 100 of them want to see a popular movie at a peak time, then there is no reason not to save communication costs by storing that movie in each metropolis. In Chapter 5, Applications, we consider some alternatives that reduce the system cost a lot while reducing the function only a little. However, the server continues to be strongly affected not only by the hard drive's storage capacity required to store hundreds or thousands of movies, but also by the need to store a popular movie hundreds of times.

The small number of data streams per hard drive also makes it extremely important to use a hard drive's data rate efficiently. For example, suppose that a large, fast hard drive has a peak data rate of 3 M Bytes per second when it is actually reading data, and consider what is required to achieve a data rate of 2 M Bytes per second, averaged over many minutes for many users' data streams. What makes this difficult is that, before it can read the next part of each user's data stream, the hard drive must move its heads to the radius of the track on which those data reside (called the *seek*) and then must wait for the part of the hard drive surface that contains the start of those data to rotate around under the head (called the *search*). While a hard drive is seeking and searching, it cannot read any data. Some hard drive advertisements specify the average seek time, typically about 12 ms, which is actually the time that a head requires to travel one-third of the way from its innermost position to its outermost position. The ads do not often specify the hard drive's rotation rate, typically 3600 revolutions per minute or 60 revolutions per second. The time that the hard drive takes to complete one rotation is thus one-sixtieth of a second or 16.6 ms. The average search time is half of one rotation, or 8.3 ms. Thus the time a hard drive requires to start reading the next user's data stream is

$$12 \text{ ms} + 8.3 \text{ ms} = 20.3 \text{ ms}.$$

In order to achieve an average data rate two-thirds of the rate at which the hard drive reads, after it has found the data, the hard drive must spend twice as long reading the data as it took finding the data. Thus it must read at least 40.6 ms of each user's data stream before going on to seek, search, and read another user's data stream. At a data access rate of 3 M Bytes per second, each time the hard drive begins to read, it must read

$$(40.6 \text{ ms}) \times (3 \text{ M Bytes/sec}) = 122 \text{ K Bytes}$$

to keep one user satisfied until it can get around to doing another read for that same user.

Thus 122 K Bytes, about ⅛ of a M Byte, turns out to be a very important number for multimedia servers. It is the smallest unit of video data that a multimedia server and network can handle efficiently. Because the amount of video that this represents is

$$(122 \text{ K Bytes})/(150 \text{ K Bytes/sec}) = 0.8 \text{ sec,}$$

it is also close to the smallest amount of video that any user could require. Of course, for different hard drives, the smallest unit for video data could be about a factor of two larger or smaller.

Is 122 K Bytes close to the unit of information for which today's hard drives and file systems are optimized? Not quite. Most hard drives are formatted for a sector length of 512 Bytes, and most file systems move and buffer data in 512-Byte blocks. Manufacturers of hard drives and designers of computer file systems assume that a typical application wants to read or write about 512 Bytes from one part of one file before going on to read or write some other part of the same file or a different file. Using today's hard drives and file systems, the smallest quantity of video data that is either practical or desirable requires reading

$$122 \times 1024 \text{ Bytes/512 Bytes} = 244 \text{ sectors.}$$

Today's hard drives waste the space that they use for all but one of those sector headers, and today's file systems waste the time that they spend handling all but one of those blocks.

This 244-fold increase in the smallest meaningful block of data illustrates the quantitative changes that operating systems and hard drive controllers require in order to handle multimedia efficiently. Operating systems also need qualitative changes in order to optimize handling of the isochronous and synchronous properties of audio and video (Vin and Rangan, 1993).

Hard Drives Rather Than CD-ROMs

Because a great deal of digital video will appear on CD-ROMs, it is reasonable to ask whether CD-ROM drives could substitute for some or all of a multi-user multimedia server's hard drives. The answer comes from an analysis similar to the one we just went through for a hard drive. A single-speed CD-ROM drive reads 150 K Bytes per second when it is actually reading, so it can supply continuous video to only one user. To serve even that single user, it must read continuously. A double-speed CD-ROM drive reads 300 K Bytes per second, which is the rate of two video data streams. However, in order to supply different continuous video streams to two users at once, it too would need to read continuously. Thus it would have no time left over for moving its head back and forth between where the two users' data streams exist on the disc.

However, a triple-speed CD-ROM drive reading at 450 K Bytes per second would be able to serve two users if it could spend two-thirds of its time reading and one-third of its time moving back and forth. How much data would the triple-speed CD-ROM drive need to read at a time, for each of two users? A typical triple-speed drive can find a given point on the disc in 200 ms. If the drive reads data for r ms each time it finds one of the users' data streams, then its activity consists of 200 ms finding the first user's data, r ms of reading, 200 ms of finding the second user's data, and r ms of reading. Then this cycle repeats. To get r, we note that in each cycle the drive is actually reading for $2r$ ms and that this time must be two-thirds of the cycle's total time, which is $200 + r + 200 + r$, so

$$2r = (2/3) \times (\ 200 + r + 200 + r).$$

Solving this gives $r = 400$ ms. Reading for 400 ms at the triple-speed rate of 450 K Bytes per second gives 180 K Bytes as the amount of data that the drive must read and buffer for each of the two users in each cycle. Again, this is a reasonable amount of data, although it is far more data than most existing file systems now handle as a unit. Figure 3.3 shows a timeline for the process just described.

Our last two calculations indicate that a typical hard drive has two significant advantages over a triple-speed CD-ROM drive. First, after it finds what it is to read, the hard drive reads at 3 M Bytes per second rather than at 450 K Bytes per second. Second, the hard drive finds what it is to read in an average of 20.3 ms, rather than 200 ms. The hard drive is quantitatively more suitable than a CD-ROM drive for a multiuser multimedia server because of these factors of 6.7 and 9.8.

The fact that a server can write new data onto a hard drive, whereas a person must physically replace a CD-ROM disc, is an advantage for the hard drive, but it is not as big an advantage as you might imagine. Even writing at a continuous rate of 3 M Bytes per second, the time that a hard drive requires

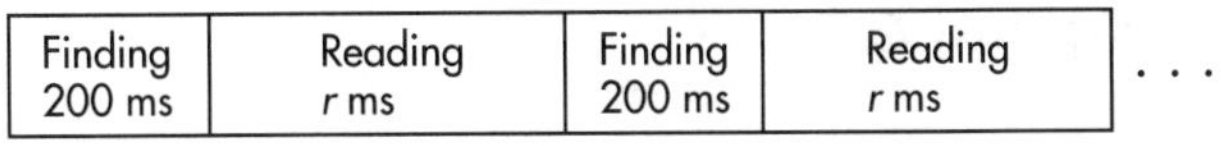

Finding 200 ms	Reading r ms	Finding 200 ms	Reading r ms	. . .

Figure 3.3 Timeline for CD-ROM.

to write an 800-MB movie, is almost four and a half minutes. During that time, the hard drive's resource is fully occupied, so it might as well be a CD-ROM drive that is open while someone changes the disc.

Thus, if a CD-ROM drive had a 6.7 times faster data rate and a 9.8 times shorter access time than the drives that we used in our last two calculations, it would pose serious competition to hard drives in servers. Won't inevitable technological progress provide these improvements over the next several years? Yes and no. CD-ROM drives are already available that have transfer rates 6 times the rate of the original drives and thus twice the rate of our triple-speed drive. However, six-speed drives have approximately the same access times as the original drives. In fact, spinning the disc faster to achieve a higher data rate exacerbates the CLV problem that causes the long access times, as we discuss in Focus 3.1.

Foreseeable derivatives of today's CD-ROM drives are likely to remain more suitable for individual use than for use in servers that supply video to many users. Such derivatives include higher-density compact disc proposals by Sony and Philips and by Toshiba and Time Warner that led to digital video disc (DVD) technology (Lammers, 1995). In their pursuit of greater capacity than CD-ROMs attain, these proposals are likely to continue to use the CLV recording method and have correspondingly sluggish access times.

Other sorts of optical drives, which are not limited by any requirement for compatibility with CD-DA discs, may be suitable for use in servers. Such optical drives must operate more like hard drives, particularly in using CAV rather than CLV. This is perfectly reasonable. For example, laser discs have included CAV as well as CLV formats ever since two competing standards came together under one umbrella in 1978. The CAV laser discs, also called *standard play*, allow special effects and computer control by using one revolution to read each frame of video. The CLV laser discs are called *extended play* because, although they put one frame on each inner track, they put three frames on each outer track, and put intermediate numbers of frames on the tracks in between. As a result, a CLV disc can contain one hour of video on each side, rather than a CAV disc's half-hour, but a CLV disc is far less amenable to special effects and computer control. Another reasonable change to improve the reliability of higher-speed, denser optical discs is for manufacturers to hermetically seal the discs inside housings, rather than subjecting them to users' fingerprints and dust particles, which limit the lifetime and reliability of a CD-ROM.

Hard Drive Design Criteria

Hard drives and their associated electronics will require some redesign in order to be optimal for use in multimedia servers. For example, today's advanced hard drives occasionally detect that they have either heated up and expanded or cooled down and contracted. At such times, they stop whatever they are doing, perform an extensive thermal recalibration, and take up where they left off. Today, when a hard drive is supplying text and programs, no user notices if an access takes an extra fraction of a second. However, when a multimedia server is supplying video or audio, all users will notice if their data streams stop for a fraction of a second. Multimedia servers will need to tell their hard drives when to take thermal recalibration breaks (del Rosario and Choudhary, 1994; Reddy and Wyllie, 1994).

Multimedia servers may also refuse to allow a hard drive to take error-correction breaks. Designers of hard drive systems assume that a hard drive

---

Focus 3.1   CLV and CAV.

The CD-ROM standard inherited a peculiarity from its CD-DA parent that makes a CD-ROM appropriate for reading a single stream of video or other media for a single user but inappropriate for reading several different streams for several different users. The peculiarity is that the CD-DA and CD-ROM standards maximize the amount of music or data that a disc will hold by always recording the same number of bits per linear inch. This is called *constant linear velocity* (CLV) recording.

In order to read a constant number of bits per second, a single-speed drive rotates the disc about 500 revolutions per minute (RPM) when it is reading near the center of the disc and rotates only 200 RPM when reading near the outside. A CD-ROM drive's long access time results from the fact that, whenever it moves the head, it must make a matching change in the rate at which it spins the motor and the disc. Although the head is light and easy to move, the disc and motor are heavy and hard to accelerate or decelerate. A triple-speed drive must change speeds between 1500 RPM and 600 RPM. A six-speed drive must change speeds between 3000 RPM and 1200 RPM. It requires careful engineering to avoid increasing access time when going from single speed to triple or six speed. Decreasing the access time by a factor of 9.8 in order to make the CD-ROM drives compete with hard drives for use in multiuser multimedia servers is not in the cards.

Contrast the CD-ROM standard's CLV recording with the way a hard drive records data. The hard drive runs at a *constant angular velocity* (CAV) no matter whether its heads are near the center or near the outside. A hard drive can have a short seek time because its seek takes only as long as it requires to move its heads; it need not change the rotation speed. It can also have a short search time, because it can spin rapidly, typically 3600 RPM. ■

must correct every error, even if the correction process takes so long that the hard drive stops transferring data for an entire revolution before it can resume reading. After all, a delay of about 16.6 ms is insignificant in comparison to an incorrect bank balance. However, if a multimedia server stops a video data stream for 16.6 ms, in order to correct one bit of a frame, the cure is likely to be worse than the disease. A gap in an audio data stream may be even more disconcerting. The best solution is to improve a hard drive's error-correction process so that it can correct an error on the fly and continue reading. The reason is that, as we have seen, video compression often records an index frame and then records many successive frames as changes to that index frame, before recording another complete index frame. As a result, one wrong bit may affect what a user hears or sees for a significant time. A server may need to trade off higher compression allowed by fewer index frames against more expensive hard drive electronics that can perform error correction on the fly (Costlow, 1994).

The demands on a server depend partly on the server's intended application. In the video-on-demand application, users are likely to be extremely unforgiving of glitches or any other type of unreliable service. Business information users may be somewhat more forgiving. The physiological principle that is involved here is that a billboard must be attractive in order to capture a driver's attention, whereas a sign that says "Fire Exit" need not have a fancy font to capture the attention of a theatergoer who smells smoke.

File System Design Criteria

An affordable multimedia server must use its hard drive resources efficiently, because the hard drives themselves represent a very significant expense. For example, if a 1-GB hard drive costs $700, a movie occupies 810 MB, and each movie need be stored only once, then the hard drives for a library of 1000 movies would cost a total of

$$\$700 \times (810 \text{ MB}/1000 \text{ MB}) \times 1000 = \$567,000.$$

Associated adapter cards, physical housings, power supplies, and other items would increase this cost significantly. At a 7 percent annual interest rate, if the hard drives are used 12 hours per day, then the debt service for each hour of use is

$$\$567,000 \times 0.07 \times (12/24) \times (1/365) = \$54.37,$$

which is perfectly reasonable if the hard drives are shared among 100 or more users.

A hard drive represents two resources, storage capacity and data rate, which it must use efficiently. Just as an airplane seat is a wasted resource unless a passenger is sitting in it at takeoff, so a hard drive's data rate is a wasted resource unless the hard drive is transferring data, and a hard drive's storage capacity is a wasted resource unless it contains frequently accessed data. A hard drive's resources are mostly wasted if it spends most of its time either waiting for a request or seeking and searching or if its data rate is used to play the same small fraction of its contents repeatedly. If a server's hard drives cost only a few thousand dollars, like a personal computer, there would be no problem in wasting the hard drives' resources while waiting eagerly to serve the next user request. However, because a server's hard drives cost as much as a mainframe computer, economics requires owners to keep the hard drives busy making money. Individual applications of multimedia servers require careful design in order to use hard drive resources well. For example, a video-on-demand server may need to put a popular movie on a hard drive to use up most of the hard drive's data rate, but fill the hard drive's unoccupied space with less popular movies.

The next section discusses trends in the development of servers to show how they split their functions and optimize use of their hard drives and other resources.

TRENDS

Upon being asked why he robbed banks, a famous felon is supposed to have replied "Because that is where the money is." For the same reason, there is a strong trend for hardware and software makers to turn many types of computers into multimedia servers. Like other important trends in multimedia, this trend is driven by supply as well as by demand. That is, each computer vendor is trying to find a role for its own sort of hardware or software, as Fig. 3.4 indicates.

The types of computers that vendors are turning into multimedia servers are as follows:

- High-end personal computers, sometimes in groups, using high-volume, low-cost components

- Workstations with high-performance RISC processors and UNIX operating systems, often in symmetrical multiprocessing (SMP) configurations, and usually with unique hardware that handles video and audio

- Mainframe computers or large minicomputers

- Massively parallel supercomputers

Fortunately for different computer vendors, different market segments demand different sorts of multimedia servers. We next discuss three segments of the multimedia server market that appropriate types of computers can serve.

The first market segment contains departments of approximately 5 to 40 people connected by way of a LAN. Most departments in this segment already have file servers that are simply large personal computers. These departments' typical multimedia applications include desktop access to training and help, which the addition of video makes more educational and more helpful. Novell, IBM, Starlight, and Microsoft are actively attempting to add software to their basic software offerings for personal computer servers that will make the servers suitable for delivering video and other media to departments, over LANs, with little or no change to hardware.

The second market segment contains companies that want to deliver movies on demand, other video on demand, home shopping, news, and many other multimedia services to homes. Many vendors in many industries are preparing to court this segment using servers based on three types of computers. For example, IBM, Digital Equipment Corporation, Hewlett-Packard, and Silicon Graphics, Inc., base servers on their workstation product lines, namely, RISC System/6000, Alpha, Precision Architecture, and MIPS, respectively. IBM bases another server thrust on its ES/9000 mainframes and its large AS/400 minicomputers. NCube, along with Oracle for software, and IBM base servers on massively parallel supercomputers. Mi-

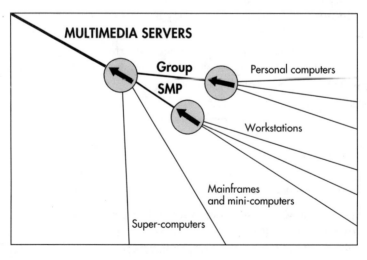

Figure 3.4   Convergence of servers.

crosoft's server software can scale up to this market segment by running on a large number of personal computers.

The third market segment has requirements that are, in some sense, the union of the first two segments' requirements. This segment contains business enterprises (including educational and governmental institutions) that operate multiple sites. At each site are one or more departments with LANs. The business needs to deliver a full suite of video to employees at all sites, although presumably with a strong bias toward business information rather than entertainment. Moreover, businesses in this segment may have a strong interest in video conferences. A business in this segment needs personal computers as departmental servers and also needs one or more of the other three types of computers as enterprise servers. Database companies such as Oracle and Sybase are adding support for digital video to their base offerings, partly to appeal to this segment.

These three market segments thus provide opportunities to use a wide variety of computers as multimedia servers. The following examples constitute a snapshot of current video server trends. By selecting the examples that we have mentioned and that we shall discuss in more detail, we do not mean to imply that they are the best as we write this or that they will be the best when you read this. We selected them to represent important trends in multimedia servers. We cite current specifications and prices to give you a feeling for orders of magnitudes and to allow rough comparisons. You should expect continual improvements and should get up-to-date information before making any purchasing decisions (Clancy, 1993).

Personal Computer Hardware and Starlight Networks' Software

Starlight Networks, Inc., produces software that runs on a dedicated, industry-standard personal computer. The software and computer constitute the Starlight Media Server, which can hold up to 100 GB of video. This is 190 hours of digital video, with associated audio, compressed to a typical data rate of 1.2 Mbps. One server can supply a total of up to 50 Mbps, as 42 different video streams, to 42 active users. In typical setups, the server connects to an Ethernet switched hub through either an FDDI backbone or several Ethernet connections. The hub then supplies each user with the requested video, over a dedicated Ethernet connection. Each user's computer runs Starlight client software and employs either hardware or software to decompress the video stream that the client receives from the server.

Starlight provides both StarWare and StarWorks video network server software. StarWare is a NetWare loadable module (NLM) for a Novell Net-

Ware server. NetWorks runs on a UNIX-based server and is compatible with NetWare and other network environments. Either product manages network resources to assure that the server delivers acceptable video. For example, before beginning to transfer video and audio from the server to a user, the software reserves bandwidth that will suffice for completing the user's request. Either product uses a lightweight protocol that allows a relatively low-performance processor to supply video data streams with a relatively large total data rate (Tobagi and Pane, 1993; Smalley, 1993).

Starlight licenses StarWare or StarWorks for a price that depends on the total rate at which a particular server can supply video. It licenses StarWare for $4495 or $8750 to support 6 Mbps or 12 Mbps, respectively, and it licenses StarWorks for $8750, $14,995, or $24,995 to support 12 Mbps, 25 Mbps, or 50 Mbps, respectively. For comparison at the high end, the software that supports 50 Mbps requires server hardware that contains at least a 50-MHz Intel 486 processor and 25 MB of RAM. The several thousand dollar price of such hardware, without hard drives, seems small in comparison to the price of the software. However, a group of hard drives that can contain a total of 100 GB of video cost roughly $30,000.

Personal Computer Hardware and IBM's Software

IBM's LAN Server Ultimedia is an extension to the IBM LAN Server product that requires Advanced OS/2 LAN Services. It can support video on the same server and LAN that support other media, and it uses OS/2's task-priority mechanism to assure sufficient processor and hard drive resources. On a token ring LAN, it also allows a network administrator to allocate bandwidth to video data and to other data to avoid degrading performance on a heavily loaded network. On an Ethernet LAN, it does the best it can but is more likely to run successfully if the Ethernet is dedicated to video. It supports up to 100 GB of video data and can send up to 40 different video streams to 40 active users. It can support up to 10 users on a single token-ring segment. It supports clients that run DOS, OS/2, and Windows, along with suitable video decompression. Its software license costs $3195 for one server (Pollili, 1994a, b).

Personal Computer Hardware and Novell's Software

Novell's NetWare Video is a NetWare loadable module. It uses load balancing, scaling, and video buffering to support video on the same server and network that support other media and is sufficiently aware of the nature of video to scale or degrade gracefully. As a network's load increases, it decreases the number of frames per second that it delivers to each user, by dropping frames. It plays all the accompanying audio at the isochronous rate and keeps the video synchronized with the audio. This scaling requires significant cooperation from software in each client. It supports both Apple's QuickTime and Microsoft's Video for Windows. NetWare Video is not merely a file and print server (Willett and Damore, 1993).

NetWare Video can support up to 24 clients at one time, with up to 6 clients per Ethernet segment. It required some changes to NetWare and may become a standard part of NetWare. In the meantime, a NetWare Video server software license costs $1100 for 5 clients, $1990 for 10 clients, and $2975 for 25 clients.

A company that uses Novell's NetWare Video (or Starlight's StarWare) on a video server, and also uses Lotus Notes, can integrate video into its Notes environment by using Lotus Video for Notes. Video for Notes runs on an IBM OS/2 Notes server. The video server and Notes server cooperate to store video clips on hard drives or on CD-ROM discs. In the spirit of Lotus Notes, Video for Notes avoids replicating video needlessly. On a slow network, a server can download a complete video clip to a user's hard drive so that the user's computer can play the downloaded video at the correct isochronous rate. A Video for Notes server software license costs $2695. For corresponding client software the license costs $120 (Barney, 1994, 1995).

Personal Computer Hardware and Microsoft's Software

Microsoft's Tiger video server software runs with the company's Windows NT Advanced Server on a cluster of personal computers. Tiger stores a movie or other piece of video as stripes. The server breaks up the movie's data stream into several stripes and writes each stripe on a hard drive attached to one member of the cluster. As Tiger plays back this movie, each computer reads the corresponding stripe. As Tiger plays one second of video, consisting of roughly 1.2 million bits, each computer contributes a fraction of the required bits. The software assures that the aggregate of the computers' stripes forms the movie, just as a suitable aggregate of black and yellow stripes might form the image of a tiger (Alsop, 1994).

Striping makes it possible for a cluster of computers to supply a high aggregate data rate without requiring any one computer to supply a high individual data rate. Striping thus allows a user to scale a server to a particular peak data rate by employing a suitable number of personal computers. Running on a few computers, Tiger can supply video to a department. Running on a large cluster of computers, it can supply video on demand to homes.

Thus Tiger may apply to a CATV company's or telephone company's trial or full deployment. A company can purchase the personal computers that have the best performance per dollar at a given time, rather than requiring computers that either have a particular brand or have the highest available performance.

By writing redundant stripes, Tiger allows the server to recover from the failure of a hard drive or of a computer. If one computer ceases to contribute its stripe to the aggregate data stream, the software can start up a different computer that has the same stripe on a different hard drive, without interrupting the user's video data stream.

On the borderline between the Tiger server and whatever delivery network connects the server to users, multiple stripes must merge to form a complete video data stream. In a typical installation, one or more ATM switches perform this function. Like the personal computers, the ATM switches are scalable, to handle a wide range of peak data rates, and are more or less available off the shelf.

Tiger's cluster of personal computers is not an instance of symmetric multiprocessing. One or more master scheduler computers control one or more computers that handle individual stripes of video. Microsoft calls the latter *Tiger Cubs, hard drive servers,* or *continuous-media servers.* Within one computer, however, Tiger can take advantage of Windows NT's symmetric multiprocessing and fault tolerance. Tiger's product name and pricing are uncertain at the time of writing. You may know it as Microsoft Media Server.

Hewlett-Packard's Hardware and Software

One way to produce a server that will support many video data streams is to employ powerful workstations rather than economical personal computers. University researchers sought to take advantage of a high-end workstation's 9-MBps system bus to support about 60 video streams. To exceed a single hard drive's data rate, they experimented with striping a video stream's data across up to 28 hard drives. They found that 1 hard drive could sustain a data rate of 1.3 MBps, which suffices for about 8 video streams. They found that 2 hard drives could sustain 2.3 MBps, or 15 streams. However, adding more hard drives failed to increase the data rate, because 2.3 MBps saturated the workstation's memory bandwidth. They found that their system organization wasted the bandwidth of 26 of the 28 hard drives. Their organization even wasted most of the bandwidth of the system bus, which they had expected to be the bottleneck (Drapeau et al., 1994).

After similar experiments, Hewlett-Packard elected to bypass video streams around the workstation part of its HP Media Stream Server. To move video data, HP designed a highly specialized Video Transfer Engine (VTE) using LSI Logic's ATM chip. The resulting server can support from 60 to beyond 10,000 video streams, with a data rate of up to 3 Mbps per stream. The server's workstation initiates video streams in response to user requests and also handles such functions as user authorization and billing. HP and HP's value-added partners supply the software that runs on the workstation. HP supplies all the specialized real-time software that runs on the VTE. The VTE handles each user's VCR-type commands, such as pause. Thus these highly interactive commands, like the video itself, bypass the server's workstation (Stiefel and Klein, 1995).

IBM's Workstation Hardware and Software

IBM's Ultimedia Server/6000 runs on IBM's RISC System/6000 workstations, IBM's AIX version of UNIX, and IBM's MultiMedia file system. Like LAN Server Ultimedia, which runs on personal computers, Ultimedia Server/6000 relies on bandwidth reservation to assure that it does not begin an operation it cannot complete. It uses a variable degree of closely coupled multiprocessing to support from 50 to thousands of video streams and also to tolerate failures. Various sorts of routers or switches connect video streams from one or more RISC System/6000 workstations to one or more networks (Patterson, 1994).

Special software for the Ultimedia Server/6000 creates a video file system that changes pointers rather than copying video. The software can create and erase a video file, but does not edit or copy such a file. An application program can select any portion of a video file by setting up a start pointer and a stop pointer. Such a portion is called a filament of video. The application can then concatenate several filaments to make up a strand of video and can play several strands in synchronism to make up a rope. This approach allows applications to manipulate small pointers rather than huge video files.

Silicon Graphics' Hardware and Software

Silicon Graphics, Inc., takes a software approach to multimedia servers, eschewing special-purpose hardware. Its standard Challenge server hardware can simply overwhelm video's problems with bandwidth. One fully expanded Challenge XL server, with 36 symmetric processors on one bus, supports a theoretical maximum input-output bandwidth of 1.2 Gbps. This works out to about 8000 video streams of 1.2 Mbps each. In practice, one such server is limited to four network adapters, which can support about 60 streams each. Thus a ring of eight Challenger servers suffices for a field test that involves 4000 homes, not all of which will have an active user at any one time. In Chapter 7, we describe the Time Warner trial in Orlando, Florida, which uses such a ring of servers.

Digital Equipment Corporation's Hardware and Software

Digital Equipment Corporation's product line includes Alpha Servers that are suitable for workgroups, departments, and enterprises and that play the respective roles of personal computers, minicomputers, and mainframes. These servers employ different numbers of Digital's Alpha processor chip, which has a modern architecture designed to handle streams of binary data. For example, Alpha is particularly adept at performing some types of digital video compression and decompression without adding special-purpose processors. Digital builds multimedia servers that can supply from tens to thousands of video streams using Alpha servers, high-speed network switches, interactive gateways, hard drive arrays, and tape libraries. A typical server's storage hierarchy can hold popular movies in instantly accessible memory, hold somewhat less popular movies in hard drive arrays, and hold a large library of movies in a tape library. Because the product line includes fast processors, high-bandwidth network components, and some special video hardware, software can assure that the servers deliver video and audio isochronously (McGee, 1994).

IBM's Minicomputer Hardware and Software

Industrywide sales of minicomputers that cost over $1 million have been declining at about 20 percent per year. Manufacturers of these relatively powerful and well-supported systems would dearly love to find new applications that minicomputers perform better than do networks of personal computers. A multimedia server, which requires high input-output bandwidth and large amounts of hard drive storage, may be such an application. IBM's AS/400 can support hundreds of GB of storage and can supply well over 40 digital video data streams to OS/2 clients, while running business applications.

An AS/400 can also control a large number of sources of analog video that drive a CATV head-end. The head-end, in turn, can use F-couplers to send up to 70 channels of analog video over the same wires that simultaneously carry token-ring signals. IBM's Ultimedia Video Delivery System/400 provides an application programming interface with which an application can integrate video with other functions. A user's terminal can be as simple as a telephone and a television set or as sophisticated as a personal computer running OS/2 and Multimedia Presentation manager (Schroeder, 1994).

Although such a minicomputer is probably not the most economical dedicated video server, adding video server functions to an existing installation may be reasonably economical. Moreover, the price of even an expensive processor may be negligible in comparison to the price of the hard drives that hold a large amount of video.

IBM's Mainframe Hardware and Software

Once upon a time, multimillion dollar mainframes provided processing power more economically than did any other type of computer. Then, in the 1970s, minicomputers began to provide processing power for fewer dollars per million instructions per second ($ per MIPS) than did mainframes. In the 1980s and early 1990s, personal computers improved the $ per MIPS still further. However, if a mainframe processor constitutes less than one-tenth of the price of a video server system, then it would be possible to save at most 10 percent by using a more economical processor. That is, if the server's hard drive farm costs 10 or 20 times as much as does the processor, then there is no overwhelming reason to economize on the processor. Mainframes have always excelled at controlling large numbers of input-output channels that connect hard drives and networks. As a result, input-output-intensive video servers may be better uses for mainframes than are more processor-intensive applications.

IBM's LAN File Services running on Enterprise Systems/9000 mainframe hardware can deliver up to 1000 video data streams by way of token ring or Ethernet networks. Corresponding software allows the same hardware to deliver several thousand streams over networks suitable for trials of video on demand to homes. Moreover, the ES/9000's hard drives can hold thousands of digitized movies. A given hard drive may connect to eight different processors over eight tails, which adds flexibility and reliability.

Research on video software helps make the hardware more effective. For example, software can read the compressed form of a popular movie from a hard drive just once, in order to supply different video streams to dozens of users. Users can start the movie at slightly different times and can take advantage of such controls as pause and fast forward. The software reads video from the hard drive into successive main memory buffers, then sends video from these extremely high-speed buffers to different users at different times. Hard drive and main memory thus form two layers in a multilayer storage hierarchy that can include tapes and other devices. Research into real user statistics helps make good use of such a hierarchy. Researchers who work on ES/9000 servers in Hawthorne, New York, enliven their days by competing with researchers who work on RISC System/6000 servers in Almaden, California.

NCube's Massively Parallel Hardware and Oracle's Video Server Software

Oracle's video server software approach does not rely on particular underlying hardware. The software runs on hardware from NCube, Hewlett-Packard, Sequent, and Sun. It can run on combinations of hardware, such as NCube's for video streams and Sequent's for billing. In fact, Larry Ellison, Oracle's CEO, says that Oracle's video server software approach is suitable for any hardware that a potential customer for large video servers could desire.

What type of hardware should such a customer desire? We summarize this section on trends in video servers by discussing Ellison's opinions on this subject, as reported in several lengthy interviews. Although we might equally well cite any vendor's comparisons of its own products to competitors' products, Oracle's hardware independence, together with its arguably preeminent position as a supplier of software to trials of video on demand, make Ellison's opinions especially significant. However, as you consider the following summary, you should keep in mind that Ellison has a large financial interest in NCube and that Oracle has won significant contracts involving hardware from either NCube or Hewlett-Packard (Ellison, 1994; Schwartz, 1994).

Ellison expresses the opinion that the lowest possible cost per video stream will come from server hardware that includes nonconventional, high-bandwidth, low-cost switches. He cites two leading examples of such switches in Hewlett-Packard's VTE and in NCube's massively parallel supercomputers. He asserts that a server based on either company's hardware can cost as little as $200 to $250 per video stream.

Ellison contrasts such a nonconventional video switch to a conventional computer or symmetric multiprocessor. Whereas the nonconventional switch provides many paths between hard drives and networks, a conventional system may have a single memory that acts as a bottleneck for the entire system. He estimates a price per video stream of $2000 to $3000 for Silicon Graphics' SMP servers and asserts that, to be competitive, SGI must improve either its price or its speed by a factor of 10.

Ellison also contrasts NCube and HP to Microsoft's Tiger. Microsoft uses individually packaged and powered ATM switches connecting individually packaged and powered personal computers. Although NCube uses ATM as its interface to the network, the latest NCube system uses economical large-scale-integration chips for interprocessor communication. HP's VTE uses ATM chips rather than separate ATM boxes. Mr. Ellison guesses that Tiger's cost per stream is approximately $2000 to $3000. What makes this interesting is that Microsoft has a target price of $20 to $30 per stream. The cost per digital video stream is a crucial measurement for a video server. Mr. Ellison conjectures that Microsoft's target price applies to a future system that will integrate many processors and many ATM chips within a single package. He notes that such a result would amount to a massively parallel computer that includes a nonconventional video switch.

From this perspective, video servers show two opposing trends. One trend is toward using conventional hardware products, such as personal computers and ATM switches. This trend is based on the hope that large sales volumes and vigorous competition will assure that conventional products have the advantage of rapid improvements in performance and price. The opposite trend is toward using nonconventional hardware optimized for delivering many video data streams at low cost. This trend is based on the hope that designers can take advantage of the fact that video and the other media have only very specific requirements and require essentially no general-purpose processing.

As video server volumes increase, the two trends will cease to be opposite. Nonconventional server hardware will enjoy sales and competition similar to those of personal computers, with resulting rapid improvements in performance and price.

CRITICAL SUCCESS FACTORS

The factors that are critical for successfully achieving the vision for distributed multimedia system servers include:

Function: Perform the function of supplying large quantities of media, including isochronous media and synchronized media.

Fit: Fit within a customer's operational environment while providing necessary management and operational functions and without unnecessarily disrupting ongoing activities.

Price: Have acceptable prices of acquisition and operation.

Scalable Design: Provide a wide range of capacities with a small number of different designs.

Upgradable Design: Allow a provider to support more customers and content without discarding equipment that the customer has already installed.

Flexible Design: Support different types of storage and storage hierarchies in order to serve different demands and take advantage of different prices.

SUMMARY

Multimedia servers may easily turn out to be the largest, most expensive, and most complex computers ever assembled. For example, a server that contains a repository of digitized movies may be significantly larger than any of today's mainframe-based airline reservations systems. There is likely to be a market for a large number of expensive servers. The complexity and size of a server system tends to require the efforts of several cooperating companies.

Multimedia servers require different hardware and software designs from the previous decade's file servers. The hardware must support large numbers of isochronous video data streams. The software must support the real-time nature (rather than batch or transaction nature) of the tasks that deliver media. Multimedia servers are likely to become deeply involved in running applications and handling details of data, such as time stamps, whereas the last decade's servers were more likely to accept, store, and retrieve files without any involvement in the files' contents. For this and other reasons, some multimedia servers are likely to run application programs as well as store information such as digitized media. Although general-purpose designs facilitate changing from one application to another as customers make their desires known, special-purpose designs may be necessary to move large volumes of information economically.

The multimedia server design that will turn out to be most prevalent has yet to be determined. It is not clear whether there will be a single design or many different ones that are optimal for different applications and capacities. Multimedia servers must meet separate challenges for different applications, such as high data rates for live sports, high storage capacity for movie libraries, and high interaction rates for training and games. It may be unreasonable to expect a single design to scale to fit such diverse applications at any given time. As relative costs of different parts of a server system change over time, optimal server designs for particular applications will continue to change, as designs have changed over the past decade.

Table 3.2   Telephone numbers.

Company	Voice telephone
Microsoft	(206) 882-8080
Novell	(801) 228-9813
Starlight Networks	(415) 967-2774
Sybase	(510) 596-3500
DEC	(508) 486-7111
IBM	(914) 766-4204
NCube	(415) 593-9000
Oracle	(415) 506-4176

REFERENCES

You will find providers to be the most useful references concerning individual products, as we did. Table 3.2 gives some of the telephone numbers that we used.

Alsop, Stewart. 1994. "Microsoft's Tiger Beats the Stripes off Oracle's Server." *InfoWorld,* May 23, p. 24.

Barney, D. 1995. "Lotus Ships Video for Notes." *InfoWorld,* January 30, p. 7.

Barney, D. 1994. "Video Notes Put to Test at NYU." *InfoWorld,* December 26, p. 45.

Business Week. 1994. "Mainframe Makers Hope to Cash in on the Digital Video Market." January 24, p. 92.

Clancy, Heather. 1993. "Integrators Target Niches in Video-Server Market." *Computer Reseller News,* December 13, p. 2.

Costlow, Terry. 1994. "Redesigned Disk Drives Go to the Movies." *Electronic Engineering Times,* January 17, p. 37.

del Rosario, Juan, and Choudhary, Alok. 1994. "High-Performance I/O for Massively Parallel Computers." *IEEE Computer,* March, p. 58.

Drapeau, Ann, et al. 1994."RAID-II: A High Bandwidth Network File Server." *IEEE Computer Architecture News,* 22, no. 2, p. 234.

Ellison, Larry. 1994. Interview. *Upside Magazine,* September, p. 17.

Gemmell, D.J., and Han, J. 1994. "Multimedia Network File Servers: Multichannel Delay-Sensitive Data Retrieval." *Multimedia Systems,* 1(6), p. 240.

Huynh, K.D., and Khoshgoftaar, T.M. 1994. "Performance Analysis of Advanced I/O Architectures for PC-based Video Servers." *Multimedia Systems,* 2(1), p. 36.

Keeton, K., and Katz, R.H. 1995. "Evaluating Video Layout Strategies for a High-Performance Storage Server." *Multimedia Systems,* 3(2), p. 43.

Lammers, David. 1995. "Sony Says HD-CD Will Transform Multimedia." *Electronic Engineering Times,* January 2, p. 4

McGee, Marianne. 1994. "Alpha's Big Break May Be in Video." *InformationWeek,* March 21, p. 20.

McWilliams, Gary, and Hof, Robert. 1994. "They Can't Wait to Serve You: Mainframe Makers Hope to Cash in on the Digital Video Market." *Business Week,* January 24, p. 92.

Norris, Guy. 1995. "Boeing's Seventh Wonder." *IEEE Spectrum,* October, p. 20.

Patterson, Alan. 1994. "Hongkong Telecom, IBM Map Video Effort." *Electronic Engineering Times,* August 1, p. 20.

Pollili, S. 1994a. "IBM Beefs Up Features and Capacity of Its Video Server." *InfoWorld,* February 7, p. 5.

Pollili, S. 1994b. "Video Server Exploits Cable." *InfoWorld,* February 21, p. 41.

Reddy, A., and Wyllie, James. 1994. "I/O Issues in a Multimedia System." *IEEE Computer,* March, p. 69.

Ryon, Bruce. 1994. "Multimedia Market." *Dataquest,* San Jose, CA.

Schroeder, Erica. 1994. "IBM to Release VideoCharger Server Subsystem." *PC Week,* April 18, p. 63.

Schwartz, Evan. 1994. "Demanding Task: Video on Demand." *New York Times,* January 23, p. 14.

Smalley, Eric. 1993. "Novell Shines Spotlight on NetWare Video NLM." *PC Week,* November 29, p. 10.

Stiefel, Malcom, and Klein, Stanley. 1994. "Serving up Video." *OEM Magazine,* January, p. 30.

Stix, Sary. 1994. "Trends in Transportation." *Scientific American,* May.

Tobagi, Fouad, and Pang, Joseph. 1993. "StarWorks—A Video Applications Server." Proceedings, IEEE Computer Society International Conference, COMPCON '93.

Vin, H., and Rangan, P.V. 1993. "Admission Control Algorithms for Multimedia On-Demand Servers." *Network and Operating Systems Support for Digital Audio and Video.* Third International Workshop Proceedings 1993. New York: Springer Verlag.

Willett, Shawn, and Damore, Kelley. 1993. "Novell and IBM to Deliver Multimedia to LAN." *InfoWorld,* November 29, p. 1.

Chapter 4

End-User Devices

BACKGROUND

In this chapter we discuss end-user devices, which connect to servers and also to other end-user devices by way of delivery networks, as Fig. 4.1 shows. Although servers and delivery mechanisms might conceivably converge to a few recognizable designs, end-user devices will remain widely diverse. A single ideal end-user device is no more likely than an ideal vehicle. Just as a given traveler may need a bicycle, automobile, bus, truck, or jet airplane at any one time, a typical multimedia user will need to own or use many different types of multimedia devices.

As multimedia end-user devices become more tightly integrated into more facets of daily life, their diversity will increase. Size will range from large enough to see clearly from 100 yards away to small enough to wear as jewelry or carry in a pocket like a wallet or a paperback book. Some devices will be integrated unobtrusively into desks, night tables, living room furniture, and automobile dashboards or steering wheels. Others will need to be armored to survive in public places such as schoolrooms, airport waiting rooms, airplane seats, automotive garages, libraries, hospitals, and malls. Most important, users will continue to need devices that operate near the face, like a telephone, for privacy and to avoid disturbing other people; they will need devices that operate like a computer screen, at arm's length, for detailed viewing and keyboard control; and they will need devices that operate across a room without physical contact, like a television, for comfortable lounging and shared use. Figure 4.2 notes that media converge, although devices do

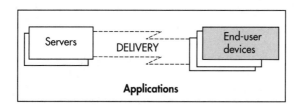

Figure 4.1 Context of end-user devices.

not. End-user devices will become more universal as digital technologies break the chains that tied particular devices to particular networks and to particular media. These chains come with strong links, as Table 4.1 shows.

Table 4.1 shows that most of us think of a telephone as operating near the face, handling only audio conversations, and connecting to a copper twisted pair or cellular delivery system. We think of a computer as having a screen that will tolerate close scrutiny, handling mainly serious linear text with occasional graphics and perhaps a few images, and connecting to a local area network or telephone line and accepting mailed diskettes and CD-ROMs. We think of a television set as suitable for viewing from a comfortable sofa, handling incoming video entertainment, and connecting to a coaxial cable or antenna. As an illustration of how closely television is associated with entertainment and with coaxial cable, a cable company executive once confidently asserted that entertainment should travel over a cable company's network rather than over a telephone company's network, as if coaxial cables were inherently more entertaining than twisted pairs of wires.

Such links among end-user devices, purposes, media, and networks are unnecessary and undesirable. They are unnecessary because converting media to digital form makes it possible to send all the media over the same network to any end-user device, and they are undesirable because they force end users to deal with a hodgepodge of incompatible devices rather than viewing distributed multimedia as a single system. Moreover, the links make it extraordinarily difficult to exchange media among devices. Thus the present situation forces users to select among media based on which end-user de-

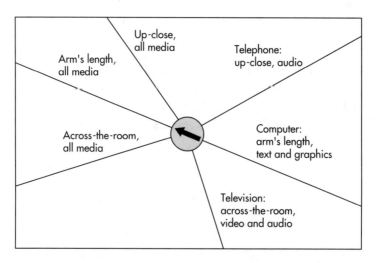

Figure 4.2 Partial convergence of end-user devices.

Table 4.1 End-user device capabilities.

End-user device Capability	Telephone	Personal computer	Television set with set-top box
Distance	Near face, for privacy	Arm's length, for high detail	Across room, for sharing
Connect to	Twisted pair Wireless	LAN Twisted pair Postal service	Coaxial cable Wireless
Media	Audio	Data Text Graphics	Video Audio
Choices of content	Many	Many	Few
Primary purpose	Conversations	Business and individual entertainment	Individual and group entertainment
Social equivalent	Whispered secret	Reading a book Small meeting	Lecture Meeting Football game

vice they have available, rather than based on which media are most effective for their purposes. Interoperability standards are the best approach to breaking such links.

VISION FOR THE NEXT DECADE

End users, businesses, and government regulators have quite different, although not necessarily inconsistent, visions for end-user devices (Davis, 1994; Forman and Zahorjan, 1994; Gibbs, 1994; Gleick, 1995; Hwang, 1994; Waldrop, 1993; Agnew and Kellerman, 1996).

End Users

An individual end user sees available end-user devices as if they were the entire distributed multimedia system. Whatever is right or wrong with the entire system appears to be right or wrong with devices that the user encounters at home, at work, and in public places. Thus a user's vision for a device is her vision for the entire system, including servers, delivery network, and end-user devices. According to this vision, distributed multimedia must be affordable, must be available when needed, present a coherent single system view, allow her to see and hear desired content, and accept and transmit content that she creates.

Affordability   The vision of affordability for distributed multimedia, including its end-user devices, applies to accessing training and information in a business context as well as to accessing entertainment and personal business services in a home or other personal context. Affordability depends strongly on who makes the actual payments and how visible the payments are, as well as on what the user compares the expense against. Relevant costs include the indirect costs of learning enough to purchase, install, use, repair, and upgrade hardware and software, as well as the direct purchasing costs.

The amount of money a person is willing to pay for a service, whether as a lump sum, as installment payment, or in rental fees, depends strongly on the overall perceived value of the service, which includes the content, the device, and all the rest of the system. Users want a sense that multimedia gives them acceptable return on their investments in equipment and time, not only in the monetary sense but in a business sense. They want multimedia to produce savings relative to other ways of improving their effectiveness of business or quality of life. Although business users are more likely to make formal cost/benefit tradeoff calculations, individual consumers make informed purchasing decisions based on what they consider to be good values.

Multimedia's perceived value may depend strongly on price comparisons. For an MBA candidate deciding whether to pursue the degree by way of an interactive network and end-user device, rather than by moving to campus, the candidate may easily justify a $3000 outlay for the device by comparing it to the expenses of moving and paying two years' room and board. By contrast, a sports fan deciding whether to obtain the function of controlling camera angles when viewing football games, rather than settling for an on-site crew's camera decisions, may find it harder to justify a $3000 outlay in comparison to a $3.00-per-month rental for a television set-top box.

The whole concept of multimedia may seem more affordable if the end-user device appears to replace or be part of something that is more expensive. Basing decisions on price comparisons and on the perceived fitness of things is familiar to all of us as consumers. We somehow feel better about buying an expensive sound system along with an expensive car, even though buying a less expensive car would leave more cash available to buy the sound system. This human tendency, along with the notion that an end-user device seems to embody an entire system, makes it crucial that the end-user device should replace an expensive computer or an entire television set such as HDTV, rather than replacing only a cheap telephone or a small set-top box on an existing television set. Suppose that a person's price expectations are based on having bought a $4000 computer and a $50 telephone several years ago. This year's video purchase may seem to be a bargain in the form of a $3000 computer, whereas it would seem to be an extravagance in the form of a $1000 phone with video.

Another way to predict what consumers are likely to perceive as affordable is to compare the price of multimedia content, in person-hours of use, against what people already expect to pay for similar information and entertainment experiences. The tricky part is deciding which experiences are similar. The best we can do is point out some reasonable boundaries. No known multimedia content is as entertaining as a live Broadway play, as relaxing as an expert massage, as engaging as a theme park, or as educational as a face-to-face discussion with a great and knowledgeable teacher. Multimedia content uses fewer media and provides less interaction than the preceding examples, so people expect to pay less for multimedia than for these experiences. But because multimedia uses more media and provides more interaction than a paperback book, textbook, movie rental, or newspaper, people expect to pay more for multimedia than for books, movie rentals, or newspapers.

Table 4.2 places multimedia content, the italicized row, in the context of more and less expensive experiences. You might want to provide your own numbers and work out results that are meaningful to you. In particular, you should compare the prices and perceived values of typical multimedia content to your other experiences.

Multimedia's value may depend not only on cost comparisons but also on time comparisons. When an activity is neutral or even negative, a user will pay more to complete the activity in less time. This applies both to personal activities, such as purchasing uninteresting essentials or filling out income tax forms, and to business activities, such as processing a customer transaction or deciding whether to buy a foreign currency. Here, affordability depends on how much a user's time is worth and on the value of opportunities the user would lose by spending more time. In principle, using audio and video allows a user to interact with the rest of the world at a higher bandwidth than would be possible using only text, so multimedia should increase productivity. In practice, determining where ordinary personal computers have produced significant productivity gains has proven difficult.

Single System View   An end user's vision includes viewing the entire system as a unified whole. A user need not normally be concerned with which part of the overall system happens to contain given information or how the system stores that information. When a user needs to distinguish different parts of the system from one another, such as when deciding to

Table 4.2 Affordability of experiences.

Characteristics Experience	Price ($)	Person- hours	Price per person-hour
Consultant	1000	7	143
Massage	50	0.5	100
Broadway show	45	2	22
Theme park	30	6	5
Typical multimedia content on a CD-ROM	*36*	*10*	*3.6*
Video rental (for 2 movies)	5	3	1.7
Paperback book	7	5	1.4
Textbook	70	90	0.78
Newspaper	0.35	2	0.18
Prodigy on-line service	30.00	30	1.00
Transcontinental telephone call	16.20	1	16.20
Cable service	50.00	100	.50

make do with a slightly less convenient form of information that is available much more cheaply, the parts must nevertheless continue to appear to be parts of the same system. A single system view includes being able to report a suspected malfunction to one person who will accept the problem in the name of the system rather than pass the buck.

Any user will have frequent occasion to move from one end-user device to another, such as to achieve greater privacy from other users, to achieve greater sharing with other users, to move from home to work, to alleviate monotony, or to circumvent a defect. When moving from one device to the next, the user must either continue to see the same single system view or understand why that is not possible. The multimedia vision precludes solutions as clumsy as carrying around a diskette containing work in progress. For example, a user who orders a desk lamp from his interactive television shopping facility would need linkage to the home financial transaction records probably stored on his home computer rather than on his set-top box.

When moving from one device to another, the user must remain the same user, as seen by other users of the system. One obvious way in which today's system fails to provide a single system view is that a typical telephone number stays with a device rather than going along with the person whom others want to call. The end user's vision for the future entails being able to accept communications on any available device without taking overt action to leave a forwarding number and certainly without requiring communication partners to keep track of the number of the device that is nearest to him.

As sophisticated end-user devices become more ubiquitous, it becomes more essential for each user to be able to access the same single system view all the time, rather than having to deal with different systems depending on whether the user is at home, at work, on vacation, in the hospital, or anywhere else. Physical location means less and less about what that user needs to do next. Thus, just as it is no longer necessary to provide some information only over telephone networks and other information only over CATV networks or local area networks, it is no longer desirable to provide particular information only to work locations and other information only to home or college locations. Working at home avoids unnecessary commuting, and conversely handling small amounts of personal business from a work location both compensates for time spent working at home and reduces physical time off from work. Without having to leave home or workplace, users can also pursue lifelong education and training for successive jobs as well as for pleasure and improved quality of life.

What will end-user devices of the future look like? Any descendant of today's public pay phone should serve as an office, study desk, or home office, not only with full function but with full convenience. Such a public device with a screen should allow a user to identify himself or herself. The device should then obtain information that personalizes the device for that user, either locally from a magnetic-striped card or remotely over the network, so that the next screen the device shows the user is exactly like the screen the user would see at home, work, or anywhere else. Given this personalization capability, relatively few end users would need to carry such devices as laptop computers, containing screens and other parts that make the devices inconveniently large. Today's small steps toward this capability include pay telephones that accept a spoken command such as "Call Tom" after finding who is using the device. This involves not only accessing the user's voice-recognition training file but also determining whom the user means by Tom.

Note that having access to work, educational, and personal information from many locations does not mean having only a single network. Rather, it means that different networks must interoperate. Each network will need to access information that exists in the intersections of work, educational, and personal contexts. End-user devices will need to display and manipulate data from all three contexts. However, the vision of a single system view does not imply existence of a single system. In fact, the question of single system view, as it applies to the number of connections that run into a home or business, has bedeviled the history of telecommunications.

Many of the end users' specific requirements are likely to affect software that runs in an end-user device. Some of these functions will split with hardware or even move entirely to hardware. Some may move to servers. Achieving the overall vision will require moving many new software functions into the devices' operating systems, making such functions available to all applications in a uniform fashion. Some of the functions and requirements likely to affect software follow.

- Easy-to-learn and easy-to-use interfaces that users can personalize and customize

- Intuitively usable tools for users to identify, obtain, and manipulate personalized interactive multimedia information easily and productively

- Intuitively usable tools for users to prepare multimedia content and multimedia requests

- The ability to conduct transactions wherever the user is, with appropriate user authorization and authentication

Some of the vision's requirements for supporting end users' use of video include having software that allows users to perform the following actions.

- Retrieve video either slowly, as for movies on demand, or rapidly, as for training applications.

- Control camera angles in television shows.

- Insert her own video easily, either in annotation mode or in the mode of completely new creation.

- Select and retrieve on demand not only movies, but old television shows, recent news shows, and sports attractions.

- Interact with television programs or movies in stimulating and interesting ways such as by altering plots by choosing different outcomes at various points throughout a story, or alter a character's personality, such as from passive to domineering. Note that this makes producing programs vastly more complex and difficult.

- Allow a user to request additional information about a specific point, such as in-depth news interpretations or additional sports statistics.

Businesses

We have seen that an individual end user envisions an entire system as embodied in one or more end-user devices and that most end users have similar visions because they all employ these devices for work, education, and personal use. Business, that is, companies, on the other hand, envision end user devices as distinct from delivery networks, servers, and content. Moreover, different companies have significantly different and conflicting visions for end-user devices.

Device Providers Companies that provide end-user device hardware and software envision being able to build on their already installed bases and competencies. Each such company hopes to achieve product differentiation that will turn its own products into de facto standards and thereby produce large sales volumes and profits in the consumer or commercial marketplace. A large installed base may be an advantage or a detriment. Some companies see opportunities to sell inexpensive additions to expensive installed products; others worry about responding to new opportunities in ways that require existing customers to scrap installed products.

Many companies see large volumes as their only hope for maintaining acceptable profit levels as technological progress turns their existing product lines into low-profit commodity items. Others find that multimedia is becoming part of the price of admission to their product areas.

Equipment manufacturers' visions diverge, of course, in the details. Telephone suppliers say that successful devices must be as easy to use as telephones. They point out that they have the world's largest installed base and have been interactive from the outset. Video game suppliers point out that their devices have the fastest and most interactive graphics and video support at the lowest price. Television set-top box makers feel that, because of their experience with high-bandwidth networks, they already have the hard part licked. Different computer suppliers point to different highly flexible systems and huge recent improvements in their prices and price performances.

Each company hopes that its own approach, technology, design strength, and installed base will evolve into the most pervasive end-user devices. To achieve that goal its own products must be both compatible and incompatible with most other devices. The devices should be compatible, so that they will play the same content as most other popular devices, but it is their unique features that will sell a particular poduct. Either the devices must play the same content better than competitors' devices can or they must be able to play important content that competitors' devices cannot play. Clearly, only one company can achieve this vision. Unfortunately, as many companies strive to, they create turmoil rather than creating standards that allow devices to interoperate.

Because most companies know that no one of them has enough competence and capital to do the whole job, they envision successful partnerships and joint ventures among equipment makers, such as between the manufacturer of set-top boxes and the maker of high-end computer workstations. Equipment makers also investigate whether they should form partnerships with network operators and content providers. We discuss this subject in detail in Chapter 6, Providers.

Companies and groups of companies all find that achieving their vision is difficult because they are uncertain which functions end-user devices of the future will need to perform. As an interim approach, many plan a series of easily modifiable modular products. The modular versions are ideal for test installations because companies can customize and combine the modules relatively quickly in response to any conjecture about what consumers want and are willing to pay for. For example, the set-top box that Time Warner uses in its trial in Orlando has an earlier Scientific-Atlanta set-top box recessed in its top left corner.

If any one combination becomes sufficiently popular, companies have an opportunity to redesign that combination for lower manufacturing cost as a less customizable and nonmodular product. Often, such redesign replaces some flexible but expensive software-based parts by less expensive, fixed-function, hardware-based parts. In other cases, the redesign involves combining several boxes in order to share a single package and power supply.

Companies that provide software envision object-oriented products that reduce development costs by facilitating reuse of parts of existing software. They expect to find hypertext integrated into underlying operating systems, for general use as well as for help screens, along with support for all media, to unify and simplify development. Software companies also envision application development tools that support cross-platform development and project-management software that supports the entire application development process of planning, producing, assembling, distributing, and supporting software for end-user devices.

Content Providers Companies that produce multimedia content envision a huge number of devices in the homes of consumers and on the desks of information workers. They look forward to identical interfaces (for application programming, network, etc.) that will enable them to create a single form of content that works on all devices. Not yet sure what types of content users will buy, they envision that these interfaces must be highly flexible in order to support types of popular content that have not yet been invented.

Content providers are severely discomfited by not being certain what functions end users will buy or what hardware designs will become popular or survive. One current approach, developing content that will play on both Intel-based systems and Apple Macintosh systems, becomes complex when developers who use Macintosh find that most of their customers use Intel-based systems on which the content works, but does not work quite as well as on Macintosh systems.

There are two general approaches to making end-user devices more flexible, in order to achieve content providers' vision. One approach is for manufacturers to make the devices more programmable at a lower level, so that content providers can modify more details of the devices' intelligence. But increasing a device's programmability may increase its component cost. For example, a video decompression chip that supports many different algorithms by means of different software tends to be larger and more expensive than a chip that implements a single algorithm in fixed-function hardware. The programmability approach to flexibility also exposes lower level interfaces. For example, the original CD-I multimedia format from Philips Electronics N.V. included within each CD-ROM disc actual programs. These programs used a particular microprocessor's instruction set and a particular operating system's function calls. This approach to flexibility requires a very low level of standardization. Nevertheless, making many devices programmable produced the microprocessor, one of the most notable success stories of the century. The other approach is to move intelligence out of end-user devices into servers. Content providers can change hardware and software in servers with less impact on customers than changing end-user devices would cause.

Companies as Multimedia Users   Most businesses are potential consumers of end-user devices. Companies envision using these devices to gather information, train their personnel, and in general to transact business more productively and efficiently. Many realize that appropriate end-user devices are key to hiring and keeping good employees. Entrepreneurial companies envision end-user devices as sources of new products and services in vacant niches. Service companies see business opportunities in supporting end-user devices in businesses and even in homes, where people do not want the hassles of dealing with installing and upgrading hardware, operating systems, databases, and network protocols. (Attempts to avoid the same hassles drive designs, such as network terminals, that require no configurations on customer premises.) One such service is to configure end-user devices for specific user applications. Other services include handling authentication, billing, and all sorts of monitoring. Energy utilities envision end-user devices that can accept networked instructions to cycle off hot water heaters and air conditioners at times of unusually high demand.

Government Regulators

In addition to purchasing end-user devices such as employee workstations and public kiosks for the purpose of improving delivery of their services, governments at various levels attempt to provide regulations that are in the public interest. A key purpose of future regulations will be to ensure universal access to information. Government regulators understand that universal access to distributed multimedia systems—by end users who may also be content providers—could become a great equalizer, whereas restricted access could significantly and unacceptably amplify existing inequities. Many also understand that a lowest common denominator approach to universal access, that is, arbitrarily forbidding anybody to have a function unless everybody has it, could harm national competitiveness and have other deleterious consequences.

Although an interface standard for end-user devices is complicated, to be concrete we consider just the part that determines how a network must represent video and audio in compressed digital form for transmission to and from end-user devices. Consider the following three possible outcomes.

From the viewpoint of universal access, the worst outcome would be a single, unregulated, proprietary, closed, de facto standard interface between all end-user devices and their networks. If one company, for example, controlled use of the algorithm that all end-user devices employed to decompress information from the network, then that company could determine which information was compressed into a form suitable for putting onto the network. They could refuse to compress information prepared by particular individuals or groups. They could also determine who could obtain or employ end-user devices. They could close out other potential providers of equipment and compression services, to maintain artificially high prices. They could frustrate attempts to reverse engineer their compression and decompression products by making frequent undocumented software changes, such as requiring a new password every month, and by making occasional major required but undocumented hardware changes. They could build in mechanisms for deciphering users' encrypted information and even for tracking users' travels. Government regulators would feel behooved to step in if they saw such a monopolistic situation developing.

A somewhat less undesirable outcome would be the evolution of thousands of incompatible but open standard interfaces. For example, if each region that has its own zip code ended up with its own compression and decompression standard, then anyone who wanted to supply a piece of content nationwide would need to pay for thousands of expensive compression operations. This outcome might be tolerable for a mass market item such as a major movie or a popular television show, because it would be comparable to today's practice of distributing separate movie prints or program tapes to theaters and television stations. However, it would be prohibitively expensive for any piece of content aimed at a niche market, because no one zip code would have an audience large enough to pay back its cost of compression. The result would amplify inequity by limiting access to the largest providers. Government regulators would have to step in to protect individuals and minorities from the tyranny of the majority.

The best outcome, from the viewpoint of universal access, would be a single, regulated, open standard interface between all end-user devices and their networks. Regulators would have the same powers over this third outcome as the monopolistic company had over the first outcome, but would presumably use the power more nearly in the public interest. Regulators could assure that many companies knew the standard well enough to build compression and decompression devices, driving down the prices. Many content providers would be able to afford a single compression operation for each title, either by buying equipment or by employing a service bureau. Regulators could specify standards that helped law enforcement agencies to decipher encrypted information and locate users, and forbid standards that did not.

These three potential outcomes show that one or a few regulated open standards are optimal for achieving regulators' vision for equal access to multimedia. This may not be the optimal outcome for other stakeholders, however. One of its drawbacks might be that it could work too well, depriving citizens of rights they traditionally enjoy only because governments cannot afford the expense of tracking what everybody is doing all the time. Citizens might well prefer to have a monopolistic company using their past travel records to send them advertisements for future vacation sites rather than having a government use such records to disallow their tax deductions.

A single regulated standard has other potential drawbacks. Having one open standard removes some of the motivation for businesses to invest in innovative algorithms. It is difficult to convert to hardware and software that implement even a vastly better algorithm. There must be some provision for people who need and can afford much higher function to pay for it, without requiring them to subsidize universal access to such functions. For progress to occur, it is important to resist standardizing prematurely before an acceptable standard is available, to avoid destroying the motivation for innovation, and to avoid limiting everybody's capabilities to a lowest common denominator.

A cautionary word on the subject of premature standardization comes from the leading supplier of equipment, such as devices for encrypting video to the cable and satellite industries. Hal Krisbergh, president of General Instrument Corporation's communications division, warns that standardization of set-top operating systems would limit deployment of technological advances and freeze the current state of technology, thereby significantly diminishing the availability of new services to consumers (Amt, 1994).

STATE OF THE ART

We next consider end-user devices that are common today, as a base for discussing changes that will be necessary to achieve the vision for distributed multimedia.

Consumer Marketplace

Table 4.3 illustrates the size and nature of the U.S. market for some end-user devices. Unless otherwise noted, figures are for 1992.

Types of Devices

Tables 4.4 and 4.5 express today's state of the art of end-user devices. Table entries express relative ease or difficulty with which people who are neither media professionals nor computer professionals can perform each function

Table 4.3 Size of U.S. consumer marketplace.

Millions	Item
94	Total households
140	Telephones
150	Color television sets
67	Videocassette recorders
16	Video cameras
21	Personal computers in homes
0.7	CD-ROM-equipped video game devices in 1993
17	Multimedia computers of all types in 1995
4.9	CD-ROM-equipped video game devices in 1995
< 0.5	Personal Digital Assistants

Sources: First six items (GISTICS Inc., 1993), last item (*Information Week*, 1994).

Table 4.4   End-user devices' media capabilities.

End-user device Capability	Telephone	Personal computer	Television set with set-top box
Receive and present to user:			
Text	No	Easy	Incidental to video
Graphics	No	Easy	No
Image	Easy (fax)	Easy but typically with limited colors	Incidental to video
Audio	Easy	Hard to add, rather hard to use	Incidental to video
Video, low quality	Possible but unusual	Easy	Easy
Video, high quality	No	Very hard	Easy
Create, edit, and transmit:			
Text	Numbers easy, letters hard	Easy	Quite easy
Graphics	No	Easy	No
Image	Easy (fax)	Quite easy	No
Audio	Easy (edit is hard)	Hard	No
Video, low quality	Possible but unusual	Very hard	No
Video, high quality	No	Very, very hard	No
Store for later use:			
Text	No	Easy	No
Graphics	No	Easy	No
Image	No	May be hard	No
Audio	Easy (answering machine)	Moderately hard	No
Video	No	Hard	No

Table 4.5   End-user devices' other capabilities.

End-user device Capability	Telephone	Personal computer	Television set with set-top box
Distance	Contact with face, for privacy	Arm's length, for high detail	Across room, for sharing
Connect to	Telephone, wireless	LAN Telephone Mail	Cable, wireless
Flexibility	Low	High	Low
Price	Low	Medium	Low
Portable forms	Quite common	Common	Unusual
Reliability	Very high	Low (due to complex software)	High
Purpose			
Entertainment	Low	Medium	High
Education	Low	Medium	Medium
Information	High	High	Medium
Business	High	High	Low

using each type of device. Ease or difficulty depend on the skill levels that users must develop as well as the price and availability of the equipment that users must acquire. Distributed multimedia is important to the extent that it is useful to normal consumers whose interest lies in fields other than media, computers, or networking and who have middle-class household budgets.

As Tables 4.4 and 4.5 indicate, no existing end-user device handles all media well or connects to all networks. Improvements are likely to come in the form of incremental improvements to computers, telephones, and televisions. Today's associations will persist due to habit, long after they have become unnecessary. There will be a strong historical precedent for a device that operates near a user's face to connect to a circuit-switched twisted pair, and for a device that operates across a room to connect to a frequency-division multiplexed coaxial cable. Both designers and end users will benefit from considering which such associations are necessary and which merely used to be necessary.

Famed industrial designer Raymond Loewy coined the phrase "most advanced yet acceptable" (MAYA) to summarize users' desire for something that looks not only advanced and improved but also familiar and comfortable (see Loewy, 1979). Although he applied the MAYA principle to designing department stores in the 1920s, it applies equally well to designing hardware and software for the late 1990s. MAYA prescribes a fine line between a device that looks too much like its ancestors, so that a user cannot see that it has additional functions, and a device that looks too different from its ancestors, so that a user cannot see what its functions are. Users are likely to reject a completely new design, simply because it is too different.

In his book *The Evolution of Useful Things*, Henry Petroski (1992) debunks the idea that form follows function, making a strong case for the idea that, instead, form follows failure. He shows that each new design is an attempt to correct some perceived failing on the part of an older design by meeting particular user requirements. The wide variety of conflicting requirements, such as a desire for both higher function and lower cost, leaves room for an endless stream of such improvements. Just as there is no one type of paper clip that satisfies all users, so there will be many different end-user device designs.

Although we expect most end-user devices to be evolutionary improvements on today's computers, telephones, and television sets with set-top boxes, we must consider the possibility of all-new devices that are not recognizable descendants of any existing devices. There may be reasons to design a new device from the ground up. There is no reason to believe or disbelieve that such a device will be built within the next decade.

Hardware

Figure 4.3 shows a composite of many hardware units that may appear around or in a generic end-user device. It employs round corners to denote peripheral units that may appear as separate boxes and square corners to denote functions that are likely to be hidden inside a central box. The triangle is the multiplexor that we discussed in the section entitled Media Combinations in Chapter 1. The circle labeled *local storage* at the bottom of the figure includes not only hard drives but also floppy diskettes, CD-Recordable discs, CD-ROM discs, and Digital Video Discs, although the arrows that point downward do not apply to read-only forms of storage. Note that storing media on local storage is functionally equivalent to storing media on the world of remote servers at the top of the figure.

You will recognize the figure's other boxes that implement functions that we discussed in previous chapters. The display adapter converts images from digital form to analog form that can drive a computer display. Audio capture and playback adapters convert audio from analog form to digital

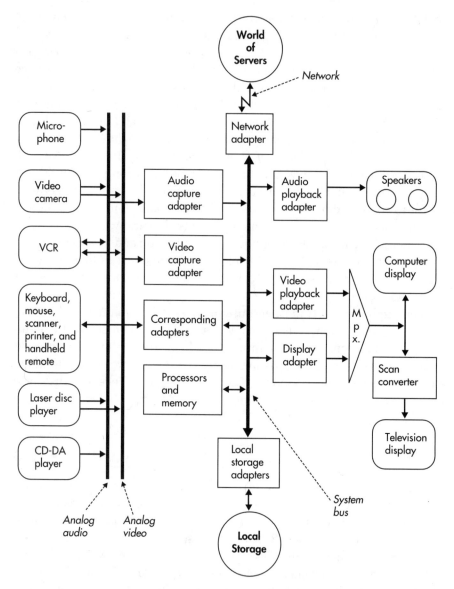

Figure 4.3   General device hardware.

form and from digital form to analog form, respectively. Video capture and
playback adapters perform the corresponding A-to-D and D-to-A functions
for video and also usually compress and decompress the digital video. Network adapters include modems for telephone lines, CATV cables, or local
area networks. The scan converter may be necessary to convert a signal suitable for driving a computer display (typically specifying amounts of red,

green, and blue for successive pixels) into any of several types of signals suitable for driving a television display.

A typical end-user device includes only some peripheral units and only some functions. Even if all five sources of analog audio were available, for example, only one would usually be connected at a particular time. Thus, in Chapter 2's terminology, these buses employ circuit-switched multiplexing, usually implemented by unplugging and plugging connectors, whereas the system bus and the multiplexor's output signal employ time-division multiplexing.

One way you can use Fig. 4.3 is to trace data paths. For example, the data path for capturing sound starts with the microphone, proceeds through the audio capture adapter, system bus, and local storage adapter, and ends with the digital audio on the local storage, which is usually a hard drive. The data path for playing back previously captured or synthesized digital audio starts at the local storage, proceeds through the local storage adapter, system bus, and audio playback adapter, and ends with the speakers. Note that a line with a one-way arrow shows the primary direction in which a connection carries information although, for example, an audio capture adapter actually accepts control information from the system bus as well as sending digital audio to the system bus. Any particular end-user device includes an appropriate subset of the devices and functions in Fig. 4.3. Some examples of useful subsets are as follows.

A digital set-top box requires a network adapter, such as for a digital CATV cable or satellite; an audio playback adapter; a video playback adapter; a scan converter (in the form of an NTSC encoder); a device adapter for the infrared link from a handheld remote device; and processors and memory, perhaps including some authentication, decryption, or descrambling units in pluggable modules to improve security. A set-top box that presents a graphical user interface must add a display adapter and a multiplexor, which determines the parts of the television display that receive text, graphics, or images and the parts that receive video.

A digital telephone has a network adapter, such as for a local loop or CATV cable, a microphone, an audio capture and playback adapter, speakers, a keyboard of 12 or more keys, and corresponding adapters, as well as processors and memory. An answering machine adds local storage and its adapter to a digital telephone, and a fax machine adds a scanner and printer.

A personal computer with no special multimedia hardware and no network includes keyboard, mouse, and printer with corresponding adapters, a display adapter, a computer display, local storage, local storage adapters and, of course, processors and memory.

As you select or develop end-user devices, you will note that physical packaging of both peripheral units and internal functions into electronic circuit cards or boxes can vary widely. For example, a normal digital audio adapter contains both an audio capture adapter and an audio playback adapter and may also contain a CD-ROM drive adapter. Internal functions may appear on a device's main electronic circuit board or on adapter cards that plug into sockets that provide access to the system bus. It is common, although not universal, to package a VCR in the same box as a video camera, thus creating a camcorder or handycam. A video capture adapter and a video playback adapter are often packaged separately. A video capture adapter is often useful, even without any special hardware that acts as a video playback adapter, because a computer's normal processor and display adapter can show video with a quality that is acceptable for many purposes. Having a video playback adapter without a video capture adapter is common, as well, particularly in a simple set-top box. If a device has both a video playback adapter and a display adapter, then it needs a multiplexor, which is often packaged as part of the video playback adapter. A video in a window adapter is actually the combination of a video capture adapter, a video playback adapter, and a multiplexor. Several available display adapters include the video playback adapter and multiplexor functions.

In Fig. 4.3 we avoided clutter by omitting a few important connections and devices. A suitable laser disc player can connect to a computer's serial port in order to receive commands, such as a command to play video and audio between two specified frame numbers. In addition to the connections shown, a laser disc player's analog audio and analog video outputs frequently drive a separate television display and speakers without passing through a computer at all. Audiocassette recorders and digital audiotape (DAT) recorders are other peripheral devices that can play or record analog audio. Some end-user devices include magnetic-stripe readers that read credit cards or key locks for security.

Figure 4.3 glosses over some details about the analog audio and analog video buses that will become intensely interesting if you find yourself plugging an end-user device together from component parts. Focus 4.1 mentions some details. Far more such information is available elsewhere (Agnew et al., 1996).

One of the most useful general principles that you should consider when either purchasing or designing multimedia hardware is that it is best to implement as many functions as possible in software. That is, whenever possible, perform a function by running special-purpose software on the device's general-purpose main processor. Following this principle yields flexibility, because it is usually far easier to alter software than to replace hardware. The same principle yields economy, because investing in a faster main processor speeds up many functions, whereas investing in special hardware speeds up only a particular function. For example, an early Apple Macintosh computer had very shallow adapters, meaning that it contained a minimum amount of

FOCUS 4.1 Connecting analog audio and video.

The analog audio bus near the left side of Fig. 4.3 can represent two different kinds of connections and a third type can appear at the top right. A typical microphone produces a weaker signal than do the other devices, so a typical audio capture adapter has a separate microphone input jack that provides extra amplification for weak signals, in addition to the line input jack that receives the other signals. An audio playback adapter's speaker connection, shown at the top right, may be suitable for a line input connection, for recording a device's audio output. This signal is suitable for driving speakers only if the speakers include amplifiers. An audio playback adapter may include a second speaker connection suitable for driving unamplified speakers.

All three sorts of analog audio connections tend to mix ⅛-inch phone connectors with phono (also called RCA) connectors. This situation assures electronic supply houses of a continuing source of revenue from selling adapter plugs. The names of connectors are fundamentally meaningless; we supply them only to help you find appropriate cables and adapters.

The analog video bus near the left side of the Fig. 4.3 can represent no less than five sorts of connections. A VCR usually has a radio-frequency (RF) input connection for a CATV cable or antenna, with a type F connector, and has a tuner with which it can select one of many incoming analog video and audio signals. It uses a corresponding RF output connector that carries the selected signal as either Channel 3 or Channel 4. A consumer-grade VCR or other such peripheral device often uses a composite video signal, which runs on a single coaxial cable with one pin in the attached phono plug. A *prosumer* (professional-consumer) device often uses a Super-video or S-video signal that runs on four wires within a single cable with four pins in its DIN plug. A television display that includes either sort of video input connection is distinguished by the name *television monitor* or *video monitor*, whereas one that has only an RF input connection is called merely a *television set*. A professional video device often uses a component video signal that runs on three or four separate cables with individual BNC plugs. A digital cassette tape recorder or camera may include a fifth type of video connection that replaces analog video by digital video.

Whereas the three sorts of analog audio connections differ mainly in signal strength, the five types of video connections differ mainly in resolution. For example, composite video is significantly better than RF, and S-video is significantly better than composite video. The video signals are so different that you cannot buy a trivial adapter plug to convert from one to another; to get higher-resolution connections, you buy more-expensive hardware. The connection from the scan converter to the television display may be any of these five types. As a result, a scan converter can drive a VCR, which is useful in case you want to make a tape that shows activity on a computer display. ∎

special hardware for each adapter and used its main processor to control every detail of the adapters' operations. Today, Intel vigorously advocates using its main processors to perform most digital functions, at least in low-end hardware. They term this design *native signal processing* (NSP), and use it instead of adding *digital signal processing* (DSP) hardware or other special-purpose hardware (Wilson, 1995).

Despite this excellent principle, an end-user device is likely to require special-purpose multimedia hardware for three interesting reasons. First, analog-to-digital conversions and digital-to-analog conversions require special hardware to accommodate each medium's unique analog form. This explains unique audio capture adapters, audio playback adapters, and video capture adapters. Second, several multimedia functions may require more speed than affordable general-purpose hardware can provide. For example, a normal display adapter, which converts digital images to analog signals that control the intensities of a computer display's red, green, and blue beams, may not have sufficient speed to convert compressed digital video to the same three analog signals. This explains unique video playback adapters. Another example is that software running on a main processor may not be able to convert graphics to images sufficiently rapidly to keep up with a user's requests for successive windows in a graphical user interface, let alone keep up with three-dimensional (3-D) animations. This explains graphics accelerators.

The third reason for special-purpose hardware is that an end-user device may need hardware to perform functions that software could perform perfectly well, if software were available. For example, most personal computers have specialized hardware that implements a single bit-map font that converts text to an image with 80 characters per line and 24 lines per screen. After a computer has booted its operating system and launched a word processing program, of course, the computer can use software to implement fonts with a wide variety of sizes and styles. However, before a computer has booted its operating system, it may need to display progress messages or error reports. Special bit-map font hardware makes this possible. Similar special hardware in every television set now sold in the United States translates up to 480 bps of closed-caption text for display at the bottom of the screen (Jack, 1993).

Performance

It is often important to assign numbers to the performance (speed of handling information) of an end-user device's general-purpose hardware, such as its main processor and hard drive, as well as of its special-purpose multimedia hardware, such as its video capture adapter and display adapter. Such numbers will help you decide among competing solutions to a particular problem, when you are either designing or purchasing an end-user device.

You can get quantitative information about performance by asking three types of questions. First, you can ask for individual numbers, such as the CD-ROM drive's transfer rate, the hard drive's access time, and the processor's clock rate. Second, you can ask how the device performs on particular benchmarks that include applications for which you want to use the device. Third, you can ask whether the device meets one of the standard specifications such as Multimedia Personal Computer 3 (MPC3). We continue by noting the types of answers you might get in response to questions about benchmarks and standards.

Some benchmarks measure processing power, which is particularly important if the device uses its main processor to decompress digital video or rotate a 3-D object as part of displaying animation. Even a specification of millions of instructions per second (MIPS) actually represents the result of a benchmark. For example, if you measure only multiply instructions, you get a smaller number of instructions per second than if you measure only additions. Any valid MIPS specification requires an application that contains a reasonable mixture of instructions. Similarly, a useful general benchmark specification requires one or more suitable applications. A manufacturers' organization named the Standard Performance Evaluation Corporation (SPEC) developed benchmarks for processing power. Its specifications for floating-point and integer performance, SPECfp92 and SPECint92, are compilations of about 20 application programs. Motorola rates the 80-MHz 601 PowerPC chip, used in some Apple computers, at 85 SPECint92 and 105 SPECfp92. The 100-MHz P54C Pentium processor, used in some Intel-based computers, delivers 100 SPECint92 and 81 SPECfp92. Dhrystone is an integer benchmark that measures both processor performance and compiler efficiency. It applies only to processing integers within a system's cache. Other benchmarks measure 3-D vector performance, such as how many vectors or triangles a computer can send to its screen each second. Still other benchmarks measure the number of frames per second that an end-user device's main processor can prepare when performing software decompression of digital video of a particular resolution.

More sophisticated benchmarks measure complete operations, such as the total time an end-user device requires to comprehend a user's input, find and prepare what the user requested, and deliver the results to the device's screen and speakers. Many useful product comparisons report the results of running such benchmarks on competing products. One typical example ran a complete operation that involved loading Microsoft's *Encarta* multimedia encyclopedia, performing a Boolean search, scrolling a time line, and loading an image and a video clip. If you are selecting an end-user device or multi-media content, your best measure of performance is a comparison of relevant benchmarks (*Multimedia World,* 1995). Results of such a benchmark depend strongly on whether an end-user device has special assist hardware for functions that the benchmark uses and on whether the selected software takes advantage of that hardware.

A standard specification attempts to provide an overall measure of an end-user device's performance. Table 4.6 shows two of the most relevant specifications. Note that the most important difference between 1993's MPC2 and 1995's MPC3 is that the latter specifies a particular degree of performance in decompressing and playing back digital video. Such specifications are extremely valuable because they are easy to use. The Software Publisher's Association (SPA) provides the MPC specifications to guide its members, hardware providers, and end users. End users can look at a simple logo to determine a device's capabilities or a title's requirements, rather than needing to compare a dozen individual numbers that have confusing units. For example, not all end users know that increasing a CD-ROM's transfer rate is good, but that increasing its access time is bad. Content providers can begin creating titles that use MPEG-1 as soon as a reasonably large number of users have purchased devices that bear the MPC3 logo. In a nutshell, the MPC specification that most end users have available at a given time is the state of the art of computer-type end-user devices. But don't blink. A joke says that whatever processor the SPA selects for its latest specification becomes obsolete in a few months.

Table 4.6 MPC specifications.

Requirement	MPC2	MPC3
Memory size	4 MB	8 MB
Processor and speed	486SX, 25 MHz	Pentium, 75 MHz
Hard-drive size	160 MB	540 MB
CD-ROM transfer rate	300 KBps	600 KBps
CD-ROM access time	400 ms	250 ms
Audio playback	16-bit, FM, MIDI	16-bit, wave-table, MIDI
Video playback	No specification	MPEG-1 hardware or software 30 frames per second 352 by 240 pixels 15 bits per pixel

Software

Multimedia software forms a synergistic marriage with multimedia hardware in which each partner strengthens the other partner's weak areas. Each partner's state of the art does contain significant weak areas, partly as a result of several decades of development during which the most important media were nonisochronous text and graphics. One of software's weakest areas is the lack of real-time operating systems that could handle efficiently large volumes of isochronous audio and video. Hardware strengthens this area by providing increasingly powerful and affordable processors and storage, which allow distributed multimedia systems to handle audio and video by what amounts to brute force. In most areas, however, it is hardware that is the weaker partner, so software does most of the strengthening. This is particularly true because users must be able to run most software on several generations of installed hardware, connected to slow networks, even if software creators' hardware happens to be the high end of the most recent generation, connected to a fast network. The state of the art of multimedia software, like many marriages, is thus based on making the best of an imperfect situation and remaining hopeful about possibilities for improvement in the future.

Stand-alone personal computer hardware provides reasonably good support for multimedia that is distributed on CD-ROMs. Significant numbers of potential users have obtained powerful end-user device hardware that contains audio adapters with speakers, displays that can show high-resolution images, and processors that have sufficient performance to decompress reasonably high-quality digital video.

Recently, however, the Internet and the World Wide Web (WWW, or the Web) have become important for distributing multimedia. WWW is a very large-scale distributed hypermedia system in which links can extend beyond navigating within a single document and can extend far beyond a single server. Clicking your mouse when pointing at part of one page may invoke a second page that exists only on a server halfway around the world. Explosive growth of interest in World Wide Web pages has caused a temporary step backward in hardware's support of multimedia software. Through no fault of the software, the state of the art of multimedia distributed over today's networks is static and dull, although extraordinarily wide-ranging, in comparison to multimedia distributed on CD-ROMs.

It is unsurprising that Web pages lack CD-ROMs' many high-resolution images, audio, and video, when you compare an Internet user's 9.6-Kbps modem connection against a single-speed CD-ROM's data rate of 1.2 Mbps. For example, using such a modem to download a typical image as a JPEG-compressed 150-KB file takes about two minutes, whereas a single-speed

CD-ROM drive can read the file in one second. Moreover, compared to the preceding two examples, today's state of the art includes telephone line modems that are only about three times as fast, whereas CD-ROM drives can be six times as fast. In order to match the speed of even a single-speed CD-ROM drive, a network needs to reach T1 speed.

Of course, this step backward in hardware's support of software is only temporary. Although faster network connections will be forthcoming, there is no prospect of CD-ROMs that contain as much content as is available over networks, and networks have the unique advantage of delivering timely content or even real-time content.

We discuss the state of the art of stand-alone and networked multimedia software from two viewpoints. Before we consider what several software providers are doing, we consider what is going on in the following software layers.

- Content, including titles and applications

- Tools for developing and running content

- Operating systems, including services and user interfaces

- Network protocols and hardware support, including device drivers

In general, it does not pay to accept these layers as accurate descriptions of the real world, because a typical multimedia software product is likely to include functions that slop across several layers. For example, installing a CD-ROM that holds a game or encyclopedia may install not only an application program but also software for decompressing digital video and performing other functions, without even checking whether a later and compatible version of the tool is already installed. As a consequence, we occasionally spend a day installing a half-dozen such CD-ROMs, carefully making each one work in turn, and then find that the first few no longer work. Despite this caveat, it is useful to discuss several of these layers separately.

Content   Each new distribution method requires content creators to develop correspondingly new techniques. Just as early movie producers had to learn that a wide variety of camera positions works better than pointing a single camera at a stage play from front-row-center, today's creators of stand-alone and networked multimedia content are learning what works, given hardware that typical prospective customers have available.

Multimedia content distributed by the two major methods now has significantly different states. For stand-alone multimedia, creators have had several years to learn how to make good use of the capacity and data rate of a CD-ROM. One of their most useful techniques is to find plausible excuses for using video on only a small fraction of a screen. For networked multimedia, however, creators are just starting to master a difficult and frustrating environment. They have learned to reduce an image's number of colors to the bare minimum, and to compress an image as much as possible, while still maintaining acceptable quality. They have also learned that end users dislike either seeing the image's lines painted from the top down or seeing the prior screen until after the entire image downloads. One useful technique involves first painting several widely spaced lines and then going back to paint intervening lines. An alternative technique first paints the user's screen with a low-resolution image and then gradually increases the resolution. (These techniques occasionally go by the respective names *interlace* and *progressive scan*, although we have seen that those names properly refer to the two forms of raster scan in which you either scan odd and even lines or else scan all lines in numerical order.) Content providers are experimenting with proprietary extensions to MPEG audio and video compression algorithms that allow them to download small amounts of audio or video quickly and to stream larger portions in real time. Even with such proprietary compression and the fastest modems, however, the resulting audio and video are barely acceptable. We discuss many forms of distributed multimedia content in Chapter 5, Applications.

Tools   At this layer, too, we see significantly different states for software that applies to stand-alone and networked multimedia. Many excellent stand-alone multimedia authoring systems are available for personal computers, both Macintosh and Intel-based, and a few proprietary ones are available for game machines. An authoring system helps you to create and edit some media and also helps you combine media with interactivity. Two good examples of authoring systems are Macromedia's Director and Asymetrix's Multimedia ToolBook. The former has versions that run on both Intel-based and Apple Macintosh computers and can help convert content to play on both of these platforms. More-specialized tools help you do a better job of creating and editing media than you can do with the facilities in typical authoring systems. Two good examples of such tools are Adobe's Photoshop for creating and editing images and Adobe's Premiere for editing digital video on either type of personal computer. Other specialized tools run only on powerful workstations, although they produce content for use on more conventional end-user devices. For example, Silicon Graphics' Wavefront is an animation tool that runs on Silicon Graphics' workstations.

For multimedia on the Internet, in addition to traditional information retrieval tools such as Gopher, Veronica, and Wais, there are tools for creating and browsing (viewing) WWW pages. To create a Web page, an author can use an editor such as Microsoft Word to enter text that contains hypertext markup language (HTML) tags, which refer to other text documents and images. HTML is a dialect and subset of the standard generalized markup language (SGML). For example, a line that uses tags to refer to a map of Owego, New York, might be

```
<A HREF="http: //www.owego.edu/owego.jpg"> click to view.</A>.
```

To see a page that contains such an image, you invoke a browser that is appropriate for the page's version of HTML.

Multimedia tool providers are responding to content providers' pleas for minor and major improvements to make tools more compatible with networks. Netscape Communications, Inc. is leading the drive to extend HTML in the direction of multimedia. Other tool providers are endowing some Web browsers or viewers with the ability to play back stand-alone multimedia authoring systems' content that appears in an HTML document. Conversely, providers of some stand-alone multimedia authoring systems are adding the ability to embed a Web page's universal resource locator (URL) so that a user can invoke that page from what would otherwise be stand-alone multimedia content. Although providers are eager for exclusive features, they do not want to become so exclusive that only a few users will have the specialized browsers needed to view their home pages. If standardization, porting, and interfacing efforts succeed, a user will be able to use one of today's commercial stand-alone multimedia authoring systems to produce content that includes hyper links to other content throughout the world.

Tool providers are also experimenting with techniques for displaying dynamic Web pages without sending large quantities of data over networks. Techniques include using animation rather than natural video, referring to data that already exist on a user's device, and using a lean, platform-independent language to specify what a user's device needs to assemble dynamically, as the user browses a WWW page, to reveal the page.

Many tool providers are seeking roles in which they can set standards and make profits by sending distributed multimedia over the Internet and World Wide Web. Figure 4.4 shows a bag of tools. It is not clear how these and other tools relate to one another and which ones will survive.

When you are trying to make sense of a bag of tools, it is worth noting that each provider has a strong tendency to devise new tools that fit well with its installed base of tools and with its employees' areas of expertise. For

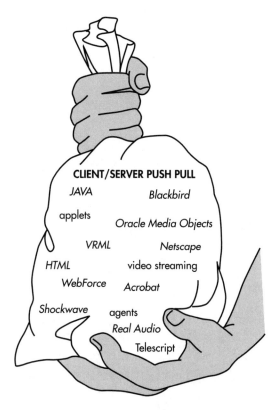

Figure 4.4   A bag of tools.

example, Microsoft views the world from a Windows base, IBM and Oracle have host mainframe and database viewpoints, Novell and Netscape Communications see the world as growing out of network operating systems, and Adobe builds on its Acrobat and Postscript desktop publishing tools. AimTech, which provides authoring systems for developing stand-alone computer-based training content, is trying to avoid being left out in the cold by seeking and announcing affinity with multimedia delivered by way of the Internet. Focus 4.2 notes characteristics of some state-of-the-art tools of which you can make some sense by considering each provider's heritage.

An agent is a useful tool based on the metaphor of a helpful person such as a secretary that can assist in finding products or employing services on electronic networks. Like a human assistant, an agent may free a user from repetitive actions, provide problem-solving intelligence, and point out better plans for attacking an information retrieval problem. The current state of the art for agents is a wide variety of existing macros, together with screen recorders and scripting languages that help users prepare their own macros or customize ex-

FOCUS 4.2 Some multimedia tools.

Java from Sun Microsystems

- Is an interpreted object-oriented language suitable for creating small pieces of applications called applets that are embedded in HTML files and that actually run on end-user devices equipped with suitable Java enabled browsers.

- Is based on C and C++ languages, but without some dangerous features.

- Has a Basic interpreter and class support that occupy 40 KB of storage with an additional 175 KB for thread support and basic standard libraries.

- Allows for a virtual machine on any end-user device running the HotJava browser.

- Is being beta tested with only rudimentary development tools.

QuickTime virtual reality (QTVR) from Apple, where virtual reality means the ability to use cursor keys to move up, down, backward, or forward and also to use keys to pick up objects. With QTVR, a creator

- Takes pictures in several directions from a fixed center point.

- Captures and refines images.

- Stitches images together by morphing edges, to get a 360-degree, 3-D look.

- Converts to a compressed QTVR movie format.

- Embeds hot words or nodes in the result.

- Embeds additional QTVR movies such as to allow rotating a vase in a museum.

Virtual Reality Modeling Language (VRML) from Silicon Graphics, (where virtual reality has the same meaning as above)

- Is a markup format for nonproprietary platform 3-D.

- Could be an extension to HTML.

- Could use URLs in VRML environments.   *(cont.)*

FOCUS 4.2 Some multimedia tools. (*cont.*)

Real Audio from Progressive Networks

- Allows live transmission with real-time audio encoding.

- Has had 450,000 copies of its Real Audio player downloaded by potential users.

- Uses 9.6 Kbps to transmit high-quality audio, compressed from 1.2 Mbps.

StreamWorks from Xing

- Allows live transmission with real-time audio encoding.

- Offers varying transmission rates from 9.6 Kbps to T1 speed.

- Provides video transmission at 28.8 Kbps for two to three frames per second, CD quality at ISDN line speed, and NTSC quality at T1 line speed.

- Supports MPEG with proprietary extensions.

Telescript from General Magic, owned by Apple, Sony, Motorola, Philips, AT&T, and Matsushita

- Provides software that allows devices such as television sets, personal computers, and cellular telephones to communicate across networks.

- Gives each user an agent.

- Sends agents from the user's device onto the network.

- Presents an interface with icons representing parts of the electronic community. ■

---

isting macros such as to produce a custom mail filter. The future holds promise of agents that can learn from a user's past actions and gradually become proactive (Wayner, 1994). Some other typical tools are as follows.

Oracle has developed Media Objects, an authoring software tool for creating multimedia interactive services and CD-ROM-based applications for use with Oracle's media server and television set-top boxes. Media Objects uses the metaphor of a stack of cards, where each card represents a full screen of information and controls. The resulting applications are portable and run on various intelligent set-top boxes.

Sybase is offering a product called Gain Momentum, which Gain Technology developed. Gain Momentum allows users to decompress video in real time on high-performance workstations. Developers can build links, graphics, video, audio, and animation.

Operating Systems   Operating systems such as Microsoft Windows, Apple's Macintosh OS, OS/2, and UNIX have been gradually integrating improved multimedia functions, multitasking, lightweight threads, fast context switches, small streamlined kernels, and language environments optimized toward presenting information to the user. However, this evolutionary approach may not suffice, and a revolution may be required to produce real-time operating systems. One new approach started with Script X, which Kaleida (absorbed by Apple) designed from the outset to accommodate video and computers. It may be too late and too hard for some to learn. Another approach is based on real-time kernels that are smaller and employ faster context switching than is possible with existing operating systems. Arguments about the relative merits of revolution and evolution involve the natural desire of companies that have no current winner to start with a level playing field, whereas companies that have current winners want to benefit from their installed bases. Some relevant examples of operating systems are as follows.

Before Windows 95, Microsoft Windows had relatively poor display performance, compared to using the facilities of DOS. This is why most popular, fast-paced games ran directly on DOS. Microsoft and Intel had previously developed a display control interface (DCI) to allow application programs to use the graphics display interface (GDI) to talk more directly to display hardware. For Windows 95, Microsoft developed direct draw, which gives better display performance than applications had when using DOS directly. However, direct draw is not backward compatible with DCI, so display adapters required new device drivers to work at all (Ozer, 1995).

Microsoft's MIMOSA is an object-oriented operating system, intended as a successor to Modular Windows. It is designed for high-bandwidth, full-switched interactive television systems.

Microware developed a widely used real-time operating system, OS-9. Later they developed a digital audio and video interactive decoder (DAVID) development package that contains all the software necessary to design an MPEG decoder in a set-top box for interactive digital television.

Geoworks in California has introduced GEOS, which is a lightweight, object-oriented operating system aimed at electronic organizers, fax machines, intelligent telephones, PDAs, and set-top boxes. Geoworks says its focus is on highly cost-effective solutions, whereas general-purpose personal computer or workstation operating systems use unnecessarily large amounts of processing power and memory.

Network Support Network support is improving as changes to transmission control protocol and Internet protocol (TCP/IP) make these protocols more appropriate for streaming large quantities of isochronous media to one user or to several users at once. With today's protocols, downloading a Web page with several images requires a great deal of handshaking—that is, many calls and acknowledgments. Future protocols may make it possible to open a pipe and send all the data. Eliminating unnecessary handshaking from the protocols would decrease downloading time significantly. Further improvement is possible by eliminating the slow start feature of today's protocols. Any transmission now starts with a relatively low data rate and later switches to a higher data rate. This was appropriate in an era when a typical transmission contained a few dozen to a few hundred Bytes, but it wastes time in an era when a typical transmission is a large file. Multicasting protocols will improve the efficiency of sending the same information to many users at one time. For example, if you are in New York and want to send a large file to several hundred users in Los Angeles, you would prefer to send the file across the country once and have something near Los Angeles distribute it to the individual users. MBONE is one tool that allows multicast of multimedia.

Software Providers We now proceed from discussing multimedia software layers to illustrating the state of the art for some software providers, both businesses and the academic community. Table 4.7 summarizes what some providers say about their current approaches. Note that providers change their plans rapidly as they learn more about what is required and what makes good business sense.

Standards

The layers of software in end-user devices include several interfaces at which standardization could provide significant benefits. We next discuss these interfaces in decreasing order of importance.

The end-user interface is the most important interface to standardize because it affects users most directly. If each application creates its own unique end-user interface, then multimedia users could find themselves in the position of purchasers of today's CD-ROMs, for each of which they need to learn a different operating paradigm.

The next most important interface to standardize is the logical interface between end-user devices and networks. Although their physical interface, with its connector forms and voltage levels, is likely to be unique for each type of network, the networks' logical interface need not be unique. For example, if the successors to CATV, broadcast, and CD-ROMs use different

Table 4.7 Providers' approaches.

Provider Attribute	Microsoft	Kaleida	Microware	Apple	General Magic	Sun	Geoworks	Oracle	Internet and academia
Major goal	Participate fully in information highway	Cross-platform development tools	Sell operating systems	Software for information highway	New OS for PDAs, then WWW	Servers Java	New OS for information highway	Multimedia client-server database support (client can be set-top box)	Multimedia information communication and information access
Major target device	Set-top boxes and personal computer server	Cross-platform	Set-top boxes, then PDAs	Set-top boxes and WWW	PDAs and WWW	Was set-top boxes, now WWW	Set-top boxes	Client-server environment, then network terminal	Personal computer and workstations
User friendly	High priority	For developer	For developer	High priority	High priority Telescript	For developer	High priority	For developer	Low priority
Scalable	Yes	Transportable	Transportable	Transportable	Transportable	Transportable	Low priority	Yes	Low priority
Cost effective	TBD	Yes for development	Yes	TBD	Yes	Yes	Yes	Yes	Not goal
Low system resources	TBD	Not a goal	Yes	TBD	Yes	Yes	Lightweight	Not a goal	Not goal
Object oriented	Evolving	TBD	TBD	TBD	TBD	Yes	TBD	TBD	Partially

(cont.)

Table 4.7 Providers' approaches. (cont.)

Provider Attribute	Microsoft	Kaleida	Microware	Apple	General Magic	Sun	Geoworks	Oracle	Internet and academia
Cross platform	No	Yes	No	No	Evolving	Yes	No	Evolving	Yes
Unique function in low levels of OS	Yes	No	OS-9 is real time	Yes	Yes	Machine independent	Yes	No	Yes
User's choices presented in new ways	TBD	NA	NA	Yes	Yes	TBD	Yes	TBD	Yes
Enhanced navigation tools	TBD	NA	NA	TBD	Yes	Yes	Yes	Yes	Yes
Enhanced information creation and retrieval tools	TBD	Not a goal	TBD	TBD	Yes	TBD	TBD	Yes	Yes
Application to all media	Yes	Yes	Yes	Yes	Yes	Yes	Yes	Yes	Yes
Development tools	TBD	Yes	DAVID	TBD	TBD	TBD	TBD	Yes	Yes
Evolution	Yes	No	No	Yes	No	No	No	Yes	Yes
Revolution	No	Yes	Yes	No	Yes	Yes	?	No	No

video compression algorithms, then end users might need to purchase and connect different devices to play different program sources, with serious detriment to both cost and convenience. One useful proposal makes each end-user device sufficiently intelligent to receive video that has any available resolution and frame rate and convert the video to whatever resolution and frame rate the particular device can display.

In a sense, the Internet itself is a collection of standards for interconnecting networks. The Internet's most fundamental standards are transmission control protocol and Internet protocol, the famous TCP/IP. One of the many other standards important to Internet users is MIME, a multimedia E-mail standard that defines a range of media types and encoding methods.

The third most important interface to standardize is the application programming interface inside an intelligent end-user device or inside an application server. Having multiple incompatible programming interfaces in different devices might require end users to purchase only corresponding applications, as they did for Intel-based personal computers and Apple Macintosh computers. Several other interfaces should be standard for devices that accept removable media such as CD-ROMs and diskettes.

Because consumer products can generate large sales volumes, the most important standards are those that affect an individual end user. It is less important to standardize interfaces that affect only software and hardware developers. As a result, each of a reasonably large number of different interface definitions can eventually have sufficiently large sales volumes to justify the required separate investments. Standards help software and hardware developers mainly by increasing early volumes for particular designs, so that adequate sales volumes build up more quickly. It is in this early phase that standards can also be detrimental by preventing or delaying innovations that were not available when standards were set, but that nevertheless are necessary for acceptable performance, function, or cost.

HISTORY

In general the history of end-user devices is one of divergence rather than of convergence. A representative example is the proliferation of telephone devices that followed the breakup of AT&T, with its consequent encouragement of connecting other manufacturers' devices to local exchange carriers' local loops.

As with other consumer markets, companies propose new end-user devices but consumers dispose, that is, they decide whether or not to buy. For example, Picture Phone, introduced at the 1964 World's Fair, never sold significant quantities. Thirty years later, AT&T's VideoPhone, similarly, may or may not sell. Intelligent set-top boxes, which are more like computers with CD-ROM drives that use television sets as their displays, than like cable frequency selectors, have not been outstandingly successful. The many competing interactive CD-ROM formats, such as Commodore's CDTV, Philips's and Sony's CD-I, Tandy's VIS, and Kodak's Photo-CD (which allows people to see their photographs on television sets) have had trouble both in attracting creators to write titles for them and in attracting consumers to buy drives that play them.

Today's personal computers had highly diverse ancestors. At the risk of slight oversimplification, designers of the original IBM PCs optimized their hardware and software for text and coarse color graphics; designers of Apple Macintoshes designed for text, graphics, and monochrome images; and designers of Commodore Amigas designed for video. Successors of PCs included PS/2s that delivered significantly better graphics and somewhat better images. Still later ones improved images by increasing the available number of colors and also made audio and video adapters available. Successors of Macintoshes added color and improved resolution for images, made audio standard, and added video adapters.

Designers of the original PC, announced in August 1981, optimized their hardware and software for text that scrolled from top to bottom, like teletype machines. The standard displays were restricted to placing 256 different letters, numbers, and special symbols in a grid that consisted of 80 characters per row and 25 rows. Some of the special symbols, such as vertical line characters, allowed a coarse form of graphics. In the mid-1980s, IBM actually based the design of a graphical user interface software product on such character graphics, believing that few users would pay for the available low-resolution color displays that could address each pixel individually.

The original Macintosh, announced in February 1984, not only provided such an all-points-addressable screen but also included hardware and software that gave applications rapid and standard ways to draw high-resolution graphics as well as many different text fonts. The screens could produce good images, as well, although only in black and white.

Commodore designed the original 1985 Amiga A1000 and subsequent computers to present video on interlaced television screens. The computers included powerful hardware to support such common functions as filling a region with a color and moving several small sprites over a fixed background. As we shall see, video displays are so different from personal computer displays that a computer designed for video tends to perform that function far better than does a computer designed for text and graphics.

These different ancestors produced significantly different organizations in today's personal computers. We have noted that a user can read text at about 42 Bytes per second, whereas a compressed video data stream is roughly 150 K Bytes per second. An uncompressed video data stream is roughly 100 times faster still. Using the compressed video rate, we see that the ratio between typical data stream speeds is

$$(150 \text{ KBps})/(42 \text{ Bps}) = 3571.$$

Such a large factor requires qualitatively different designs, rather than merely making quantitative changes to the same design. For example, video requires different bus organizations, rather than merely faster buses. Amigas have a bus structure that makes them particularly amenable to video adapters such as the NewTek Video Toaster, which produces broadcast-quality video special effects. For contrast, the standard way to add such video capabilities to an Intel-based personal computer is to first add an Amiga computer and then add the Video Toaster adapter to the Amiga.

Table 4.8 presents some dates when end-user devices first became available to consumers in the United States. Edison recorded "Mary Had a Little

Table 4.8 Commercial introduction of end-user devices.

Date	Event
1874	Remington typewriter
1877	Telephone connected to switchboard
1896	Gramophone audio record player
1946	Black-and-white television set
1948	Ampex audiotape recorder
1954	RCA color television set
1960s	Computer terminal
1972	Pong video game
1981	IBM Personal Computer
1980s	Consumer camcorder, cellular telephone, CD-DA
1984	Apple Macintosh
1985	Commodore Amiga
Early 1990s	AT&T VideoPhone
1993	Multimedia Personal Computer

Lamb" on a tinfoil cylinder in 1877. It was almost 20 years before Berliner started selling spring-driven Gramophones that played plastic discs. CD-DA discs did not supplant Berliner's general technology until about 90 years later. Typewriters lasted even longer than plastic disc recordings. Word processors partially supplanted typewriters around 1980, but word processing programs on personal computers did not bury typewriters until about 111 years after typewriters first became available. By comparison, color television appears to have supplanted black-and-white television relatively rapidly. However, it took color sets 18 years to outsell black-and-white sets. Consumers were still buying 5 million black-and-white sets per year 30 years after the introduction of color sets.

Perhaps the oldest still-significant end-user device is paper, manufactured by matting together vegetable cellulose fibers. Table 4.9 shows some dates for paper. The millennia that this end-user device required to achieve its present vigorous maturity makes the 90-year complete lifetime of the phonograph look like a flash in the pan and makes the 20-year adolescence of the personal computer look even shorter. It is in this context that we must estimate when new end-user devices will become prominent and eventually completely displace older technologies.

DIFFERENCES

When companies and end users buy personal computers, technological progress allows them to purchase either far more performance and capacity for the same price or purchase the same performance and capacity for far less money. However, there has been no corresponding major increase in their ability to use such computers to access audio or video over networks. Exist-

Table 4.9 Timetable for paper.

Date	Event
105	Ts'ai Lun first made paper in China
1150	First paper making factory established in Spain
1495	First paper factory established in England
1690	First paper factory established in America
1990s	The United States and Canada the world's largest producers of paper and paper products

ing networks are only gradually increasing their content that is available in media other than text. The only network that has a vastly improved ability to deliver multimedia to homes is the postal service, as a delivery mechanism for CD-ROMs. Achieving end users' vision for distributed multimedia systems requires more than this.

Perhaps the largest gap between what end users might envision for multimedia end-user devices and the corresponding state of the art occurs in the area of ease of use, including ease of installation. End users expect products to be as easy to use as are telephones and television sets. State-of-the-art products that enable end users to create, store, and transmit digital video with synchronized digital audio are instead personal computers with elaborate and intractable configurations of hardware adapters, display accelerators, device drivers, operating systems, operating system extensions, graphical user interface programs, application programs, speakers, microphones, video cameras, attachment cables, and cable adapters. Such devices challenge even experts in media and in computers to set up a new one in less than a month, to add a feature to one in less than a week, to transport one and make it work again in less than several hours, or to keep one running long enough to complete an hour-long demonstration in a workshop. Published evaluations of a random sample of popular computer-based video games report that an expert is doing well if she can get more than half to operate at all on a given computer. End users get lots of practice driving to electronic supply stores for cables and adapters, logging onto bulletin boards to download revised device drivers, and above all listening to music while on hold at telephone help desks. A speaker-phone that allows users to type with both hands while conversing with a help desk operator is one of the most important peripheral devices for a multimedia computer. An end user has the choice between purchasing a computer that does exactly what he wants it to do and never adding a function or learning a wide variety of demanding techniques for determining why a new function does not work and how to fix it. The phrase *plug-and-play* embodies the difference between what is necessary in order to achieve the vision for end-user devices and today's state of the art of such devices. Most of today's personal computers don't have it, and all forms of consumer electronics need it.

TRENDS

Following sections discuss a baker's dozen of trends that affect all end-user devices and particular types of end-user devices. We begin with a section that notes relevant general trends in our society. We next discuss the effects on end-user devices of faster processors and buses, driven by improvements in the performance of digital electronics. The next three sections focus on displays, including clever designs that reduce hardware costs and make the most of slow networks, mix computer and television displays, and make television displays more like both movie theater screens and computer displays. Subsequent sections discuss trends to improve telephones, set-top boxes, and game devices. The last four trends concern taking advantage of miniaturization to move functions from desktop to pocket, improve the ability of different end-user devices to work together, reduce total cost of ownership by making devices more dependent on networks, and leverage corporate alliances to produce the best possible end-user devices.

Changing Environment

End-user devices must change continually to keep up with the rapidly changing environment in which we use them. Some important environmental changes are as follows.

More people spend more of their working time in their homes. More homes have personal computers equipped with multimedia hardware and software. Networks such as Internet and on-line services such as America Online, CompuServe, and Prodigy are becoming extremely popular. Companies and governments are increasing their use of WWW for delivering information and services. Educational environments use more computers, multimedia products, and networks. Mixtures of education and entertainment, sometimes called edutainment, are becoming more significant reasons for home purchases of multimedia computers and multimedia content. End-user devices with increasing computation and communication capabilities are appearing in public locations such as airports and municipal offices. More homes and businesses have fax machines, VCRs, video cameras, and other devices that would be significantly more useful if they could work well together. Interactive television in the United States is suffering a short-term downturn, perhaps as a result of promising more than it could deliver within consumers' attention spans, whereas it is moving ahead strongly in Europe and some other regions.

Faster Processors

Perhaps the least subtle trend is toward end-user devices that are (at least under the covers) economical personal computers with faster processors. Increasingly powerful personal computers are becoming suitable for performing multimedia functions that were previously possible only using engineering workstations. A workstation is often characterized by a reduced instruction set (RISC) processor, an operating system that is some version of UNIX, and specialized hardware that accelerates rendering of 3-D graphics to create animation. Workstations are increasing in performance yearly, retaining some lead over personal computers in terms of integer, floating point, and graphical performance. However, as the trend toward faster personal computers passes a particular function's performance requirement, that function migrates from workstations to lower-priced and easier-to-use personal computers. For example, in the early 1990s, impressive demonstrations showed high-end workstations reading compressed full-motion, full-screen digital video from their hard drives and using their main processors to decompress the video. Now the fastest personal computers can perform this highly useful function.

Workstations are common in the contexts of engineering design, academic research, and the federal government. People working in these contexts often develop prototypes of a product on workstations and then wait for personal computer performance to catch up before deploying large volumes of the product. With IBM's and Apple's introduction of the PowerPC RISC chip, which is capable of emulating personal computers' Intel 8386, 8486, and Pentium complex instruction set computer (CISC) processors, entire systems may be built that appear to be both personal computers and workstations in the same physical box. There is a trend toward merging the best features of RISC and CISC processors onto a single microprocessor chip, to further converge these technologies. In another sort of convergence, Microsoft's high-end NT operating system runs not only on the CISC 8x86 processors but also on such RISC processors as PowerPC and Digital Equipment Corporation's Alpha.

The path that leads toward processors that will perform important multimedia functions more quickly has several steps. The first step increases general-purpose processors' clock frequencies and data path widths. Fifteen years after a typical processor used a 4.7-MHz clock rate and processed 8 bits at a time, we now see clock rates moving from 100 MHz to above 200 MHz and data paths widening from 32 bits to 64 bits. The second step starts with a general-purpose processor and adds a few special-purpose multimedia instructions. Intel's P55C Multimedia Pentium and Sun's Ultrasparc are examples of taking this step. For example, Ultrasparc has several instructions that perform functions on all of the red, green, and blue dimensions of a pixel at the same time, rather than requiring three successive instructions. A group of 30 additional instructions allow the processor to decompress full-motion MPEG-2 digital video. The third step yields a digital signal processor (DSP) chip, which contains data paths that are particularly adept at performing several functions that relate to digital media, but which is not suitable for running a general-purpose operating system or a complete application. High on this step is the Mpact Media Engine from Chromatic Research and Toshiba. Its many data paths, controlled by a very long instruction word (VLIW) program, carry all the elements of several vectors at once, in order to accelerate 2-D graphics, 3-D graphics, audio, fax, fax modem, telephony, and video conference functions (Ristelhueber, 1995). The fourth step follows this path to its end, reaching a single-purpose chip, such as one that performs only MPEG-2 decompression but performs that function exceedingly rapidly. At least one chip manufacturer seems to put one foot on each of the second and third steps by simply packaging DSP data paths on the same silicon chip that contains a computer's main processor. There is a clear trend to take these steps, but there is no clear trend to stop on any one of them.

Faster Computer Buses

We have noted that audio and video require significantly higher data rates than do text, graphics, and images, which were the media that personal computers were originally designed to process. As a result, there is a trend toward providing a personal computer with a special, fast bus for functions such as video decompression that need higher speed, rather than a trend toward increasing the speed of a personal computer's main device attachment bus.

Table 4.10 illustrates the peak transfer rates of several important personal computer buses. In the late 1980s, IBM and other manufacturers attempted to replace the industry standard architecture (ISA) bus by the micro channel architecture (MCA) or extended industry standard architecture (EISA) buses, which could transfer information three or four times faster. In the early 1990s, it became clear that the ISA bus was sufficiently fast to attach slow devices, such as modems and printers, but the MCA and EISA buses were not sufficiently fast to attach fast devices, such as displays, hard drives, and optical networks. This realization led to the development of the peripheral component interconnect (PCI) bus and Video Electronics Standards Association (VESA) or VL bus. The trend is to provide both an ISA bus and a fast bus. Whereas an inexpensive adapter card can upgrade a typical personal com-

Table 4.10 Personal computer bus transfer rates.

Bus	ISA	MCA	EISA	VESA	PCI
Width, in bits	16	32	32	32	32
Peak transfer rate, in MBps	8	20	33	66–130	264

puter to handle high-color or true-color displays, and processor upgrades are quite common, about the only way to provide a fast bus is to replace the computer.

There is a similar trend toward providing high-speed external peripheral interfaces, in addition to existing slow interfaces such as serial and parallel ports. The most promising such high-speed interfaces are serial storage architecture (SSA), Fiber Channel, and IEEE 1394 also known as Firewire (Costlow, 1995).

High-Color and True-Color Displays

There is a trend toward displays that can show 65,000 colors or 16 million colors. This amounts to a trend away from displays that use palette tables to show only 16 or 256 colors. In the sections of Chapter 1 in which we described images and video, we discussed the characteristics that a computer display must have in order to show these media with acceptable quality. We noted that a display's perceived quality depends not only on its resolution— that is, its number of pixels per row and its number of rows per frame—but also on its color depth—that is, the maximum number of different colors that it can show at one time. We noted that a typical computer that people bought in the 1980s can display a palette of only 16 colors, which is perfectly adequate for displaying graphics but is inadequate for displaying images. We also noted that a typical computer that people bought in the early 1990s can display a palette of 256 different colors, which is marginally adequate for displaying images. Not surprisingly, as images are becoming increasingly important, there is a trend toward high-color and true-color computer display systems, which can handle far more colors and display significantly better images. However, there is more to it than that. The type of display that uses a palette table is particularly poor for displaying video. In this section, we discuss why display systems with palettes are so poor for video and why they are, nevertheless, so common.

The characteristics of a display depend not only on the tube or other screen but also on the display adapter electronics, which are usually packaged inside a computer. The electronics for any display that shows 16 or 256 colors includes both a frame buffer and a separate memory called the palette table or color lookup table (CLUT). Software places an image in the frame buffer and places a carefully selected palette of colors for the image in the CLUT. That is, bits in the frame buffer describe a pixel and bits in the CLUT tell what color the bits in the frame buffer mean. Changing the bits in the CLUT to bits that represent an optimal 256-color palette for each image, before changing the frame buffer to the bits that will display that image, allows such a display to show a moderately respectable image by using only 256 colors. However, the necessity to leave the CLUT unchanged while displaying the many successive images that make up a video clip accounts for the difficulty that such a display has in showing video. When slowly displaying a succession of images, the hardware can load an optimal palette for each image; but when rapidly displaying video, a single palette must suffice for all the images that make up the clip.

Figure 4.5 and Focus 4.3 show and tell how a CLUT works. Focus 4.4 discusses why economic necessities in the 1980s made computers with CLUTs so common today.

Unfortunately, when you consider creating multimedia, you must realize that typical computers that consumers can afford today are significantly better than typical computers that consumers are using today. Moreover, network speed often limits the number of colors that you should use in an image that you create. The same economy that drove computer designers to use small frame buffers drives creators of World Wide Web home pages to use images that have only 16 colors. A full-screen image that contains 307,200 pixels displays significantly faster if the image has only 4 bits per pixel than if the image has 24 bits per pixel. This advantage is independent of whether users who access the home pages have VGA computers or true-color computers.

The optimal end-user device for you depends on whether you are primarily a creator or consumer. If at all possible, you should employ a true-color computer to capture or paint images, even if others will display the images on S-VGA computers that are limited to 256 colors or will use net-

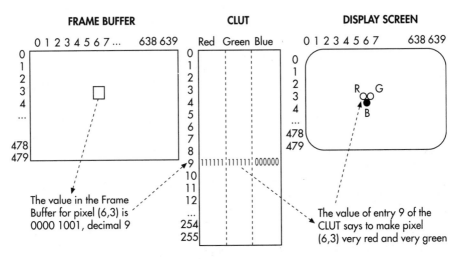

Figure 4.5 Color-lookup table design.

FOCUS 4.3 CLUT operation.

An S-VGA display adapter provides a mode in which it can display any of 256 colors at each of 640 by 480 pixels. As Fig. 4.5 shows, both the frame buffer and the display screen have 640 entries per row and have 480 rows. The CLUT has 256 entries. The image happens to have a bright yellow pixel in column 6 at row 3. As the display's raster scan approaches this pixel, the adapter reads the corresponding Byte from the frame buffer and finds the value 9. The adapter uses that value to look up the desired color in the CLUT. The CLUT contains six bits that tell how red the pixel is, another six bits that tell how green the pixel is, and still another six bits that tell how blue the pixel is. In this case, the adapter finds that the CLUT says to make the pixel as red as possible, because 111111 is as large as the red field of the CLUT can get, and also says to make the pixel as green as possible, but says to not make the pixel at all blue.

If the display screen is a cathode ray tube (CRT), the adapter feeds each of these three six-bit numbers into a corresponding digital-to-analog converter to get the three analog voltages that it sends out through a cable to control the display tube's red, green, and blue electron beams (originally called cathode rays) as the beams paint the given pixel. A liquid crystal display (LCD) performs the same function in a different way. For pixel (6, 3), the analog voltages that control the red and green beams are as large as they can be and the voltage that controls the blue beam is as small as it can be. The result is a bright yellow pixel. (With a magnifying glass, you could see the individual red and green spots; from a normal viewing distance, you see yellow.) The adapter then hurries on to read the value in the frame buffer's next entry to the right, as the raster scan approaches the next pixel, and so on, to completely refresh all pixels as often as 72 times per second.

The CLUT design limits the number of colors the display can show at one time. The 8 bits in each pixel's entry in the frame buffer limit the number of entries in the CLUT to 256. The 18 bits that make up each entry of the CLUT limit any pixel to one of $2^6 \times 2^6 \times 2^6 = 262,144$ colors, which is respectably large. However, the 256 entries in the CLUT further limit a screen to using only 256 of these colors at any one time. The 256 colors that the CLUT's 256 entries describe constitute the palette, that is, the set of colors from which a given screen can select the color of each pixel. If several images are present on the screen at one time, those images must, of course, share the same palette of colors. Software changes the palette by changing the entries in the CLUT. The hardware allows the software to change the palette between successive images, but the hardware is not fast enough to allow the software to change the CLUT between successive images that make up a video clip. Moreover, whenever software changes to a new palette, the screen tends to give an annoying flash. Thus, although a display adapter that uses a CLUT may be acceptable for displaying images, it is poor for displaying video. ∎

FOCUS 4.4 CLUT economics.

But why did designers ever use a CLUT in the first place? The answer is that a small frame buffer and a tiny CLUT cost significantly less than does a large frame buffer with no CLUT. Thus, an S-VGA display adapter, which has a frame buffer that stores only one Byte for each pixel and has a CLUT, costs less than does a high-color adapter, which has a frame buffer that stores two Bytes for each pixel, or a true-color adapter, which has a fame buffer that stores three Bytes for each pixel.

If your screen displays 640 by 480 pixels, and your frame buffer stores three Bytes of information about the color of each of these 307,200 pixels, you need about one million Bytes of frame buffer memory. Hardware reads this memory about 18 million times each second, so it must be fast memory. In the late 1980s, when a typical computer had only a few megabytes of main memory and read that memory only about 1 million times per second, a frame buffer that was almost as large as the main memory and was much faster, would have cost as much as all the other pieces of the computer combined. Storing only eight bits per pixel in such an S-VGA computer required less than $\frac{1}{3}$ MB of frame buffer and kept the cost of the display adapter in line with other pieces.

Prices have declined sufficiently that a typical consumer can now afford a computer that has significantly more than 1 MB of main memory. Such a computer's main processor now reads main memory about as rapidly as special hardware reads the frame buffer. Thus, a consumer probably can afford at least a high-color computer with a $\frac{2}{3}$-MB frame buffer storing two Bytes per pixel. Even true-color computers with resolutions greater than 640 by 480 and three Bytes of frame buffer per pixel are not completely outside the consumer price range. In either case, the frame buffer stores each pixel's actual color, rather than storing an address of an entry in a CLUT where the adapter hardware must look up the pixel's color. High-color displays and true-color displays do not need CLUTs. In many cases, a relatively inexpensive adapter card will upgrade a typical S-VGA computer to a high-color or true-color computer, without changing the relatively expensive display tube. ∎

works that favor 16-color images. Your last step in creating an image may invoke a Paint program's powerful option that reduces an image's color depth to eight (or four) bits per pixel. This program selects the very best 256 (or 16) colors for the particular image and may also use dithering to make the image look better to users who are sufficiently far away from their screens. Similarly, when you create a video clip, you may need to produce a palette that is a reasonable compromise for all the images that make up the clip. In either case, you are unlikely to get acceptable results if you limit yourself to 256 or 16 colors from the outset.

The trend toward high-color displays or even true-color displays, which replace displays that employ palette or CLUT tables, is rapid for people who primarily create multimedia content. However, this trend is frustratingly slow for people who primarily play content that others create. The trouble is that old computers do not rust out. They continue to operate as their designers intended them to function, long after their functions have become obsolete.

Mix Computer Displays and NTSC

A strong trend exists toward mixing the functions of personal computers and television sets. It is often desirable to use a personal computer to display analog video, occupying either the full screen or a small window. Conversely, it is often desirable to use one or more television sets to display a computer's output, for example, to enable a class to see the display. Although some personal computers, such as Apple's Macintosh AV models, have these capabilities as standard features, typical computers require additional hardware, such as a video in a window adapter and a scan converter, to perform these functions.

As you participate in this trend, you should not underestimate the differences between the signal that a computer sends to its display tube and the National Television Standards Committee (NTSC) video signal, which a television station, video camera, or videocassette recorder sends to a television set. Converting a computer display to NTSC form can lead to disappointments. In Chapter 1, we noted that interlace makes a television display unsuitable for showing a horizontal line that has a height of only a single scan line, because such a line flickers annoyingly. We also noted that television screens have lower resolution than do typical computer displays. Consider a computer screen that contains a one-pixel-wide vertical line. After converting the screen to analog video, which has lower effective bandwidth, the line probably disappears altogether. Small text can contain many such narrow lines. Any text with more than about 40 characters across the screen is unreadable on a typical television set.

Another major difference between computer displays and television screens is that a television set cannot display the bright, saturated colors that computer screens typically employ for text and graphics. Focus 1.2 notes that a computer represents a particular color as corresponding amounts of each of red, green, and blue, whereas analog video expresses a color as a combination of luminance, hue, and saturation. A computer transmits color to a display on three wires that give amounts of red, green, and blue, whereas analog video transmits the entire signal on one wire, either as radio frequency or as composite video, or on two wires, as Super-video or S-video. In radio frequency or composite video, a hue is a particular phase of a color carrier signal, of which the amplitude is the saturation. As a result, a computer can display a far wider range of saturated (strong) colors than can a television display. Moreover, whereas a computer can display alternating stripes of saturated colors as well as alternating stripes of black and white, NTSC severely limits the resolution at which a television set can display different colors.

Thus the main disadvantage of using personal computers as bases for multimedia end-user devices is that typical ones require major changes to handle video and other media well. Making such changes may well be easier than starting from scratch. However, the result may cost more because parts of personal computers may stay around long after they are known to be inapplicable. Starting from a partially applicable base also adds an unnecessary level of complexity.

For really good video, personal computers with display subsystems that were optimized for graphics, rather than for natural images, must handle video separately from graphics. Such computers must merge the two media on their way out to the display tube, as we showed in Fig. 1.7. They perform this merging after they convert the graphics from digital to analog form, so the merging process is called *analog multiplexing*. Merging graphics and video together in digital form in a single frame buffer, which is called *digital multiplexing*, would give better results. However, this would require a complete redesign of a personal computer's display adapter with very fast buses, resulting in still higher costs. As hardware prices continue to decline, the trend toward digital multiplexing will accelerate.

High-Definition Television

HDTV represents the trend to converge three technologies. Its designers attempted to take the latest and best features of television, computers, and movies. First, its principal role is to replace the antiquated television broadcast standards, NTSC in North America and Japan, PAL and SECAM elsewhere. Second, its transmission is exclusively digital, like computer networks, no matter whether it travels by way of terrestrial broadcast, satellite broadcast, CATV cable, or other wired networks. Its screens have high definition, higher than today's typical computer screens. Third, its most visible change from NTSC and computers is a larger aspect ratio (display screen width divided by height) that more closely matches the wide screens in movie theaters. In the rest of this section, we discuss the effects of HDTV's wide aspect ratio, digital presentation, and high definition.

HDTV's aspect ratio illustrates the problems and compromises that convergence can involve. Essentially all HDTV proposals have emphasized an aspect ratio of 16:9. Designers explained that this is more theaterlike than NTSC's aspect ratio of 4:3. Indeed, 16:9 sounds larger and more impressive than does 4:3. However, only the ratios matter. When you divide 16 by 9 and divide 4 by 3, you get 1.77 and 1.33, which are easier to compare to the actual aspect ratio of 2.4 that many big-budget movies employ. Figure 4.6 shows HDTV's proposed aspect ratio as the shaded rectangle, which has a corner marked with 1.77. This is indeed wider than the smallest rectangle, marked with 1.33, which corresponds to today's television and computer screens. However, HDTV's rectangle increases the width by less than half the amount that would be required to cover the figure's widest rectangle, which would allow display screens to show an entire movie. Like today's television, although to a lesser extent, HDTV will be forced to show only the center portion of a movie, pan back and forth to show important action that occurs near the edges, or show blank regions above and below the movie in the dreaded letterbox format. To reduce this problem, the American Society of Cine-

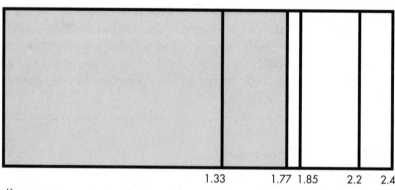

| | 1.33 | | 1.77 | 1.85 | 2.2 | 2.4 |

Key:

1.33 Television and computer displays (4:3)

1.77 HDTV proposal (16:9)

1.85 Narrowest theatrical movies made in the last 40 years

2.2 70-mm movies

2.4 Panavision anamorphic wide-screen movies

Figure 4.6 Aspect ratios.

matographers has recommended that HDTV employ an aspect ratio of at least 2.0 (Wolfe, 1995). Nevertheless, for the rest of this section, we will continue to assume the 1.77 aspect ratio.

Unlike NTSC, HDTV is a digital medium. Whereas NTSC samples a scene as a succession of horizontal scan lines, but uses continuously varying analog signals to represent brightness and color along each line, HDTV samples a scene as scan lines, samples the intensity and brightness along each scan line as a succession of pixels, and uses digital values to express each pixel's brightness and color. One consequence of HDTV's digital nature is a simple measure of horizontal resolution. Whereas we noted in Focus 1.5 that NTSC broadcast television has a number of lines of horizontal resolution that is approximately equivalent to 350 pixels per row, HDTV simply has a number of pixels per row.

How many pixels per row would you think an HDTV screen requires? For a given screen height, an HDTV screen is a little wider than an NTSC screen, so the HDTV signal needs a few more pixels per row than NTSC's approximately 350 pixels. Dividing HDTV's aspect ratio of 1.77 by NTSC's aspect ratio of 1.33 and multiplying the result by NTSC's number of pixels per row gives 466 pixels per row for HDTV. Then why did HDTV's designers decide upon either 1280 or 1920 pixels per row? Why did they increase the number of visible scan lines from NTSC's 480 to either 720 or 1080? The answer to both questions is that designers expect you to sit closer to an HDTV set than to an NTSC set. Sitting closer and viewing a screen with a wider aspect ratio make a movie appear more realistic. If NTSC makes you feel that you are watching actors through a small window, HDTV should make you feel that you are part of the action. Presumably, the same effect would make a game, business video conference, or family video conference more interactive.

Focus 1.3 used a physiological result to quantify the idea that, if you get too close to an image, you see pixels rather than the image. Focus 4.5 uses the same result to indicate how close you must sit to an HDTV set in order to take advantage of its high resolution.

Not only is HDTV digital video, but it is compressed digital video. Compression allows a broadcast station to transmit an HDTV signal at 20 Mbps over the same 6-MHz-bandwidth channel that now carries a lower-resolution signal. Some broadcast companies, however, would like to use digital video compression in different ways. They might like to transmit 10 standard definition television (SDTV) signals over one such channel. Alternatively, they might like to use the channel for one or two SDTV signals and a lot of other information that customers will pay to receive. SDTV proposals use the same 480 visible scan lines as NTSC, so they are suitable for viewing from the same distances as today's television sets and computer displays.

FOCUS 4.5 How close is close enough?

As aspect ratio measures a screen's width in terms of the screen's height, viewing ratio measures your eye's distance from the screen in terms of the screen's height. If your computer screen is 8 inches high and you view it from a distance of 16 inches, your viewing ratio is 2. If your television screen is 30 inches high and you watch it from across the room, 15 feet away, your viewing ratio is 6.

In Focus 1.3, we noted that you can see individual pixels when your viewing distance is less than about 2000 times the size of each pixel. If each of your S-VGA computer screen and NTSC television screen has 480 scan lines, you can see individual pixels when your viewing ratio is less than about

$$2000/480 = 4.16.$$

That is, you can see the scan lines when you sit closer than about 4.16 times the height of the screen. This critical viewing distance is 33 inches for the computer screen and 125 inches or 10.4 feet for the television screen. For the distances we assumed, you can see the computer's individual scan lines clearly, but you could move almost 5 feet closer to the television set without seeing any scan lines.

Now suppose that you replace the screens on your computer and your television set by HDTV screens of the same heights. Multiplying the two screen heights by the old and new aspect ratios shows that your computer screen's width increases from 10.6 inches to 14.1 inches and your television screen's width increases from 40 inches to 53.1 inches. (You might want to stop reading, make similar calculations for your actual computer screen and television set, hold a ruler up to the screens, and decide how excited the extra widths would make you.)

Suppose further that each of your new HDTV screens had 1080 scan lines, rather than 480. Now you can see the scan lines when your viewing ratio is less than about

$$2000/1080 = 1.85,$$

which means your critical viewing distances are 14.8 inches from the computer screen and 55.5 inches or about 4.6 feet from the television screen. From your original viewing distances, going to HDTV makes your computer screen look somewhat sharper, because you are now just beyond the distance at which your eyes can resolve individual pixels, but HDTV makes your television screen look absolutely no sharper. Sitting 15 feet away, you were 5 feet beyond the critical distance; now you are 10 feet beyond the critical distance. In neither case do you see any scan lines or other significant effects of limited resolu-

(cont.)

FOCUS 4.5 How close is close enough? (*cont.*)

tion. To check this, glance back at Fig. 1.4 and note that the two images look about equally good, when you are far enough away that your eyes do not see the pixels in either image.

Now we can answer this focus' question. For our examples, you can see that your new HDTV computer screen is sharper than your old S-VGA screen whenever your eyes are within the S-VGA screen's critical distance of 14.8 inches. You will see that your new HDTV screen is sharper than your old NTSC screen if you move up within the NTSC screen's critical distance of 10.4 feet. In fact, to make the most of your investment, you should move to 4.6 feet from the HDTV television screen, which is the closest you can sit without seeing scan lines or pixels. In general, what HDTV's higher resolution is all about is that it allows you to decrease your viewing ratio from 4.16 to 1.85.

If you want a head start on HDTV television, just move up so that your viewing ratio is 4.16, that is, move in to a viewing distance that is 4.16 times your NTSC screen's height. If you like that and want more, HDTV is for you. If you wanted to sit 15 feet from the screen, you would need an HDTV screen that is 15 feet/1.85 = 8 feet high and is therefore 1.77 × 8 feet = 14 feet wide. You might prefer to get a smaller HDTV screen and rearrange your viewing room so that you sit closer. ■

One SDTV proposal uses 640 pixels per scan line, which makes computer manufacturers and users very happy. However, another SDTV proposal uses 704 pixels per scan line, which makes computer people squirm. The trouble is that 704/480 = 1.46, which matches neither today's 1.33 aspect ratio nor HDTV's 1.77 aspect ratio. Yet the proposal suggests using 704 × 480 for both aspect ratios. How can that be done? By using pixels that are not square! That is, this proposal involves transmitting a 1.33 aspect ratio signal by making each pixel higher than it is wide and transmitting a 1.77 aspect ratio signal by making each pixel wider than it is high. This is not a desirable convergence technology. With square pixels, computer graphics that involve circles always show up with circles, although the sizes differ on different screens. Without square pixels, computer programs need separate routines to make circles look circular on different display devices. Similarly, images require special processing to avoid letting rectangular pixels make people and automobiles look squashed or stretched.

The Federal Communications Commission (FCC) recognizes that the most important part of HDTV may be the increased flexibility that digital transmission allows. FCC Chairman Reed Hunt has proposed to emphasize this part by changing the name from HDTV to digital television (DTV) (Leopold and Yoshida, 1995). Others use advanced television (ATV) as an even less specific name.

Higher-Function Telephones

Expanded telephones are beginning to extend the state of the art well beyond plain old telephone service (POTS). Many telephones now store numbers that a user can dial with few keystrokes or even with voice commands. Some public telephones have display screens that show operating menus in selected languages. AT&T's VideoPhone adds a screen that shows color video at between 5 and 10 frames per second, over normal telephone circuits.

Both VideoPhones and fax machines use symmetric digital compression and decompression algorithms, which have been key to making video and image transmission acceptable and will be key to further improvements. VideoPhone also uses audio compression in order to integrate video with audio over a single normal connection.

A user can partly integrate image with audio by employing the same local loop for either fax or voice. However, using one local loop for both purposes is clumsy, because either use ties up the loop for the other use. Moreover, it can be unclear whether a person, a fax machine, or an answering machine should answer a ringing telephone. Some information services allow a customer to place a telephone call from a fax machine and use its touch pad to request that information be faxed back on the same connection. Many information services accept calls and touch-tone specification of the information desired (Day, 1995).

Typically, neither fax nor audio is well integrated with computers. Few computers have even an interface to dial voice calls. Many computers with laser printers sit beside fax machines, which contain printers that produce lower-quality printouts at higher cost, and which contain scanners that would enable the computers to create images.

AT&T's Sage proposal is a revised telephone that contains software and circuitry to manage digitized information coming into a home. This unit would accept plug-in cards that mimic an existing application or connect to another device. It would store messages, act as a set-top box to use a television receiver as its display, connect a personal computer to a network, connect a video camera to phone lines to send video calls. Sage extends the telephone to become an open-architecture communications platform (Ziegler, 1994).

AT&T's Picasso telephone can compress and transmit an image stored on a personal computer, cassette tape, Photo-CD-type CD-ROM, camera, or document scanner, in real time, with a telephone as the end-user device. Picasso is thus a mixed-media migration device for people who do not have ISDN. Its use imposes no extra network service charge. This is a special case of a more general vision of an advanced telephone as a private branch exchange (PBX) that manages all of a home's digital communications.

More-Powerful Set-Top Boxes

There is a trend toward extending the functions of a set-top box far beyond its present functions of selecting one signal from the many signals on a cable and, if necessary, decoding or deciphering the selected signal. At least one trial's set-top box has more processing power than does a high-end personal computer. What do the dinosaurs in *Jurassic Park* have in common with the 3-D graphical user interfaces in Time Warner's trial in Orlando, Florida? Both result from the processing power of a Silicon Graphics workstation!

Designers can model the visible surface of a fictional dinosaur or of a cylindrical band of numbered television channels as an enormous collection of points in three-dimensional space (equivalent to giving each point's distances north, east, and up, relative to a given point of origin) and specifying a color or texture for each part of the surface. A computer can determine the appearance of the model's surface from a given viewpoint and, if the model moves or the viewpoint changes, can compute changes in the model's appearance. Because personal computers have not yet become sufficiently powerful to perform the required computations within reasonable times, producers of *Jurassic Park* and developers of Time Warner's trial in Orlando selected Silicon Graphics workstations to do the computations more quickly. In the former case, the workstations' high cost did not matter; in the latter case, the price should drop to acceptable levels before the trial gives way to massive deployment.

Giving a set-top box the power of a workstation is an extreme case of the trend toward more powerful set-top boxes. Although Silicon Graphics' is not the only RISC-based workstation slated for set-top box duty, many trials of video on demand settle for significantly less expensive set-top boxes. Such boxes may present only two-dimensional graphics (giving each point's distance right and down, relative to the top left corner of the display screen) or simple text menus. No matter whether the interface uses 3-D graphics, 2-D graphics, or text, such a set-top box runs an application program that presents a user with choices, receives the user's response, and decides what screen or program to show the user next. By this definition, a personal computer or workstation becomes a set-top box when connected to a television display just as, from a different point of view, the television display becomes a computer's peripheral device.

One reason to favor a trend toward set-top boxes with more processing power is the enormous ability of software to change a processor's function. For example, given a processor with an interface for controlling several VCRs or video cameras, there is no reason for a customer to purchase a separate setup in order to perform nonlinear editing, such as combining selected parts of two different tapes to make a third tape. See the References section for articles about many important set-top boxes.

More-Powerful Game Devices

Today's trend is toward video game units that have rapidly increasing hardware performance along with specialized hardware that assists graphics, audio, and video. The video assistance applies primarily to animation, but also may include natural video. Many such units connect to home televisions, similarly to set-top boxes; others contain their own display screens. Their ease of use suffices, at least, for teenage boys. They are not general-purpose, open, programmable computers, and they are not often viewed as general-purpose end-user devices suitable for homes or businesses, but they contain many powerful components that could appear in set-top boxes and personal computers. On benchmarks that compare display capabilities, relatively inexpensive video game machines often perform better than personal computers and perform about as well as some workstations. Game machines' hardware specifications, too, can be impressive. The hardware components of two impressive game machines are as follows.

Atari's Jaguar

- Processor runs 55 MIPS.

- Screen displays 16 million colors.

- Special-purpose hardware renders 3-D polygons.

- System bus is 64 bits wide and has 106.4 M Byte per second peak bandwidth.

- A 64-bit RISC graphics processor performs shading and rotation.

- Programmable object processor provides video functions, a sprite engine, pixel-mapping, and character-mapping.

- Digital signal processor executes 27 MIPS.

- Sound is CD-DA-quality including stereo.

- High-speed synchronous interface connects by way of a modem to a high-performance network such as a CATV cable.

- General-purpose MC68000 processor performs control functions.

- Price is about $200.

3DO

- Processor is 32-bit, RISC architecture, moving to the PowerPC.

- Includes CD-ROM drive

- Includes two graphics-animation processors

- Displays 64 million pixels per second with interpolation

- Digital signal processor handles simultaneous sources of audio data without burdening the main processor or other system resources.

- Includes video processor and math co-processor, and digital video encoder

- Peak bandwidth is 50 M Bytes per second.

- Price is dropping through $700, which is inexpensive for the function it provides, but nevertheless too expensive for limited use in entertainment.

More Handheld Devices

As access to familiar end-user devices becomes increasingly important, there is a growing trend toward more devices that users can carry around with them. Examples of handheld devices are Sony's Data Disc Man, which plays electronic books distributed in a form that looks like a smaller version of CD-ROMs, Apple's Newton, which is a personal digital assistant (PDA) that specializes in recognizing its user's handwriting, Hewlett-Packard's 200LX palmtop, and HP's Omni laptop. Among the hardware components represented in such devices are the following: infrared transmitter and receiver; personal computer memory card international organization (PCMCIA) or PC card expansion slot; serial port connector; LAN connector; main printed circuit board; and battery with external unit for line power and recharging. Such a device may come packaged with a sleek small case weighing under one pound, compact enough to fit in some pockets. The size of the LCD screen is severely limited by case size. The device may have a pen input region, usually the LCD screen.

The Apple Newton has an ARM RISC processor with 46 instructions and a 25-MHz clock. Operating from 18 to 25 MIPS peak, it is a 0.8- to 1.0-micron complementary metal oxide semiconductor (CMOS) chip. The processor has its own custom software and end-user graphical user interface (GUI).

A user who carries a portable device can be sure to have a familiar unit anywhere and any time. Such a device may perform many functions without communicating with other devices but may allow wired or wireless connections when communication is desired. The device might look more like a paperback book than like a computer.

All the compromises that make a handheld device small and light enough to carry create corresponding disadvantages that devices in fixed locations do not have. The most general disadvantage is a small screen, because the normal size screen typical of almost every fixed device would, by itself, disqualify the device from being handheld. The next most general disadvantage is lack of a standard keyboard because, again, a full-sized keyboard alone is too big to carry. Equally obviously, a device that must be portable needs a battery. Both size and weight limit the time that a battery can power the device. Less obviously, there is little reason to foresee development of a handheld battery that can supply enough power to broadcast a meaningful duration of live full-motion video, so such devices' interaction will not include a return path of video within this book's vision horizon.

Standard Control Interfaces

There is a trend for set-top boxes, television sets, VCRs, and other components that make up an end-user device to respond as parts of a single system to a single set of controls. Focus 4.6 provides a scenario that illustrates today's problem of a collection of successive afterthoughts. Standardizing the control interface could help to solve this problem.

The 1992 Cable Act charged the Federal Communications Commission (FCC) with ensuring compatibility among CATV networks and consumer electronic components. One goal was to enable consumers to purchase set-top boxes at retail stores, as a way of encouraging competition and reducing prices. A joint committee of the Electronics Industry Association (EIA) and the National Cable Television Association (NCTA) responded to the Act's challenge, working with members of the Interactive Multimedia Association (IMA), Video Electronics Standards Organization (VESA), and Digital Audio-Video Council (DAVIC). This diverse committee produced a

FOCUS 4.6 A control scenario.

You buy a cable-ready television set, that is, one that knows the frequencies of CATV channels, as well as broadcast channels. You get with it an infrared remote control unit that can change channels, brightness, volume, and so on. You connect your new set to the cable, tell the set to use the cable frequencies, and sit down to watch.

Some time later, you decide that you want to record programs for later viewing, so you buy a VCR. You disconnect the cable from your television set, reconnect the cable to the new VCR, and run a short piece of coaxial cable from the output of the VCR to the television set. Now you use the VCR's remote control unit to change channels. The VCR converts whatever channel you select to Channel 3 (or perhaps 4) and sends the selected signal to the television over the new piece of coax. You leave the television set tuned to Channel 3 and continue to use the television set's remote control to set brightness and volume. You learn to enjoy using the VCR's remote control to program the VCR to turn itself on at a given time, change to a given channel, and record for a given interval.

Still later, you subscribe to a few of your CATV company's additional channels. Your VCR cannot receive these encoded or enciphered channels. As part of the channels' additional cost, the CATV company provides you with a set-top box that can decode or decipher the new channels. You disconnect the cable from your VCR, reconnect the cable to the new set-top box, and run a second short piece of coax from the output of the set-top box to the input of the VCR. You tune the VCR to receive Channel 3 and use the remote control unit that came with the set-top box to select channels.

Because you dislike juggling three remote controls, you buy a universal remote control that knows how to command the set-top box to change channels, the VCR to record and play, and the television set to change brightness and volume. You pause briefly to admire the standardization that allows all three devices to work together and even use identical coaxial cable connectors. Although you realize that connecting the VCR ahead of the television set was an afterthought and that connecting the set-top box ahead of the VCR was another afterthought, it seems that aside from a little signal degradation and wasting the money you paid for channel-selection capabilities in the VCR and the television set, you have not lost much. The universal remote control is a third afterthought that seems to take most of the sting out of the first two. *(cont.)*

FOCUS 4.6 A control scenario. (*cont.*)

Having programmed the VCR to record two shows, you go out for the evening. When you return, you find that the VCR did not record your shows. You realize that you programmed the VCR to switch to the shows' successive channels. The VCR switched from Channel 3 to the channels you specified, on which the set-top box put no signal, so the VCR recorded two hours of nothing whatever. You find that the afterthoughts cost you some function, after all. Your VCR can accept a program that includes desired times and channels, but your set-top box cannot accept a program, and your VCR cannot command the set-top box to switch channels.

A specialty retailer offers to sell you a prosumer VCR that has a wire running to a small unit that can control your brand of set-top box. The unit consists of an infrared transmitter that sits in front of the set-top box's infrared receiver. You are not quite sure whether this fourth afterthought is clever or absurd. You have heard that your CATV company is about to change to newer set-top boxes that receive digital signals. You are considering buying a digital direct broadcast satellite unit that has its own set-top box for selecting channels. You wonder if the prosumer VCR will know how to command the two new boxes, let alone switch from one to the other. Next, you realize that each of the two new boxes has its own infrared remote control unit that contains functions that your not-so-universal remote control never heard of, so your coffee table will again be cluttered with remote controls. Somehow, standardizing the coaxial cable connectors on set-top boxes, VCRs, and television sets no longer seems to be sufficient. You need a standardized way to control all the parts of your system. ■

draft specification based on a bus that gave all connected components access to not only television signals but also commands from a user's remote control unit.

In early 1995, the NCTA insisted on modifying the draft standard to allow every CATV company's component to bypass the control part of the bus. The kindest comment was that this bypass would make the draft standard, at best, irrelevant. Members of the committee are not sure whether they should be most worried that the FCC might step in and decree a standard, that Congress might repeal the 1992 Cable Act and remove that impetus for members of the committee to work together, or that consumers might stop buying products that do not work with other products. Everyone involved realizes that the draft standard applies only to one-way analog video, rather than to the more interesting two-way digital video. The trend toward convergence of companies that wrongly consider themselves to be parts of different industries is not a smooth one.

Less Self-Sufficient Devices

The total cost of owning a personal computer can be astonishingly high, when you include not only its purchase price but also the time and money that you spend acquiring the skills necessary to install and upgrade its software and the time you spend performing other chores such as backing up its data. Although a high cost of ownership and a high skill level may be appropriate for a self-sufficient computer, they may not be tolerable for a more network-oriented end-user device that plays a role more like that of a set-top box or a telephone.

One way to reduce the cost of owning an end-user device is to make the device less self-sufficient and more dependent upon a network. By moving some or all of a device's storage or processing to a central location, it should be possible to reduce the device's purchase price and also to take advantage of the economy of scale that exists for many maintenance chores.

It has been said that anything that three people do is a trend. If this is true, then making (or at least discussing) less self-sufficient devices qualifies as a trend. Leaders of IBM, Oracle, and Sun say that they plan to sell such devices for roughly $500 under such names as InterPersonal Computers (IPCs), Internet computers, Net computers, or Net-ready PCs. Part of the appeal of the trend toward less self-sufficient end-user devices is that this trend could become the next paradigm shift, akin in importance to the earlier shift from mainframes and minicomputers to personal computers. Everyone knows that, after a paradigm shift, companies that were followers have a new chance to become leaders; therefore many companies seem to feel that it is time for a shift. Conversely, leaders seldom retain their lead after a paradigm shift, so Microsoft and Intel see no need to change today's personal computer paradigm. Less self-sufficient end-user devices are attractive for technical reasons in addition to political reasons.

Chapter 3's section titled More Options for Function Splits discussed three positions at which a network could separate an end-user device from a server. As Fig. 3.2 shows, it may be useful to place a network (1) between a file system and an application program, (2) between two parts of an application program, or (3) between the display part of an application program and a display screen. Replacing a self-sufficient personal computer by an end-user device that has a network in any of these three positions would reduce the cost of the device. Moreover, by shifting functions from a user's home or office to a central site, such a strategy would allow professionals to assume the burden of some maintenance. The benefits and network requirements, of course, depend strongly on which of the three places you put the network, that is, on where you split the function between an end-user device and a server.

Using a network in the first position, between a file system and an application program, effectively moves hard drives and file system from an end-user device to a file server. This allows many users to share a single copy of a data file or program file rather than having to maintain and upgrade separate copies of the information on each of their individual personal computers. However, only a good local area network has sufficient bandwidth and interactivity to make a remote server's hard drive appear to be almost as fast as a user's own local hard drive. Downloading a large file over today's wide area networks is notoriously slow, so getting all your program and data by that route would be intolerable until network bandwidths increase significantly.

Using a network in the second position, between two parts of an application program, effectively moves hard drives, file system, and most of an application, but not the part of the application that drives the display, from an end-user device to a partial applications server. This allows the resulting end-user device to have a less expensive processor without requiring an enormous network bandwidth. For example, an application program can compute a collection of points that make up the surface of a 3-D object that a user wants to see and can transmit the points' coordinates over the network in relatively compact form. The display system in the end-user device, running on an inexpensive but powerful special-purpose processor, can then expand these points into a fully rendered view for display on the screen. Another example is an applet, which Java downloads for execution in end-user devices.

Using a network in the third position, between the display part of an application program and a display screen, effectively moves everything except the display screen (with associated video decompression hardware, corresponding functions for other media, such as an amplifier and speakers, and a network interface) from an end-user device to an applications server. This strategy eliminates essentially all user setup complexity and allows professionals at central sites to perform essentially all maintenance. A service provider could even replace an application server's processor by one with a different architecture, and make a corresponding change in software, without affecting end users. Placing an ultimate multimedia network, capable of transmitting unique digital video streams to and from each user, between the display system and the display screen would not reduce overall system speed. However, today's networks have insufficient economy, bandwidth, and interactivity to make this approach attractive, as we discussed at length in Chapter 2. Note that without the requirement for interactivity this approach amounts to HDTV. Without the requirement for high bandwidth, such as in a system that relies on text alone, this approach amounts to the dumb-terminal system designs that were ubiquitous around the 1970s.

Each of these three network positions has significant advantages. Position 1, network between file server and application program, is likely to remain important only in cases where both the end-user device and the server have hard drives. For example, service providers such as Prodigy continually download necessary programs to hard drives on users' devices. Position 2, network between two parts of an application program, is likely to become increasingly popular, particularly among the many people who want to access networks without acquiring sufficient skills to operate and maintain complete personal computers. It is likely to dominate in developing countries and other contexts in which $500 is affordable and $2500 is not. Position 3, network between application program and display screen, will become important gradually, as high-bandwidth fully interactive networks become available and affordable.

Reducing the cost of each end-user device, by making each one more dependent on a network, would help a typical household to afford a reasonable number of such devices. To this end an individual home might have two layers of devices. Tucked away in a closet, an intermediate server that has a moderate degree of self-sufficiency might communicate with several different devices that have less self-sufficiency, sending different content to and from several different screens, as well as communicating with one or more wide area networks. One advantage of using an intermediate server as the interconnection point for several different screens within a home is the opportunity to share information, such as a common list of telephone numbers and addresses, or to transfer a telephone number from an advertisement to such a database. Thus, an intermediate server may be an attractive alternative to both having several fully self-sufficient personal computers in a home and having only end-user devices that are fully dependent upon outside networks.

Significant Alliances

Alliances to create, market, and support end-user devices are being formed. Table 4.11 documents this trend. Note that General Instrument and Scientific-Atlanta are the largest and second-largest set-top box developers and manufacturers.

Table 4.11   End-user-device alliances.

Partners	Purpose	End-user-device highlights	Status
IBM and Bell Atlantic	Early trials	PowerPC; MPEG-2; Microware's David running on OS-9	In development
Microsoft, Intel, and General Instruments (1993 agreement)	Interim product to be completed in 1994 for cable multiple system operators to get into interactivity early	Windows Adaptation on 8x86 architectures and General Instrument adaptation Digi-Cipher and MPEG	Ongoing
3DO, U S WEST, and Digital Equipment Corp.	For U S WEST trials in Omaha, Nebraska, in 1994	Set-top boxes based on 3DO technology	In development
Nintendo and Silicon Graphics	Goal to develop a $250 high-performance game machine	Based on Silicon Graphics' Indy 3-D graphics desktop system	In development
Silicon Graphics, Time Warner, and Scientific-Atlanta	Major trial for interactive cable in Orlando, Florida, with set-top boxes and video servers for video on demand and home shopping	MPEG and MIPS' R4000 derivative	Deployment late 1994 in large trial in Orlando
Silicon Graphics and Kodak	Special effects	Kodak's digital film system for movie studios	In development
Microsoft and TCI	Entering test with partners' employees	Microsoft's Tiger based on Windows NT and ATM switch	

(cont.)

Table 4.11 End-user-device alliances. (*cont.*)

Partners	Purpose	End-user-device highlights	Status
Kaleida passed to IBM, Apple, and Scientific-Atlanta	Goal is set-top box for consumer marketplace	IBM's Power PC Apple's Open Doc IBM's SOM objects Kaleida's ScriptX	Ongoing
Apple, Oracle, and NCube	Client to Oracle's system, goal is possible industry standard	Ease of Use Quick Time extension	Ongoing
Scientific-Atlanta and 3DO	Several projects with IBM, Silicon Graphics, and Time Warner scheduled to be tested by U S WEST in Omaha	Leader in set-top boxes	Ongoing

CRITICAL SUCCESS FACTORS

Critical to the success of multimedia end-user devices envisioned for the next decade are the following factors.

Attractiveness: Devices that appear physically attractive to purchasers.

Functionality: Devices that appear to do whatever is required for both accessing and creating desirable multimedia content.

Human factors: Devices that the customer finds easy to acquire, learn, set up, use, and maintain.

Affordability: Devices that are perceived as affordable and as a good value by the customer.

Video quality: Devices that present video of acceptable quality.

Customer support: Devices that have excellent support services, including one-stop support without finger-pointing.

Provider's profitability: Devices that allow providers of hardware, software, content, and related services to remain profitable in most years.

Provider-friendly architectures: Devices that are built using open, flexible, and scalable architectures with standards that facilitate interoperation of existing devices, without stifling innovation of new devices.

SUMMARY

As separate representations of all five media converge on a single digital form, as prices of digital devices decline, and as separate networks converge on a single digital network, it will become unnecessary to have separate end-user devices for telephony, computation, and television. However, separate devices for private conversations, intensive work, and casual group viewing will remain desirable. Bringing the advantages of multimedia end-user devices to the mass market will require minor increases in performance and major increases in all aspects of ease of use. The following scenarios summarize quandaries that end-user devices pose to members of the mass market.

Video Devices   Mary Smith wants to know if she can use a particular end-user device to make video telephone calls to her daughter in Des Moines. Mary wants to send information that she has collected in planning a family trip to Disney World next year. She also wants her daughter to be able to send video of her new granddaughter.

Mary would like to know if she should purchase an end-user device now or wait until a rumored new video standard appears in six months. She realizes that purchasing one of these devices will not suffice, because her daughter will need some compatible device. Mary is concerned about buying an expensive device that may become obsolete in the next year or two. She wonders whether there will be a way to upgrade whatever she buys.

Interactive Information Devices   Barry Greggor's multimedia service company has been creating stand-alone multimedia presentations and kiosks for businesses in his city for four years. The company specializes in education and training. It also created the airport kiosks that welcome visitors to the area. Barry is interested in some way to add recent information to the kiosks. He would like to develop some prototype content for interactive television. Barry wonders for which of the proposed end-user devices his company should create content.

REFERENCES

Agnew, P. W.; Kellerman, A. S.; and Meyer, J. 1996. *Multimedia in the Classroom.* Needham Heights, MA: Allyn & Bacon, ch. 2, 13, and 14.

Agnew, P. W., and Kellerman, A. S. 1992. "Plugged in." *Computerworld,* May 11, p. 111.

Amt, Fritz. 1994. General Instrument Information Kit. General Instrument Corporation, 2200 Bayberry Road, Hatboro, PA, (215) 674-4800.

Cole, Bernard C. 1994. "Video ICs Inch Toward High Integration." *Electronic Engineering Times,* June 27, pp. 53–90.

Cole, Bernard C. 1995. "Set-top Is Pandora's Box." *Electronic Engineering Times,* January 30, pp. 52–54.

Costlow, Terry. 1995. "Designers Face Serial Challenge." *Electronic Engineering Times,* January 23, p. 1.

Davids, Meryl. 1994. "TV on a Platter (Interaxx Television Network)." *CD-ROM World,* April, pp. 48–53.

Davis, Arnold. 1994. "The Digital Valet, or Jeeves Goes Online." *Educom Review,* May/June, pp. 44–46.

Day, Rebecca. 1995. "Busy Signal—VideoPhone Under Construction." *OEM Magazine,* January, pp. 42–52.

Forman, George H., and Zahorjan, John. 1994. "The Challenges of Mobile Computing." *IEEE Computer,* April, pp. 37–47.

Gibbs, W. Wayt. 1994. "Heads in the Cloud." *Scientific American,* February, pp. 110–113.

GISTICS Inc. 1993. "Interactive Index—Milestones Along the Information Superhighway, Facts, Figures and Figments." *Morph's Outpost on the Digital Frontier.* Orinda, CA: Digital Frontier, November, p. 5.

Gleick, James. 1995. "Watch This Space." *New York Times Magazine,* July 7, p. 14.

Hwang, Diana. 1994. "Choosing the proper input device: Far more than just keyboards." *Computer Reseller News,* August 15, pp. 65–72.

Information Week. 1994. "BIS Strategic Decisions." June 13.

Jack, Keith. 1993. *Video Demystified, A Handbook for the Digital Engineer*. Solana Beach, CA: HighText Publications, p. 178.

Leopold, George, and Yoshida, Junko. 1995. "FCC Plays Activist in Digital-TV Push." *Electronic Engineering Times*, January 23, p. 1.

Loewy, Raymond. 1979. *Industrial Design*. Woodstock, NY: Overlook Press.

McMamee, A. Miles. 1995. Microware Information Kit. Microware Systems Corporation, 501 Silverside Road, Suite 11, Wilmington, DE 19809, (302) 792-8360.

OEM Magazine. 1995. "Inside the Set-Top of Boxes, Bandwidth and Business." Jericho, NY, June (ISSN 1071-8990).

Ozer, Jan. 1995. "Microsoft Fast-Forwards Video Strategy." *PC Magazine*, September 12.

Petroski, Henry. 1992. *The Evolution of Useful Things*. New York: Random House.

Ristelhueber, Robert. 1995. "It's Show (and Tell) Time in Race for Multimedia PCs." *Electronic Business Today*, October, p. 27.

Scientific American. 1994. May, p. 110.

Scientific-Atlanta Annual Report, One Technology Parkway South, Norcross, GA 30092, (404) 903-5000.

"The Great Communicator." 1993. *Discover*, October, p. 74.

Waldrop, M. Mitchell. 1993. "PARC Builds a World Saturated with Computation." *Science*, September 17, pp. 1523-1524.

Wayner, Peter. 1994. "Agents Away." *Byte Magazine*, May, pp. 113–118.

Wilson, Ron. 1995. "Intel to Relaunch NSP Multimedia." *Electronic Engineering Times*, November 13, p. 234.

Wolfe, Alexander. 1995. "Feuds Fulminate, as Feds Finish Up HDTV." *Electronic Engineering Times*, August 7, p. 1.

Yoshida, Junko, and Costlow, Terry. 1994. "Group Races Chip Makers to Set-Top." *Electronic Engineering Times*. February 7, pp. 1, 102.

Yoshida, Junko. 1993. "Infotainment—Hopes to Make Family Interactive." *Electronic Engineering Times*, March 29, p. 41.

Yoshida, Junko. 1995."PC Makers Aiming for Living Room Seat." *Electronic Engineering Times*, January 2, pp. 1, 14.

Yoshida, Junko. 1993. "Set-Top Box Could Be Budget Buster." *Electronic Engineering Times*, November 29, pp. 1, 8.

Ziegler, Bart. 1994. "Future Phone?" *Business Week*, January 24, p. 37.

Chapter 5

Applications

BACKGROUND

The forces that are driving distributed multimedia are primarily improvements that technological advances make possible, rather than applications that potential users consider necessary. As we noted in Chapter 1, no one has yet identified a killer application or a killer suite of applications that will allow today's separate information industries to produce significantly greater profits and revenues by converging than the industries now produce separately.

In this chapter, we discuss eight categories within which today's industries are seeking attractive applications and application suites in order to increase revenues and profits.

1. Desktop video conferences with collaboration

2. Multimedia store and forward mail

3. Consumer edutainment, infotainment, and sociotainment

4. Shopping and advertising

5. Digital libraries

6. Video on demand

7. Educational and health applications

8. Hybrid applications

To address the question of what applications users will want and will be willing to pay for, we devote most of this chapter to scenarios in which fictional characters use what may or may not become typical applications. One point that should not be lost when reading through these scenarios is that the context of the applications differs from today's single-purpose applications or even suites of applications. Not only do the people in the scenarios expect to interact with integrated application suites, but they expect the ability to conduct transactions based on their personal preferences (personaliza-

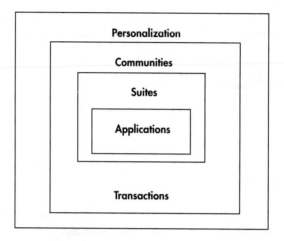

Figure 5.1 The applications' context.

tions). Two additions are critical. The first is the context of applications envisioned: the supporting presence of a virtual community of people to consult through E-mail, chat rooms, forums, or the equivalent. (See Fig. 5.1.) The second critical addition is the support services essential for making the application completely successful. Support services range from providing the customer enough preliminary information so that the customer feels comfortable purchasing that application's offering in the first place, to having it delivered on-line or very rapidly by mail.

We begin by presenting a scenario for each of the eight application categories. In the Vision for the Next Decade section, we present scenarios that involve mixing applications in several categories. In State of the Art, we discuss several specific applications within each category. The History section mentions some key dates for those categories that have a past as well as a future. The Differences section lists some impediments to moving from the state of the art toward the vision that apply to all application categories. The sections titled Trends and Critical Success Factors list directions in which each category appears to be heading and factors that will determine the degree to which applications in each category will succeed.

We do not intend for these application categories to constitute a complete taxonomy of possible applications that the converged information industry could provide. There is a possibility that some killer application will appear outside all of our categories. Moreover, the categories overlap. For example, the applications in category 3, which serve consumers by mixing entertainment with each of education, information access, and socialization, must ultimately include digital libraries and video conferences. Perhaps some important applications will form a killer suite of uses that invoke an unexpected synergy among applications in several categories.

Developers and users have different views of what an application is. From a developer's point of view, an application is the next to highest software layer in a layer chart such as Fig. 5.2. An application's upper boundary is an end-user interface. An application's lower boundary is the application programming interface that lower layers provide. In general, an application runs partly in one or more end-user devices and partly in one or more servers.

From a user's point of view, an application is everything that the user sees of both the software and the hardware, including the delivery network and any other support services. Because the application invokes lower layers' functions, in a sense the application includes the inner parts of the system. Insofar as a user directly commands tools that form part of the base operating environment, these tools are part of the application. As operating system and tools developers recognize common application functions, these functions gradually migrate from multiple implementations in applications to a unified implementation in the operating environment. Some of the most ubiquitous functions even migrate all the way into hardware. A user should see no difference as a result of such migrations.

It is helpful to view multimedia applications as a convergence of today's content and titles, such as movies and books, of today's computer application programs, such as word processors, and of today's network services, such as POTS and on-line bulletin boards. Although there are many more examples of each type, consider just one example. A multimedia book should have the following features. Besides text, the book has other media that the author created, including not only text, graphics, and images but also audio and video, to make the book's content clearer or more enjoyable. Programs should be built-in to help a user navigate through the author's media (besides tables of contents and indexes that merely assist page flipping). With other programs, such as expression evaluators and simulators, users can experiment with the book's concepts (as opposed to dry formulas, static graphs, and nonoperating flow diagrams). A network interface would allow the user to obtain further details about any desired part of the book's material (unlike a list of references) and to obtain recent postpublication information as well. The multimedia book should incorporate a creation tool that a user can use to add related content while maintaining the book's style and tone, either for the user's own benefit or for others. Also valuable is a notepad into which the user can copy and paste notes, which automatically generates citations for information selected. With a corresponding network interface any user of the multimedia book may become a partial co-author of a subsequent edition, derivative work, or sequel.

END USER
    End-user interface

APPLICATIONS
    Content
    Titles
    Solutions

SUPPORT TOOLS
    Multimedia authoring tools
    Software engineering management tools
    Systems administration
    Application enablers
    Programming language compilers
    Hypermedia and hypertext linking tools
    Agent tools
    Browsers
    Tools for capturing, creating, and editing graphics, image, and video

DATA MANAGEMENT FACILITIES
    Object-oriented, relational, and hierarchical databases
    File systems
    Hypermedia link support in operating system
    Agent support

Base operating system and network operating system

Batch, interactive, or real-time support

Input-output device drivers
Hardware interface

Hardware, including end-user device, server, and delivery

Figure 5.2   Software layers.

Arguably the most far-reaching collective impact of multimedia applications will thus be the blurring and gradual disappearance of lines that now separate readers from authors, moviegoers from producers and directors, program users from programmers, and, in general, amateurs from specialists. Multimedia makes only a few new functions possible for specialists, but multimedia makes many functions easy and economical for amateurs. With few exceptions, anything an amateur can do with today's multimedia personal computers, specialists such as military people and movie producers could do a decade or two ago with enormously expensive unique multimedia hardware and supercomputers. Multimedia lowers the admission fees to clubs that only specialists used to be able to afford.

Distributed multimedia promises to make publication easy for millions of amateurs, rather than barely possible for the far fewer specialists who can now establish reputations and get funding that enables them to embark on producing a movie, publishing a book, writing a program, or creating any other sort of content. We assert without proof that the best content that millions of amateurs will be able to create and distribute by means of distributed multimedia will be significantly more valuable than the best that today's far fewer specialists can create. Of course, the average value of future amateurs' content will be significantly lower than the average value of present professionals' content, if only because economic pressures now prevent bad books and movies from ever seeing the light of day. Thus your outstanding problem with using multimedia content will be finding the tiny fraction that has high value to you at a given moment.

A successful multimedia application must be both economical and easy to use. An application will fail if it requires a user to make an excessively large investment, either in money or in the time and effort required to learn to use the application. Requiring a large investment limits the application's users to specialists, which destroys the fundamental advantage of multimedia applications.

Today, getting a book, essay, or poem into bookstores requires a very strong push, as does getting a movie into theaters or television channels. Multimedia applications will greatly reduce the amount of push required to make creations that use multiple media available to large numbers of people. The result will be useful only if other multimedia applications allow people to pull what they want and need, easily and cheaply. It would not be an improvement to merely replace the requirement for a few strong pushes by the requirement for many difficult pulls.

Multimedia's driving technologies, mainly digital electronics and fiber-optic communications, are making more and more functions sufficiently economical for consumers to use. However, making applications sufficiently compelling that consumers will want to use them, and sufficiently easy that consumers will be able to use them, is more than a matter of hardware. Making applications compelling and easy to use will require vast amounts of inspiration and perspiration. Again without proof, we assert that the very best multimedia applications are likely to result from empowering millions of amateurs to contribute applications to the world of on-line information. That world must therefore be open to amateurs who create applications.

Desktop Video Conferences with Collaboration

Scenario   Charles Goodman lives in Cleveland, Ohio. His daughter and her baby live in Albany, New York. Goodman routinely conducts business meetings using video conferencing. What he enormously enjoys much more is his daily video conference between his home and his daughter's home. The baby already recognizes her grandfather's face on the computer screen. As he reads her a story, she responds to his oral prompting by pointing at specific pictures. The pictures and her pointer appear in both Cleveland and Albany. Goodman intends to include his son, who lives in Florida, in a future video conference. These video conferences allow members of an extended family to share one another's lives, despite their physical separation.

Definition   Desktop video conferences with collaboration involve transmitting live real-time video and audio over a network. Transmission may be two-party (one on each end) or multipoint (many participants). Users can see and modify common shared visual materials, such as photographs, word processor screens, and spreadsheet screens.

Video conferences make severe demands on a network, for three reasons. First, high-quality video requires far more bandwidth than does audio. Thus video conferences tend to be far more expensive than POTS, because many network operators charge more or less in proportion to bandwidth as well as in proportion to the time for which a user ties up that bandwidth. Users can reduce communication costs by settling for lower-quality video and by performing more sophisticated video compression and decompression. Hardware-assisted compression can significantly increase users' investment in equipment.

Second, video conferences require a network to provide a constant delay, because each of video and audio is an isochronous medium and because these media must be synchronized with each other. For example, sending the end of a video clip with less delay than the beginning of the video clip is as bad as sending the end with greater delay. Similarly, sending audio earlier than the video with which the audio must synchronize is as bad as sending the audio later. Today's predominantly text-optimized networks provide best-can-do delivery that is a disaster for video conferences.

Third, video conferences require a network to provide a short delay, because this is a real-time application. One or more people are actually present at each end of the connection, at the same time. People can interact with other people over a network that has a total delay of less than about ¼ of a second. The value of a video conference drops sharply when the total delay becomes so long that users feel the need to say, "Over," each time they finish a thought and expect another party to start talking. A sharp drop in value, when delay exceeds some characteristic number, is the defining characteristic of such real-time applications, which also include rocket guidance and numerical milling machine control.

Multimedia Store-and-Forward Mail

Scenario   Cynthia Lemon is reviewing and annotating Tom Keefe's chapter from a book for which she is overall editor. She uses her multimedia E-mail system to enter audio for general comments. She uses text, graphics, and image to mark up corresponding media in Tom's chapter.

After working through the chapter, Cynthia uses video to make a sandwich in which the bread is tasty, even if the meat is tough. She makes a video clip of her face and voice as she starts with an encouraging summary of her comments that Tom will see and hear before he reads her detailed annotations. She makes another video clip that Tom will see and hear afterward. In this video, she compliments his work and prioritizes the areas on which he should concentrate, to insure that his next draft will be his last draft.

Cynthia combines the two video clips, Tom's original chapter, and her annotations into an ordered compound multimedia document and sends the result through her local service provider's gateway onto the Internet and then to Tom's local service provider. Tom can access the document at his leisure, play it over as required, and clip pieces out of it as he updates his chapter.

Definition   An application in the multimedia store-and-forward mail category allows users to create, modify, and receive documents that contain multimedia. Nearly everyone should be able to create mail that contains not only text, but also graphics, images, audio, video, and hypermedia links. Sending such mail should be easy, efficient, available, and economical.

Mail applications make much less severe demands on a network than do real-time video conference applications. Mail can tolerate a network that has low bandwidth and that introduces long delays. Delays can occur in the slow connections that forward the information, in compression and de-compression, and on hard drives that store the information between times when the information is forwarded. Although quick delivery is more valu-able than long-delayed delivery, only the actual playback must present isochronous media at the correct rate and must synchronize audio and video with each other and with text, graphics, and images. In a sense, reestablishing the media's original isochronous rate and original synchro-nization, as the network presents the information to the receiver, constitutes endowing the network with a constant delay, even though that delay may be hours long.

Mail's value drops smoothly as delay increases. This is in sharp contrast to any real-time application, where the value drops sharply at some critical point at which the delay becomes, in some sense, intolerably long.

Making relatively gentle demands on a network does not necessarily make multimedia mail economical. One minute of good-quality compressed video requires roughly 9 MB of information, independent of whether a net-work whisks the information over a high-bandwidth T1 line in 1 minute in real time or dribbles the information over a 24-times-slower voice-grade line in 24 minutes. Insofar as a carrier charges proportionally to bandwidth and proportionally to time of tying up the bandwidth, sending a given amount of video rapidly or slowly costs about the same. Although a slower line costs fewer dollars per minute, economy of scale often makes a faster line more economical, when measured in total dollars per bit sent. If a network can store mail and can wait to forward the mail over spare capacity or at night when rates are lower, mail can be somewhat cheaper than real-time trans-mission. However, renting space on the hard drives that store the video counteracts some of mail's cost advantage.

The most fruitful methods for making multimedia mail more economi-cal are to use video that requires fewer Bytes per minute of presentation, that is, to accept lower-quality video, and to use more powerful compres-sion and decompression algorithms. Of course another approach is to sign up for an economical multimedia E-mail service. One way is to look for a flat-rate service.

Consumer Edutainment, Infotainment, Sociotainment

Scenario   Janet and Nathan are senior citizens. Although they live thou-sands of miles apart and have never met, they communicate daily over E-mail. They personalize their messages with animated pictures of them-selves, which they create in response to their feelings and moods. The self-images that they project may have no relation to their actual appearance, gender, or even species. As the famous *New Yorker* cartoon has it, "On the Internet, nobody knows you're a dog." Janet and Nathan use E-mail to discuss mostly their triumphs and sometimes their failures. They use the network to play interactive games against remote computers, against each other, and against other players. They then use the network to discuss the games' outcomes. When they are not engaged in this activity they sometimes enjoy participating in choosing their own plot twists in interactive on-line books and movies. Sometimes they participate with other people around the country in jointly selecting stories' endings. When something newsworthy or merely interesting occurs in their communities or lives, Janet and Nathan place their own video clips on the network for general viewing. They remember when they were couch potatoes; they are glad they became mouse potatoes.

Definition Consumer edutainment, infotainment, and sociotainment begin with education, information, and socialization; they all end with entertainment. Entertainment helps consumers distinguish these applications from work, even when the results are useful and productive. Moreover, making tasks entertaining encourages consumers to spend more time on the tasks and to achieve more significant outcomes. As a result, consumers are willing to pay more for the mixed opportunities than they would pay for the sum of useless, dull, boring entertainment, stultifying education, dry information, and barely keeping up with social obligations. Such a whole that is greater than the sum of its parts is the synergy without which multimedia networks will fail miserably.

On-line service providers offer personal computer users the opportunity to get timely information about news that ranges from stocks to weather and sports, download files that contain related background information, access other service providers by way of gateways, participate in user forums and discussions, exchange multimedia E-mail, and even participate in rudimentary video conferences. This participation, along with information access, is particularly important and in fact, may be the critical element to most of the application categories. Clearly, this application category overlaps the previous two categories.

Applications in this category have network requirements that fall between a video conference's severe demands and multimedia mail's tolerance for low bandwidths and long delays. Entertainment people know that they must never let a consumer see or hear dead air, which is when nothing is happening. They are highly expert at filling unavoidable delays with transitions, such as with a previously prepared image and voiceover. They can cover reasonably short delays, if the delays are constant. For contrast, we have noted that some computer people tend to commit blunders such as filling a gap, for which information has not yet reached an audio buffer, by replaying the contents of the previous buffer. The stammering that results is arguably the only solution that could be worse than leaving dead air.

Some familiar service providers are Prodigy, America Online, CompuServe, and the Internet itself. IBM and Microsoft have recently started others. Many local access providers provide access to Internet as well as local features.

Shopping and Advertising

Scenario   Kristan is investigating travel destinations and travel service providers for her vacation this spring. She has specific requirements and constraints. She loves gourmet restaurants but is on a strict wheat-gluten-free diet. She loves scenic drives but hates mountain roads that lack guardrails. She wants to use her on-line service with its information databases and its forums, to help her decide where to go. She then wants to have a personalized application conduct whatever transactions are necessary to turn her vacation plans into a pleasurable and economical reality.

Definition   An application in the shopping and advertising category targets some portion of the catalog shopping market, which is approaching $100 billion annually in the United States. Many applications in this category reach a consumer in her home; others apply to in-store kiosks. As the name indicates, any such application is a two-sided coin. The consumer's side of the coin involves pull, in that the consumer uses the application to request information about products and services that interest her, along with enough detailed information to enable her to choose among those products. Choosing could also involve the customer's consulting with people on a forum or sending out a comparison agent as well. The advertiser's side of the coin involves push, in that the advertiser uses the application to tell a potential consumer about products and services that she might buy if she knew about them.

The two sides share many common interests. Both want to avoid advertisements for products and services that the consumer is sure to not buy; the consumer doesn't want to waste time reading such advertisements and the advertiser doesn't want to waste money sending them. Both sides want the consumer to interact with the application. The consumer wants to be able to ask questions and get answers without needing to peruse answers to other peoples' questions. The advertiser wants to avoid opening up subjects that might include drawbacks about which the consumer neglects to ask. Both sides want to use the application to complete a transaction with an order and a payment. The consumer may have a specific requirement for very fast delivery and may be willing to pay a premium for it.

The two sides have divergent interests as well. An advertiser wants to present products and services in the most advantageous possible light, whereas a consumer is at least as interested in drawbacks as in advantages. An advertiser wants to accumulate as much information about the consumer's tastes and purchases as possible, to target interesting products and services. A consumer demands privacy. A consumer wants to select among alternative products and services from many manufacturers, dealers, or other providers, based on a uniform presentation of easily comparable information. An advertiser wants to exclude alternative products that the consumer could buy from alternative suppliers, especially if the advertiser is paying for the consumer's network access.

Digital Libraries

Scenario Bernardo Torres is beginning research for his doctoral dissertation on the subject of the influences of Latin American dictators on Spanish authors and vice versa. His search begins with several of the world's electronic digital libraries although he will also search traditional (paper) libraries whose contents have not yet been digitized. He plans to contribute his completed research to one or more digital libraries, not only as a hypermedia book, but also as extensive multimedia annotations to relevant documents that already exist in the digital libraries. At the same time that he hopes to gain some royalties from on-line access to his book, he would like to enable students like himself to pay less than commercial customers. Bernardo's academic future depends on publishing refereed papers. He hopes that he can publish these papers electronically by placing them in digital libraries, but he suspects that he will need to publish them in paper journals of record, as well as publishing them on-line.

Definition A digital library application allows users to interact with a large body of on-line information expressed in appropriate media. Users of such an application employ a network to select information, to access information, and moreover, to add information. Libraries digitize their content not only to make the content more easily available to users over a wider area, but also to give users access to old or rare materials without gradually destroying the materials.

A digital library differs from a paper library in many important ways. By far the most fundamental difference is that distributed multimedia will make it vastly easier for almost anyone to contribute content to the world's aggregate digital library, just as almost anyone can now post a note on a computer bulletin board or contribute to a forum. Whereas a paper library is essentially a read-only memory, a user's interaction with a digital library may include not only accessing what others created but also contributing content for others to access. Such content can include not only new content but also commentary on existing content. Adding a user's information is by far the most sophisticated way in which a user can interact with a body of information.

Although an individual digital library may be as selective as any of today's paper libraries, a typical user may have access to many digital libraries that accept content on many subjects from almost any source. The worldwide digital library could accumulate masses of content that no editor has culled and no peer reviewer has blessed. Thus, in comparison to paper libraries, a digital library might decrease a user's difficulty of adding information and increase a user's difficulty of selecting valuable information from a mass that is irrelevant, illiterate, or even erroneous.

The next most fundamental difference is that a digital library supports much more frequent interaction than does a paper library. A paper library's typical patron may travel to the library several times per month and may check out six books on each trip. A digital library's typical user may select a new piece of information several times per minute and may select as little as one paragraph or one image at a time.

Another important difference is that today's editors make sure that each paper book is self-consistent and complete. A user can check out no less than an entire paper book. A digital library's users tend to assemble their own eclectic virtual books. A user who is searching for information may read a paragraph here and a chapter there. A professor who is preparing a text for her class may select seven chapters from seven books or select from content that never formed part of any traditional book.

A digital library's users tend to cover a wide geographical area. The library's level of funding need not be commensurate with the number of people within easy commuting distance of a paper library's location. A digital library, itself, may be distributed over a wide area, with enough duplication to improve reliability and availability. A good digital library application allows users to ignore most boundaries among different digital libraries and among different physical locations of one library.

Video on Demand

Scenario   Paul is spending a cold evening at home watching interactive video. He selects a news program that concentrates on technical developments rather than on human interest stories. During a news item about In-dia's telecommunications industry, he requests in-depth background information, then returns to the point at which he had digressed from seeing the news commentator. Paul need not know that his last demand involves accessing a stored and delayed version of what had been a live feed before he digressed, but which is still in progress. He doesn't mind paying high fees for this unique video stream, because his livelihood depends on information about technical developments. After seeing his fill of news, he decides to spend the rest of the evening watching an exciting World War II movie. Paul's wife Angie comes in from the den, where she has been using a network to teach a distance-learning course on the social effects of multimedia. Several of her regular students, including one in Japan, participated in a live video conference in which they asked questions and discussed answers. The video-on-demand application recorded the entire session, including the students as well as Angie and her presentation materials, so that other students could subsequently demand the material at their convenience. This is particularly convenient for one student who is asleep in Greece and a local student who works evenings. Those students will record their comments as video that Angie can demand later. After completing the semester's work, Angie plans to add hypermedia links to her recorded material. After she electronically publishes the resulting multimedia textbook, students will be able to interact with the book much as if they had been able to interact with Angie during the original live sessions.

Angie enjoys war movies only if they have a hero who ends up alive and victorious. Paul and Angie select a suitable movie using an intelligent video selector application. This application keeps a record of movies that Paul and Angie have liked and disliked. Not only can it use this information to select a movie that either of them is likely to enjoy separately, but also it can select a movie that both of them are likely to enjoy together.

The first movie they select exists only in a tape archive. The application offers to digitize the movie and download the movie to a tape in their home, so Paul and Angie can see it sometime next week. This sort of waiting to digitize archives on demand applies to all digital library materials, not just to movies on demand.

For this evening's viewing, Paul and Angie agree on a more recent movie. The video selection application offers them three methods for delivering this movie. For a significant fee, they can see the movie starting in 15 seconds. This choice will give them full control of pauses, rewinds, fast forwards, and digressions, just as Paul had for the news video, because no other viewer will be seeing the same video at the same time. However, no other viewer will be sharing the video's cost, either. Alternatively, for no fee beyond their telephone carrier's base cable service, they can join a broadcast of the selected movie that happens to have started 5 minutes ago on

Channel 396. For a small fee, they have the third alternative of joining a broadcast that will begin in 10 minutes, which the server sets up to meet the needs of several other viewers who have selected the same movie and more viewers who will soon select it. Based on information that Paul and Angie usually go for intermediate-cost entertainment, the application offers the third method as the default. Paul pushes Execute on his remote control and washes the dinner dishes to make good use of the 10-minute wait, which saved him several dollars.

Definition   A video-on-demand (VOD) application offers a user the opportunity to select exactly the one video stream the user wants, even if no other user wants the same video stream at the same time. (See Focus 5.1.) Without interfering with any other user, the user can change that video stream, such as rewinding to see a good part again. The user can select a completely different video stream, as frequently as several times per minute.

Because no conceivable or affordable infrastructure of broadband communications and video servers could support as many separate video streams as there are potential users, video on demand relies heavily on the fact that users can greatly reduce their bills by settling for less interactivity or

---

FOCUS 5.1   Helping customers choose movies.

To imagine some of the challenges of bringing this application to reality, think of the challenge of devising excellent ways for customers to select movies. Assume 10,000 movies are available. Customers may want help making selections. A value-added feature of a VOD service might provide ways for customers to make selections that are better than other options. Now, some customers may want to select by a description rather than by title: "The one where the ape climbs the Empire State Building." Some want to select any of a general set of movies: "Any James Bond movie I have not seen lately." Some want a lot of help in making the selection: "Some movie that is pretty close to one of my ideal movies" or "Something pretty far out, for variety, but still acceptable to me." Some have seen everything old and will select from new releases. Some want to select by lead actor or by director. Some want a "great books" type tour of movies. A given person's desires change widely from day to day. On one day he may want to select a movie that pleases one of his favorite critics, and on another day, one that pleases his mother-in-law. Often, the selection must please a group, not just one person. ■

near-video-on-demand (NVOD). Most of the time, most users will accept being limited to selecting one of several hundred channels, which professional video programmers have decided to broadcast at published times, as long as the users have a convenient way of selecting an interesting channel. Some of the time, most users will have special needs that they can fill by requesting video that will start at a fixed time. They may need to wait a few minutes or a few days. An earlier start time means a larger fee, because fewer other users will have time to sign up for the same video. At least occasionally, many users will insist on true video on demand and will be willing to pay the significantly higher fee that this choice entails.

Free market economics may be allowed to optimize providers' investments in infrastructure and operations that will deliver high interactivity to users who are willing and able to pay larger fees. Insofar as governmental regulators view wide choices of video and prompt start times as vitally important to citizens' lives, regulations may cause users who can afford higher fees to subsidize users of lesser means. Like other resource-transfer mechanisms, this one must not prevent users from seeing the different costs of different degrees of interactivity. Video on demand can work if users who actually need such a high degree of interactivity demand it, but not if everyone demands it all the time.

Educational and Health Applications

Scenario   Tom Mansfield continues to brush up on his knowledge of Securities and Exchange Commission (SEC) regulations by subscribing to a distance-learning forum on the subject. His children find that their access to the Children's Research Forum provides active learning, friends, and fun. His brother Charlie, who is currently roaming the world as a salesman for jogging shoes, is working toward his MBA in a joint program among three of the world's leading business schools. His sister, Marla, a nurse, wife, and mother, is enrolled in interactive and on-demand educational activities on the subjects of advanced cardiac techniques, cake making, and raising a mathematically gifted child.

At work, Marla uses telehealth and telemedicine facilities to give patients in their small and remote hospital many advantages that otherwise would be available only in a large metropolitan hospital. Telehealth helps her provide health services and related services; telemedicine helps her deliver clinical services. Marla acts as a physician's extender for both primary care and specialty services. She talks to and examines local patients and communicates with remote physicians. Along with improving the quality of care, she finds that telehealth saves patients money by significantly reducing relocation to tertiary care centers. She also finds that telehealth reduces her feeling of isolation and gives patients confidence in her rural hospital.

Definition   Educational and health applications take their definitions from these two respective niche markets. Each niche is sufficiently large to have a major role in driving distributed multimedia applications.

As parts of education we include kindergarten, elementary school, middle school, high school, college, and lifelong learning of the nature that people get well before needing the information that they learn. We also include training, which tends to occur in relation to employment and which people get much closer to the time when they need the information, such as just before they start a new job. The extreme case, called just-in-time (JIT) training, may occur as people begin an unfamiliar task or may occur a few seconds after people get into trouble and find that they need help.

Many people believe that classroom lectures, the staple of traditional education, are not meeting current needs. Moreover, traditional classroom lectures are becoming more expensive at the same time as alternative delivery mechanisms are becoming less expensive. Unlike lectures, distance learning or on-line education can provide education when and where necessary. Most on-line education does not yet take advantage of multimedia. Unless it is delivered over a local area network, satellite, or cable, the medium involved is almost exclusively text. For example, institutions such as the New School for Social Research in New York City, the University of Phoenix, and Nova University offer complete courses that rely entirely on telephone lines, modems, and text. Research and experience support the effectiveness of such instruction. Britain's Open University, the National Technological University (NTU), Mind Extension University (MEU), and some other institutions use satellites or cable to transmit video courseware. Their return path from the students to the institutions is quite narrow and is often limited to text. NTU sends courses from 45 engineering schools to over 400 companies. MEU plans to extend its cable reach to over 50 million homes.

Elementary and high school educators began using interactive multimedia on laser discs long before other potential users discovered multimedia. Several companies have attempted to use schoolchildren's familiarity with multimedia in schools to persuade parents to buy multimedia personal computers and titles for their homes as educational investments. Multimedia training is one of the most successful multimedia business applications. It is one of the uses of multimedia for which a company can most easily develop a business justification.

Health care is a growth industry in the United States, if for no other reason than the demographics of an aging population. It is also a service industry that uses vast amounts of critical information. Multimedia applications that involve interacting with multiple media promise to make information more accessible to the service providers. The multiple media make information more meaningful. The interactivity allows service providers to focus in rapidly on information they need. Networks help consolidate and distribute information that various workers generate and use in different locations both within one hospital and around the world (Kling, 1994).

Services that telehealth has delivered successfully include radiology, pathology, pediatric cardiology, psychological evaluation, sharing of patient data, information services from medical libraries, continuing staff education, and administrative teleconferences.

Hybrid Applications

Scenario David and Tom often watch professional football, particularly the Buffalo Bills' games, in Tom's living room. At the start of this season, they bought a football reference library on a CD-ROM to help settle the heated arguments that are the primary reason they enjoy watching the games together. The disc contains a wealth of scores, statistics, images of players, videos of interviews with major players, and animated diagrams and video clips of key plays. However, of course, the disc's statistical information ends at the end of the preceding season.

Each time David and Tom start using the disc, software that came as part of the application on the disc automatically uses Tom's modem and telephone line to dial an on-line service. The application has noted that its particular users usually ask for statistics on the Bills, on teams the Bills are scheduled to play in the next few weeks, and on teams that have won-lost records close to the Bills' record. Thus the software tells the on-line service to send information about what those teams have done since the last download, including partial results of games in progress. Because the CD-ROM is not changeable, the application downloads the new information onto the hard drive inside Tom's computer. The application also downloads a few images from the Bills' last game. However, to minimize the network time and charges, the software downloads only an index of other available updates.

While watching the next game with David, Tom makes a typically confident assertion contrasting two quarterbacks' ratios of touchdown passes to interceptions. David replies with a typically detailed quantitative refutation. They use Tom's computer to call up the relevant statistics, based on contents of the CD-ROM and all information already downloaded to Tom's hard drive, which of course support David's position. However, the application presents a button indicating that the index says one of the numbers may have an update and asking for authorization to log on and download the latest information. Tom decides the network charges will be worth the possibility of vindicating his assertion and gives permission. The new information shows that Tom's assertion has become correct since David last memorized the statistics, so each of the two parties claims a moral victory.

The mutual close call has piqued the two sports fans' interest in this particular ratio. Before they go back to watching the game, they draft a note about the ratio for the on-line service's bulletin board. They also ask the application to ask the on-line service to notify them if the ratio changes. An hour later, the computer beeps and its screen shows that David has become right, again.

Definition   An application belongs in the hybrid category when it falls between today's typical methods of accomplishing its function and tomorrow's potential methods of accomplishing the same function by using fully interactive video over a true multimedia network. Such an application makes good use of existing networks to give users significant advantages, but also presents significant disadvantages relative to applications of a true multimedia network.

The preceding scenario's application has the following advantages and disadvantages, which place it squarely in the hybrid category. Advantages of the application are as follows.

- It makes good use of the U.S. Postal Service's ability to transmit a reasonably large volume of information at low cost by delivering a CD-ROM. After receiving a CD-ROM, a user has rapid and extremely economical access to the information that the disc contains.

- It also makes good use of on-line networks for overcoming a CD-ROM's two large drawbacks: (a) An on-line network allows a user to select small portions of a total amount of information much larger than would fit on any reasonable number of CD-ROM discs. (b) An on-line network allows a user to access information that can be updated every minute, whereas information on a CD-ROM may be weeks or even years out of date.

Disadvantages of the application may, depending on implementation, include some of the following.

- It runs on a computer that is in Tom's den, whereas his large screen television set is in his living room.

- It uses a separate control unit from the television's wireless remote control.

- It displays answers on a separate screen from the television's screen.

- It has a unique user interface, which only Tom has mastered.

- It has variable delays between inquiry and answer, depending on whether underlying data are already inside the user's computer or requires access to the network.

- Its video clips from previous seasons are few in number, short, small-screen, and slightly grainy and jerky, limited by the capacity of the disc.

- Its video clips from the current season are even fewer and shorter, limited by the network's bandwidth and the user's willingness to wait for and pay for long download times.

- It must ask the users whether a particular inquiry is sufficiently serious to warrant the delay and price involved in logging on to get the very latest information.

- To use the application, David and Tom must be in Tom's home. They could carry the CD-ROM to David's home, but only the hard drive that is fixed inside Tom's computer has the information they already downloaded.

Interestingly enough, the preceding scenario has an almost exact mirror image in which a user logs onto an on-line service. The service sends occasional instructions for the user's computer to display media, already in the user's home on a CD-ROM, that relate to what the user is doing on-line. This mirror-image scenario has almost identical advantages and disadvantages. The only significant difference is that, instead of the last two disadvantages that we just cited, the mirror-image scenario has the disadvantage that users must remain logged-on during the entire time they employ the application.

Hybrid applications are examples of the famous 80–20 rule, which asserts that it is possible to reach 80 percent of perfection with 20 percent of the effort that would be necessary to reach perfection. The preceding scenario's application might well meet David's and Tom's needs 80 percent as well as an application that has none of the disadvantages we have indicated. Removing all the application's disadvantages would surely increase its cost even more than five times.

Such applications will be important to the commercial development of true distributed multimedia applications. Companies will invest hundreds of billions of dollars in interactive video network infrastructure only if they can be confident that consumers will pay for corresponding applications. Companies are justifiably suspicious of marketing surveys that require customers to attempt to visualize effects of major qualitative improvements in the ways various products perform functions. Using such applications allows consumers to gain actual experience with major qualitative improvements. After experiencing such applications, consumers are much more likely to know whether they would pay for true distributed multimedia applications. In most cases, removing the disadvantages of hybrid applications involves only quantitative improvements, which consumers can visualize relatively easily.

VISION FOR THE NEXT DECADE

Different stakeholders have significantly different visions of what distributed multimedia applications can do for them in the next 10 years. We next discuss the visions of individual users, businesses, and governments, in that order.

Individual Users

Customer requirements are by no means the major impetus driving distributed multimedia. However, because only consumer applications can draw enough revenue to pay back necessary investments in infrastructure, consumers do hold veto power over the deployment of large-scale interactive video networks. Surveys, studies, history, and results from focus groups indicate that individual users may have the following sorts of visions.

Individual users envision working with applications that allow them to append their comments, insights, questions, and requests to documents. These documents range from letters and business reports to family albums. Individuals will not have to spend huge amounts of time and effort becoming professionals or specialists in creating video or other media. This change is a significant part of erasing the line separating amateurs from professional content providers. Users also want to create original multimedia content and applications and to distribute their creations over wide area networks to friends, family, and business associates.

Users envision applications that are far easier to use than existing ones. They hope for far less hassle than applications currently entail, particularly with installing new applications, maintaining and upgrading them, and even removing old ones. They have the same hope for applications that they come across in their work, in dealings with governments and educational institutions, in retail establishments, and at home.

Users envision applications that help them make personalized choices and execute the resulting transactions without re-entering information. Users want to feed back to their applications how well they liked each choice so that the applications can become increasingly helpful to them in making their choices in the future. Users also want to access such applications when and where they need them, rather than having the applications tied to separate computers in offices, malls, government bureaus, or libraries. A single application to access and manipulate information from many sources would be desirable. Among these sources should be live, human, on-line help as well as stored information from competing on-line information suppliers and information about competing products. Users want to be able to select either only the information of immediate interest to them or background and contextual information as well. They want information presented in the most appropriate media that include graphics, images, audio, and even full-motion video, as well as text, without incurring exorbitant delays or expenses.

When users buy information, they expect to get whatever programs they need to make the information useful. They want enough consistency among various applications so that what they learn about one application carries over to the next application they use. For example, if they buy an encyclopedia, they expect to get the computer that accesses it or else get the programs that enable all sorts of existing computers to access it. They want assistance in deciding what specific pieces of information mean to them and assistance with the choices they need to make. They insist that their applications respond sufficiently rapidly to let them continue with an unbroken train of thought, even if the computers and data are remote. Users envision that either applications come with a virtual community or it will be easy to find the associated virtual community.

Users envision a high degree of privacy, ease of use, and economy. They do not want others to use personal information about them to send them junk electronic mail. They refuse to spend hours learning to use a tool, or relearning the use of a tool after being away from it for a month. They will allocate no more than a few percent of the cost of the product they are choosing to pay for an application that helps them make the choice.

Perhaps most important, users envision seeing a single system image, rather than seeing a collection of unnecessarily different applications. Users do not want to supply information repeatedly, even when competing organizations need the same information. They do not want to have to know that different information is in different data files, that different organizations put information in data files with different formats, that different programs manipulate those files, that different operating systems support those programs, and that different hardware runs it all. They expect distractions from making choices to keep discreetly out of sight. An operating system message that emerges from a tool's user interface is as surprising and as unwelcome as steam that emerges from the hood of an automobile. Users should see differences among remote and local databases only as a well-phrased warning that employing some particular remote source of information will be unusually expensive. All the separate applications involved must work together to present the appearance of a single system that helps the users make choices.

Users want one simplified hypermedia bill or invoice for their use of applications even if many providers are involved. Users may want to see additional details that are available through the hypermedia links.The following scenarios further articulate individual users' possible visions.

Select a Rental Apartment   I need to find a place to live and I have some definite requirements. The location must be within 15 miles of my workplace. I cannot pay over $650 per month, including utilities. I want a quiet building with a pleasant view all year. I want to be no higher than the third floor. I need to move in by next month with a six-month lease that I can break if my job moves, with at most a small penalty. I will not sign a lease for any apartment that I cannot see in final condition. If several apartments meet these requirements, I will make a judgment based on subjective combinations of requirements.

I want a multimedia application to act as my independent agent and help me find an apartment. The application should access advertisements in all local newspapers and real estate listings, rather than relying on any single source of on-line information. The application should act as a filter so that I need consider only apartments that meet all my requirements.

When easily available on-line information about an apartment meets all requirements, the application should probe further. It should use its network to obtain images or video clips. It should then contact actual people to obtain less easily available answers. For example, if provisions for breaking the lease are not available as coded information on-line, the application might send a form E-mail letter requesting a copy of the lease by E-mail, fax, or mail. The application need not be capable of reading a lease and determining the provisions. However, the application should know whether I am capable of doing so. If not, the application should be equipped and authorized to engage counsel and get an answer. If the counsel is, in fact, artificial intelligence, I don't want to hear about it.

The application should accumulate information about whom to contact for each piece of information concerning each suitable apartment. If I want to try to negotiate a change in the lease, I want to be able to initiate a telephone call or preferably electronic mail to the rental agent without looking up her number or address.

Since I have rented several apartments in recent years, I want the application to compare each reasonably suitable apartment with my previous apartments, concentrating on features that I reported I especially liked or disliked.

After eliminating unsuitable apartments, I would ask the application to set up appointments for me to see apartments. The application should select an optimal sequence, not only considering driving time, but allowing for my desire to sample the complete spectrum of apartments. After seeing a sample of apartments from the outside, then I want to see the two or three that are most likely to satisfy my needs on the inside. The application should then get driving directions and a map for finding each apartment. I must not need to tell a separate route-finding application the addresses of the apartments or the order in which I want to see them.

After I have made or confirmed my choice, the application should help me complete the transaction by signing the lease and making guaranteed payments, without my having to take time off from work to appear in person. Finally, after a few weeks and again after a year, the application should ask me to report what I like and dislike about the selected apartment, so it can be even more helpful next time I move (Croal and Stone, 1995).

Buy Fall School Clothes   Because none of her friends happen to be available for a mall-crawl, Susan decides to access an on-line multimedia application to select and buy an outfit that looks similar to a friend's outfit. She begins by entering a rough sketch of the outfit. She wants her application to determine what is available from several of her favorite stores and catalogs. She wants items filtered so that she sees only those that look similar to her sketch and that are available in her measurements and in her price range. Susan has bought clothes on-line for several years. Having been careful to report how she liked each item, she can count on the application's filter to emphasize items similar to ones she has bought and liked. The application can notice and use gradual changes in her tastes, and use information about changes in buying patterns of people her age. Since Susan reported that a very recent purchase was the correct size, the application decides not to ask Susan to specify her latest measurements. Instead, it applies a rule of thumb to approximate her growth measurements.

The application shows Susan video clips of several outfits that meet her requirements, in several of her favorite colors. To see how she would look in each, without going to a public dressing room, Susan asks the application to superimpose an image of her face on the video and to scale the models to her measurements. She discusses the potential purchases with her friends by way of a fashion bulletin board. The application makes it easy for her to send video of the outfits, along with text and audio.

Susan makes tentative selections and receives a consolidated summary with side-by-side pictures, prices, care characteristics, return policies, along with when, where, and how she could get each item. Susan uses this summary to make her final selection and completes the business transaction, including paying for the items. She decides not to pay an extra premium for overnight delivery. Later, she will continue her practice of saying how well she liked each item, including how well it fit, so that the application can help her make better choices in the future.

Establish a Diet and Exercise Program   Jane and John each employ an on-line self-help application. They specify their respective needs and preferences for diet and exercise. Jane is somewhat overweight and somewhat over 50. She needs to consult a diet doctor. The application notes that she should not undertake an exercise program without passing a thorough physical, so she needs to consult a general practitioner as well. She is quite fussy about whom she consults. The application sets up video interviews with suitable professionals.

John's needs are simpler. The application notes that he needs to jog three times each week and reduce his cholesterol intake. He requests information about safe nearby places to jog, including video clips that will help him select the most attractive scenery and best maintained paths. He also requests information about restaurants with suitable low-cholesterol menus, atmosphere, and prices, and requests suitable recipes that are simple to prepare at home.

Jane and John employ different applications to select among many possible activities. Filters make sure that they need consider only alternatives that are applicable and safe. Jane signs up for appointments. Later, she feeds back her opinions about the results. The application uses her responses to improve future suggestions that it will make to her and to others who have somewhat similar needs.

Jane and John store their medical records on their respective home computers. They set up agents to answer questions when an application requires access to their records. However, they instructed the agents to refuse to transmit the actual records to any other computer and to refuse to answer a series of questions that appear to be trying to get too much information.

Select a Vacation Site   The Chins want to spend Christmas vacation with a group of three families and several friends. They need to select a location that each member of the group will tolerate and that most members will like a lot. Ages of group members range from 25 to 50 and interests range from skiing to watching scenery and reading by the fire. Several members need to make good use of frequent flyer mileage, bonus points, coupons, and various other promotions they have accumulated over the past year.

The Chins instruct an application to make suggestions based on information about places where each person has vacationed, and about how each person liked each place, as well as on information about what places appeal to people of similar ages and general interests. The application suggests locations along with videos and cost estimates for each. The Chins discuss the suggestion with members of the group and with people who have been to each location. They exchange text and video, both in real time and in relevant forums and bulletin boards.

The discussions allow the group to choose a location. Each member then uses the application, and information the application already collected, to choose detailed travel itineraries and accommodations. They use the application again to make and pay for the corresponding reservations.

Entertain a Niece   Mary is babysitting her niece. Mary's sister suggested finding an activity that would be enjoyable for Mary and educational for her niece. Mary's profile of favorite recreational activities is already part of a distributed multimedia application's data. Mary adds her niece's age and interests and requests suggestions. The application suggests a game. Because Mary has come to trust the application, she instructs the application to download the game and order a pizza.

Select a Movie   How can I intelligently and satisfactorily select one movie that meets my needs for this evening? I enjoy several different sorts of movies. Sometimes I feel like seeing an old favorite; sometimes I want to see almost any new and popular movie that is within my range of acceptability; sometimes I want to see something completely off the wall. If I have not seen the latest sequel of a favorite series, then I surely want to consider that. I want the concept of "movie" generalized to include not only theater attractions but also current and past television shows, live sports and news, and even educational material.

I ask an application to make suggestions. I may need to see video previews (trailers) of several suggested movies before I make my final selection. I may want to select a movie using equipment that may range from just a telephone and a television set to a multimedia-equipped personal computer with a two-way high-speed link.

After I select a movie, I want the application to do whatever is necessary to get it for me to view at the time I want it, at minimum cost. I want the application to determine whether an available free programming channel is broadcasting the movie at any time before the start time I selected. If that is the case, I want the application to record the movie for me on a time shift tape that is always ready in my end-user device. If the movie is not available free, I want the application to find the least expensive pay-per-view source. The cheapest delivery might consist of having a tape delivered to my door, downloading the movie to tape at 3:00 A.M. when network time is least expensive, or transmitting the movie as I watch. Later, of course, I will tell the system how well I liked the movie, to improve the system's ability to help me choose movies that I will enjoy in the future.

Typical Menus The following examples indicate the sorts of screens an application might present to a user in the above scenarios, to meet users' visions of easy-to-use applications. Figure 5.3 shows a top-level menu of

```
MAIN MENU
  • Movies on demand
  • Television programming
  • Messages
  • Shopping
  • Information services
  • Games
  • Anne's customizer
  • Anne's hot news
```

```
MOVIES ON DEMAND
  • Anne's agent
  • Movie catalog
  • Order
```

```
MESSAGES
  • Video phone
  • E-mail
  • Voice mail
```

```
TELEVISION PROGRAMMING
  • Interactive television
  • What's on television
  • Anne's television
```

```
INFORMATION SERVICES
  • Internet
  • Anne's news filter
  • Anne's hot list for information
  • Anne's university library
```

```
ANNE'S CUSTOMIZER
  • Synchronize with PDA for trip
  • Filters
  • General agents
  • Credit card information
```

Figure 5.3 Anne's personalized application interface.

functions and several lower-level menus. For example, selecting "Movies on demand" from the top-level menu shows the lower-level menu of which the title is "Movies on demand."

Of course, a screen designer could offer the option of customized picture icons and 3-D representations, rather than text, and an interface designer might offer help in personalizing a committee of software agents. Anne likes mostly text.

Businesses

Businesses, that is companies, envision different advantages from distributed multimedia applications, depending on whether the companies are commercial content providers or commercial users. We next discuss visions for companies that play these two roles.

Commercial Content Providers Commercial content providers envision leveraging their expertise by feeding multiple end-user devices, such as personal computers and interactive television sets, over all available networks. They want standards that will allow their titles, and all other sorts of multimedia applications, to play on computers and set-top boxes from all manufacturers. The resulting large sales volumes will enable providers to make acceptable profit margins despite high costs of developing interactive content and despite the need to keep consumer prices low.

Many companies provide multimedia content now mostly on CD-ROMs. Between 1993 and 1994, 22.8 million CD-ROMs were sold with about 10,000 separate titles. One selection of the top 100 CD-ROMs included titles from the following providers (*PC Magazine*, 1994).

Knowledge Adventure	Viacom New Media
Sierra On-Line	Living Books
Microsoft	Grolier Electronic Publishing
Time Warner Interactive and Warner Interactive	Simon & Schuster Interactive
	Davidson & Associates
Broderbund	Voyager Company
LucasArts Entertainment	The Learning Company
Paramount Interactive	

See Focus 5.2 for a best-sellers list.

New content providers will emerge. Some will be entirely new companies. Others will be new parts of traditional publishing houses, movie studios,

FOCUS 5.2   Some best-selling CD-ROMs in 1995.

Magazines and other sources publish lists of popular titles. One list in the August 1995 *NewMedia Magazine* contained the following items:

Myst, a game, from Broderbund

Dark Forces, a game, from LucasArts

Encarta '95, an encyclopedia, from Microsoft

Street Atlas USA 2.0, from DeLorme Mapping

LionKing Animated Storybook, from Disney Interactive

Interactive Encyclopedia '95, from Compton's NewMedia

NBA Live '95, about the National Basketball League, from Electronic Arts

Family Tree Maker Deluxe 2.0, from Banner Blue

70 Million Households Phone Book, from American Business Information ∎

and personal computer companies. Still others will be partnerships, such as between telephone companies and companies in other industries. For example, Ameritech Corporation, Bell South Corporation, and Southwestern Bell Corporation have signed a deal with the Walt Disney Company to create interactive video programming for future telephone usage. Disney is considering software titles based on its animated movies. We discuss partnerships in a broader context in Chapter 6, Providers.

Users of Multimedia Applications   Businesses envision using multimedia applications to interact more efficiently and effectively with employees, customers, suppliers, and other companies. They want to expand their markets and market shares by gaining access to the rapidly growing on-line community. They hope to market to millions of people, concentrating on people who are actually potential customers, and targeting appropriate advertising messages to particular groups of potential customers. Especially in retail and service sectors, businesses hope to combine marketing with completing transactions, both to take advantage of impulse purchases and to reduce their operating costs.

Nordstrom, an upscale department store chain with headquarters in Seattle, Washington, expresses the opinion that, by the end of the century, businesses can offer a customer the opportunity to hold conversations with a personal shopper by way of the customer's television set (*Business Week*, 1993). Nordstrom also envisions combining interactive shopping with movie watching. If, while watching a movie at home, you see some item of clothing that you like, you can pause the movie and purchase the item.

Some companies feel that they have no choice but to start working toward distributed multimedia. Major industries recall the business impact of being left out of previous innovations. Publishers recall their late reaction to paperback books; telephone companies recall their reaction to each other and to LANs; and computer companies recall their late reaction to personal computers and then to laptops. Companies feel that they should at least participate in some prototype experiments, make some announcements of intent, or create a home page in the Internet's World Wide Web (WWW or the Web) in the hopes that some customers will hear that the page exists and perhaps use a browser such as Netscape's Navigator to browse the information.

Companies that select and purchase applications their employees use envision increasing employees' productivity and quality of service. After a decade of heavy expenditures on information systems, many companies are still wondering when these increases will commence. Business conditions make it increasingly difficult for a typical company to bring together employees who work on a particular task, either in the same physical location or in the same organizational unit. A typical task requires cooperation from employees at several sites who are in several organizations, often in separate companies. However, a typical task lasts too short a time for a company to recover the expenses involved in moving employees or even in reorganizing.

Companies envision using multimedia applications to create virtual locations and virtual organizations that cost little to create and that nevertheless work about as well as moving employees to a common physical location under the same organizational unit. Experience indicates that challenging tasks require spontaneous informal communication. If communication requires formal effort and appears to be expensive, one employee will tend to guess about what other employees are doing. By creating a virtual location, in which one employee can see other employees and ask casual questions, distributed multimedia applications can avoid the expense of straightening out results of wrong guesses.

CD-ROM drive vendors were surprised by their relatively slow penetration to employees' desktop computers. One conjectured reason is that information system managers feared a loss of productivity to highly attractive computer games distributed on CD-ROM discs.

In general, companies also envision expanding their use of multimedia for training and video conferences.

Governments

Statutes require governments to make a great deal of information available to citizens. With respect to some information, statutes go so far as to require governments to achieve optimal visibility to the right audience, to collect and process responses, and to make the responses available. For example, the National Science Foundation's (NSF's) requests for proposal (RFPs), and also the resulting proposals, must be especially well publicized. NSF reports that it has been tinkering with electronic grant handling since 1985. Ten years later, it was deploying software to enable grantees to use Internet to transmit the administrative portions of their grant applications, determine the status of their applications, manage cash flow, and submit final reports. Reviewers, too, will be able to use the system to send in their comments (Mervis, 1995).

Governments must also educate and train many thousands of people who have widely differing skill levels and learning styles. Governments envision multimedia applications that can take good advantage of the economies and benefits of the information superhighway.

In some of the many reports on the National Information Infrastructure in 1994, Commerce Secretary Ron Brown asserted that the federal government will focus on the seven key application areas of manufacturing, electronic commerce, health care, education and lifelong learning, environmental monitoring, and libraries.

STATE OF THE ART

Network bandwidth, interactivity, availability, usability, and affordability limit the state of the art for essentially all application categories. We next discuss the state of the art for each application category.

Desktop Video Conferences with Collaboration

Full-screen full-motion video, of the sort found on CD-ROMs, requires a data rate of at least 150 KBps or 1.2 Mbps. Real-time symmetric compression and decompression on consumer-grade computers give only quarter-screen full-motion video at 1.2 Mbps. This is the baseline number for judging the quality of digital video in a video conference.

A typical home's only two-way communications link is a voice-grade analog telephone local loop with a modem that can send and receive at most about 28.8 Kbps. The factor of 64 by which quarter-screen digital video's data rate exceeds a typical home's available data rate expresses the state of the art of consumer video conferences. Some offices have 128-Kbps ISDN lines. Even such a well-equipped office falls short of the aforementioned digital video data rate by a factor of 10. An office endowed with an expensive T1 link or ISDN Primary Rate Interface link can send and receive quarter-screen full-motion digital video. An office that has a LAN that links to a T1 or Primary Rate ISDN gateway has the same capability.

Some early uses for video conference applications are general meetings, technical problem solving, training, customer support, engineering design, and marketing and sales. We next discuss some interesting prototypes and products that solve real problems.

IBM's Person to Person/2 (P2P/2) is an early product for desktop video conferences. Figure 5.4 shows a typical screen.

Augusta Tech in Augusta, Georgia, uses P2P/2 for collaborating with the University of Michigan's Department of Medicine over the Internet. The in-

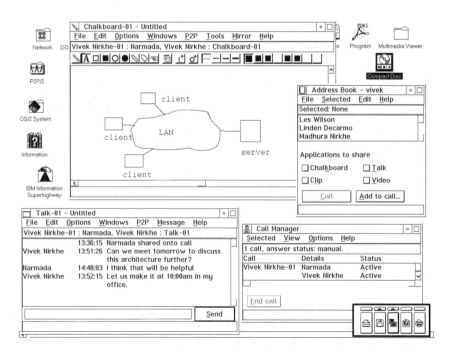

Figure 5.4 A Person to Person/2 Screen. Reprinted with permission of IBM.

stitutions share high-quality medical images, including computerized axial tomography scans (better known as CAT scans). Augusta Tech can take advantage of expensive medical-imaging equipment without having to purchase it. Sessions utilize both P2P/2 for OS/2 at the University of Michigan and P2P/2 for Windows at Augusta Tech. Augusta Tech is also implementing P2P/2 to enhance communications and information sharing between the Department of Adult Technical Education and the main campus.

The Gertrude Stein Repertory Theater in New York City uses P2P/2 and Action Media II cards (which capture, compress, and decompress video using a precursor to Intel's Indeo compression technology) to share dance routines with others in remote locations. P2P/2 has made possible spontaneous artistic collaboration among directors, costume and set designers, production managers, and cast members scattered around the country. College art departments have held collaborative workshops with schools in East Los Angeles and the South Bronx to develop new routines. P2P/2 allows everyone involved to work together without physically being together.

Internet Video Conferences   The Internet has at least two efforts that are relevant to video conferences, the Internet Engineering Task Force's Multicast Backbone (nicknamed MBone) and Cornell University's project, CU-SeeMe. MBone is a virtual network that implements multicasting, whereby one computer sends information to several destination computers simultaneously. Clever routing avoids redundant transmission to groups of destination computers that are remote from the sender but close to one another. Some popular application tools that use MBone are visual audio tool, video conference system, network video, and white board. MBone Audio allows anyone to start a conversation. Because audio and video require more bandwidth than does text, MBone strains many networks and increases demands for resource control and real-time traffic control.

The authors of Mosaic are enhancing it to allow a lecturer to multicast control information to students' Mosaic programs. Typical MBone trials employ fewer than five frames per second.

CU-SeeMe over the Internet is one of the least expensive methods for delivering global electronic distance education. CU-SeeMe provides useful video conferences at minimal cost, for users who have access to the Internet. See Focus 5.3 for details.

AT&T's WorldWorx Solutions   AT&T's service involves a broad alliance among many vendors that has the goal of expanding the market for desktop video conferences by permitting systems with different equipment to work together. The service includes ISDN and strongly supports the H.320 standard which we discussed in Chapter 1. Intel and AT&T have agreed to work together

FOCUS 5.3 CU-SeeMe details.

CU-SeeMe runs on Apple Macintosh and Intel-based personal computers. Reception requires only a connection to the Internet and either type of personal computer that has a screen capable of displaying 16 levels of gray scale. Transmission requires, in addition, a video camera, either an Apple AV-Macintosh system or a Macintosh system with a SuperMac VideoSpigot board, and either Quicktime and SpigotVDIG extensions added to the Macintosh system folder or the Intel-world equivalents.

CU-SeeMe is available free under copyright from Cornell University and its collaborators. A version is being marketed commercially as well by White Pine Software, Inc. It works with any connection, but it works better with faster connections such as the best university LAN gateways to the Internet backbone. Its proprietary protocol wisely refrains from retransmitting failed packets and supports its own brand of multicasting, rather than using MBone. With a fast connection and a lightly loaded network, it can deliver about 12 frames per second in a 160×120 pixel window or about 8 frames per second in a 320×200 pixel window. The resulting video, although somewhat jerky and small, is usable for many purposes. Usable early releases required users who wanted audio to establish an additional POTS connection, but recent releases offered audio as an option. A reflector, which is an associated program that runs on a UNIX server, allows one-to-many, several-to-several, or several-to-many conferences. Cornell's research objectives include determining whether these options are necessary for effective research collaboration. ■

to enable AT&T to support Intel's favorite compression-decompression algorithm, Indeo, in multipoint video conferences across WorldWorx networks.

Acquiring an Application   Equipping a desktop personal computer to handle two-way video presents a significant challenge. A typical shopping list includes the following items.

- A video camera suitably placed to view the user and occasionally view other objects of interest

- Speakers and a microphone with a stand

- Compression and decompression hardware, usually in the form of an adapter card for the personal computer

- User-friendly application software to handle the communications with other personal computers, send and receive real-time video, manage the sharing of a chalkboard or other shared function, and send messages such as text or multimedia files

- Some sort of high-speed connection and the corresponding adapter for the computer

Figure 5.5 shows Palmer Agnew operating a desktop conferencing set-up at Binghamton University. Notice the small video camera on the top of the personal computer.

Multimedia Store-and-Forward Mail

Computer companies such as IBM, Microsoft, and Apple own all or portions of on-line services such as Prodigy, Microsoft Network (MSN), and EzWorld. Other companies provide on-line services by riding on other carriers' infrastructures, such as Dow Jones News/Retrieval Service and Access Atlanta.

Prodigy and America Online are general-purpose on-line services targeted at the consumer marketplace. CompuServe targets users who are

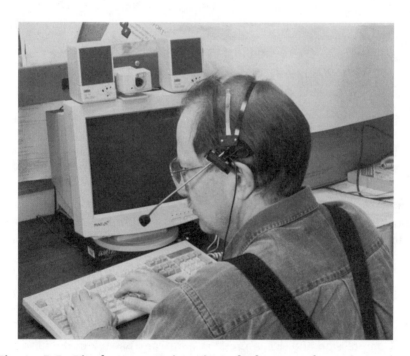

Figure 5.5   Binghamton University's desktop conferencing setup.

more computer literate or more experienced. Sierra-On-Line, renamed Imagi-Nation Network and purchased by AT&T, is targeted at game players of all ages.

The three major providers, Prodigy, America Online, and CompuServe have vigorously built memberships and have attempted to add more media and functions to increase their market share. Prodigy Services Corporation claims close to 2 million subscribers. CompuServe has 2.5 million sub-scribers and America Online had 1.5 million subscribers (*Washington Post,* sidebar, 1995). A more recent survey shows America Online's vigorous mar-keting bringing its subscribership up to a leading 3 million subscribers. These numbers can be compared with hardcopy *Newsweek*'s 3 million plus subscribers in 1993.

A DataQuest survey (Binghamton, New York, *Press & Sun-Bulletin,* side-bar, 1994) reports that E-mail is the most frequently used on-line service. Nearly 40 percent of on-line respondents regularly use E-mail, whereas fewer than 10 percent use on-line banking.

On-line services provide user interfaces that range from those that restrict users to seeing and entering text to GUIs that present colorful menus and hy-pertext. A service that provides high-resolution images risks getting the rep-utation of being slow. One solution is to provide downloadable images, video, and audio, which users request only when they are not in a hurry. A more general solution is to obtain faster communication lines and modems. Some services provide text chat mode for real-time conversations as well as bulletin boards that store messages. Figure 5.6 is a sample of a Prodigy screen. Such screen interfaces are undergoing continual evolution to attract more customers.

Acquiring an Application   Our week's mail often includes several offers to join one of the major on-line service providers. A new home computer may come loaded with software to access one or more of these services or the Inter-net. A typical package offers to automatically dial an 800 number and obtain a local access number for the purchaser usually in exchange for a credit card.

Internet's Multipurpose Internet Mail Extensions (MIME) handles net-work multimedia mail for Internet users. With MIME-compliant E-mail soft-ware such as Eudora for personal computers at both ends, it is possible to send any medium by attaching the medium's binary file to an E-mail mes-sage and dumping the pair into a file. Compressing the file saves bandwidth but is optional.

Lotus Video Notes allows users to incorporate video into their E-mail. The Notes application stores documents separately from text on a video-ready server and provides simplified tools for editing the video clips. The application also provides an API for third-party add-ons. Lotus uses Distrib-

Figure 5.6 Prodigy screen interface © Prodigy Service Company 1995. Reprinted with permission.

uted External Object Storage (DEOSS) as a video-management framework to allow users to access the video files across a WAN. Users can click on an object and watch the corresponding video stream off the server without having to download huge video files to their workstations.

Several word-processing applications allow authors to import video and audio files and send an entire document through many E-mail systems as a binary file. Recipients can view such a file if they have suitable multimedia hardware and software, preferably identical to the author's hardware and software.

Consumer Edutainment, Infotainment, Sociotainment

In many homes that have personal computers and modems, using on-line networks to communicate with other people now consumes more time than does watching television. Television increasingly plays the role of providing provocative conversation subjects for such on-line communication, adding a social dimension to television's entertainment role.

Major on-line services provide access to fact sheets on stars of television shows and provide access to on-line forums in which users discuss the shows with one another and sometimes with the stars. A small but increasing number of broadcast and cable television shows have their own on-line forums, 800 telephone numbers, 900 telephone numbers, or WWW pages. Everyone involved expresses astonishment at the popularity of on-line discussions of television shows. One communications marketer accounts for the 10,000 messages received per week relating to a single television show as resulting from the fact that viewers fall in love with the program's stars. Viewers seem to have an insatiable demand for information about their beloved stars. Another explanation is that watching a television show is an inferior simulation of interacting with real people, whereas using an on-line network to discuss a show is actually interacting with real people.

As a second example whereby on-line networks make entertainment increasingly social, at least one game network set up E-mail as an afterthought to allow users to select remote partners and adversaries. This game network found that users spend more time using the network to discuss the games than to play games.

Many companies in the publishing industry provide E-mail addresses or WWW home pages, which users employ to make their access to information and education more entertaining. Several metropolitan newspapers operate or participate in forums on major on-line services and Internet for customers to discuss the news with the newspaper staff. Newspaper professionals use forums to debate the optimal form for future on-line, on-demand newspapers. Several newspapers have announced on-line production service. Access Atlanta, from the *Atlanta Journal-Constitution*, is one such service that users can access using Prodigy. The business model divides revenue between Prodigy and Access Atlanta, based on access time, along with a monthly fee for specific access to this service. Many publishing companies have extensive on-line plans, activities, and ideas on how to make money on-line while preserving the money they make with paper and ink.

PED's *The Journalist* is an example of news on demand. The software runs on personal computers in conjunction with the on-line infotainment provider. It employs text, graphics, and images, but as yet no audio or video. To use this application, you must subscribe to an on-line provider and purchase *The Journalist* software for less than $50. With the tools of this software you can design the format of your own newspaper. You specify when you want the software to log on to your on-line provider and what information you want the software to download and insert into your personal format.

The Wall Street Journal has started a similar service called *Personal Journal—Published for a Circulation of One*. It costs $12.95 for one personal edition every business day and 50 cents for extra downloads. You specify favorite columns, specific companies, and stocks and mutual funds for your paper.

The commercial on-line services are moving beyond providing only text for communications. Focus 5.4 describes some early efforts.

Acquiring an Application Equipment for combining entertainment with education, information, and socializing includes the following.

- A suitable modem running at least 9.6 Kbps for Prodigy, CompuServe, America Online, or Internet without Netscape or comparable browser, or at least 19.6 Kbps for Internet with Netscape or comparable browser

- A suitable delivery provider, preferably with a local telephone number

- An on-line service's software and perhaps third parties' add-on pieces

- Additional software for special connection protocols such as Serial Line Internet Protocol (SLIP), Point-to Point Protocol (PPP), and TCP/IP for World Wide Web access

Shopping and Advertising

Since its inception, Prodigy has presented unsolicited advertising in the forms of images and animation as well as text. Users can order some but not all advertised items, often without re-entering credit card and shipping address information. The Home Shopping Network has agreed to bring its products to the Prodigy service. There will be a bulletin board for members to share their experiences with the products and to ask questions of each other and of the Prodigy Home Shopping Staff.

Advertising on the Internet is recent and controversial. Will it be effective or not, where effective means making money? Are the fancy Web pages with more than just text, which many think are required to attract attention and distinguish one company's products from another's, simply too slow with today's available bandwidth? Can Web-page creators learn tricks and techniques to make today's dull, static Web pages compelling and effective with today's bandwidth, server, and playback device limitations? Is the "mall" the right metaphor? Will companies bow to customer surveys and lower prices of goods and services purchased over the network? Will companies allow computer agents into their malls to facilitate customer comparison shopping? Early indications are that there are many window shoppers, but few buyers. Nonetheless, many companies are rushing to develop World Wide

---

FOCUS 5.4 Early steps toward more than text communications.

Efforts to include additional media in on-line services include the following.

Audio: Apple's eWorld now provides Speak. This new function allows a user to listen rather than read text and listen to chat.

Images: Prodigy is working with a film developer to digitize photographs so that users can attach digitized photos to E-mail. Users can also attach sound clips to E-mail.

Slow video: Apple's eWorld plans to include the ability to display frequently refreshed still images that simulate very slow video, one frame every 30 seconds. This video can accompany real-time chat. CNN will be the first to use this technology.

3-D Animation: CompuServe plans a simulated 3-D environment for chat called WorldsAway. Real-time text dialogue appears above the user's simulation, a digital actor's head. Representing the user, the digital actor can show facial expressions and gestures and pick up objects in a room. The proposed HTML extension, Virtual Reality Modeling Language (VRML), allows people to communicate using 3-D images. WorldsChat on Internet uses VRML. Chat still is in a voiceless text box. ■

Web home pages that contain catalogs of merchandise. Figures 5.7 and 5.8 show typical home pages, in which boldface type indicates hotwords that users can select to link to other pages.

Internet has lacked the intrinsic security, privacy, and reliability necessary for most commercial uses demanding these features. Commercial connections vary in price from $20 per month for a light dial-in connection to $65,000 for a corporate T1 connection.

CommerceNet is a nonprofit consortium of cooperating partners based in Silicon Valley. Their goal is to create an electronic marketplace in which companies transact business over the Internet. They are solving business, security, reliability, and other problems that now prevent using Internet for routine commercial and business communications, including monetary transactions. The technology they are developing will enable electronic commerce on the Web, including a Secure-HTTP protocol for digitally signed or private Web transactions. To start their operation, the U.S. government's Technology Reinvestment Project provided $6 million. CommerceNet's recommendations for Internet connectivity include 28.8 Kbps as a minimum, 56

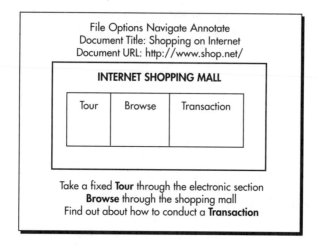

File Options Navigate Annotate
Document Title: Shopping on Internet
Document URL: http://www.shop.net/

INTERNET SHOPPING MALL

Tour	Browse	Transaction

Take a fixed **Tour** through the electronic section
Browse through the shopping mall
Find out about how to conduct a **Transaction**

Figure 5.7 An Internet screen.

Kbps or 128 Kbps for medium use, and T1 for a large group that requires frequent access to images. CommerceNet provides a storefront listing for $1250. A company's information resides on the company's servers.

Mecklerweb was a proposal for an Internet-hosting service that would have provided companies with places to advertise their wares and services. It was to be the first large-scale vehicle for the sort of discreet, soft-touch advertising that is consistent with Internet traditions. Mecklerweb was to provide servers for Fortune 1000 companies and charge about $25,000 per year for 20 MB of space containing full multimedia including video clips. Digital Equipment Corporation was to supply Alpha AXP servers, disk drives, and system integration resources. Users were to see a free, slick, point-and-click, full-color, hypertext interface built on Wide Area Information Servers (WAIS). The project ended because it did not have an adequate business case as much as it tried. Others that we describe may well have suffered the same fate by the time you read this.

CD-ROMs are a particularly attractive form in which to distribute catalogs, especially when a disc works with an on-line service that can update prices and process orders. CompuServe uses such CD-ROMs to augment its text-oriented on-line shopping mall. More and more software companies distribute demonstration versions of products on free CD-ROMs and use networks to sell passwords that unlock the complete versions that are also present on the discs.

Acquiring an Application   To try a typical shopping service, and many other services that combine on-line access with a CD-ROM, consider getting an account number on CompuServe and either telephoning (800) CDROM89

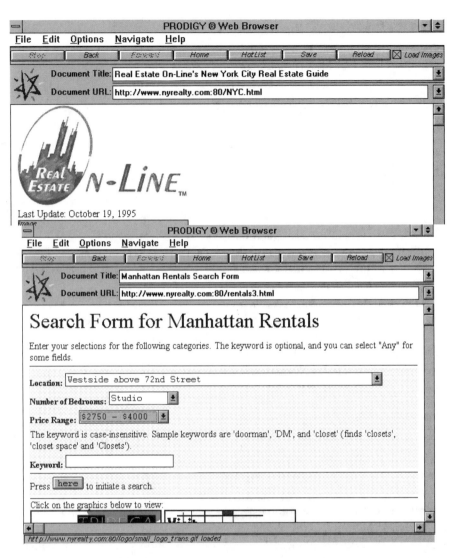

Figure 5.8 Screens of Real Estate On-Line's Real Estate Guide on the Internet. http://www.nyrealty.com. Reprinted with permission.

or logging onto CompuServe and executing GO CCDSUPPORT. You might also check out this chapter's references for a World Wide Web page called the "Hall of Malls."

Joan Warner reports (*Business Week*, 1993) that home shopping by way of television and 800 numbers remains a mere blip on the retail sales scene, accounting for just 1 percent to 2 percent of the shopping population. The replacement of store shopping by on-line shopping is far from imminent, even if interactive on-line home shopping grows exponentially.

Digital Libraries

Many libraries have moved from card catalogs to networks and terminals that allow users to search lists of books and periodicals. Automating acquisitions, circulation, and catalogs allowed libraries to keep up with an accelerating flow of information without hiring additional clerical staff. Even at similar costs, libraries found it easier to obtain funding for automation than for salaries. On-line catalogs satisfied most users, although some users bemoaned the loss of reader's feedback such as finger oil stains marking the most frequently touched cards, and others noted that an error in entering a book's card made the book about as inaccessible as would burning the book.

A digital library is much more than a library with an on-line catalog. A digital library keeps all or most of its assets in digital form, accessible to researchers and other users by means of networks and various sorts of terminals or personal computers. Along with digitized books and periodicals, a digital library consists of a search-and-filter engine, a storage facility, digitizing stations for new assets, internal and external networks, and the business piece that deals with billing, managing copyrights, and royalty payments.

Most digital library efforts have the status of pilot tests custom designed to support particular environments. All such efforts face moderately monumental problems. We next discuss two key problems of digitizing information and accessing information.

Digitizing Little of the world's information exists in digital form. Before users can access information over a network, someone must digitize the information by scanning it or photographing it with a digitizing camera. These procedures result in images, which preserve appearance, formatting, and illustrations, but which consume vastly more storage space and network bandwidth than would the equivalent amount of text. Several pilot projects have found that users require text as well as the image forms, especially for purposes of indexing, searching, browsing, scanning, preparing concordances, and editing. Economical conversion of images of printed pages to text requires optical character recognition, which is often far from perfect.

Digital library pilot tests use different strategies for digitizing existing material, depending on whether their primary purpose is access or preservation. For access, they tend to digitize content only when some user requests it, and often they then go on to create the text form as part of the same process. For preservation, they tend to begin with items that are most significant and are closest to having been destroyed by time and usage. They may defer conversion to text until their entire collection is safely preserved in the form of images stored on at least two physically separated systems. In either case, users will make use of a digital library only after the library builds up a critical mass of information that users can access online. As a result, most digital library projects require a massive up-front investment.

One survey found that the amount of information suitable for inclusion in libraries was doubling every 20 months and was getting out of control (Piatetsky-Shapiro and Frawley, 1991). Thus the problem of digitizing information includes the rising volume of new material, as well as the backlog of preexisting material. Fortunately, authors create a significant fraction of today's material in digital form, so libraries have a chance to obtain digital form directly rather than applying scanning and character recognition to an analog form. Carrying this one step further gives libraries an opportunity to serve their users better by capturing more content and different content than authors ever considered publishing on paper. Examples include massive tables of original experimental data, video of experiments, and simulation programs that users can run to try further experiments.

Concerns with digitizing literature and works of art include the extent to which the ease of making perfect digital copies dilutes original owners' rights and intentions and also the loss of quality that results from viewing images on-line with low resolution and inexact color. Artists, particularly, worry about users judging art works from inferior on-line presentation. However, even text suffers some degradation. Paper books have a typical contrast ratio of 120:1 and have 1200 dots per inch resolution, whereas most electronic media have significantly less contrast and resolution, with the result that on-line text appears less crisp than does printed paper. Business concerns include access control, authentication, copyrights and royalties, privacy, distribution and redistribution rights, and who pays costs of digitizing information.

Accessing   Other significant challenges exist in developing applications that facilitate precise and timely access to massive amounts of digitized information. The success of these applications depends on developing new ways of categorizing, indexing, archiving, and organizing electronic information. As more nonprofessional authors find it easier to contribute more material that no referee or editor has checked for content or style, digital libraries will find it harder to keep up with the challenge of helping users find valid, relevant, and readable information.

Finding digital information on-line is quite difficult, even with tools such as Mosaic or Netscape. Recall that these are graphical browsers for documents on the Web. When a user accesses a document in the Web with a browser, the user sees the icons that represent hypertext and hypermedia links to other documents in the Web that the document's authors included in the document. Mosaic is the work of Marc Andreessen, now of Netscape

Communications, and colleagues, then at NCSA in Urbana-Champaign, Illinois. NCSA versions of Mosaic are free. However, Mosaic style browsers are rapidly going commercial and are not just provided by Netscape Communications. Graphical browsers require high-speed connections to the Internet. A speed of 14.4 Kbps is hardly adequate for this use (Witten et al., 1994).

Before World Wide Web and its browsers, the Internet had Gopher, Archie, Veronica, and WAIS, which provided some help for users by offering various forms of keyword searches.

Recent advances in compression technology have made full content retrieval viable, including not only text but color images. See Focus 5.5 for details.

On-line commercial services are moving to provide full-text retrieval searches of various kinds. There are tradeoffs. For example, CompuServe decided to use a proprietary search engine that indexes text and performs searches based on content rather than searches based on natural language. This engine required less training time and less effort to integrate into their existing services.

Other problems that relate to access include the fact that most libraries still have only dumb terminals. There is no standard for access with personal computers or any other equipment. Many users lack the time and courage to master new search techniques.

Large test projects are under way in institutions such as Syracuse University, Cornell University, Carnegie-Mellon University, and Virginia Polytechnic Institute and State University. The Carnegie-Mellon application involves developing protocols to allow huge numbers of workstations to access digital information simultaneously in distributed libraries. Brief descriptions of some of the other projects follow.

Syracuse University   The Syracuse application's objectives are to determine the extent to which intelligent retrieval, which is now possible only with

---

FOCUS 5.5   Full text indexing.

Witten et al. (1994) report that the processing required to compress and invert a document on-line is approximately 4 MB/minute or 250 MB/hour on Sun's SunSPARC 10 Model 512. Starting from scratch, it takes eight CPU-hours to build a retrieval database from a 2-GB collection of text. It takes less than two minutes to compress and index a small 4-MB collection. Retrieval, including decompression, occurs at 50 MB per minute. ■

the assistance of a trained human librarian, can be automated and to investigate development, impact, and policy issues associated with creating the first significant digital library collection of learning materials for K–12 educators and students.

The Syracuse developers are working on what they call a Digital Librarian, which will attempt to retrieve information based on what a user's query means, rather than merely on what the query says. They base their work on the ARPA-funded DR-LINK natural language processing (NLP) approach to representation and retrieval.

Cornell University Staff at the Cornell University Library Department of Preservation and Conservation have spent several years experimenting with determining the best equipment, setup, software, and infrastructure for preserving library holdings. They report that "digital computer output that meets national standards for quality can be produced from 600 dpi binary scanning." Higher-resolution scanners, and scanners that record gray-scale information rather than binary scanning of black or white, make the scanning process significantly slower and more expensive. They also report that "binary scanning can reproduce many categories of printed illustrations and archival material in a manner superior or comparable to the quality obtained with standard light lens photocopy and microfilm."

Cornell librarians have experimented with providing access to their scanned images over the Internet from a variety of workstations. They found it necessary to define a unique infrastructure that employs a UNIX-based, X-Windows, Digital Library client. For each document they enter text search fields such as author, title, and catalog identifier. They identify chapter headings, tables of contents, indexes, and other parts of the document that help users navigate. Cornell quotes an early 1990s contract for converting 35-mm film to 500-dpi images at 35 cents per page. In production, technicians scan books at a rate of 5 pages per minute. Scanning costs for a 300-page, lightly illustrated book, including labor and equipment, average around $30, over the past decade. Access costs average about $1.00 but depend heavily on the equipment chosen (Kenney and Personius, 1992).

Virginia Tech Virginia Polytechnic Institute and State University's Project Envision aims to build a user-centered database around the literature of the ACM, the IEEE Computer Society, some Addison-Wesley publications, and other sources. They will share this information with other universities over a wide area network (Fox et al., 1993). The first step is to determine what users want and can use, and to investigate problems relating to operating digital libraries, by means of a pilot test using SGML and HyTime.

Interviews with early users indicate two things: Users do not select videos because users cannot browse or skim video, cannot easily locate a desired segment of video, and have no video table of contents. Also, users appreciate the opportunity for E-mail dialogues with colleagues that yield fuzzy pointers to information on-line such as, "Why don't you try to access a Web page for a company called Verity to see what they are doing for on-line searches?"

In 1994 the Commonwealth of Virginia allocated $5.2 million to create a virtual library. This project links Virginia's 51 public universities and colleges. It may be the most extensive such project in the country.

Bibliothèque Nationale de France   Philippe Aigrain of the staff of the Bibliothèque Nationale de France writes in his preprint for the workshop "Digital Libraries: Current Issues" (1994) about key issues for the design of the Bibliothèque's image and sound digital library. He reinforces others' assertions that the biggest time and cost bottleneck in a large library project is the digitizing or transfer process, citing the following cost ranges for digitizing important media.

- $1 to $4 per page for printed text material, at 600-dpi resolution

- $100 to $500 per hour for audio, using MPEG-audio compression

- $10 to $50 per color image, at 2048 × 3072 resolution, using JPEG compression

Aigrain predicts a trend toward on-demand digitizing of media other than text. He indicates that users need applications that support previewing or prehearing, filters, user annotation, and indexing. His group has experimented with applications that allow segmenting video according to time chunks and then allowing selection by chunk. The Bibliothèque's catalog and database associate a document with a visual representation of its contents that is useful for browsing and retrieving. Based on their work, they expect scholarly users to require a multimedia workstation that handles the following media. Specifications such as these can get outdated very quickly. However, they illustrate what very advanced pioneer and early adopter digital librarians feel are appropriate in 1994.

- 2000 digitized images, 1 GB, JPEG compressed

- 4 hours of digitized sound, 2.7 GB for uncompressed CD-DA quality

- 3 hours of JPEG AVI compressed digital video, 12 GB

- 8 GB of MPEG-2 compressed video at 4 Mbps

- 3.6 GB of JPEG AVI compressed video at standard interchange format (SIF) resolution

Some University Grants   Table 5.1 lists six universities to which NSF awarded $24.4 million in 1994. The focus areas and content emphasize the wide variety of problems that must be solved to advance this application category's state of the art.

Acquiring an Application   Neither a potential user nor a potential digital library manager can come close to buying a shrink-wrapped general-purpose digital library application. Library managers attend highly technical conferences to determine when funding and technology will allow them to go on-line. Users simply keep track of what is available by way of their on-line forums or by way of trade journals.

Table 5.1 University grantees.

University	Focus area	Content
Carnegie-Mellon	Automated categorizing techniques for digitized images and video	Digital video with emphasis on math and science
University of California, Berkeley	Electronic helpers that can visit potential digital information locations	Environment
University of Michigan	Software agents that work with and for the user to find information, including costs	Multiple media with emphasis on earth and space science
University of California at Santa Barbara	Search techniques for digital images	Geography and maps
Stanford University	User requests that search multiple libraries transparently	Technologies for a single integrated virtual library
University of Illinois	Capability for users to add links to existing digital information	Engineering and science journals and magazines

Video on Demand

Of all distributed multimedia application categories, video on demand, meaning movies over broadband networks, attracts the most hype. Potential users can easily imagine combining a television channel, which is convenient, with a videotape rental store, which provides a wide variety of content, with a VCR, which provides a degree of interactivity. Potential suppliers respond with pilot tests that are only slightly more convenient than driving to a video store and that provide only slightly more choice than do television channels.

Some surveys indicate that users are insufficiently enthusiastic about this application category to justify spending a significant fraction of $1 trillion to rewire networks for just this purpose alone. One survey ranked video on demand below participating in on-line elections (Piller, 1994). The survey results may indicate that the people surveyed were trying to give answers that would please their mothers or the vice president. In any case, video on demand may turn out to be a loss leader that customers can understand and that draws customers to other, more profitable, services.

Acquiring an Application   A potential provider of content cannot select off the shelf video-on-demand platforms to place the content on, but rather must work with manufacturers or system integrators to put together a test system. A key concern is the investment required to digitize enough video titles to interest potential customers. This investment must be written off, if the selected compression method fails to become one of the few ultimate standards. A critical concern, of course, is where to get the video to digitize. A potential user has no choice other than to move into an area conducting a video-on-demand trial.

Educational and Health Applications

EduPort is a leading state-of-the-art demonstration project targeted toward education. It consists of video content on a video server connected to schools by fiber-optic cables and ATM switches. In the schools, teachers use wireless control pads to select video clips and to do dynamic hyperlinking and bookmarking.

Dr. Miriam Masullo and colleagues at IBM's T.J. Watson Research Center in Hawthorne, New York, conceived and constructed EduPort as a digital library demonstration to help teachers bring relevancy and depth to the learning environment. (See Focus 5.6.) They believe that teachers and students can benefit from real-time on-demand access to historical information in the form of digitized video, audio, and images. They foresee large storage repositories of general educational content and specific curricula, with universities and K–12 teachers as major contributors.

EduPort's creators obtained and digitized more than 100 clips of public domain video for their demonstration from such sources as the T.J. Watson Research Laboratory, AAA, the Kennedy Center, the Smithsonian Museum, the National Gallery of Art, the FDR Library, and NASA. The clips suffice to get educators thinking about the possibilities of such capabilities and to elicit their participation in building up an application-development environment and a meaningful set of educational materials.

Senator Bob Kerrey sponsored an EduPort demonstration installation at Lincoln High School in Lincoln, Nebraska, in 1994. The University of Nebraska provided space and time on its campus server. A channel-attached IBM PS/2 Model 95 personal computer ran as the front-end processor (FEP), supporting 60 concurrent video streams through four token-ring connections. Lincoln Telephone and Telegraph provided the wide-area network connectivity to Lincoln High School through the company's LAN Emulation Services over fiber-optic lines. The high school selected video that appeared on a large electronic blackboard. The teacher was free to walk around the room, interact with students, and select materials that added to class discussions. The teacher could also answer extemporaneous questions by bringing up relevant video clips in real time on demand.

Such attractive and impressive demonstrations raise several questions. How can such information be disseminated to more than just a few lucky schools that just happen to be in cooperation with some universities, some computer and communication companies, and the government? How critical is the cooperation of universities to the advisement of technology such as this at the K–12 level? How can information be kept current? How can the materials be tightly integrated with existing and future curricula? How can a teacher identify appropriate video for on-demand retrieval? How can teachers be trained to add and manage dynamic hyperlinks in the vast sea of information? In response to the latter question, EduPort's creators organized information into media blocks that contain combinations of objects consisting of video clips, images, and text. Teachers spent evenings selecting and combining media blocks to correspond to the curricula the teachers expected to discuss the next day (Masullo, 1993).

Some businesses have been able to justify distributed multimedia expenditures for use in either creating or using multimedia computer-based training. Businesses select among the following approaches to deliver such content.

FOCUS 5.6   Interview with:

Dr. Miriam Masullo

Senior Researcher at IBM's T.J. Watson Research Laboratory

What are the frustrations?

This is a very important issue to bring out. The biggest frustration is having to deal with the incomplete information or lack of knowledge (in this area) by decision makers with funds to deploy. For example, last year a group convened in Washington to discuss the future of digital video. At that time our project in Nebraska was already demonstrating to the world the benefit of digital video, and the world was assimilating the message of the power of digital video technologies for education.

This past year the same group produced a report that establishes the need for pursuing these broadband and digital video technologies for the advancement of our information infrastructures and for advancing education. However, during all that time the Nebraska message was ignored by every funding agency in Washington. Worse than that, it was also ignored by organizations in corporations who routinely provide funds for educational efforts, who did not understand the power and future of these technologies and did not even understand their own company's role in all this.

Unless we infuse some knowledge into the decision makers that have it in their power to break or make our future based on technology, we will become a Second World nation quickly. We will continue to support efforts that do not have the potential to propel us into the future, because we are stuck with borderline advancements in changing the paradigms rather than drastically advancing paradigms.

It is no longer the decision makers in the educational establishments who are involved, but every decision maker who funds schools who is now liable for their mistakes. The report had not been produced on time to back up our initiative. We were too early. In fact, we were so early that at the time we had digital video libraries used in real-time on-demand in the classroom; the WWW was not even popular. Now the race is on to make the Web real-time interactive as opposed to store and forward.

What have you found by talking with people from around the world?

This is an interesting piece of the puzzle. What I have personally experienced is that the Nebraska project is very inspiring to people around the world who would not otherwise perhaps take an active interest in these technologies. Experiences and projects in places such as New York and California, for example, do not seem to touch upon the hopes and expectations of people from South America, Korea, South Africa, and the agricultural provinces of Europe. Even people around the United States are intrigued by what we have done in Nebraska, and I find that intriguing.

Recently I gave a talk in Korea on the role of digital libraries in education. When I told them that students in Nebraska don't get to see the ocean or walk the halls of the great museums in our nation's capital, the audience in Korea gave the project a standing ovation. What they were expressing is joy at the existence of proof that none need be left out.

There is also a tremendous desire to leapfrog into the future—to bring these technologies to the backroads of the world, and use them to solve serious deliberately created inequalities, not unlike those that exist in parts of our own nation.

There is a portion of the world that views technology as a great equalizer, and there is a portion of the world that sees beyond that (in my opinion to what is more likely to happen) a shift in the distribution of power. But nobody knows which way it will go.

What skills do children have to learn?

Students need to become inquiry literate. Current lack of practice in digital libraries applications is high. In many cases, misguided expectations are leading students to believe that they will have access to world class scientists any time they want. How will scientists, researchers, and experts, a very select very small group, be able to respond to questions from potentially thousands, even millions of students? The issues are not being dealt with realistically. This will retard the application of the technologies because the paradigms sought are impossible, defeating. All students must understand the issues at some level of sophistication. Students must learn to deal with emerging technologies, something that is different from the very stable, very slow changing setting of the classroom. Students must know the differences among communica-

tions and information technologies, e.g., television broadcasts, digital media, the Internet, JTV, and video on demand services of the future, and be able to form a vision for how changes in these technologies will affect their lives.

What have you learned, both good and bad, from your work in deploying your prototype digital libraries?

The main lesson for me was the confusion that I found out there concerning the technologies. We have known for a long time that many in the education community are still highly bewildered and confused about the role and impact of technology in education in general. So I was prepared for that, but I was not prepared for questions like How is video on demand different from television? and Why do we need this when we have VCRs? Since I was coming from a technology environment, the fundamental lack of understanding surrounding the issues was an important lesson I learned. It doesn't matter how real or powerful these new technologies are if people have no idea what we are talking about.

How can we be convincing?

It turns out that the most important problem to solve is to provide a way for people to envision the possibilities. Without that, nothing is doable. This is a case where the sword is mightier than the pen. We need action. We need to demonstrate the possibilities with real-life projects to help the teachers, students, parents, and decision makers envision. Talking and meeting about it will only add to the confusion.

(cont.)

FOCUS 5.6 (*cont.*)

What was involved in setting up EduPort? Where did the information come from? Was it hard to get?

The media came from several organizations that have large inventories of content in the public domain and that have great interest in seeing the information well used. In some cases there are mandates to make content available to the public. So these organizations were willing to explore this new route, EduPort's digital library, for sharing information. The media was not really hard to get, given that we had a legitimate project, that we were a reputable organization, had the endorsement of a public figure, and were able to demonstrate our technical skills. It was very time consuming and labor intensive to cultivate these relationships. Time is required to build trust among content providers and technologists. No shortcuts are possible, but every second is worth bringing our legacy of content to the rightful owners, the students. Every single point of contact with the potential information provider required personal attention, a demo using large amounts of hardware, and travel to their location. Sometimes the point of contact required a visit to the T.J. Watson Research Laboratory, where they had to be hosted. It takes time and special skills to build relationships and sustain them over the time that is required to carry out a project such as this one. Money, by the way, was not a major inhibitor at this stage, not that we had any, but extended funding from a company, the possibility of a grant, and things of that nature were not even a consideration. These organizations did

not become involved because they thought they were going to get money or equipment, but because they were intrigued by the technology and eager to become involved with what they considered had an element of goodness associated with it and a possibility for greatness in the future. Also, sharing knowledge and information with people that they would not otherwise be able to reach was a major inducement to participate.

What are some of the critical pieces of investigation that need to be performed in the next few years to make prototypes and visions of digital libraries real?

We need people to use the technologies so that we can come to understand really what it is we are doing. From the technical perspective, this might be called usage patterns and applications; from the human perspective, it is called doing something that enhances the quality of life.

What are the critical inhibitors that prevent every community from having a digital library?

Right now the inhibitor appears to be connectivity, the inability to be able to reach with the kinds of broadband networks that are needed. In many ways this is a problem similar to electrifying rural America, which took 40 years to do. We don't have that much time now; the dimensions are different. We need to turn this inhibitor into an asset by using the time to understand the problem and to digitize the content. We can also build local infrastructures now, that as the connectivity develops will become regional infrastructures and eventually we will have the national infrastructure that we seek. But we must balance the growth of the communications infrastructure with the growth of the information infrastructure. Just worrying about connectivity will lead to massively being connected to nothing. We need to understand what it is that we are connecting to and for what.

What new skills do educators need, to enable this kind of technology in the classroom?

I feel very strongly that the inquiry skill is where it is all at. We need to learn those skills, to learn to teach them, and then to teach them. Learning how to manipulate the current end-user devices is not an endeavor of lasting value. These devices are ephemeral in nature. Learning to harness information by first learning what questions to ask, when to ask them, and how to ask them is the skill that is at the heart of the information revolution. Certainly, creating information is not what the information revolution is all about; that has been going on forever and is now going out of control. It is in the how-to-find-it and how-to-use-it where the real challenge lies. We are supporting much effort in the finding aspects of all this—but what is the driving force?

Do parents have a role?

Regarding what is happening in the world today, every person has a role. With respect to education, parents have the same role that they always have, responsibility for the education of their children and advocacy for the education of every child. That will not change, but under the current climate it will take different forms. Since this information revolution is very tightly coupled with on-line telecommunications, we would expect that becoming more involved with the education of our own children and taking more responsibility should be made easier by the simple enhancement of connectivity. Advocacy, however, will be made more difficult because it will require decision making of a more complex kind, involving technology issues, that again, is very confused, very difficult to sort out.

As you have discussed digital libraries with people all over the world, what has impressed you about what people in other countries are thinking and doing?

The thing that stays with me and never ceases to amaze me is the impact that this project in Nebraska, in the heartland of the country, has had on the hopes and goals of people all over the world. What I found was that when I told people that in Nebraska students don't get to see the sea or walk down the halls of the great museums in the nation's capital, but yet they were able to do this and get access to information that students even in the nation's capital do not have access to (digital video on demand of archival value); all of a sudden the reaction shifted to that of players and stockholders, rather than that of audiences listening to what

(cont.)

FOCUS 5.6 *(cont.)*

others were doing. They identified with it. This project touches the minds and hearts of so many people.

We have had people from all over the world come to Nebraska to see what has been done there, important, powerful, and skilled people. They are not impressed with the technology, which they can see in any laboratory of any university or research center. They are impressed with what we have done with it. If you come to Nebraska you will see a borrowed obsolete PC, a makeshift rear projection room, and a few teachers who are excited and hopeful. We are not impressing anyone with technology, but rather with human potential and spirit. It was the right place, the right time, the right level of resources (almost none), and the right formula (leadership and vision) for delivering the message that this can be done and that it is a good thing to do.

Should we be aware of some exciting developments in related research areas that might reach production in the next decade? It is so difficult to impress anyone with exciting research areas anymore. It seems that nothing research can do will ever compare with special effects and the world of fiction. Anticipating the future with fiction plays an important role in human ingenuity, energizing our capacity for dreaming and then making dreams realities. But we have taken that so far that even at the speed at which technology moves, speeds that make it impossible to implement what is doable, we will never be able to implement what is not doable but already expected. Expectations of technology are too high, while our ability to implement existing needed technologies is very low, creating a confusing paradox in the American consciousness.

- Installing content on each personal computer and sending infrequent video updates over the company's existing local area networks

- Setting up a dedicated media server and local area network for training that uses video. In 1995, HP and Oracle offered media server software off the shelf. IBM, Sun, Sybase, and Microsoft announced intentions to provide such software or had shipped beta test versions.

- Sharing existing local area networks with other applications. This brute-force approach occasionally inconveniences other users.

Several companies reported that multimedia gave students excellent results, in comparison to conventional training methods. Results included more consistent learning, higher comprehension and retention rates, learning in a shorter time, and more convenient scheduling. These results could justify installing a dedicated local area network and server for computer-based

If you had $1 million to give to a community to prepare for digital electronic libraries, for what would you advise them to use it?
I would put together a plan for creating a self-sufficient local infrastructure that connects to key places in the community maximizing human access. I would include a business plan for selling special services through that infrastructure so that when the $1 million is used up we would be able to sustain and grow the project.

If you can only afford to keep track of a few periodicals or forums or equivalent, which would you recommend for our readers in this area?
Newspapers are doing the best job so far of keeping us informed of progress as things change daily. The problem there is

recognizing those changes, the news that affects this area, and that is sometimes only noticeable even to the experts. Changing and current events as reported by the technology observers in the daily media are very effective because an almost daily update mechanism is needed to understand what is happening.

Other than that, the relevant publications are only now emerging. For instance, the *International Journal of Educational Telecommunications* printed its first issue in 1995. We need more focused publications like that one. Conference proceedings are always a good source of relevant information. All the well-established conferences in the areas of education, multimedia, and telecommunications also have special-interest groups or workshops that focus on digital libraries and education. ∎

Printed with permission.

multimedia training, along with the front-end expense of developing computer-based training content. The reference provides model business cases (Fetterman and Gupta, 1993, Chapter 7).

Health Multimedia network applications can provide remote access to health care providers and to databases. A hospital may accumulate from 3 GB to 100 GB of CAT scan and X-ray data each day. (See Focus 5.7.) Legal requirements mandate archives that can accumulate TeraBytes of data. Health care can thus require large-capacity storage as well as large-bandwidth networks.

Different sectors of the medical community employ several disjoint systems, as a result of many years of gradual evolution. The good news is that more than half of all diagnostic images use digital techniques. The bad news is that workstations suitable for viewing high-resolution images are scarce and paper reproductions are poor. However, economical personal computers are appropriate for many purposes, including teaching.

FOCUS 5.7 Sizes of digitized images.
A computerized axial tomography (CAT) scan examination may result in 512 by 512 pixels for each of 64 slices, with 2 Bytes per pixel, for a total of 32 MB of data per examination. A patient may have several examinations. A typical X-ray has far higher resolution, although only a single image. ■

Yale University uses multimedia in its Introduction to Cardiothoracic Imaging class. Multiple concurrent users access a digital server that contains over 800 diagnostic images, 100 medical illustrations of normal anatomy and anatomical landmarks, and several dozen digital videos of echocardiography, explanatory animations, and magnetic resonance imaging. Yale's campus Ethernet system is perfectly adequate for still images, but only occasionally provides acceptable frame rates for digital video.

The University of Wisconsin in Madison has developed a Comprehensive Health Enhancement Support System that serves as a networked information resource for at-home patients.

The University of South Carolina School of Medicine worked with partners such as the local integrator, CAE-Link, and PictureTel Corporation of Danvers, Massachusetts, to create a system for Winnsboro Rural Primary Care. The system provides video conference capabilities to help primary care physicians contact specialists in other cities.

Atlantis Software's ReadySetGrow! medical software has interactive animation and sound effects covering the first five years of life. The software provides diary areas in which users can enter information.

Johns Hopkins University has a prototype ATM network to transfer CAT and magnetic resonance images. They expect to support video consultations from archived on-line patient records. Their challenges are to provide sufficient speed to transfer images in seconds rather than hours and to provide sufficient intelligence to identify, display, and archive the information for easy retrieval. They are collaborating with others, such as the Institute of Systems Science of the National University of Singapore, to meet these challenges.

Remote diagnosis and treatment face serious obstacles that have little or nothing to do with technology. A conference on Breaking the Barriers to the National Information Infrastructure heard that physicians' major concerns are as follows (*Network World*, 1994).

- Insurance for nonpayment for services

- Insurance for malpractice

- Licenses to practice across state lines

- Costs of getting started

- Long-term return on investments in equipment

- Privacy

- Disturbing traditional doctor–patient relationships

Acquiring an Application   Hospitals and other health care providers tend to rely on integrators to supply complete verified applications, sometimes including hardware as well as software. They face a major challenge of making many individual applications work well together.

Hybrid Applications

Because there are no widely deployed multimedia networks, the state of the art of almost all application categories tends to be hybrid. Some examples of state-of-the-art activities are as follows. Users can

- Share their thoughts during and after television broadcasts over on-line services.

- Use CompuServe to send comments to a radio or television talk show.

- Shop from home by waiting until the television home-shopping channel shows a desirable item and then using POTS to complete a transaction.

- Buy a CD-ROM such as *Microsoft's Baseball,* which automatically dials a for-fee service to obtain the latest statistics and scores.

- Play games over a network, against computers or against human opponents, then use the network to discuss the play with competitors and partners.

HISTORY

Through the 1980s, different industries obtained, created, and transmitted content in characteristically different ways.

Publishing: Publishing houses contracted with authors to create content. They then edited and printed the results and distributed books to retail outlets. Newspaper publishers developed their own content, contracted with wire services for outside content, and used the various other news services.

Telephone: Telephone companies provided only connections. Their common carrier monopoly did not allow them to own content and did not allow them to influence what content they would deliver.

Television and Movies: Television and radio networks obtained much of their content from production companies and produced some of their content, such as local news. CATV networks obtained much of their content from broadcast television networks and stations, obtained some content from syndicators and production companies, and produced a few public service programs. Movie companies dealt with independent producers and acted as distributors and loan guarantors. (In earlier decades, movie companies produced much more of their content.)

Computers: Computer companies developed content in-house and contracted for content from outside authors.

Distributed multimedia is extending the concept of content to encompass the broader concept of applications and associated services. Distributed multimedia is also converging the above-named industries' sources of content and methods of delivery. These changes make histories of application categories more relevant than histories of individual industries. We next look at the history of each category of applications.

Desktop video conferences with collaboration have a relatively long but not very successful history so far. As Table 5.2 indicates, neither industrial nor consumer applications in this category have been successful. The most closely related applications that have been successful are centralized industrial video conference rooms. These rooms did not allow the parties to participate in video conferences from their desks and did not allow the parties to collaborate on creating documents. The historical message is that large amounts of time and hype do not suffice without economy and quality, in this case, adequate video quality.

Multimedia store-and-forward mail, as Table 5.3 indicates, has a long and increasingly successful history. This application category, unlike the previous one, was genuinely useful when limited to text, which early networks could deliver with acceptable economy and quality. The success of text allowed providers to introduce other media gradually. Whereas E-mail that includes text, graphics, and a reasonable number of images is now about to leap the chasm that separates early adopters from the mass market, relatively few users—only the pioneers—have sufficient equipment and skill to record or even play binary files that contain audio and video. However, a look at the history of this category makes us confident that these two demanding media will make it across the chasm eventually.

The history of consumer edutainment, infotainment, and sociotainment in Table 5.4 shows that an appropriate mixture of facts and fun appeals more

Table 5.2 Some video conference history.

Date	Event
1964	AT&T announced the VideoPhone at World's Fair.
1970s	Vendors proclaimed that the VideoPhone and related applications were just around the corner.
Mid-1980s	Use expanded gradually from expensive executive video conference rooms to smaller organizations, due to less expensive integrated circuits and somewhat less expensive networks.
1991	PictureTel introduced a small full-color group video conference system priced below $20,000.
Early 1990s	AT&T reintroduced the VideoPhone for about $1200.
1994	Intel, AT&T, IBM, and others began emphasizing desktop products such as Intel's ProShare and IBM's desktop video conference products. High price and low availability of networks hindered sales.
1995	Declining hardware prices, agreements on standards, and agreements on the part of some major software providers to work together to provide integrated solutions gave reason to show some small sign of optimism for the next few years.

Table 5.3 Some E-mail history.

Date	Event
1969	CompuServe began as a time-sharing text service for businesses that needed remote access to mainframe computers. ARPANET (earlier Internet) started.
1972	InterNetworking Working Group (INWG) started to address need for establishing protocols. The chairman was Vinton Cerf.
1982	INWG established TCP/IP standard.
1988	IBM, Sears, Roebuck and Co., and CBS began Prodigy.
1991	WAIS and Gopher released to help retrieve information on the Internet.
1994	Prodigy claimed close to 2 million users. It noted that its users prefer E-mail and bulletin boards over home shopping. It adjusted pricing accordingly. It continued to have difficulty being profitable.
1994	Major E-mail services announced various forms of access to Internet, expanded and easier-to-use mail facilities, and gateways to other services.
1995	All of CompuServe, America Online, Prodigy, and Internet added users and features at prodigious rates. Some estimates place the total number of Web sites at almost 1 million with over 40 million people worldwide using Internet. Many surveys show that E-mail is the most widely used application.

Table 5.4 Consumer edutainment, infotainment, sociotainment.

Date	Event
Late 1880s	Nintendo was founded in 1889 by Fusajiro Yamauchi, who made playing cards.
Late 1970s	Manufacturers sold game devices as add-ons for television sets. Sales exploded and later crashed.
Early 1980s	Warner Communications lost millions on Qube, an interactive cable television system in Columbus, Ohio, that allowed people to play games and order merchandise.
Early 1980s	Newspaper publisher Knight-Ridder Inc. lost heavily on a videotex service in Florida.
Early and mid 1980s	Videotex offerings did well in Europe, especially in France and in Japan, but not in the United States. The technology was hard to use. The services charged by the minute, rather than charging a flat rate that would have encouraged casual use. See Chapter 7 for information on related trials.
Early 1990s	Sierra On-Line found that people like talking about their game-playing skills as much as actually playing the games. Forums grew dramatically on topics ranging from help groups for nursing mothers to how to fix old Hondas.
1990s	Nintendo, Sega, and 3DO planned increasingly sophisticated game machines and also tried to leverage the installed base of personal computers. About 40 percent of American households owned game devices. Game networks grew and customers used the networks to discuss games as well as to play games. On-line services' offerings, particularly forums and chats, appeared to finally catch on and move beyond early adopters. Internet grew exponentially with Internet surfing very popular as a form of entertainment.
1994	Prodigy augmented news with audio that a suitably equipped personal computer could download and play back. CompuServe offered libraries of compressed multimedia clips for downloading. Veronis, Suhler & Associates' Communications Industry Forecast, Ninth Annual Edition (1995), indicated that per capita in 1994 the U.S. consumer on-line and Internet services accounted for 3 hours and $7 vs. 22 hours and $17 for home video games, and 1560 hours and $110.00 for television.
1995	Prodigy integrated the Web into its basic consumer services and added templates for users to add their own personal home pages to the WWW. They redesigned their pages, removing much of the blatant advertising. America Online went ahead with over 3 million subscribers. Microsoft had a significant entry with its Microsoft Network.

Table 5.5 Some shopping and advertising history.

Date	Event
1744	Benjamin Franklin produced America's first catalog, to sell scientific and academic books.
1888	Sears offered its first catalog.
1993	Sears shut down its catalog operation.
1994	Hundreds of highly specialized mail order paper catalogs such as quilting, laser paper, or archival supplies appeared in the mail.
1994	CD-ROM catalogs appeared for early pioneers.
1995	Some mail order companies offered E-mail ordering.

and more strongly to the segment of society that contributes most network users. Nonetheless the right combination at the right time is critical.

Shopping and advertising have a history of moving from mass markets, such as the Sears Catalog that dominated for so long, to smaller and more specialized markets. Table 5.5 illustrates some steps along this path.

Starting a digital library is like leaving an airplane in flight; the first step is a big one. Even digitizing a rare books collection and making the results available over a network is a large change from traditional library practice. Making full text of a large library accessible over a network is even more serious business. However, Table 5.6 indicates that digital libraries solve enough real problems to encourage some big steps.

Table 5.6 Some digital library history.

Date	Event
Early 1990s	Cornell and a few other libraries began to look to digitization for rare book preservation.
Early 1990s	Many publishers, libraries, and universities established on-line indexes. Some of these indexes were available for remote access.
Early 1990s	A few publishers, libraries, and universities digitized the full content of their collections. Many provided only text for remote use.
1994	The Vatican Library and IBM announced a project to digitize some of the Vatican's holdings.
1994	The National Science Foundation granted significant funding awards to several universities to work to make digital library set-up and access a reality.

Table 5.7 Some video-on-demand history.

Date	Event
Mid-1980s	CATV penetrated 50 percent of U.S. households.
Late 1980s	VCRs reached 50 percent penetration in U.S. households.
Early 1990s	The home video industry's revenue was twice the revenue of movie box offices. Video-game software's revenue was half the revenue of movie box offices.
1990s	Over 100,000 retail outlets sold or rented videotapes. Over 25,000 outlets rented videotapes as their only business.
1990s	Potential suppliers of delivery service started aggressively lining up movie assets or other sources to deliver.
1990s	Blockbuster experimented with digital transmission of movies to its stores from a central distribution site.
Mid-1990s	VCRs reached 80 percent penetration.
Mid-1990s	Early trials indicated that consumers would choose two movies on demand per month, but want more selections, more help making selections, and more applications than trials provided.
Mid-1990s	Many trials were under way, as we note in Chapter 7.

Video on demand is a future goal that is based on a long history of approximately similar functions that employ earlier technologies that Table 5.7 shows.

Educational applications had a surprisingly rapid takeoff. Surprisingly, many elementary schools, despite generally parsimonious funding, bought and used laser disc players, which gave interactive access to high-quality analog video educational content long before commercial users employed lower-quality digital video. Personal computers, too, appeared in schools quite early, although not in large numbers. Table 5.8 notes that education did not match early use of stand-alone multimedia with early use of even the simplest POTS networks.

Table 5.9 notes progress in medical applications driven by a rapidly growing sector of the economy that has massive requirements for more and better information and better use of costly personnel. We received Table 5.9's detailed information in response to an inquiry on Internet (Kling, private communication, 1994).

Hybrid applications make effective use of discs, networks, some end-user devices and maybe even the telephone. This synergy appeared more

Table 5.8 Some history of computers in education.

Date	Event
1978	Philips and IBM agreed on laser disc standards and started selling players and educational content to schools.
Late 1970s	Schools started buying computers for students to use.
1980s	Schools expanded their purchases of computers, reaching about one per school, but often with old and slow models. They focused on computer-assisted instruction (CAI) and simple applications such as word processing, spreadsheets, databases, and programming in BASIC, LOGO, and Pascal.
1980s	School classrooms continued to have relatively few telephones and very few computers with modems.
1984	National Technological University transmitted lectures over satellite.
1987	Mind Extension University transmitted lectures over its basic cable network.
Late 1980s and early 1990s	Industries gave grants to, or had partnerships with, universities to develop infrastructure and content for networked mainframes, minicomputers, and personal computers. Some universities with key developments were MIT with Project Athena, Carnegie-Mellon University with the Andrew File System, and the University of Michigan with the Institutional File System.
1990s	Presence of personal computers in schools increased, with typically five in a classroom rather than one in a remote laboratory. Presence of multimedia and interest in the Internet increased.
1993–1994	Schools spent almost $1 billion for personal computers during this school year. Still too many schools were without sufficient computers or staff trained to use computers.
Mid-1990s	A strong home market developed for multimedia personal computers that run educational and edutainment programs for K–12 students. Over 50 percent of K–12 teachers had computers in their homes.

recently than the foundations of other application categories. The closest example of the same sort of synergy was receiving a Sears Catalog in the mail and placing orders by telephone. Making do sometimes can work out very well. Table 5.10 illustrates what newer technologies make possible.

Table 5.9 Some history of medical applications.

Date	Event
1959 through 1971	University of Nebraska used two-way closed-circuit microwave television for medical treatment and education, to sites on campus and to a state mental health facility 112 miles away.
Late 1950s through 1970s	Lockheed, National Aeronautics and Space Administration, and National Public Health Service used two-way video to a mobile van in a remote Papago reservation, both to provide health care and to do research on providing medical services to astronauts in space.
1966	An Anchorage, Alaska, hospital used the ATS-1 satellite to provide routine medical services to rural sites by means of black-and-white television.
1968	Massachusetts General Hospital used interactive television to provide health services at Boston's Logan Airport medical station. They reported a 1 to 2 percent variance between telemedicine diagnoses and in-person diagnoses.
1980s	Telemedicine activities in the United States declined, only to blossom again in the early 1990s.
1993	Some insurance carriers recognized remote consultation and began paying as if a patient had been with a physician.
1993	U.S. Department of Defense demonstrated telemedicine among three sites, a MASH unit in Fort Gordon, Georgia, University of Virginia Medical Center in Charlottesville, Virginia, and Walter Reed Army Medical Center in Washington, DC. Robotic devices provided tactile feedback for a surgeon performing remote surgery. This added the unusual medium of touch to the five more common media.

Table 5.10 Some hybrid application history.

Date	Event
1994	Microsoft announced and shipped CD-ROMs that could log on and get up-to-date information supplements.
1994	CompuServe announced and shipped their periodical CD-ROM magazine, which included easy log-on to their on-line service.
1994	Several mail order companies accompanied their traditional paper catalogs with CD-ROMs that facilitated ordering.
Mid-1990s	Radio and television talk shows added E-mail participation to traditional telephone participation.

DIFFERENCES

Some of the characteristics of the state of the art for all categories of applications that differ widely from the vision for those categories are as follows.

The vision demands integrated applications and contexts, but even single good applications are in the future. Overzealous news services and industry providers' public relations departments have set unrealistically high levels of expectation for quick deployment and successful penetration. Distributed multimedia applications suffer more than stand-alone applications from interoperability problems and multiple or missing standards. Consumer applications suffer more than business or industrial applications from hard of (the opposite of ease of) acquiring, installing, and use. Complex business, political, and legal processes that must accompany these applications raise new issues and affect more individuals. Simply digitizing existing information is a major challenge in itself and rights management is required to ensure quality applications. Successful business models delivering value and satisfaction to the customer and dollars to the provider are currently being developed.

TRENDS

We return to the application categories to list trends that can lead from today's state of the art toward capabilities in the vision. Provider trends by application category follow.

Desktop Video Conferences with Collaboration

- The trend toward economical multipoint connections and multicasts (instead of point-to-point connections), all with collaboration on computer-type applications, makes desktop video conferencing more affordable.

- Providers' agreement on more and better application programming interfaces (APIs) allows different vendors to produce software add-ons, including stability enhancements.

- Providers' agreement on standards such as H.320 (including H.261) encourages cross-platform interoperability and thus increases the number of people who can participate.

- Research results on effective use and minimal requirements for lowest cost are starting to come out of projects at MIT, Berkeley, Cornell, AT&T, IBM, Intel, and PictureTel.

- Costs are declining but still too high for most consumers.

- Faster lines are increasingly available, but there are not yet enough lines for more than pioneers and early adopters and they are not available in smaller cities.

- Desktop video conferencing communities are emerging from pioneers and early users after almost 40 years since AT&T's introduction of the VideoPhone.

Multimedia Store-and-Forward Mail

- Providers are adding features that make multimedia store-and-forward mail easier to use.

- Use of appending binary files for holding compressed audio or video is increasing. However, even where audio and video are present, it is still much too hard for most people to create, send, and receive multimedia mail.

- More gateways among different services allow a user to access many services without placing many separate telephone calls.

- Trials are in progress and more are planned with E-mail that includes compressed audio and video after a history of years of being able to send only text.

Consumer Edutainment, Infotainment, Sociotainment

- Emphasis is likely to increase on ease of purchase, set-up, learning, maintenance, and use of edutainment, infotainment, and sociotainment to attract more than early adopters and more than college-educated males.

- Emphasis continues on increasing performance or giving the appearance of increased performance through clever programming techniques.

- As they gain competence and experience, developers are producing more attractive, less boring content as well as content appropriate to the limitations of the hardware, available bandwidth, and software.

- New forums and real-time chats that appeal to a broader spectrum of the marketplace debut frequently.

- Query tools are improving, particularly those used with enhanced WWW browsers and other search engines.

- Graphical user interfaces, including shopping mall or home metaphors, are becoming more usable and intuitive.

- Hyperlinks are extending across services.

- Value-added applications and services available from on-line providers offer more to users than the less expensive Internet access.

- Agents, such as those created by using General Magic's Telescript language, are evolving beyond simple macros.

- Users' ability to perform extensive and precise background searches are expanding by means of software agents or equivalent.

- Suites of integrated applications are combining consumer edutainment, infotainment, and sociotainment across providers and end-user devices and are including the ability to conduct transactions.

- Early production use of programming tools such as Java and VRML and authoring tools such as Macromedia's Director embedded in Web browsers are making static Web pages dynamic and thereby more appealing to consumers while not waiting for faster delivery vehicles. Early use of these tools requires very skilled creators.

Shopping and Advertising

- Trends in advertising and sales include development of better tools to help small businesses create and place on the Internet electronic brochures, company information, and related information that mix text, graphics, images, audio, and video.

- Various services on Internet are expanding even without remuneration to avoid being left out.

- Growing pains and legal hassles are continuing.

- Many experiments with new applications for shopping and advertising are likely to fail, some to succeed.

- Providers are experimenting with shopping applications and advertising targeted to specific niches.

- Tactics to entice targeted customers to browse, participate, and be counted in specific on-line sites are continuing to improve.

Digital Libraries

- More pilot tests to prioritize innovation in digital libraries are preceding standardization, cost reductions, and wide-scale dissemination.

- Standards and sharing of digitized library content are gradually emerging.

- Innovations in compression and digital representation of information are making possible improvements in digital library applications.

- NSF and other government agencies are funding more activities.

- New on-line metaphors are available in addition to the old metaphor of a digital page of text.

- More digitized information is available as time goes on.

- Announcements are expected of early automated ways to effectively manage copyrights satisfying the end user as well as copyright owner.

Video on Demand

- Pilot tests are offering more selections than a typical video store, including a greater selection of movies and other applications.

- More attractive and usable end-user interfaces for selecting video are being developed.

- Users are able to demand current television shows, including live news and sports, as well as movies.

- Network upgrades are deploying fiber-optic cable nearer to more homes, reducing the investment increment required to provide such applications.

- As standardization of video compression increases, pilot tests can share the cost of digitizing material.

Educational and Health Applications

- Larger tests funded by grants and partnerships among users, major companies, and universities are featuring educational and health applications.

- As results of these tests are integrated into educational environments and curricula, obstacles of equipment, training, and politics are slowly overcome.

- Long-distance learning applications are expanding, with educators providing content and distributing the content to schools.

- Developers are experimenting with educational content specifically for distributed multimedia rather than merely reusing content designed for another environment.

- Providers of educational materials are beginning to acknowledge that the proliferation of computers in the home, and parental interest in educational and edutainment, can mean good business. Educators are also acknowledging that children without computers at home can be significantly left out if schools do not provide all students possibilities of exposure to computers.

- Some companies, realizing the proliferation of multimedia computers at home, are suggesting to employees that they use company-produced multimedia training at home.

- Some debuts of pay-for-learning systems are including some elements of multimedia, E-mail, and real-time chat.

- Acceptance and knowledge of the benefits of telehealth and telemedicine are growing.

Hybrid Applications

- CD-ROMs containing hypertext and other media with optional, mostly text, updates over networks are augmenting but not replacing paper publishing.

- Among additional hybrid applications are talking telephone books with 900 and 800 numbers.

- Developers are learning, even from tests that have disappointing results.

- Applications are migrating into home computers and set-top boxes, as long as it remains more economical to generate sequences of screens near the user than to send unique screens to each user over a network.

- Using Java and Hot Java and similar languages sent from a server to the client computer are further extending the hybrid concept.

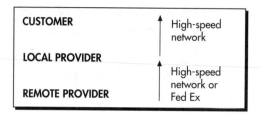

Figure 5.9   Options for receiving a movie.

One of the most important trends in distributed multimedia is for commercial providers to improve hybrid applications incrementally. For example, we noted that one such application, *Microsoft's Baseball,* is a CD-ROM that transparently logs the user onto an on-line service to get the latest baseball statistics.

Consider a hypothetical CD-ROM application that has a database of movies. Suppose that this application could accumulate information about the extent to which a customer enjoyed each movie that she saw in the last two years, so that the application could confidently suggest a movie that she would enjoy next. Imagine, further, that the application can access an on-line service transparently so as to request a movie and a start time from a nearby video-on-demand provider who commits to availability within 24 hours.

Suppose that the application requests a movie that is not available on the local provider's computer's hard drive. The local provider passes the request to a remote provider, which replies by sending the movie to the local provider by way of either ATM lines or Federal Express overnight delivery. The local provider then loads the movie on its server's local hard drive and prepares to send the movie to the user's set-top box. Figure 5.9 illustrates these options, which could take this hybrid application in gradual stages from using only today's existing infrastructure to using a highly advanced delivery system.

Next Steps for Users

Table 5.11 suggests some reasonable next steps for potential users of the application categories based on provider trends and users' vision.

As authors, we ourselves expect to take the step from being pioneers to being early adopters of most application categories within the next year. We have already taken this next step for hybrid applications. In our rural location, we do not expect to have video on demand for several years.

Table 5.11 Next steps for individual users of applications.

Application category	Possible next steps for individual users
Desktop video conferences	Decide on your personal thresholds for price, function, and quality. Watch for price reductions and suitable network availability. In your work environment, check whether avoiding travel or getting immediate assistance in business matters justifies current prices.
Multimedia store-and-forward mail	Track the cost of sending media along with text on-line, and compare to the cost and delay of mailing a CD-ROM or CD-R or other multimedia storage device via U.S. mail or an overnight express courier. Experiment with authoring your own multimedia content that includes audio and video so that when multimedia E-mail becomes available and desirable you will be ready.
Edutainment, infotainment, and sociotainment	Lobby with your network delivery providers, whether phone or cable, for faster networks. Experiment with hybrid applications and on-line services. Compare values of alternative ways of spending your entertainment dollar.
Shopping and advertising	Try out some of the early efforts to provide on-line shopping and compare to alternatives. What would make these efforts attractive to you?
Digital libraries	Consider becoming a trial supplier of content, perhaps a home page or even a trial supplier of a digital library, for information that you create or have available. Learn what is required to digitize your holdings. Identify what the value added could be.
Video on demand	Participate in a trial, as provider or user, and determine the extent of improvement to your lifestyle or business.
Education and health	Be aware of what is available in your schools and medical facilities. Use on-line services to stay aware of what is available. See if you have a business case for using distributed multimedia to train employees.
Hybrid applications	Get some and experiment. Provide feedback to the provider.

CRITICAL SUCCESS FACTORS

The factors that are critical for successfully achieving the vision for multimedia applications include:

All Application Categories

Entire Application: Perceived affordability and availability of the entire application as seen by the customer.

Bandwidth: Affordable and available bandwidth to support these applications.

Desktop Video Conferences with Collaboration

Scalability: Scalable delivery services, so each user can trade off quality and function against cost.

Communication Partners: Critical mass of desired communication partners with whom to conference.

Multimedia Store-and-Forward Mail

Human Factors: Ease of installation and use for creating and receiving multimedia mail.

Enough People: Critical mass of users equipped to send and receive each other's multimedia mail.

Consumers Edutainment, Infotainment, Sociotainment

Wonderful Content: Compelling, dynamic content better than today's often dull, static offerings.

Wonderful Development: Easier and more affordable content development for the provider.

Human Factors: Ease of acquiring, installing, learning, and using for the customer.

Competitive: Competitive cost per entertainment hour in comparison with other entertainment alternatives.

Standards: Standards to alleviate content creators' and users' fears of investing in content and equipment that will soon become obsolete.

Shopping and Advertising

Commercial Infrastructure: Efficient, effective, and secure business transactions and backroom processing behind the shopping and advertising applications.

Business Models: Working business models that provide ways to make money with these distributed multimedia applications.

Optimized Total Shopping Process: A total shopping process that allows the customer not just to select and order, but also to determine how the product will be delivered to him and at what speed.

Widespread Appeal: Compelling reasons for almost everyone, not just 18- to 40-year-old white males who are typical computer users, to use these applications and like these applications.

Digital Libraries

Appropriately Formatted Digitized Information: Critical mass of useful, easily accessible digitized information (information that is beyond traditional on-line versions of printed pages, that is, composite documents with hypertext, reusable objects, simulations, etc.).

Search, Retrieval, and Use Methods: Methods for finding and manipulating digitized information economically and easily.

Sharing: National cooperation for sharing content and standards.

Managing Ownership and Payments for Use: Efficient and effective ways to manage ownership and appropriate payment for use of content.

Video on Demand

Personalized Choice: Significantly more personalized choice of content than neighborhood video rental outlets.

Better Services: Prices and ease of use comparable to or better than those of today's cable services.

Educational and Health Applications

Publicized Advantages: Clarification of advantages and superiority to justify initial setup and recurring operational costs.

Existing Operations: Smooth integration with previous, existing operations.

Training: Training of educators and the medical community in how to create, customize, and use these applications for maximum benefit.

Economic Viability: Assurance of economic viability for providers and consumers, including liability insurance for health personnel and educational institutions who can pay without resorting to grants or one-time industry partnerships.

Wonderful Content: Compelling and useful content for users, that is, the patients and students, with demonstrated effectiveness.

Hybrid Applications

Superior Applications: Clear improvement over previous ways of accomplishing similar functions.

Lower Cost Delivery: Significantly lower cost than corresponding uses of full, high-speed multimedia networks would currently provide.

Marketing Hook: A hook to catch first-time customers.

Wonderful Wide Range of Content: Compelling content and more variety of content.

SUMMARY

Multimedia applications bring in revenues that companies can weigh against necessary investments in multimedia infrastructures. No known single application can assure profitable operation by outweighing an investment of a large fraction of several billion dollars for delivery networks, servers, end-user devices, and content. Profits must come from suites of applications, covering several application categories, and no doubt from applications that no one has yet invented or taken seriously. Profits may come from applications appealing to very specialized niche areas. Furthermore, it may be true that the very successful suites of applications on-line will have associated with them virtual communities of people.

Who can select applications? Technologists are unlikely to select suitable applications based on what they would find most interesting and challenging to develop. Potential customers are unlikely to describe optimal combinations of services that they can barely imagine using. Companies make only marginal contributions by expanding horizontally or vertically into one another's current markets. Governments can help mainly by making some uses of resources more attractive than others and by standing out of the way.

Without an underlying plan, the best hope may be that companies will elect to reduce costs by using advanced technologies to deploy general-purpose infrastructures. The same technologies will incidentally allow companies to increase capacities significantly for small additional costs. Both large-scale-integration digital electronics and fiber-optic cables have the highly desirable property of having a relatively weak coupling between the application layer and lower implementation layers. Like digital computers, it is possible to make digital networks more capable without knowing much about the applications that will eventually use the increased capabilities. If this chapter has a moral, it must be to deploy networks that can support general applications in all eight categories, rather than misapplying technological improvements merely to reduce the costs of today's special-purpose networks or placing all the eggs in one application category's basket. Slow, steady evolutionary progress, perhaps fueled by the euphoria over Internet and other on-line services, and continued improvement in multimedia content and associated programming, will eventually get us there.

REFERENCES

Advances in Digital Libraries (ADL) Yearly Workshops. Prof. Nabil Adam, Rutgers University, Newark, NJ. adam@adam.rutgers.edu.

Aigrain, Philippe. 1994. Bibliothèque Nationale de France (preprint materials). Distributed at the 1994 Advances in Digital Libraries (ADL) Yearly Workshops. Contact Prof. Nabil Adam, Rutgers University, Newark, NJ. adam@adam. rutgers.edu.

Business Week. 1993. "Retailing Will Never Be the Same." pp. 54–60, July 26.

Cogger, Richard. CU-SeeMe. Cornell University, Ithaca, NY. R.Cogger@Cornell.edu.

Croal and Stone. 1995. Internet Apartment Access. "Cyberscope," *Newsweek*, August 21, p. 10.

Designing Hypermedia Applications—special edition. 1995. *Communications of the ACM*, vol. 38, no. 8, August.

Digital Libraries—special edition. 1995. *Communications of the ACM*, vol. 38, no. 4, April.

Fetterman, Roger, and Gupta, Satish. 1993. *Mainstream Multimedia*. New York: Reinhold Publishing, ch. 7.

Fox, Edward A.; Hix, Deborah; Nowell, Lucy T.; Brueni, Dennis J.; Wake, William C.; and Heath, Lenwood S. 1993. "Users, User Interfaces, and Objects: Envision, a Digital Library." *Journal of the American Society for Information Science*, 44(8):480–491.

Gillespie, Robert G. 1994. "Everything You Always Wanted to Know About Internet Pricing (but Were Afraid to Ask)." *Educom Review*, November/December, pp. 42–43.

"Hall of Malls," http://nsns.com/mousetracks/hallofmalls.html, maintained by New South Network Services in Tallahassee, FL.

Kenney, Anne R., and Personius, Lynne K. Project Managers. 1992. "Digital Capture, Paper Facsimiles, and Network Access." The Cornell/Xerox Commission on

Preservation and Access, Joint Study in Digital Preservation, Report: Phase I, January 1990–December 1991. Cornell University Library, Ithaca, NY.

Kling, Barry. (MSPH), Director of Continuing Education. 1994. Private communication, School of Medicine, University of Missouri-Columbia.

Mann, Charles. 1995. "Regulating Cyberspace." *Science*, vol. 268, May 5, pp. 628–629.

Masullo, Miriam. 1993. "Multimedia On-Demand and the Organization of Education Systems." *Proceedings of IFIP WG 3.2 Conference on University Uses of Visualization.* CA: Elsevier Science Publishers B.V., July.

Mervis, Jeffrey. 1995. "Electronic Documents, NSF Moves into Fast Lane to Manage Flow of Grants." *Science*, vol. 267, January 13, p. 166.

Multimedia Systems Magazine. 1995. Special issue, *Content-Based Retrieval*. Vol. 3, no. 1.

Network World. 1994. September 19, p. 41.

NewMedia Magazine. 1995. August, p. 117.

NSFNET—The National Science Foundation Computer Network for Research and Education. 1990. IBM, GK21-0104-00, Milford, CT.

PC Magazine. 1994. Vol. 13, no. 15, September 13.

Piatetsky-Shapiro, G., and Frawley, W.J. (Editors). 1991. *Knowledge Discovery in Databases*. Cambridge, MA: MIT Press.

Piller, Charles. 1994. "Dream Consumers Want More Than TV Overload from the Information Superhighway, but Will They Get It?" *MacWorld*, October.

Press & Sun-Bulletin. 1994. Binghamton, NY. September 18, p. 8E.

Stix, Gary. 1994. "The Speed of Write." *Scientific American*, December, pp. 106–111.

Waldrop, M. Mitchell. 1994. "Culture Shock on the Networks." *Science*, vol. 265, pp. 879–883, August 12.

Warner, Joan. 1993. "Home Shopping Has to Beat the Siren Song of the Store." *Business Week*, July 26, p. 60.

Washington Post. 1995. D1, January 17.

Witten, Ian H.; Moffat, Alistair; and Bell, Timothy C. 1994. "Compression and Full-Text Indexing for Digital Libraries." Newark Digital Library Conference, Newark, NJ, May 11.

Chapter 6

Providers

BACKGROUND

In this chapter we focus on the providers of content, products, and services for distributed multimedia. All companies involved are becoming part of a single, converged industry, in which many companies compete to provide one customer's content, products, or services.

In this background section, we discuss the framework in which providers operate and give some illustrative tasks, companies, and numbers. In the Vision section, we present a specific vision for each of several categories of providers, along with significant impediments to achieving the full potential of their vision. We present the state of the art for each category and for several representative companies. In the History section, we discuss some financial numbers. We hope you will look back on this small sample of numbers as we progress on the road to achieving the vision. In the Differences section, we note the wide gap between the vision and the state of the art. We then discuss trends, including both forming alliances and developing in-house skill bases. We finally list some critical success factors common to all categories of providers.

To structure this discussion, we must make clear that we include individuals as providers and not just as users. Individuals wear different hats, providing multimedia as part of their personal lives, as employees in companies, or as officials of governments.

The framework that we introduced in the Preface notes that providers must consider all aspects of distributed multimedia even if their specific efforts address only some small part of the framework. Figure 6.1 recapitulates this framework. Providers must consider whether to develop or procure applications, hardware and software products, delivery vehicles, and several sorts of services. Making that choice in the future may be much harder than it is today. For example, consider a fairly typical mid-1990s distributed multimedia offering, a supermarket information kiosk that displays images of foods, prices, store locations, and recipes. It includes a very small amount of video and audio in which the store manager welcomes customers to the store and strongly recommends the store's deli section. Customers select foods of

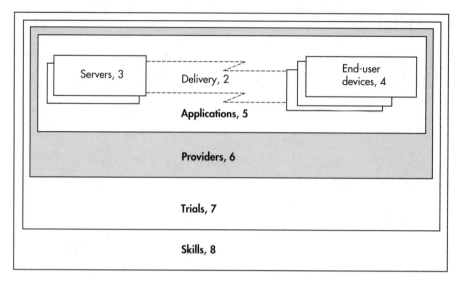

Figure 6.1   Framework.

interest by scrolling down an alphabetized list of foods, positioning the cursor on the desired food, and pressing Enter on the kiosk's keyboard. The kiosk can receive occasional small text updates and maintenance over a network, either a LAN or some type of communications line. This information kiosk can be replicated in several locations inside the store and in various similar supermarkets across the city. The server that holds the updates and maintenance releases is a personal computer at the supermarket's headquarters. The end-user devices, or the kiosks, are also personal computers. Although creating such an information kiosk is a simple project, each of the creation tasks shown in Focus 6.1 may involve a different provider with a different set of skills.

Now let's consider the case where the end-user devices happen to be television sets with set-top boxes located in customers' homes. The server is a computer capable of supporting many streams of video. There is a suite of applications for the end user, including home grocery shopping or "supermarket kiosk in the home." This distributed multimedia system enables the end user to conduct a transaction from his living room couch; he can purchase a pound of pastrami and have it delivered quickly. The network is some form of hybrid fiber coaxial cable or even switched-digital video. A customer's interface is no longer an alphabetized list of bologna, ham, and cheese, but rather a three-dimensional animated store in which the customer can navigate using a remote control device while sitting on a couch. A small sampling of some providers that could be involved, in the future, in creating this sort of distributed multimedia system is shown in Focus 6.2.

Distributed multimedia is both carrot and stick to business. The carrot is a company's chance to expand market share into an expanding industry. The

FOCUS 6.1 Supermarket kiosk creation tasks.

Completing a wide range of tasks yields a network of information kiosks in three supermarkets.

- Develop a concept for the kiosk.
- Research the information the kiosk will present and then develop a concept for the kiosk.
- Plan and develop the design.
- Plan services such as updates and routine maintenance.
- Design the system configuration including the network.
- Select the network provider, kiosk's computer hardware, and kiosk's peripheral equipment.
- Obtain permission to use copyrighted media.
- Produce and digitize video and music then edit video and music together with narration.
- Scan images and develop graphics and animation.
- Assemble total multimedia content and integrate the entire environment.
- Design the kiosk enclosure.
- Install kiosks and LANs.
- Tune system performance and train service providers.
- Test the system with real users and rework as necessary.
- Deploy the system.
- Develop additional content and distribute it over the network. ■

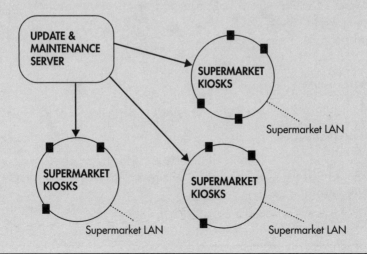

FOCUS 6.2 Possible providers for "supermarket kiosk in the home."

Some companies that may provide parts of distributed multimedia systems are as follows.

End-user devices

- Hardware—Scientific-Atlanta, General Instrument (GI), VLSI Technology, Interactive Digital Solutions (IDS), Hewlett-Packard (HP)

- Operating systems—Microware, Microsoft, Integrated Systems, Scientific-Atlanta

- Other software—IBM, 3DO, Silicon Graphics, Motorola, Sun

- Authoring systems and tools—Macromedia, General Magic, Kaleida, XAOS, Netscape

Servers

- Software—Oracle, IBM, Sybase, Starlight Networks, Microsoft, Novell, AimTech

- Hardware—HP, IBM, Silicon Graphics, Digital, Ncube, Compaq, Sun

Delivery

- Telephone—All RBOCs, GTE, Sprint, AT&T

- Cable—Time Warner, TCI, and almost all other multiple system operators (MSO)

- Some power utility company networks

Applications

- Publishing—Access Atlanta, *Newsweek*, *USA Today*, *Wall Street Journal*

- Entertainment—Splash, GTE-Main Street, Walt Disney, TELE-TV Media

- Shopping, business advertising—Shoppers Express, CommerceNet, Nordstrom

(cont.)

FOCUS 6.2 Possible providers for "supermarket kiosk in the home." (*cont.*)

Applications

- Overall content—Time Warner Interactive, Viacom Interactive

- On-screen program guides—StarSight

- Information Provider—CompuServe, Prodigy, America Online, Internet

Infrastructure provider; integrator; support systems

- AT&T, ICTV, IBM, Andersen Consulting

Help on getting started

- National Information Infrastructure Advisory Council, IMA, Oregon Multimedia Alliance, CommerceNet

- Firewall Security Corporation

- Test beds—Sprint Test Track, Bell Atlantic, BBN's National School Network Test bed ■

stick is the fear of losing current market share to other companies as technological changes expose once-secure niches to competition. For example, as technology makes it possible to deliver plain old telephone service (POTS) over CATV cables and to deliver video over local loops, each of the telephone and cable industries would like to expand into the other's territory while not giving up any of their own turf. Both would like to take revenue from videotape rental stores.

Enormous annual revenues are at stake, as Table 6.1 illustrates. Table 6.2 shows some correspondingly large investments. Tables 6.3 and 6.4 are other indications of the size and location of the dollars involved. Table 6.3 provides some insight into the trillion dollar estimate of annual revenue that has appeared frequently in the press; Table 6.4 provides the relative sizes of interested providers. These numbers will not be current when you read the book, and the precise numbers are controversial or unavailable even as we write the book, but the orders of magnitude will remain relevant. The numbers in these tables come from newspapers, numerous periodicals, companies' annual reports, and some of the references at the end of the chapter.

Table 6.1 Approximate values of typical market segments (1993 unless noted).

Revenue ($/year)	Market segment
12 B	Videotape rental industry
5 B	Movie theater tickets
22 B	CATV (connects to 63 percent of, or 50 M, homes)
80 B	Telephone industry
25 B	Fees paid for local access by long-distance carriers (AT&T, MCI, etc.) to local carriers (RBOCs, etc.)
9 B	Telephone yellow pages
7.8 B	Cellular telephones (11 M customers and 100 K jobs in only 50-MHz total bandwidth)
3.7 B	Personal communication services (PCS), by 1996
12 B	Classified advertising
31 B	Broadcast and cable advertising
100 M	What NBC pays its 200 stations to carry its advertisements
70 B	Catalog and home shopping
1 B	QVC's share of video home shopping industry; Home Shopping Network additional
1.1 B	Revenue from auctioning electromagnetic spectrum
270 B	U.S. defense budget
3.5 T	John Scully's estimate of the interactive information industry in 2001, that is, television, telecommunications, computers, consumer electronics, publishing, and information services
9 B	Information services
530 M	On-line services in 1993
8 M	Sierra On-Line and AT&T's game network
28B	Gambling
14 B	Video game cartridges

(cont.)

Table 6.1   Approximate values of typical market segments (1993 unless noted). (*cont.*)

Revenue ($/year)	Market segment
47 B	Books, magazines, and newspapers
8 B	Records, tapes, and audio compact disks
18.2 B	Estimated market for interactive programming in 1998
1.3T	Estimated telecommunications market in the year 2001
270 B	Typical defense budget in mid-1990s

Table 6.2   Approximate required investments.

Cost ($B)	Over years	Investment
150	15	Rewire for fiber
2	4	TCI to run fiber to 90 percent of its 10 M customers and eventually to provide a LAN and large media servers
5	4	Develop an undefined information highway

Table 6.3   The trillion dollar industry.

Revenue, 1994 ($B)	Segment
600	Producers/providers
42	Packagers include newspapers, on-line services, and networks
125	Distributors include AT&T, MCI, Sprint, resellers, RBOCS, and MSOs
100	Network equipment suppliers
60	Consumer electronics manufacturers

Source: Kraemer, 1994.

Table 6.4   Relative sizes of providers, by 1992 revenue.

Revenue ($B)	Industry
82.3	7 RBOCs (long-distance companies together generate slightly smaller revenue)
21.5	Cable industry
44.2	Newspaper publishing
25.8	Broadcasting industry
26.0	Motion picture industry

Source: Communications Industries Report, March 1994.

VISION FOR THE NEXT DECADE

Individuals will create and transmit multimedia content rather than merely receive high-bandwidth information or merely respond with small amounts of text requiring only low-bandwidth connection. They are, thus, legitimate providers as shown in Table 6.5. In Chapter 8, we focus more on individuals. Companies will produce content as well as products and services. They will also use distributed multimedia to make their operations more efficient and effective. Table 6.6 subdivides the vision for corporate providers according to some of today's industries. Governments provide leadership, legislation, regulations, rulings, guidelines, filings, opinions, and appointments. Some people would add bureaucracy and roadblocks to this list as well. Table 6.7 shows visions appropriate to various levels and branches of government. In these tables, we suggest some of the impediments providers will need to overcome in order to achieve their respective visions.

Many companies believe that they can become more responsive to their customers' needs by using distributed multimedia to provide customers more expeditious delivery of information in more meaningful or more convincing media. Delivery of information that is more carefully customized will therefore be more useful for individual customers. Providers also envision using distributed multimedia to reduce distribution costs; handle more orders, or the equivalent; increase customers' impulse purchases; facilitate faster collection of money at lower costs; and achieve product differentiation related to differences in on-line services.

Table 6.5 Vision for individuals.

Age range	Vision	Impediments
General	Communicate more effectively and pleasurably. Converge the communications and information access capabilities of schools and workplace with home facilities. Create and participate in on-line communities of common interests.	Skill to create interactive multimedia content High cost of and complexity of equipment Difficulty in dealing with some other providers
Preschool	Construct multimedia similar to today's crayon drawings for early learning, to prepare for school and life—e.g., interactive videos for grandparents.	Costs prohibitive below upper middle class Requires parents as educators and monitors Requires educational and edutainment support materials
Students: kindergarten to graduate school	Create multimedia documents, rather than compositions that employ only text, for more effective and efficient learning. Use distributed multimedia for information access and collaboration.	Cost of wide dissemination beyond pilot projects Teacher training Difficulty attracting women and ethnic students
Adults	Produce multimedia reports and presentations rather than text documents and dull talks. Participate in two-way video for business meetings, long-distance learning, socializing, and virtual town meetings. Access and create multimedia information. Perform on-line transactions as part of employment and personal life.	Demanding new skills required to create multimedia content Combining skills from diverse industries such as computing and television Costs not low enough or quality high enough for personal use Difficulty of extending participation beyond college-educated white males
Seniors	Participate in distributed multimedia to ease and enrich later years.	Becoming comfortable with technologies seniors did not have when growing up Inappropriate human factors for seniors Simply getting started

Table 6.6 Vision for companies.

Industry	Vision	Impediments
General	Grow overall market. Increase market share and profits with tolerable risks. Protect existing turf. Use brilliant market timing. Redefine company, as needed, to please owners.	Investment capital Lack of some skills Complexity Uncertainty of offering definition Moving from the pioneering and early adopters stage to the mass marketplace
Computer	Keep revenues and profits growing by producing and selling increasingly more hardware and software with vastly greater performance and capability. Develop or otherwise motivate applications that people will feel they absolutely have to buy requiring this performance and capability. Develop new markets such as the home market, on-line information, and entertainment.	System designs and system performance required especially for video Well-deserved customer perception as providing products that are difficult to understand, acquire, install, and use Lack of standards Profit margins with intense competition from many
Telephone	Find or develop sufficient compelling, appealing content. Find markets for that content. Eliminate constraining regulations in a favorable way. Implement favorable and preferably familiar billing algorithms.	Uncertainty about what people will pay for Enormous investment and complex process required to find out Moving from a delivery utility to a growth information provider Obsolete regulations Replacing existing low-bandwidth networks and bringing new ones on-line, especially the last mile
Cable	Expand services and customer base, e.g., provide POTS and largely replace video rental stores. Capitalize on familiar entertainment type of content.	Same as above Upgrading existing one-way nonswitched networks Changing from a one-way content-providing company to a communications company Training installers for a more complex installation Changing current inappropriate billing

(*cont.*)

Table 6.6 Vision for companies. (*cont.*)

Industry	Vision	Impediments
Publishing	Increase profit from current assets by using distributed multimedia to go after broader markets. Reuse and repurpose current assets in multiple ways for playback on multiple platforms. Expand the ability to distribute future assets in many ways and much more economically.	Uncertain role, when everyone can publish content and select from a world of information Uncertainty about what to charge and how to collect Enforcing copyrights Obtaining all the rights from authors in order to ensure the ability to reuse, repurpose, and distribute in yet undefined ways Actually succeeding at reusing and repurposing content that customers will buy
Games	Expand market to more customers and platforms. Sell increasingly sophisticated games, including games that involve full-motion interactive video, multiple players and remotely located players.	Skill required to create engaging, sophisticated games Attracting enough early users to cover costs Obtaining development money Mismatch between creative desires and customers' platform capabilities Expanding the market to include customers with more money and desire to spend it on games than current market
Movie studios	Increase profit from current assets by using new delivery methods to go after broader markets such as video on demand. Provide more entertaining content such as interactive movies and digital special effects. Expand using creative talents of outside groups. Deliver movies to studios over networks.	Skill required to produce interactive movies that customers will like Uncertain market Requirement for extremely high resolution Difficulty of reusing and repurposing assets on multiple platforms that customers will buy

(cont.)

Table 6.6   Vision for companies. (*cont.*)

Industry	Vision	Impediments
CD-ROM providers	Become very profitable. Be able to easily reuse and re-purpose assets on many platforms. Create wonderful content that consumers love. Be an acceptable content form that many of today's industries would want to distribute (that is, be a supplier to movie studios, telephone and cable companies, publishers, etc.). Promote and distribute to many niche markets over broadband networks.	Most CD-ROM providers today not profitable Large technical and artistic challenges of authoring tools and hardware and software platforms Creation skills still in early stages Large upfront costs and lack of good distribution channels Cross-platform creation tools very early in their development
Broadcast television networks	Protect audience franchises. Design branded product extensions. Build advertising revenues. Create compelling content in environments hospitable to advertisers.	Limited over-the-air bandwidths Uncertain role when customers can send as well as receive video Competition from multiple sources
Consumer electronics	Expand markets for new high-function electronic devices that consumers want, need, or can be convinced they need.	Evaporating product differentiation from computers Customers preferring to consolidate their holdings to standard platforms rather than buying multiple electronics wonders of the moment
Education	Use additional delivery methods and sensory modalities to educate more people, more effectively, and more efficiently. Balance in-school or on-campus education with distance learning and just-in-time training.	High cost of upstream path for any media other than text Incomplete understanding of how people learn using distributed multimedia techniques Limited investment funding Limited educators' skills Educational politics Difficulty of creating multimedia content Tenure credit for creating multimedia content

(*cont.*)

Table 6.6 Vision for companies. (*cont.*)

Industry	Vision	Impediments
Advertising and selling	Market more effectively by targeting smaller, more focused market segments and analyzing databases of customer behavior. Use infomercials to interest customers and encourage their quick and well-informed choices. Sell more economically and thus generate more profits.	Probable need for radically new approaches to make effective use of interactive and on-line marketing. Some reluctance to use new approaches that may require selling with product discounts and offering some kinds of monetary credits for customers to partipate in advertising. Some creativity needed to live with or counter customer use of computer agents that offer customers automated ways of competitive comparisons
Libraries	Provide increasingly effective and economical information services over wide area networks. Attract large amounts of funding for research and deployment. Do not go out of business.	Uncertain role. High cost of digitizing and maintaining media. Difficulty of locating desired information
Video rental stores	Grow revenue and profits rather than lose to video on demand.	Necessity to compete on selection, price, convenience, and pleasant rental environment (cappuccino as you browse)
On-line information	Add additional media. Expand into untapped markets. Figure out how to make large profits and not just attract browsers.	Requirement for (and cost of) isochronous bandwidth. Computer phobia. Uncertain workable business models

As users of multimedia, companies ranging from large corporations to small businesses envision using distributed multimedia to improve employee functions. They envision providing better and more useful information on demand for employees, producing more effective work-group communications, creating multimedia information for internal operations, and providing improved knowledge of the marketplace through better, more immediate response from customers.

Table 6.7 Vision for governments.

Government or branch	Vision	Impediments
General	Serve the people. Look good. Get reelected. Control government spending. Improve the economy. Ensure equitable access to information. Ensure competition. Regulate monopolies. Enforce laws.	Complexity of issues Competing high-visibility problems Diversity of opinions Being outrun by technologies Figuring out who pays
Federal, executive	Set direction. Provide universal access (figure out what that means). Provide jobs. Have regulation aligned with what companies can do, rather than with their historical origins.	As above
Federal, legislative	Replace 1934 Telecommunicaions Act by more modern legislation, that is, remove artificial barriers to competition while safeguarding the public interest. Provide legislation to appropriately protect digital intellectual property.	Difficulty passing controversial legislation where each interested party wants its barriers removed first and totally while preserving its monopolies as long as possible Difficulty defining "appropriate" for digital copyright protection
Regulatory agencies	Execute laws. Encourage business. Protect citizens' resources.	Obsolete legislation Possible downsizing target
Granting agencies	Fund projects that will yield self-sustaining progress and whose findings can be disseminated elsewhere.	Obtaining high-quality proposals Getting good, concrete results Measuring results in new areas Traditional difficulties of transferring technology
State and local	Kick-start local businesses. Regulate intrastate and local carriers.	Poor match between technology boundaries and administrative boundaries Skills required Priority

This vision includes a mass of creators and a mass of viewers where at least one set of creators is inside the company. The masses of viewers, such as partners or suppliers, are either in the company or in other companies that do business with the company. Producers of content envision interoperability and standards so they can be confident that they are developing content for the most popular delivery systems or platforms. There will be many platforms that can run their content.

STATE OF THE ART

Table 6.8 presents the state of the art for people acting as individuals, that is, the progress such people have made in achieving the vision and overcoming the impediments that we gave in the preceding section. Table 6.9 and Table 6.10 present the corresponding states of the art for companies and for governments. After the tables, Focus 6.3 describes a few examples of the state of the art for governments.

Table 6.11 assesses the progress of Chapter 5's application categories in moving through the stages of marketing new technologies. The table lists

Table 6.8 State of the art for individuals.

Age range	State of the art today
Preschool	Active, enthusiastic use of home multimedia personal computers among mostly upper-middle-class families
Students, kindergarten through graduate school	Pockets of success with student-created multimedia projects in grade schools and high schools Spreading student use of Internet for E-mail and participation in forums in higher education Student creation of WWW home pages Some student creation of hypermedia; and some examples of student participation in distributed multimedia with video
Adults	Spreading participation in on-line services Pockets of success with creating on-line information where use is heavily weighted toward 18- to 37-year-old college-educated males WWW home page construction by individuals using Prodigy templates
Seniors	Some very successful participation in on-line game networks, Senior net and other forums Getting started very difficult

Table 6.9 State of the art for companies.

Industry	State of the art today
Computers	Extensive product lines of multimedia-enhanced computers with audio, CD-ROM, large hard drives, and fast processors and local buses Multimedia content on CD-ROMs Local area networks increasingly capable of delivering multimedia Some video servers for the large telephone and cable trials and the beginnings of more aggressive marketing of video servers to corporate accounts that may be the key niche market to spearhead the eventual mass market for these video servers Some set-top box efforts as well
Telephone	Trials and test beds in plan and under way (see Chapter 7) Modifications of strategies and test plans as providers learn
Cable	Trials and test beds in plan and under way including trials of cable modems and PCs (see Chapter 7) Modifications of strategies and test plans as providers learn
Publishing	Increasing distribution on CD-ROMs Traditional market exposed to nontraditional distribution and easy digital copying Some strategists hired to help decide what to do in the future
Games	Experimenting with moderately popular game networks Marketing highly popular multimedia games for stand-alone personal computers Releasing new models of 32- and 64-bit-architecture game machines Working on television set-top boxes
Movie studios	Using more digital special effects Setting up key alliances with other providers to either create or go after multimedia Testing digital network distribution to studios and theaters
Broadcast television networks	Testing combinations of E-mail and telephone with regular broadcast shows Broadcasting some amateurs' videos Developing interactive games Using on-line services
Consumer electronics	Computers with digital audio in toys for ages 6 months and up Computer menus in televisions, camcorders, and VCRs Models of digital camera, camcorders, VCRs, editing devices
Education	Binghamton University, San Francisco State University, MIT, CMU, UCLA, UC at Berkeley, UC at San Diego, IBM's Skills Dynamics, NYU's M.S. program, USC's Film School, the Art Center College of Design in Pasadena, Vanderbilt's Learning Technology Center's integrated program based upon cognitive science and technology in education, and some others offering relevant courses

(cont.)

Table 6.9 State of the art for companies. (*cont.*)

Industry	State of the art today
Advertising and selling	Early use of Internet, World Wide Web (WWW), E-mail, and on-line services Significant customer interest and media attention So far, little profit
Libraries	Exposed as other on-line sources of information become more convenient and sources of local dollars for enhancing paper libraries become targeted for tax cuts On-line card catalogs common Public access Internet terminals starting to appear Large grants to some major university libraries for five-year research studies in digital libraries
Video rentals	Exposed as video on demand promises to improve selections and prices Some optimism that video on demand may be 7–10 years away rather than merely 3–5 years away Video rental stores experimenting with digital download from central repositories to expand inventories of local video stores and with CD-ROM and game cartridge rentals
On-line information	Rapidly growing on-line service providers with Microsoft looming large as a new provider Rapidly growing WWW home pages on Internet from academia, businesses, and individuals; most users relatively young, college-educated white males; use still rather difficult and can be slow if displaying images is imperative Internet expansion especially rapidly from academic to commercial services Many on-line services adding media and Internet affinities of various kinds

these application categories by number across the top and lists the marketing of new technologies' stages down the first column. Moore's chasm separates each stage (1991). A provider's challenge is not only to move a technology, in our case a distributed multimedia application, through the stages. Providers must adroitly move across the gaps or chasms, as Moore describes in his book, using very different marketing strategies. Simply growing new pioneers or obtaining additional new early adopters does not necessarily propel providers into the desired mass market segment. During these stressful times, providers must keep their jobs, sanity, and a continued funding stream coming in for further research, development, and marketing. The entries in each cell of Table 6.11, I for individuals, C for corporations as users, and G for

Table 6.10 State of the art for governments.

Government or branch	State of the art today
All	Progress in using E-mail, even some video conferencing, and making documents and information accessible on-line primarily through Internet and on the WWW
Federal, executive	Campaigning to put the information highway on nation's agenda Grappling with issues such as defining universal service, open access, affordability, availability, intellectual property, privacy, and interoperability
Federal, legislative	Trying to modernize 1934 legislation with legislation of 1996 Intense pressure to cut taxes and reduce size of government
Regulatory agencies, mainly FCC	Grappling with cable rates and video dial tone authorization requests from the RBOCs and AT&T Pleasing neither telephone nor cable companies, who both want freedom from regulation's complexity and competitive advantage over each other
State and local	Showing progress but with some bumps along the way
Granting agencies	Funding several programs for infrastructure, digital libraries, K–12 education, incentives for small businesses, and rural telecommunications plants and services Using Internet for granting agencies' operations

the government as users of applications in the categories, are surprisingly similar at this point. The pot of gold remains in moving nimbly to the stages involving masses of customers—that is, convincing large numbers of individuals that they need such applications along with the contexts described in Chapter 5. In the near term, providers may have to settle for the more traditional inroads into companies. Therefore, what is different is the strategy of the providers in managing movement of I, C, and G through the cells of the table. Recently, for example, some providers report slowing down, as opposed to stopping, video-on-demand efforts aimed at moving individuals to the next stages through expanding, heavily hyped, but somewhat less than promised, participation in large video-on-demand trials. Instead, they intend to concentrate more attention on moving video on demand into companies for use in training. An interpretation here is that the trial providers realize that in the near term, their participation in these large trials results in selling only a small number of servers. Trial participation does serve to create much positive publicity internally that can fund needed longer-term R&D efforts.

FOCUS 6.3 Some representative examples of the state of the art for governments as providers.

Many governments and agencies are making good use of multimedia. Some examples follow.

■ California has an On-line Voter Guide funded through contributions from Oracle, Intel, Pacific Telesis, Pacific Bell, Pacific Gas and Electric, GTE, Apple, AT&T, and MacWorld.

■ The U.S. Department of Commerce's National Telecommunications and Information Administration (NTIA) awarded $24.4 million to 92 information superhighway projects in 1994. Projects ranged from virtual field trips to telemedicine.

■ The federal government provides on-line information, such as full text of key legislation, speeches, and other documents relating to federal information policy. Examples are full text of the proposed federal budget for the 1995 fiscal year and full text of "From Red Tape to Results—Creating a Government That Works Better and Costs Less," the 180-page report of Vice President Gore's Task Force on Reinventing Government.

■ There are currently over 60 federal Web sites ranging from the Social Security Administration's to the Securities and Exchange Commission's.

■ Digitized images from the LBJ photo collection, oral history holdings of the LBJ Library, references, and selected lists of materials are available.

■ Over the next five years, the federal government plans to phase out its roughly $12 million-a-year subsidy of the NSFnet and turn the job of running Internet over to four network access providers (NAPs), namely, Ameritech, Sprint, Metropolitan Fiber Systems, and Pac Bell. ■

However, it is becoming clear to many trial providers that they must look at other alternatives as well. The italicized I, C, and G indicate current movement, but the boldface letters are the cells where the majorities of each of I, C, and G, are.

The following descriptions of companies are a small sample that we selected to illustrate a spectrum of providers. We include some companies that are relatively little known, rather than dominant, because some such companies could become dominant in the first decade of the next century. The next Microsoft or IBM is lurking there, somewhere. We do not imply that we se-

Table 6.11   Stages of marketing efforts for application categories.

Application categories Stages	1	2	3	4	5	6	7	8
Pioneers	I	I		I		I, C, G		I, C, G
Early adopters	C, G	C, G	I, C, G	C, G	I, C, G	C, G	I, C, G	I, C, G
Early mass market			I, C, G		C, G			
Late mass market								
Laggards								

Key: Categories: (1) Desktop video conferences with collaboration; (2) multimedia store-and-forward mail; (3) consumer edutainment, infotainment, sociotainment; (4) shopping and advertising; (5) digital libraries; (6) video on demand; (7) educational and health applications; and (8) hybrid applications.
   I, individuals; C, corporations as users; and G, governments as users of applications.

lected the best prospects for this or the most advanced companies now. Several of these companies are in partnerships and alliances that are conducting field trials, which we discuss in Chapter 7. By the time you read this book, you will be able to see some of the results and draw some conclusions.

Microware Systems Corporation   Microware Systems of Des Moines, Iowa, founded in 1977, has 200 employees. The company creates and sells advanced real-time software for the embedded systems market. Its flagship product is OS-9, designed originally for the Motorola 68000 family of microprocessors. It sold over 2 million copies of OS-9 and OS/9000 in 1994. Its anticipated sales in 1995 are $30 million of which one-quarter comes from interactive television (ITV). Another of its products is DAVID (Digital Audio/Video Interactive Decoder), which is based on OS-9. DAVID is system software that provides a standard, highly functional, and cost-effective interactive multimedia software environment for the consumer market. Microware also offers a complete set of software development tools, networking support, and graphic user interface software for developing multimedia applications in an OS-9, personal computer, or UNIX environment. The key to this small company's success is OS-9's ability to handle multiple real-time tasks simultaneously.

Bell Atlantic, a leading innovator, selected Microware to provide the operating system for set-top boxes for early interactive video trials. General Instrument (GI), a leading provider of set-top boxes, recently licensed DAVID, leading many to ask what is the status of Microsoft's project with them. (General Instrument indicates that it is alive and well.)

Microware's goals include providing software for television set-top boxes, head-end decoders, and even PDAs; facilitating developing large-scale video servers; and supporting authoring system tools for building applications and their data structures for use in related systems.

Macromedia, Inc. Macromedia of San Francisco, California, founded in 1977, is a recognized leader in multimedia software authoring tools for stand-alone Intel-based personal computers and Apple Macintosh computers. Its flagship products include Authorware Professional and Director. Its total revenue for its fiscal 1994 year was about $30 million. Macromedia became a public company on December 13, 1993.

Macromedia has an important alliance with Microware Systems Corporation. The goal of this alliance is to develop technology that reduces the time required to convert Macromedia personal computer multimedia content for use in an interactive television environment. Converted programs run in Microware's OS-9 set-top box environment. Macromedia has another very important alliance with Netscape, the rapidly growing, aggressive Internet WWW software provider, to incorporate a Macromedia Director playback engine into a version of Netscape Navigator. This playback can result in active WWW pages rather than static pages. Macromedia calls this technology Shockwave. It incorporates many tricks for overcoming large file sizes. Macromedia has several other important alliances including those with the Home Shopping Network, Oracle, and Prentice-Hall. These alliances extend Macromedia's reach beyond Intel-based and Macintosh computers.

Macromedia's goals include continuing to be a leader in multimedia software tools across personal computers, but moving to consumer-oriented players and distributed multimedia such as Internet's World Wide Web. It summarizes its strategy as "Author Once, Play Anywhere."

CompuServe, Inc. From its base in Columbus, Ohio, CompuServe Information Services, one of the most prestigious, and one of the oldest, on-line time-sharing services, served over 2.3 million members worldwide in 1994. Its equipment, located in three buildings in northwest Columbus, has been switched from proprietary Digital Equipment Corporation software to software that uses Windows NT and SQL. CompuServe's Business Services Group works with companies to set up forums and training on a contract basis. The firm offers multimedia services by downloading audio files, or video files with audio, to be decompressed and played back later, as well as a hybrid CD-ROM application, partly to reduce the time and cost of downloading such files. Staying abreast of cable delivery, CompuServe is testing 800 number access to ISDN and testing offering ATM to commercial customers. In order to offer Internet services along with its Internet gateways on its basic service, the firm bought an Internet company. Although its major target marketplace has always been serious professionals, it is feeling pressure from the other on-line services and Internet to expand its views of its target market. It recently announced a CompuServe Lite for less technical users.

Scientific-Atlanta, Inc.   Scientific-Atlanta in Norcross, Georgia, employs 3600 people. Its core business is selling set-top converter boxes and other hardware for cable television systems. It also builds satellite communications devices and data transmission terminals and has defense contracts. Time Warner selected a collaboration of Scientific-Atlanta, MIPS Technologies, and Silicon Graphics to furnish digital set-top boxes for their interactive television trial in Orlando, Florida. U S WEST selected Scientific-Atlanta to provide yet other boxes for the same role for an interactive television test in Omaha, Nebraska. It has a partnership with Motorola and Kaleida to develop next-generation converter boxes. Ameritech, BellSouth, PacTel, Southern New England Telephone, and Swiss PTT have agreed to use Scientific-Atlanta digital set-tops using PowerTV OS in trials or deployment. This makes PowerTV OS a powerful competitor to Microware's DAVID. Scientific-Atlanta is second in world shipments of analog set-top boxes. General Instrument is first.

Scientific-Atlanta's goal is to remain involved in tests to learn what customers want and what hardware works, as well as to build relationships with partner companies. It acknowledges that there is no money in tests.

Ameritech Corporation   Ameritech, with headquarters in suburban Chicago, is one of the seven RBOCs or regional holding companies (RHCs). Providing telephone service to five midwestern states, it has total assets of $23.5 billion and it has 66,593 employees. For the first half of 1994, its sales were $6.1 billion and earnings $823.3 million. Whereas the RBOCs' earnings growth for that year averaged 5.6 percent, Ameritech's was 13.5 percent. Ameritech's CEO, Dick Notebaert, says that owning content and investing prudently in interactive activities will assure his company's future in interactive distributed multimedia.

One Ameritech proposal is for a $4.4 billion network with 390 channels allocated in the following ways:

- Assign 6 channels for each feature film, running every 5 to 30 minutes running in near-video-on-demand mode (NVOD).

- Use 70 channels for one-way analog broadcast of entertainment programming similar to today's base cable systems.

- Use 240 channels for digital multicast services of one-way broadcast of pay-per-view offerings.

- Ultimately reserve 80 channels, shared by 500 homes, for higher-priced switched-digital service.

The switched-digital service would offer downstream transport of video signals and offer a low-bandwidth upstream channel over which a consumer could send commands to order or pause a movie or to place a bet. The FCC has given Ameritech approval to proceed with the firm's plans to build interactive video networks in the states it serves.

AT&T Network Systems   AT&T Network Systems, Morristown, New Jersey, has the goal of being a systems integrator for telephone companies' video networks. It uses other companies as subcontractors, such as Silicon Graphics, which provides the Challenge video server. The AT&T Video Manager is a network element designed to tie together video servers, set-top boxes, and broadband switching and transmission systems. It manages video network connections and functions as a gateway and menuing service for providers of video information. Even if interactive television trials slow down, they still create good businesses for integrators such as AT&T that can handle the complexities.

Broadband Technologies, Inc.   Broadband Technologies, Inc., Research Triangle Park, North Carolina, founded in 1988, has the goal of being a leading provider of interactive switched-digital video hardware and software. Toward this end, it provides a Fiber Loop Access (FLX) hardware platform and advanced software that allow management, security, and customization for each consumer. FLX has two physical assemblies, the Host Digital Terminal (HDT) and the Optical Network Unit (ONU). FLX serves as an important part of a fiber-to-the-curb system. The HDT resides usually in the central office. The ONUs reside out in the neighborhoods. Bell Atlantic is currently using Broadband Technologies' FLX in its Dover, New Jersey, trials. Broadband Technologies has a joint product and marketing relationship with AT&T Network Systems. If switched-digital video becomes a widely accepted method of choice, Broadband Technologies, Inc., is in the position of moving center stage as a provider and correspondingly doing very well financially.

Institute for Academic Technology   The Institute for Academic Technology (IAT), founded in 1989, is a partnership between the University of

North Carolina at Chapel Hill and IBM. Its staff of about 45 educators and educational technologists strive for better use of information technology in the educational process. They provide workshops, customized sessions, and consultations at their IAT site in Research Triangle Park. They also provide satellite broadcasts to other sites. IAT offerings include "Multimedia Technologies," "Designing Technology Classrooms," "Exploring the World of Computer Networks," "Moving Toward a National Learning Infrastructure," and several "Designing for the Internet" workshops. Workshops generally last about three days and cost between $300 and $600 per person. A consultation for a group of up to 10 participants, such as a project review session or goal-setting session, costs $2500. In a typical year the IAT believes that its cumulative activities reach more than 50,000 academics.

Institute for the Learning Sciences   The Institute for the Learning Sciences (ILS), founded in 1989, builds interactive multimedia teaching systems that employ advanced concepts in natural language processing, interface design, cognitive science, and artificial intelligence. Dr. Roger Shank, the director, is a strong advocate of learning by doing, and the institute's goal is to incorporate advanced concepts into applications for use by governments, businesses, universities, and schools. The ILS staff consists of about 160 professors, graduate students, researchers, and computer programmers. Corporate sponsors, including Andersen Consulting, Ameritech, and North West Water Group PLC; several government sponsors; and corporate partners, including Encyclopaedia Britannica, Hewlett-Packard, IBM, Xerox, and the Museum of Science and Industry in Chicago, have invested over $35 million in the ILS. Its internship program assists transfer of information to these organizations. Interns study and work at the Institute on projects that are meaningful to their employers.

A commercial spin-off from ILS, the Learning Sciences Corporation (LSC), provides business training, education, and information delivery software that ILS designed and tested. LSC sees significant advantages of a combination of computer scientists, cognitive psychologists, and educators working together to develop software for distributed multimedia environments.

The Interactive Multimedia Association (IMA)   The IMA, headquartered in Annapolis, Maryland, is the oldest, largest, and most active trade association devoted to making multimedia happen. Since its founding in 1987, IMA's goal has been to promote the successful application of interactive multimedia in business and consumer markets and to reduce key barriers to the widespread use of interactive multimedia technologies and applications. Members come largely from commercial multimedia providers. The association acts as an information repository for its members. More important, it serves as a lobby group to bring together appropriate people who can hammer out positions to present to various formal standards groups. Issues tackled include application portability and interoperability, intellectual property rights, and technology convergence. For example, in May of 1995 the IMA submitted a draft, *Recommended Practice for Multimedia System Services*, developed in cooperation with several members representing several companies over a two-year period to the International Organization for Standardization (ISO) and the International Electrotechnical Commission (IEC). One of the key barriers that it is currently working to overcome is the difficulty consumers have in installing CD-ROMs. For IMA membership information, contact the IMA office at (410) 626-1380, or visit the Web page at http://www.ima.org.

Digital Audio-Visual Council (DAVIC)   This 200-member international council's goal is to establish standards for end-to-end distributed interactive multimedia. It is in the process of getting ready to publish a series of draft specifications.

Viacom   With over one million cable subscribers, Viacom is the nation's second largest media and entertainment company, behind Time Warner. Chairman Sumner Redstone owns over 80 percent of the company and is one of the world's wealthiest individuals, with a worth of around $6 billion. Viacom's diverse holdings include Paramount, Simon & Schuster, Inc., several theme parks, 12 television stations, 14 radio stations, MTV, Showtime, the Movie Channel, Nickelodeon, and 50,000 movies and television programs. Viacom Interactive Media performs research, development, and ultimately distribution of interactive television content, video games, and on-line services.

One of Viacom's most interesting acquisitions has been the Blockbuster chain. Having grown explosively from only a few stores in 1987, Blockbuster had over 4000 video rental stores, 500 music stores, and a database of 50 million video renters when Viacom acquired it in 1994, for $8 billion dollars and change. Today it has several joint advanced technology projects. In partnership with IBM, it is developing technology and distribution mechanisms for downloading movies and games that customers request. Movies and games will flow from large, centralized video servers to video stores across the country. Blockbuster and Viacom are thus experimenting with video on demand. Nevertheless, they feel that Blockbuster's current success and method of doing business will continue for several years. Although Viacom is involved in the distribution end, it emphasizes owning content and has indicated it will get out of the cable business.

Microsoft Corporation   Arguably the world's most successful personal computer software company is Microsoft, of Redmond, Washington. The vast majority of personal computers have Microsoft software preinstalled. However, Microsoft's increasing reliance on upgrade and replacement markets reduced its annual revenue growth from 56 percent in 1990 to 24 percent in 1993.

Microsoft targets home use and on-line services for future growth. Cofounder and CEO Bill Gates has long been a proponent of both multimedia and personal computers for everyone. Microsoft uses phrases like "information services to assist in handling daily concerns." Microsoft's marketing strategies are analogous to selling a continuous stream of razor blades or film along with selling an occasional razor or camera.

Value-added on-line networking will contribute to Microsoft's continuous revenue stream. In August of 1995, Microsoft shipped its own on-line service, the Microsoft Network, with Windows 95. Microsoft Network supports commercial transaction processing. This bundling of their on-line network with what is certain to become the most pervasive personal computing operating system within the next few years provokes fear in other on-line providers. Microsoft Network will also become an early test bed for the future interactive TV market. Microsoft announced in January 1995 that it plans to become "the world's largest commercial provider" of access to the Internet. Its initial provider is UUNET Technologies, located in Falls Church, Virginia. Microsoft recently demonstrated some willingness to bend to the outside demands for more and more Internet by announcing the intent to remarket the Microsoft Network with an emphasis on the Internet. The firm also announced that the Blackbird program, originally intended only for the Microsoft Network, would be renamed Internet Studio. It tried to purchase Intuit, which provides Quicken personal finance software to 7 million users, but backed off because of possible government action.

Microsoft's strategy includes both near-term and far-term design points and both PCs and TV set-top boxes as end-user devices. In the near term, Microsoft plans to leverage Windows and Windows NT and to add on-line options to more of its CD-ROM titles to make them hybrid applications. In the far term, it plans to provide a new real-time multitasking operating environment for two-way broadband networking. The ultimate operating system base for this environment is a follow-on to Windows NT. Its interactive television project has two code names, Tiger and Iceberg. Tiger, or Microsoft Media Server (MMS), is the video server software. Iceberg, or Microsoft Interactive Television (MITV), is the distributed operating system.

Microsoft's goals include providing a total end-to-end system-software solution that includes set-top box operating systems, server systems, user interfaces, user navigational aids, application development tools, and some content. Its planned solution will run over ATM, CATV, FDDI, or switched Ethernet networks and will support both personal computers and set-top boxes as the user interface. Microsoft's video server software competes with Oracle's video server software. Its set-top box operating system competes with Microware's DAVID, Integrated Systems' real-time system, and Scientific-Atlanta's PowerTV.

Investing heavily in interactive broadband networking, Microsoft, in contrast to many other providers, claims to know exactly what to do, when to do it, and what customers should want from interactive multimedia and from the information highway. Microsoft has announced key alliances in this area. General Instrument licenses Microsoft's set-top operating system for the LinX cable converter add-in card. Microsoft planned a major trial for 1995 with TCI in Denver (subsequently canceled) and Seattle, another with Southwestern Bell now known as SBC Communications, and one with Rogers Cablesystems, Limited, in Canada. Several providers in the systems integration, hardware, telecommunications, and personal computing markets have announced support of Microsoft's end-to-end software solution for interactive broadband networks. Some of these companies are Compaq, Intel, and NEC for servers; HP, NEC, and General Instrument for set-top boxes; Andersen Consulting, Lockheed Martin, NTT Data Communications Systems, Alcatel, and Olivetti as systems Integrators; and TCI, SBC Communications, U S WEST, Rogers Cablesystems, NTT, Deutsche Telekom, and Telstra as network operators.

Spectra.Net Communications, Inc.   Founded in 1994 in Johnson City, New York, Spectra.Net, claims to offer "a Cadillac Internet service for a Chevy price." The firm's goal is "to bring the finest in Internet Connectivity to businesses and individuals in the southern tier of New York and beyond." Figure 6.2 shows its home page logo.

Spectra.Net's president, Steve White, who comes from a marketing background, co-founded the company in a time of rapid downsizing in the southern tier of New York state as an effort to help sell the benefits of living in this area to others and to provide jobs for his family and friends in order to keep them from leaving what was once the Valley of Opportunity for the many employees of the Endicott-Johnson Shoe Company, IBM, Hughes (formerly Link Aviation), and other such companies.

Spectra.Net offers dial-in connectivity, an electronic classified advertising section, and a virtual mall for businesses to advertise. There are several options. One option, a $99.00/year simple listing, is a largely text electronic classified ad. Paying $250.00 will add a scanned-in image to this classified ad. Another option is to piggyback on top of the Chamber of Commerce's home page for $1000 per year. You can roll your own listing at a price that starts at $2500 for setup, $1000 for an included order form, and $150 per page for

The Spectra.Net Virtual Mall Directory

Figure 6.2   http://www.spectra.net—Spectra.Net's home page.

HTML authoring. A rental fee for inclusion in the Spectra.Net Virtual Mall on Spectra.Net's server ranges from $200 to $1000 per month. Despite other firms' down-sizing in the area, Spectra.Net is growing very rapidly. Scores of dial-up customers have unlimited services for $19.95 per month with a $39.95 start-up fee, but the main source of revenue for Spectra.Net is its Virtual Mall, with 18 stores and 30 more under construction. When Spectra.Net started, there were 1200 similar Internet providers. In a year, this number grew to 12,000 providers. White says, "A large inhibitor is lack of knowledge of what Internet can do for businesses." To answer this problem, Spectra.Net has a plan for seminars and workshops.

Broderbund Software, Inc.   One of the few companies making a profit in CD-ROMs in the consumer area is Broderbund Software. The multimedia CD-ROM industry is highly fragmented, with many small, as yet unprofitable companies. Broderbund has been mostly successful in the education, edutainment, and recently, adult game areas. Its CD-ROM *Myst* occupied the best-sellers lists for several months. Where outstanding content is a requirement to be successful, Broderbund has an advantage with its experience of developing or obtaining, in the manner of a publishing company, outstanding and quality-defining multimedia content. Its goal is to be a one-stop shopping center for families. It will continue to stress educational software, an area that most forecasters say will grow dramatically. This is in contrast to other areas where product definition and growth are uncertain. Broderbund

Software, Inc., has started some hybrid CD-ROM projects. With its quality content and its objectives of defining standards in the family area, it is well worth watching in the future.

Netscape Communications   Netscape Communications was founded in 1994 jointly by James H. Clark, a former CEO of Silicon Graphics, and Marc Andreesen, one of the originators of the original Mosaic, to commercialize software for PC users for the WWW. The company currently provides the most popular browser, accounting for 6 million of the 9 million browsers used. Many browsers were given away free of charge. Netscape's goal is to set the de facto standard and then become the biggest provider of Internet-oriented products. Many observers say that Netscape wants to be the Microsoft of the Internet. The company's intended product list includes more than just browsers. Planned products include software to run Web sites, find information, and provide security for Web transactions; also planned are some Web services. Netscape's IPO offering soared from $28.00 to well over $50.00 a share on the first day in one of the market's most spectacular openings. This is a capitalization of almost $1.8 billion for a company that is now selling and giving away $39.00 browsers. While admirers think this company could be in the early days of growth and impact to rival Microsoft's, skeptics suspect that the hype for the information highway overran this company and that despite Netscape's very competent and well-respected management, this company has major competitors, including Microsoft, and thus faces major risks for future growth. Time will tell.

HISTORY

The Bright Side

> The Online Goldmine—Prospecting in the Digital Frontier: Educators Strike It Rich.
>
> *(Enhance, 1994)*

The Communications Act of 1996 attempted to account for 61 years of technical progress and social change.

Larry Ellison of Oracle calculated that video servers could account for 20 percent of his $13 billion business by the turn of the century.

Europe appeared, to some people, to move ahead of the United States in volume deployment of ITV. As an example, in Germany, the cable and telephone industries are controlled by Deutsche Telekom, which appeared to help deployment. Others felt that this was not significant in the long run.

The Dark Side   Within any major complex activity, history tells us to expect false steps and mistaken projections. There have been several false steps. Here are some of them:

1994

TCI and Bell Atlantic declared in February that their more than $16 billion deal, first announced in October 1993, had collapsed. They could not make their financial model close.

SBC Communications and Cox's $4.9 billion deal, announced in December 1993, collapsed in April 1994 because of FCC regulations.

NYNEX withdrew a bid for interactive television set-top boxes as a result of the demise of the Telecommunications Reform Bill of 1994.

The Senate failed to pass a revised Telecommunications Bill after it passed the House.

1995

BellSouth announced that it decided to eliminate Oracle as a provider for video server software for its Atlanta trial of 12,000 homes in favor of Sybase, Inc. The difficulties appeared to relate to business issues and money as opposed to software function, operations, or performance. At least three interactive trials use Sybase tools. Singapore Telecom and Southern New England Telecom's trials are the others.

Rochester Telephone Corporation concluded their 52-apartment video-on-demand trial, saying that they found only minimal demand from customers for solely movies on demand. They felt that perhaps offering movies on demand with other offerings might make a difference, but they could not make a financially viable business case for just 100 movies on demand now.

The CyberMalls Corporation site that supported about 1200 Web pages for more than 70 companies closed up shop rather than continuing to support a business model they decided was doomed to failure. There was little evidence that these 70 companies were gaining exposure that resulted in any increased sales using their on-line brochures.

In Table 6.12, we note a few of the highlights or lowlights, depending on who you are, of this decade. There has been some fairly negative commentary as well. Focus 6.4 contains some of this commentary.

Table 6.12 Some stakeholders' historical moments this decade.

Stakeholders	History	Effect
Government	Republicans took over the House and Senate after 40 years.	They promised to move to less government funding and regulation.
Computer	IBM's massive loss led to downsizing and restructure. Microsoft shipped Windows '95. The Internet and WWW grew rapidly.	Competition increased for new business such as interactive multimedia, dominance in operating systems, and hardware. Major price wars benefited users and helped accelerate the adoption of multimedia computers. Major computer companies scrambled to participate in the Internet and retain their position of leadership in setting software standards, and struggled not to be left out.
Publications	In 1995, *Encyclopaedia Britannica* debuted its encyclopedia on the WWW after five years of declining sales in paper.	One of several experiments explored new, more profitable roles.
Entertainment	National Football League moved to Fox network. First end to a television season (1994–1995) with less than 60 percent of the viewing audience for the big three television networks.	This gave dramatic evidence of loss of dominance by the major three networks.
Telephone and cable	Alliances broke up after difficulty of making them work. Announced trial plans got scaled down and delayed.	The media relished reporting hype at one moment and stumbles and pauses at rest stops the next.
Users	Users experienced hype confusion, and information overload. They purchased more PCs than TVs.	Magna Carta (see section, A Government Step, under Trends in this chapter)

FOCUS 6.4 Negative commentary.

Not everyone is positive in the press.

- In the fall of 1994, Ted Turner told *Business Week* that "The fact is, every interactive cable experiment so far has failed."

- Moody's VP-senior credit officer, Stephen Gutkowski, predicts that the information superhighway would take 30 years and $240 billion to develop. He says that the cost to the telephone industry is $164 billion and the cost to the cable television industry is $75 billion (*Moody's*, 1994).

- For the next decade, the information highway will be largely CD-ROMs and on-line services such as Prodigy, CompuServe, and America Online. The Internet will evolve slowly to accommodate secure transactions, point-and-click interfaces, and sophisticated intelligent agents. It will be common in corporations long before it is common in homes. In about a decade, a vastly watered down version of the information highway will emerge.

- There is no money to be made in the near future, just huge up-front investments. There will be major battles among telephone companies and cable companies, among different computer companies, and among different on-line services companies. ■

Here are two final comments to ponder as you look back at the history of this period. Movie mogul William Fox, commenting on an early sound system for movies, said, "To have conversation would strain the eyesight and the sense of hearing at once, taking away the restfulness one gets from viewing pictures alone." The well-known past CEO of Digital Equipment Corporation (Digital) declared in the early 1980s, "The personal computer will fall flat on its face in business."

Promises

One cogent history consists of promises that various providers are making as we write this book, and that will be history as you read the book. You may want to note the progress toward implementing the broadband deployment promises in Table 6.13, based on data reported by Richard Karpin-

Table 6.13 Some promises.

Company	Broadband deployment promises	Mid-1995 status	Current status to be filled in by you
Ameritech Corporation	6 million homes by 2000, with virtually unlimited variety of programming to customers across the midwest, and 1 million homes at end of 1996	No commercial homes to date FCC application set aside to build interactive hybrid fiber coax in six other markets for now	
Bell Atlantic Corporation	9 million homes by 2000, and 1.2 million homes by the end of 1995 $11 billion pumped into broadband platforms in five years	No commercial homes to date FCC application set aside to build interactive hybrid fiber coax in six other markets for now	
BellSouth Corporation	Small trial of 7000 homes in Chamblee, GA	Recently started construction; FCC permission requested	
GTE Communications Corporation	550,000 homes over the next several years		
NYNEX	2 million lines by 1996 Beginning ATM and VOD deployed by end of 1996 Significant interactivity provided before 2000	390,000 homes in two markets	
Pacific Telesis Group	6 million homes by 2000, and 1.5 million homes by year end 1996 $16 billion hybrid fiber coax network by 2000	Going very slowly on massive checklist of milestones; got initial FCC approval only recently	
Southwestern Bell Communications Inc.	47,000 homes by 1995 Testing with Microsoft Advanced interactive network deployed in 2500 homes by mid-1995	1800 homes by year end of 1995	

(cont.)

Table 6.13 Some promises. *(cont.)*

Company	Broadband deployment promises	Mid-1995 status	Current status to be filled in by you
U S WEST Commu- nications	600,000 homes by end of 1995, and 1.25 mil- lion homes by 1996	135 homes in a trial that was not interactive, cable only initially FCC application set aside to build interactive hybrid fiber coax; also, 18 months behind schedule	

ski (1944), technology editor of *Interactive Age*. The midstatus update is from the *Wall Street Journal*, Monday, July 24, 1995 (Cauley, 1995). Table 6.14 notes some other promises, gleaned from industry sources, that you might want to track as well.

In the promises for providing delivery systems, there is at least a strong implication that the providers will someday deploy video bandwidth upstream. There is a big question about when the near future will begin and how long the near future will last. Current bandwidth planning appears to

Table 6.14 Some cable company promises.

Company	Promises	Current status to be filled in by you
Time Warner Inc.	Spend $5 billion upgrading 85 percent of its cable systems to full service net- works by the end of 1998 4000 homes in Orlando trial in 1995	
Tele- Communications Inc. (TCI)	Spend $2 billion to upgrade cable to fiber optics with 750-megahertz band- width Full-service network capabilities, by the end of 1996	

be very asymmetric despite all visionary talks. Using fiber optics in the local loop merely to simulate audio-bandwidth twisted pairs would not constitute making good on the promises. A full-service network includes at least enough upstream bandwidth to implement video on demand, but may not include enough for full-motion video conferences or even pleasant upstream sending of multimedia store-and-forward mail.

Many other important promises involve improvements in price and function of servers and end-user devices. For example, Oracle, working with Ncube and Hewlett-Packard, intends to drive servers' price for each video stream down to approximately $200 and drive the price of a set-top box down to approximately $250. Their polemics say that Silicon Graphics' servers cost approximately $2000 per video stream. Carl Lehmann, Director of Interactive Media and Electronics at BIS Strategic Decisions in Massachusetts, projects that by the turn of the century, there will be 51 million set-top boxes with 22.5 million analog boxes, 21.5 million hybrid boxes, and 7 million fully digital set-top boxes (*Interactive Week*, 1995). We encourage you to update the preceding tables as you observe progress.

For many, the important outcome is the stockholders' outcome. For stockholders, important numbers are the earnings, net income, or net sales. We provide some of these kinds of numbers in Table 6.15 for some of the key players. The Dow Jones Industrial Average at this time was approximately 3900. We invite you to see who still is a player in this area and how strong and vocal they are. In particular, there are a couple of new mutual funds, American Funds' "New Economy Fund," and Gabelli's new "Gabelli Global Interactive Couch Potato Fund." These funds are pure speculative plays in companies involved in this as of yet not completely defined business. The Gabelli Global Interactive Couch Potato Fund started in February 7, 1994, with a net asset value of $10.00 per share. It has a large collection of cable, entertainment, interactive consumer and financial services, interactive software and services, telephone, media, broadcasting, entertainment, and publishing companies. Compare these numbers with their updated versions as you read this book. See whether the overall industry sectors are in favor and whether the participants in national and state government who have set policy and funded some projects are still in office.

DIFFERENCES

Every provider of distributed multimedia, whether individual, company, or government, sees a large difference between the vision of the future and the current state of the art. Some of the most important differences involve con-

Table 6.15 Earnings of a few key stakeholders.

Sample company	Earnings	Current earnings to be filled in by you
Bell Atlantic	Net income $1.4 billion before extra-ordinary charges for accounting changes With these charges included was loss $754.8 million (fiscal 1994)	
NYNEX	Net income $793 million (fiscal 1994)	
Encyclopaedia Britannica	Sales $150 million (1994) approx.	
IBM	Net income $2.965 billion (fiscal 1994)	
Scientific-Atlanta	Net earnings $35 million (fiscal 1994)	
Macromedia	Net profit $3.1 million (fiscal 1994)	
Microsoft	Net profit $1.2 billion (4 quarters to 9/30/94)	
Oracle Systems Corporation	$2 billion in sales (1993)	
Broderbund	$112 million in sales (1994)	
Netscape Communications	Net income of negative $4.3 million on a revenue of $16 million (first half 1995) An initial public offering that soared to over $50 the first day (in mid-1995)	
Broadband Technologies	Net loss of $24.17 million on net sales of $27 million (1994) Profit projected in 1997	

flicts between telephone and cable companies, uncertainty about what customers will buy, confusion over how best to factor in this moment's current hot technologies even if they are still vaporous, and government regulations. Time frame remains a huge uncertainty. Expectations are too high; credibility too low. In fact, you may look back at the history of this decade as one of technical, regulatory, and business uncertainties, enormous complexity, sorting out, and clarifications of exactly what various stakeholders and potential stakeholders are proposing to do. Above all in importance for you to know, however, is that many smart people and significant companies are working on solving the problems.

Expectations that large numbers of customers will want to pay money for all or parts of distributed multimedia systems and to enjoy constructing and finding multimedia information with today's state-of-the-art tools and platforms are unrealistic. Today's tools are too hard to use, too slow, or simply lacking in function. Commercial providers' capital investments to start can be very high. Providers, for the most part, make very little money in trials. Providers are uncertain about what customers want and about what providers can persuade customers to buy. Many trials focus on video on demand as the cornerstone of providers' new offerings. Surveys and early trial results indicate that customers are far more interested in other applications, suites of applications, contexts, and services where video on demand would be merely one of several offerings.

Some early trial results appear to support these survey findings. Although somewhat suspect, surveys indicate that current on-line users are primarily college-educated white males and that usage is significantly lower among Hispanics and blacks. College-educated white males do not enjoy shopping, yet providers view shopping as a huge area of opportunity for distributed multimedia. Other survey analyses indicate that when two-way broadband networking capabilities become pervasive around the turn of the century or several years beyond, the primary, but far from the only, population of users will be those who are under thirty now, who have grown up with computers and are accustomed to electronic access to information and the ability to communicate with people over E-mail. Entertainment is important to this segment, but it is a second priority. As we know, the population of the United States after the turn of the century will look very different from the population in the United States for the past 30 years. It will be older and have a greater proportion of nonmajority ethnic groups, especially Hispanic groups. Table 6.16 illustrates the difficulty of treating potential users of multimedia applications as a single audience.

We hear very little about providers' work on support systems although clearly systems to collect orders and accept money are an important part of the vision. Today many of the providers view such automated backroom support systems as crown jewels of their companies. Changing any one of these systems is a major action that can take not just months, but years. As complex

Table 6.16 Current consumers.

Attribute	Primary television users for home shopping	Primary video game users	Median of on-line information users
Heaviest users	Senior citizens and housewives	Teenage boys	Males, age 37; household income $72,000; attended college
Attention level	Passive	Fast reactions	Active intellectual involvement

as some of these systems are today, they are simple when compared to what is required to provide backroom support for the distributed multimedia of the future. Focus 6.5 indicates some features of these future systems.

TRENDS

Converting all media into digital forms that the same networks can carry is lowering barriers that previously made it difficult for companies to expand into one another's markets. For example, telephone companies and cable companies have used such completely different local networks that the only way for a telephone company to expand into the cable business was to buy a cable company's network. However, now that telephone companies and cable companies are gradually replacing their existing networks by essentially identical networks, only a much lower barrier prevents either sort of company from offering services that the other sort of company previously offered. This provides company A with both the opportunity to expand into company B's markets and the risk that company B will expand into company A's markets.

A company can approach the convergence of its industry with other industries in different ways. Many companies are basing their strategies on the idea that the best defense is a good offense. Such companies attempt to encroach more rapidly than they are encroached upon. Other companies are concentrating on defense by attempting to build up barriers as fast as digital technology tears barriers down. One common material for building a barrier is a proprietary, nonstandard product. If a company can persuade customers to lock themselves into such a product, then other companies must overcome the barrier of customers' investments in that product to compete. Another mater-

---

FOCUS 6.5 Backroom operations.

Some of the backroom support functions that multimedia providers will require are as follows.

- Order entry involves millions of distributed customers' transactions using multiple payment methods.

- Invoicing and tracking settlements involve aggregating multiple providers' separate invoices. The customer, no doubt, wants one hypermedia invoice with links to details.

- Customer service records track release levels of customers' configurations.

- Maintenance and recovery

- Network management

- Financial measurements and reporting to management, stockholders, and the board

- Market data collection and analysis

- Copyright and royalty management of assets with appropriate collection of fees ■

---

ial for building a barrier is a government regulation. If a company can convince some relevant government that a barrier is in the public interest (or even in the private interest of a member of that government), then the company may obtain a legal monopoly to replace a disappearing technological monopoly.

If the good-offense approach is the one chosen, the question is how do you go about implementing it? There is the necessity of assembling groups of people, consortia, alliances, or other entities who have skills, capital, and other resources that all together suffice to provide multimedia content, products, and services. However, there is no clear trend toward a single approach for assembling such a group or what legal or business structure that group takes. Does it represent outright ownership of all parties, a strategic alliance, or minority investments in each other? Should interested individuals found a start-up company from scratch? Should a company reorganize internally and hire people or retrain to obtain required skills, as opposed to forming a partnership or alliance with other companies whose employees have required skills? Should a company integrate vertically around distributed multimedia? For example, if a sitcom will reach viewers over a telephone company's twisted-pair local loops, should the telephone company produce the sitcom? Without a trend toward one approach, we present examples of important approaches.

Form an Alliance

We begin with the approach of forming alliances among companies that have complementary core competencies. Providers have announced several hundred such alliances, including joint ventures and partnerships of all sorts. One driving force behind alliances is the desire to spread costs and share risks. Start-up costs are large, for enough content to be attractive. No one is sure of the nature of future markets, in detail or even in outline. As reflected in the previous chapters, many technical challenges remain open, many technical and business decisions remain to be made, and standards need to be defined.

Another driving force behind alliances is that successful distributed multimedia content, products, and services involve a wide variety of skills that essentially no single company possesses. For example, in the first partnership that we mention, Siemens provides ATM technology, network management expertise, intelligent network call control, advanced multimedia applications, content conversion, and MPEG encoding; Scientific-Atlanta provides set-top terminals, digital video, digital audio, and radio-frequency technologies; and Sun Microsystems provides video networking and server technologies.

Some reasonably typical examples of alliances follow.

- Siemens, Scientific-Atlanta, and Sun formed an alliance to deliver IMMXpress, a multimedia network architecture to enable cable and telephone companies to build end-to-end multimedia networks.

- Digital Equipment Corporation (Digital) and NYNEX formed an alliance to provide computers and data-storage systems for trials in New York, Maine, and Massachusetts. Digital's design provides scalable and efficient storage of video using the Alpha chip for compression and decompression.

- Hewlett-Packard (HP) and Pacific Telesis (PT) formed an alliance where HP provides video servers for use on PT delivery systems.

- U S WEST and Time Warner formed a partnership to conduct a major test in Florida. U S WEST owns 30 percent of the cable and entertainment company.

- NYNEX, Bell Atlantic, Pacific Telesis, with Creative Artists Agency offering guidance, have formed a company, TELE-TV Media, to encourage producers to provide content and develop navigator software, taking into account the new features of video-dial-tone delivery. Howard Stringer, a long-time veteran of CBS, has been hired as chairman and CEO. They have already agreed to test Microsoft's ITV operating system.

- BellSouth Corporation, Ameritech Corporation, Inc., and Disney have announced a shared ownership in a venture to develop, market, and deliver video programming to the consumer market. Each partner will invest $500 million.

- The Oracle Set-Top Alliance includes 3DO Co., General Instrument (GI), HP, Scientific-Atlanta, Microware, and over 100 other companies. Its purpose is to set minimum requirements for set-top box hardware and ensure that these systems work across a broad range of networks. Oracle's offerings are competitive with Microsoft's.

- The Grand Alliance, including General Instrument and MIT, is developing a single HDTV transmission standard.

- AT&T Network Systems and Silicon Graphics have a joint venture to integrate the various components required to deliver on the promise of interactive television. The new entity, called Interactive Digital Solutions, is to develop powerful computers and networked communications for multimedia applications.

- Silicon Graphics and DreamWorks SKG are building and operating a $50 million twenty-first-century digital studio. Paul Allen and Microsoft have minority investments in DreamWorks.

- Silicon Graphics has purchased Alias Research and Wavefront Technologies. These companies are very strong providers of animation software.

- Macromedia and Oracle Corporation reached a licensing agreement that will enable developers to use Macromedia's Smart 3D technology in Oracle's Media Objects development environment. The intent is that developers who create multimedia titles using Oracle Media Objects for Oracle's Media Server will be able to create realistic environments that consumers can explore through interactive television. Some of Macromedia's authoring tools are best sellers.

- Oracle, Lotus Development Corporation, and 3Com Corporation are forming a consulting group that will help companies plan for the interactive age and work with content providers.

- Oracle and Intel Corporations plan to integrate Oracle Media Server with Intel's ProShare video and document conferencing software. The plan involves cross-licensing and sharing intellectual property.

- TCI and Interactive Communications have formed a company called CyberMedia. Its state-of-the-art studio enables designers, programmers, producers, writers, and others to develop interactive products ranging from CD-ROM titles to interactive broadband television and computer services.

- TCI decided to invest $125 million in TCI common stock in the Microsoft Network with a 20 percent stake indicating to many where TCI thought a real business would be.

- TCI has a joint venture with Acclaim Entertainment Inc. TCI believes that an exciting application possibility is for remote users to play video games that have wonderful video quality over cable networks.

- AT&T seems to agree with TCI on the promise of games. They purchased the ImagiNation Network from Sierra On-Line. They negotiated a contract with Sierra On-Line to continue to provide interactive game content for this on-line game network.

- Capital Cities/ABC and Electronic Arts are cooperating to use the network's news, nature documentary, and children's entertainment resources to develop family-oriented multimedia content.

- Capital Cities/ABC and NTN Communications, Inc. are developing interactive games for use in hotels and restaurants.

- Disney bought Capital Cities/ABC.

Reorganize and Integrate Vertically

A company that wants to participate vigorously in distributed multimedia may elect to reorganize for the purpose. For example, IBM went through several such gyrations starting in the early part of the decade. Initially, IBM set up a multimedia group to evangelize multimedia products into every product line and to disappear three years after the products were there. Just before disappearing, this group established a group called Fireworks Partners and set up the IBM Multimedia Publishing Studio.

Later, IBM set up several task forces under the CEO's chief strategist. The task forces recommended not merely a group, but rather a Networked Applications Services Division. This was a several-layer organization with directors and managers responsible for areas such as compression technology, distributed multimedia systems design, kiosk solutions, electronic marketing services, electronic trading, video conferences, electronic publishing, agent technology, interactive television software, multimedia network design, systems management, video-on-demand trials, and multimedia applications services. Recently, IBM further emphasized their commitment to what they term network-centric computing (distributed multimedia computing) by requiring all of their units to be responsible for developing strategies, products, and services appropriate to the high priority of Internet, the Web, and other network-centric products and services. They also created a new unit for the Internet and reported that their Research Division will spend 25 percent of their budget on network-concentric computing.

As another example, Viacom has created a Viacom Interactive Media division. The division's goal is delivery of wonderful content for any format or delivery vehicle. Its assets include cable television properties, such as MTV and Nickelodeon, plus all of Paramount Communications, Inc., including Simon & Schuster, some amusement parks, and large film and video holdings. It can distribute through Blockbuster Entertainment holdings. It now includes Paramount's former R&D facilities. It has alliances with AT&T to work on interactive television delivery systems. Its content includes CD-ROM titles, interactive television, and on-line services.

Hire Needed Skills

Finding the right mix of skills and facilitating working together toward a common goal will increasingly be a challenge and opportunity for those who qualify. We refer to Chapter 8 for more discussion on this topic. As an example, for Disney, BellSouth Corporation, Ameritech Corporation, and SBC Communications, Disney has put together a group to work on navigational aids for consumers to use in selecting options. Toward this end, Disney has gathered people from its advanced technology group, its theme park design group, and its software group.

Found Start-up Company

ICTV claims it is Silicon Valley's hottest startup in the emerging interactive television industry. Its strategic partner is Cox Cable, the third largest cable operator in the United States. It claims it is developing a comprehensive, proprietary digital television system that will make possible delivery of full-service interactive television over existing cable systems and advanced telephone systems.

ICTV provides video and multimedia processing, network communications, an interactive remote control, and a unique television-like user environment. It also offers software that enables other service providers to construct compelling applications that make optimum use of the system's processing power. It has a group of about 25 highly talented engineers and a warm, cooperative, fun environment with an emphasis on teamwork, as well as company-sponsored beach parties, softball team, and hikes in Yosemite. IBM bought an equity interest in ICTV.

Offer Services and Solutions

We describe several representative offerings that may be gone, undergoing phenomenal growth, or somewhere in-between at the time when you read this.

- Dynashuttle, (212) 673-0225, will provide an on-line link from your CD-ROM to any service that you want. The company president, Richard Reisman, says that early interest has come from publishers of legal and health-care CD-ROMs, but he expects the technology to appear in games and statistics-oriented applications also.

- Virtual Vegas, (310) 829-6268, has the goal of recreating Las Vegas on a CD-ROM with a very futuristic on-line link. Its president, David Herschman, says that people will play against one another on-line and the winner will receive a suitable, legal prize. A boutique will also be available for on-line purchases.

- AT&T has created Downtown Digital, a digital production studio, in New York City. The studio addresses the entire process of developing and maintaining interactive applications for television. It is trying to marry the best of software development with television production and publishing. Its primary goal is to drive AT&T's evolving client-server architecture for interactive content providers, especially in areas of tools to manage media and bandwidth.

- Bell Atlantic Video Services Company has completed construction of its $200 million Digital Services Bureau at its video service center in Reston, Virginia. A major service of this company is taking providers' analog and digital videotapes and turning them into digital video. However, its overall goal is to facilitate wonderful distinctive programming through producing, editing, and distributing services. It has progressed from taking 150 hours to digitize its first movie to 3 minutes per minute of movie in 1995. It has expanded its capacity to be able to digitize 50,000 minutes of video per month. At this rate it would take close to a year to digitize a video rental store's holdings of 4000 videotapes of 120 minutes each.

- MCI has a Developers Lab open to outsiders to use to test new offerings.

- The University of Ottawa in Canada has a laboratory that provides services for people interested in areas of distributed multimedia where the commercial market is not yet developed. They work on multimedia news, interactive distance learning, distributed multimedia infrastructure, and other content for delivery on Canada's largest ATM test bed.

- In 1995, Encyclopaedia Britannica debuted its encyclopedia on the WWW after five years of declining sales in paper. The WWW version, with a sophisticated search engine, is available to college students of customer universities for $1.00 per student and to users of the WWW for $150.00 per year. This form of offering represents a major change in the way that this company has been providing its solutions since 1768. It is taking advantage of significantly more economical distribution methods and new billing algorithms. We included them in Table 6.15 so you can see if their strategy shows signs of financial success.

Commission a Survey

After commissioning a survey, a provider might choose to gain some good public relations (PR) on the survey by publicizing nonconfidential results and also by selling the survey to other companies. There are several market studies, profiles, reports, and various prospectuses available for sale from a couple of dollars to several thousand dollars.

Some typical results of surveys are as follows.

- Management Forum International's survey, as reported in *Interactive Age*'s October 24, 1994, issue, reports "Internet users' median age is 36 and 85% are male. They will pay for industry-specific information and specify they want good educational programs."

- Videoway Multimedia Interactive services, the University of Montreal's New Technologies Research Lab, as reported in *Interactive Age*'s October 24, 1994, issue, sampled 1000 families and found, "The most popular application is video games, which viewers spent an average of four to five hours a week playing. The second is interactive television applications such as playing along with a sporting event or game show."

- A survey's respondents felt that they would watch an average of five movies per month, but they cited voting in elections and searching reference books as more important uses. Many people have questioned these results as what "mother" would want to hear.

- *Interactive Age*'s Gallup surveys (1994) report that respondents prefer television for home shopping and movie watching but prefer computers for home banking and game playing.

- Household penetration statistics, by product, from Electronic Industries Association appearing in *TWICE* of June 1994 were as follows:

  All television—98%

  Color television—96%

  VCR—80%

  Camcorder—22%

  Home computer—30%

  Telephone answering machine—58%

  Cordless telephone—56%

  Home radio—98%

  Home satellite station—4%

  Video-game software—over 40%

- Entertainment preferences, from the *Wall Street Journal*/Centennial Survey are as follows:

  Dinner out—55%

  Movie rental—36%

  Paperback book—22%

  Tickets to a sports event—17%

  Night at the movies—16%

  Subscribe to basic cable—16%

  Hardcover book—12%

  Night at the theater—10%

  Evening at a bar or lounge—5%

  Compact disc audio—4%

- Georgia Institute of Technology has surveyed users of the WWW. The surveyers do not claim that the results are statistically valid, but their results are some of the most comprehensive and interesting to date. Over 50 percent of the respondents in the survey used platforms based on Windows and almost half of their connection speeds were at 14.4 Kbits per second, followed by 13 percent at 10 Mbits per second and 12 percent at 28 Kbits per second. This information means that most of those sampled receive images very slowly. Both the mean and the median ages are 35. Respondents' median income is between $50,000 and $60,000, with the average income at $69,000; 15 percent are women and 80 percent are white.

■ Several surveys reported in trade journals have indicated that schools, colleges, and universities have the highest hopes for using multimedia. The next highest hopes are in industries involved in health, publishing, and printing. Such businesses cite as possible benefits increased efficiency of operation, competitiveness, and job creation. Other significant applications are in national defense and law enforcement.

Offer a Conference

Conferences provide information on how consumers can use interactive video and other services, how publishers can use on-line classified advertisements and on-demand printing, and how strategic agreements between yellow pages companies and on-line services companies create new opportunities, as well as on risks and opportunities for newspapers and magazines.

Silicon Graphics presented an Authoring Multimedia for Entertainment Conference in fall 1994. It allowed attendees to hear talks on creating content for the entertainment industry and to rub shoulders with professionals who have similar interests. It even had several talks on successes in this area. Topics included entertainment licensing, how to integrate two sides of the brain for the new creative teams, and developing good interactive TV navigators.

The Multimedia Development Group, which facilitates communications among its members, and the International Interactive Communications Society (IICS), a large organization serving interactive developers, communicators, and artists, sponsor the MultiMedia Expo Conference yearly. The first conference took place in 1987. The two groups say they are at the center of "the merger of the entertainment industry, the music, film, television, publishing, cable, and home video industries with computers, the next generation of consumer electronics, games, and communications technology." Their conference features talks on shopping in the virtual mall, a digital Hollywood roundtable, and guidance on investment and returns on the digital highway.

In fall 1994, United Digital Artists offered a Multimedia Design Conference in an unusual location—the East Coast rather than the West Coast. The conference's topics were close to actual hands-on creation and included side tours of creators' studios in the New York City area.

Microware offered a DAVID Developers Conference that covered topics from how to create using their DAVID operating system and environment to future trends in ITV even beyond the set-top box. Conference sponsors included General Instrument, Motorola, Philips, and Tele-TV.

Multichannel CommPerspectives, providers of the Convergence '95 Interactive Television Conference and Expo, discussed topics ranging from the business viability of near video on demand to realistic opportunities to make money.

Many conferences appeal to different groups of people. There are conferences dedicated to helping the publishing industry find the way, to setting up alliances to pursue something, anything digital, to why and then how to create content. The costs for conference attendance are about $1000 or more for three days. This does not include meals or other travel expenses. This amount may not be affordable for many people who could really benefit. Nonetheless, interest in distributed multimedia is high and some people do have travel money. So conferences may be one good way for providers to make money.

Publish a Column, Periodical, or Book

There is an explosion of magazines, articles, and books, particularly focusing on the Internet and the Web. Some magazines last no longer than three to four months. Some are solely on-line, available only through the Web. Others are primarily distributed through printed means but have WWW pages. Some come on CD-ROMs or with CD-ROMs. Other periodicals have directed their articles toward various aspects of distributed multimedia from other possible appropriate topics for these magazines.

Publicize Demonstrations

A typical excerpt from an IBM press release about a family of demonstrations follows (reprinted with permission). Note that System/390 is IBM's large server line.

SYSTEM/390 SERVERS BRING MULTIMEDIA LESSONS TO LIFE

November 4, 1994

IBM is demonstrating new technology at the EDUCOM conference this week that is delivering engaging multimedia education to the classroom to help high school and college students boost both their understanding—and their enjoyment—of their lessons.

At the conference, IBM is demonstrating how its new System/390™ Parallel Enterprise Server, a computer with the power of a mainframe in a package no bigger than a refrigerator, can store and send to classrooms multimedia programs that can greatly enrich classroom learning. At a college, the server would be housed in the computer center or library and would send out the educational multimedia programs to classrooms.

Universities are embracing multimedia education, both as a way to enliven classroom presentations, and as a way to deliver classes at a time and place convenient to off-campus students enrolled in popular "distance learning" programs.

"It's the System/390 server that makes all this possible," said Jim Corgel, IBM's general manager of higher education, North America. "The server can store, manage and deliver the huge amount of computerized information required for large-scale multimedia presentations."

At the EDUCOM conference, three universities are demonstrating three simulated environments using the server to deliver multimedia education. They are finding that students not only enjoy the multimedia programs, but they learn more, too.

Rensselaer Polytechnic Institute (RPI)

In this simulation, RPI is showing how a S/390 server delivers video to science classes, helping students better visualize how animals interact with their environment, how new drugs attack killer viruses, and what really happened when comets crashed into an area of Jupiter that was hidden from human view. According to Dr. Jack Wilson, director of the Anderson Center of Innovation in the undergraduate program at RPI, the performance of students using the multimedia teaching tools increased dramatically. Each student's computer has full access to networked multimedia resources and data acquisition, analysis, and visualization software.

California Polytechnic State University, San Luis Obispo

The Cal Poly simulation shows how professors can pull video, pictures, text, and sound out of a vast digitized library stored on a System/390 server to create multimedia learning modules.

History students, for example, can read newspaper stories and watch news clips of famous events; drama students can watch famous actors giving award-winning performances; and political science students can watch video of government officials delivering noted speeches, all on their classroom computer.

Commission a Charter

Interactive Age reported on December 12, 1994, that the new Republican Speaker of the House of Representatives, Newt Gingrich, was looking to a new think tank, the Progress and Freedom Foundation, to map a vision for America's high-tech future. That Foundation had retained George Gilder, Alvin Toffler, George Keyworth, and Esther Dyson to write a "Magna Carta" for the knowledge age as a basis for legislative planning. Their Magna Carta notes that talking about an information superhighway is typical second-wave thinking that concentrates on rigid bureaucracies and government ownership. It recommends, instead, talking about a highly flexible cyber-space with a myriad of owners that is more appropriate for the third wave. It notes that technological progress is changing cyberspace from a natural mo-nopoly to a market in which competition is the rule.

The Magna Carta thus recommends allowing telephone companies and cable companies to cooperate. Cooperation would allow the industries to use their respective fiber-optic cables among neighborhoods and coaxial cables within neighborhoods. Requiring that the two industries compete would re-quire each to duplicate the network that the other already has in place. The Magna Carta thus suggests replacing 1934-style price and entry regulation of monopolies by a more modern use of antitrust law.

A government's willingness to even consider such intellectual U-turns bodes well for our ability to achieve the critical success factors that will allow us to take the necessary next steps toward the vision of distributed multimedia.

Take Next Steps

Table 6.17 and Table 6.18 provide another way of looking at what providers' trends might be.

Table 6.17 Companies' next steps.

Companies	Possible next steps
Computer	Structure participation in trials to result in systems that providers can economically replicate, scale up, easily modify, spin off into interim products, and convert to new standards based on new information and trial findings.
	Do not rely on trials alone but market distributed multimedia into niche markets such as just-in-time for company employees.
	Leverage installed base of systems, adapter cards, and loyal customers.
	Incorporate more multimedia functions into operating system and hardware in an evolutionary manner.
Telephone	Leverage installed base of fiber-optic trunks, copper local loops, and switches.
	Have more focused, fewer, and smaller trials.
	Display a more evident strategy for deployment when regulatory picture clears and early trial results become known.
	Explore multiple sources of or find ways of getting content.
Cable	Same as above, except leverage installed base of high-bandwidth last-mile networks.
	Use cable modems for PCs with intermediate telephone upstream connections and cable downstream connections.
Publishing	Become critical users of others' early efforts.
	Start thinking how to repurpose current inventory for digital delivery and to reuse in new digital applications.
	Actually start doing some repurposing.
	Start planning on how and what to charge for interactive delivery and interactive applications.
	Try some market tests.
	Plan acquisitions of new content to fit within all possible delivery methods and allow reuse in other digital applications.
	Expand preliminary experiments that seem to work.
Games	Carefully evaluate new end-user devices and possible timing of their adoption.
	Take advantage of improvements in game performance that are possible with improvements in personal computers and operating systems.
	Develop tactics to broaden market beyond teenage white boys.
	Continue experimentation with virtual communities of game players.
Movie studios	Plan to repurpose their current inventory and sequels for interactive applications and delivery. Study early results of others for what might work well.
	Continue investigating how they might use two-way interactive broadband delivery to assist the production process.
	Expand the use of digital effects in movies.

(cont.)

Table 6.17 Companies' next steps. *(cont.)*

Companies	Possible next steps
Broadcast television networks	Plan to repurpose the current inventory for interactive delivery to take advantage of viewer interest and loyalty. Study early results of others for what might work well. Acquire future inventory in forms suitable for new delivery methods.
Consumer electronics (CE)	Consider personal computers and add-on equipment as consumer electronics. Anticipate that video-game machines and other CE will expand their role across many application areas in the new digital world. E-mail on my camcorder? Participate with CE such as digital cameras as input devices for personal computers.
Education	Offer more courses, workshops, and seminars on distributed multimedia. Some will even be on-line. Use multimedia to teach other subjects and offer on-line information access to multimedia enriched information.
Advertising and selling	Add information content, to create differentiation and customer loyalty. Go after niches and attempt to set up virtual user communities of interest in particular products. Pay much more attention to how to attract the buyers as opposed to the browsers as the novelty of simply having your own Web page or being in a virtual mall wears off.
Libraries	Be critical users of some early efforts of others. Consider carefully what you will digitize, where you will put it, and when.
Video rental	Compete in rural and other areas without video-on-demand services. Compete on service, rental atmosphere, large computer-assisted selection, and price. Expand rental to include CDs and games.
On-line information	Add more media but provide ways for users with less bandwidth than really needed to appreciate or tolerate the results. Add strong affinity to Internet. Make more use of interactivity. Offer at least some users higher bandwidth.
CD-ROM developers	Experiment with making applications hybrid. Vigorously pursue application development environments that facilitate author once then run on several platforms. Vigorously pursue business ventures that provide lucrative and multiple delivery options.

Table 6.18 Governments' next steps.

Government or branch	Possible next steps
Federal, executive	Continue providing overall motivation and consolidation as well as a forum for discussion. Do no harm.
Federal, legislative	Revise telecommunications legislation so that major players view it as an improvement and minor and new players can gainfully participate. Consider using antitrust rather than regulating entry and controlling prices.
Regulatory agencies	Improve efficiency and speed and avoid doing harm.
Granting agencies	Strive for wider dissemination of project results.
State and local	Emulate aggressive states, such as North Carolina's providing state-wide fiber-optics connections. Host events such as "The Future of Computer Networking and Tele-communications in San Diego" to educate employees and general public.

CRITICAL SUCCESS FACTORS

Instead of presenting critical success factors for each category of providers, we note some of the most important and difficult factors that apply to most categories. These factors could lead to the desired pot of gold shown in Fig. 6.3.

Services and Content: Providers must have compelling services, content, and other products that customers will use and pay for.

Marketing: Companies must have innovative marketing that is appropriate for the stages of new introductions.

Internal Processes: Firms must have processes to provide the services, content, and products in a manner that ensures that financial objectives are achieved, including adequate infrastructure, required security, and a back office for billing, reporting, collections, and managing financial aspects, as well as efficient processes for continued development and maintenance.

Long-term Payback: Providers need sufficient patience and capital to wait for a long-term payback.

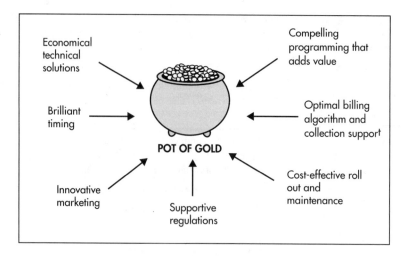

Figure 6.3 Success.

Superb Execution: They a need sensible, competitive ramp-up from providing for pioneers to the eventual, desired mass market with prudent reevaluation along the way as well as identification and marketing of products and services perhaps into niches. They need sufficient flexibility to accommodate whatever eventually becomes a successful equation.

Good Public Relations: Providers must have public relations that are visible, are prudent, and allow for managing expectations and building consumer trust.

Vision: Company leaders need plans that redirect or modify core assets and businesses as required to ensure that distributed multimedia means opportunity and not disaster or oblivion.

Regulation: Success depends on a supportive business and regulatory climate.

SUMMARY

No organization has sufficient breadth of skills and insights to provide complete distributed multimedia content, products, and services. Multimedia providers will need to combine forces and work in groups to obtain a complete solution with all of the pieces. Different categories of providers have significantly different visions and now have significantly different states of the art. All providers face the prospect that the next step from their state of the art toward their vision will require them to invest significant amounts of capital, time, and effort based on optimistic projections rather than on proven customer demand. Competing providers are stepping in significantly different directions, driven by their different installed bases and past experiences, as well as by different expectations. Not all providers' steps will turn out to have been in the forward direction. More steps will teach valuable lessons than will break even. Not all lessons will benefit the providers who paid to learn the lessons. The late 1990s are likely to see sufficiently clear directions.

REFERENCES

Cauley, Leslie. 1995. "Bell Curves." *Wall Street Journal,* July 24, p. 1.

Communications Industries Report. 1994. Atwood Group, 11600 College Blvd., Overland Park, KS 66210, March, p. 18 (ISSN 1070 4426).

Digital Delay. 1995. *Inter@ctive Week,* January 16, 1995, p. 27. Interactive Enterprises, L.L.C., Garden City, NY (ISSN 1078-7259) (609) 829-9313.

Elmer-Dewitt, Philip. 1993. "Take a Trip into the Future on the Superhighway." *Time Magazine,* April 12.

Enhance. 1994. "The Online Goldmine—Prospecting in the Digital Frontier: Educators Strike It Rich." Quote from the cover of the magazine, *Enhance—Bringing Teachers & Technology Together,* winter.

Individual. 1994a. "NYNEX, Bell Atlantic, Pacific Telesis Detail Programming Venture." FAX clipping service, Individual Inc., 84 Sherman Street, Cambridge, MA 02140, (800) 414-1000, Nov. 8.

Individual. 1994b. "Telephone-Cable Competition Could Be Costly, Moody's Forecasts." FAX clipping service, Individual Inc., 84 Sherman Street, Cambridge, MA 02140, (800) 414-1000, Nov. 8.

Interactive Age. Enterprise Computing Group, CMP Publications, Manhassett, NY, (516) 562-7383, Charles L. Martin, Jr., Publisher.

"Interactive Indices." Printed monthly in *Morph's Outpost.* (Data are provided by Gistics Inc.) Morph's Outpost Inc., Orinda, CA (ISSN 1074-6501).

Karpinski, Richard. 1944. Technology Editor's column. *Interactive Age,* October 24, p. 48.

Kraemer, Joseph S. 1994. *The Realities of Convergence,* Washington, D.C.: EDS Management Consulting Services, (202) 338-2861.

Kupfer, Andrew. 1994. "The Future of the Phone Companies." *Fortune.* (ISSN 0015-8259). October 3, pp. 94–109.

Miller, Mathew D. 1994. "A Scenario for the Deployment of Interactive Multimedia Cable Television Systems in the United States in the 1990's." *Proceedings of the IEEE,* vol. 82, no. 4 (April).

Moore, Geoffrey A. 1991. *Crossing the Chasm—Marketing and Selling Technology Products to Mainstream Customers.* (Republished by Harper Business, New York, 1995.)

Roetter, Martyn F., and Blum, Eric P. 1994. "Cracking the Consumer Market." *Upside Magazine,* April, pp. 50–57.

"How the Movies Learned to Talk" [re William Fox]. 1995. *Invention & Technology,* Winter.

Wired. Wired Ventures Ltd., Louis Rossetto, editor and publisher, San Francisco, CA, (800) 537-4618.

Young, Lewis H. 1993. "Exploring the Interactive Market—Confusion, Confusion, Confusion." *Electronic Business Buyer,* December, pp. 69–74.

Chapter 7

Trials

BACKGROUND

There are many excellent motives for conducting distributed multimedia trials rather than proceeding directly from a concept to full deployment. In order of decreasing importance, the motives for trials are economic, marketing, and technical.

Economic Motives

Consider first the economic motives for conducting trials. In Chapters 2 through 5, we discussed the major parts of a fully distributed multimedia system. For a nationwide or even large multistate regionwide deployment each of these parts could cost a few hundred billion dollars. When we include the cost of educating providers and providing necessary supporting services, the cost might well approach $1 trillion.

For the sake of discussion if we assume $1 trillion in cost and then divide this number by the approximately 250 million people who live in the United States, we get an investment of $4000 per person. Another way to view this number is to note that investing $1 trillion would consume the entire U.S. defense budget for almost four years. The nation could not afford to make such a large investment quickly, even if we were sure that we wanted widespread distributed multimedia and even if we were sure that we knew the best way to increase the bandwidth of POTS by a couple of orders of magnitude. Economics alone would dictate deploying distributed multimedia gradually, as a sequence of increasingly ambitious trials.

Marketing Motives

Consider next the marketing motives for conducting trials. Suppose that the nation's providers not only had the defense budget to invest but also knew exactly what technologies to deploy. A company would decide to invest in distributed multimedia, rather than in other opportunities, only if the market for distributed multimedia were likely to provide an adequate return on the company's investment. Only a trial with real customers can determine how much customers would pay for a particular suite of personal and business applications. Moreover, only a trial can determine how customers will react to the many possible methods of charging for service, which range from a flat monthly rate to billing for each second of use.

How much return would companies require? U S WEST is as interested in distributed multimedia as is corporately possible. It began its *1993 Annual Report* with a full page saying "U S WEST is leading a multimedia revolution that will change the way we work, learn, and play. It's easy. Whether it's movies on demand, personalized news and home shopping, or voice communications, we'll package the services *you* want. And make sure they're simple to use." The next page shows a television set displaying the elaboration "As 1, 2, 3." The report's financial highlights page says that the company's sales and other revenues in 1993 were $10.294 billion and the total assets were $20.680 billion. Excluding the effects of a one-time accounting charge, the income per share was $2.72, and the total return to stockholders beginning the year at $38.38 per share and ending at $45.88 per share plus the dividend was 25.4 percent for the year. This company also was the only communications company listed in the 1993 update of the "100 Best Companies to Work for in America." How would you manage the risk for this company in moving it from a utility company to an information-providing growth company?

Trials can determine how much more customers would be willing and able to pay for the converged services that distributed multimedia would make possible (see Table 7.1).

Trials may well show that companies know of no suite of personal and business applications that either could appeal to enough people or could be priced high enough for a few people to repay the investment that would be required. If this turns out to be true, then trials are necessary to find a smaller collection of applications that require significantly less investment than complete, fully two-way high-bandwidth distributed multimedia systems with

Table 7.1 Typical customer service bills.

Service	Price per month
Typical phone service for a household	$60
Typical cable service for a household	$50
On-line service per individual	$30

massive amounts of digitized content would require, but that can create enough revenue to pay back the corresponding smaller investment.

Technical Motives

Finally, consider the technical motives for conducting trials. Suppose that there were no problem with either obtaining required investment capital or generating an adequate return on investment. There would remain many questions about the optimal technologies companies should deploy. For example, even without a test, telephone companies and cable companies seem to agree that they want to drive fiber-optic cables deeper into the network, that is, closer to customers' homes and businesses. However, selecting the optimum number of customers that a single fiber should serve requires companies to understand more about both operational considerations and applications. As another example, how do you plan for the optimal number of subscribers that can access the server simultaneously? You certainly do not plan a server that can handle 100 percent of the customers simultaneously. Such understanding comes from trials. Similarly, although several approaches to video compression and decompression are sufficiently well known to deploy, companies need trials to determine which approaches give video that customers prefer for particular applications at minimum cost. As a third example, a server's cost depends strongly on the nature of its storage hierarchy, which may involve semiconductor storage, magnetic disks (hard drives), magnetic tapes, and optical discs. Storage hierarchy performance is notoriously sensitive to usage patterns, which only full-scale trials can determine.

Proceeding directly to nationwide or even regionwide deployment would require companies to standardize not only general approaches, such as an approach to compression, but also specific parameters, such as the number of users per fiber at each population density. The only thing worse than no standard or too many standards is a standard that is technologically obsolete before publication. The rate of technological progress is simply too rapid to freeze with a single rigid standard.

Companies that set up a trial must, of course, choose some set of working standards. Trials that begin as little as six months apart may employ significantly different standards. Companies that set up a large trial may consciously deviate from all previous trials' decisions, in an effort to set a standard and thereby gain strategic advantage. Companies that set up a small trial may consciously emulate other trials to reduce the chance of being left out on a limb. The technological reason for trials is to experiment with different sets of working standards until one set emerges as being especially good fit with the trials' economic and marketing results.

No laboratory experiments, marketing surveys, or government activities are valid substitutes for trials. Laboratory experiments have essentially no connection to what consumer products real people will buy. Although surveys determine what customers say they will buy, survey results have only a weak connection to what customers actually will buy, except when the subject of the survey is a small variation on a familiar product or service. Surveying consumers about distributed multimedia is especially unpromising, because most potential customers have extreme difficulty visualizing the subject of such a survey. Most experts have insufficient insight to replace trials as sources of economic, marketing, or technical answers. A standards group may break a tie between two alternatives that trials have shown to be more or less equally desirable. Breaking a tie avoids ending up with two standards where one would be better. In the process, a standards group representing a government may be able to bias a decision in favor of equitable access or some other agenda.

In the next section, we discuss the vision that drives various stakeholders to invest and participate in distributed multimedia trials. In the State of the Art section, we mention the industries that are investing most heavily. We next present the history of trials completed in the 1980s and early 1990s. Under Differences, we note unusual characteristics that make multimedia trials particularly interesting, in the sense of the famous curse "May you live in interesting times." The long section on Trends discusses some important trials that are underway. We then discuss critical success factors that apply to most trials.

VISION FOR THE NEXT DECADE

Companies envision a succession of trials that will answer a succession of specific economic, marketing, and technical questions and will extend their general proprietary knowledge base relative to a deployable infrastructure. Thus, companies envision trials that will evolve into moneymaking ventures. To this end, companies envision trials that will provide publicity and marketing and will whet customers' appetites for services.

Table 7.2 shows some of the reasons different categories of stakeholders participate in trials as users or sponsors.

STATE OF THE ART

Many of today's highly publicized distributed multimedia trials are expensive, complex logistically, and risky. These trials are expensive because they cannot take advantage of economies of scale. Trials are risky because, as in

Table 7.2 Incentives for participation in trials.

Stakeholders	Incentives to users	Incentives to sponsors
Individuals	Have interesting, usually painless experience, some free services or reduced rates, feeling of contributing to great events. Attractive to pioneers and early adopters of new technologies	Not generally applicable
Companies	Design their own eventual offerings or services earlier. Obtain competitive advantage over competition by means of early experience. Plan for better further use. Provide important corporate and business feedback to trial sponsors.	Succeed in trial objectives. Obtain a real and perceived head-start with competitive advantage. Expand customers and market as outgrowth of the trials. Get positive publicity.
Governments	Design their own eventual offerings or services earlier. Plan for better further use. Improve knowledge about what to fund. Provide important user feedback to trial sponsors.	Guide eventual outcome. Get positive publicity. Provide public benefit.

any scientific or marketing experiment, you learn most from your failures. You may learn that your current partners and suppliers are not the ones that you want when you move on.

Although trials could conceivably cover millions of customers, most of today's trials are primarily independent islands with little commonality and few bridges to other islands. Companies that sponsor a trial must be willing to write off the cost of the trial against the information they gain. Many of today's trials do not bring in enough revenue to pay for operations, let alone provide a desirable return on invested capital.

Partly because of the lack of standards, a trial entails the risk of investing in approaches that are destined for quick obsolescence. For example, setting up a trial of video on demand requires a company to digitize and compress enough movies and other video content to give customers a critical mass of options, although perhaps fewer options than a typical video rental store offers. A company risks selecting a compression standard that nobody will ever use again after the end of the trial. In this case, the trial must bear the full cost of digitizing and compressing the video to that standard. Even a small number of users require a reasonably large selection. Thus, on the one hand, digitizing and compressing a critical mass of video represents a particularly large cost per user, for a trial that has few users. On the other hand, if a company is losing money on each user, the company cannot make up the loss with a large volume of users.

Companies find that people are willing to participate in today's trials as users. However, companies realize that early trials risk making users very unhappy. To avoid leaving a permanent bad taste in the mouths of real customers, companies often offer free or greatly subsidized service or even use their employees as volunteer guinea pigs in early tests.

Today, providers have announced many trials and not just in the United States. Some trials have started; others continue trials begun years ago. Some companies have announced scale-downs or slowdowns of previously announced trials. Many smaller, less publicized trials are continuing in their early stages. We await the results.

HISTORY

The vision of trials' advantages has been sufficiently rosy to outweigh trials' expenses and risks for a surprisingly large number of companies for over a decade. Some of the trials and their results follow.

The 1980s

Virginia Tech   In 1984, Virginia Polytechnic Institute and State University in Blacksburg, Virginia, began requiring incoming engineering students to purchase personal computers that could handle text and graphics. This requirement was part of a trial to assess the value of students' having computers throughout their college careers. For the first time, professors at Virginia Tech could give assignments that required students to use computers, with the assurance that all students had easy and equal access to similar equipment. The network involved was sneakernet, that is, carrying diskettes. Later, several departments required their students to obtain multimedia computers. The trial was successful in all phases, despite some initial feelings that computers were expensive, applications were unknown, and student time was cheap. The trial showed significant advantages over providing a few computers in a lab and letting dozens of students wait in line for each computer. The trial showed that students learned more if they had computers available whenever a thought struck them and if they felt free to explore new possibilities at leisure. The trial also showed the advantage of assuring that users had a general capability and making determination of good uses for the capability.

U.S. Videotex Trials The 1980s' Videotex trials in the United States were generally unsuccessful, particularly in comparison with grandiose expectations. Understanding the reasons for the failures of these trials of text-based information services is important in preparing for services of the late 1990s.

- The trials priced service according to duration of use, making users feel a need to preplan their on-line time carefully and log off quickly rather than exploring other available activities, making them feel like students lined up waiting impatiently to use a lab computer.

- To users it seemed that only a little information was available, partly because they felt too hurried to determine what was available.

- Users perceived the services as dull, unnecessary, and unappealing.

- Users saw the services as trying to change their way of doing things rather than helping them solve existing problems.

- Users perceived the services as hard to use, partly because the applications were adjuncts to mainframe computers and partly because the applications lacked user-friendly education.

- The original proprietary mainframe terminals used had prices that were appropriate for custom commercial equipment rather than for consumer commodities.

- Attempts to replace proprietary terminals with personal computers occurred before the base of these computers became large or the cost became small.

- The trials seemed to indicate that only the affluent and educated could operate the equipment, partly because only such people participated.

- Trials that providers set up and priced to make money from on-line shopping determined that users instead wanted to communicate with one another through E-mail and on-line forums.

- Trials that providers set up to test interest in education found little interest.

- Surveys indicated higher user interest than did subsequent actual use.

European Videotex Trials The trials of Videotex in Europe starting in 1983, particularly in France, were generally very successful. Early subscribers to Minitel received free terminals instead of telephone books. By 1989, 16 percent of French households, which included 30 percent of the population, used almost 6 million such terminals. The early French trials determined that people wanted to decrease communication costs and save time but were less interested in accessing information. Today, almost 15 million people, almost one-third of the French population, use special Minitel terminals mostly for banking and to obtain public information.

Canadian Trials   In 1989, Le Groupe Videotron, a large cable company Canada, began limited commercial deployment of interactive television. Its trial investigated customers' usage and response to different pricing packages. The University of Montreal's New Technologies Research Laboratory helped evaluate the results. It found that 1000 families spent the following average amounts of time per week on particular activities:

4–5 hours on video games

3–4 hours on interactive participation in sporting events or game shows

1.5 hours on database services

The university found that people want expanded television service rather than new applications for computers. During this very long-running trial of interactive television service, customers paid a flat rate for the service. However, Le Groupe Videotron plans to go to transaction pricing as it enhances its offerings and equipment. It will deliver IBM set-top boxes to homes and install central equipment to process transactions.

The 1990s

Blacksburg Electronic Village   In 1993, Blacksburg, Virginia, and Bell Atlantic set up a trial to create the electronic town of the future, called Blacksburg Electronic Village. The town of Blacksburg has a population of 35,000, as well as 24,000 students at Virginia Tech. A preliminary feasibility study for the trial found that over half of the population had personal computers. The trial involved wiring the town with fiber-optic cable and installing ISDN in homes for a service charge of $8.60 per month. People who cannot afford this charge can use computers in the town library. Such library access is free, except for a nominal charge for printing. The library also provides free workshops on how to use the trial's services. The trial emphasizes text and the Internet. Users emphasize communications, both E-mail and forums, and facilitation of their daily lives. More than one-third of Blackburg's businesses and more than 13,000 of its 36,000 citizens have connections. This trial, well

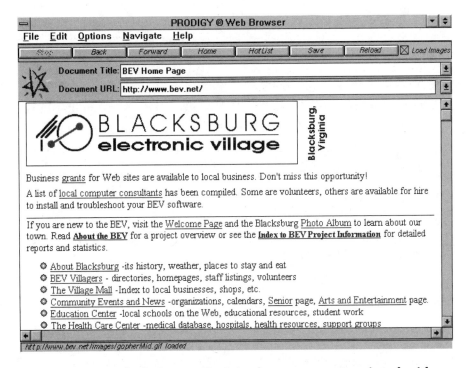

Figure 7.1   Blacksburg, Virginia, home page. Reprinted with permission.

under way, is very successful in showing how this kind of service could become a part of the very fabric of a small town (see Fig. 7.1).

Stargazer Trail in Atlanta   In the early 1990s, Bell Atlantic found the most popular viewing times are Saturday and Friday. This trial found that the key applications were movies, game shows, and children's programming.

Senatorial Suggestion   In 1991, Senators Conrad Burns, Robert Dole, and Al Gore suggested a national goal of deploying a broadband network by 2015.

Time Warner   The Quantum Cable Service trial in Queens, New York, in 1991, involved installing fiber trunks to the neighborhood of a few hundred homes, to which it provided 150 analog television channels. The system used an AT&T fiber-to-the-feeder architecture.

US WEST   In 1993, U S WEST became the first American telecommunications company to announce an alliance with Time Warner Entertainment to deliver interactive broadband services outside its territory in Florida.

AT&T   In 1993, AT&T completed an eight-month trial in homes of 50 volunteer AT&T employees. The homes were in the Chicago area and the server was in New York City. Focus group meetings produced the following findings.

- Services must be very simple to operate.

- To sell, services must be presented as advanced television, partly because users stayed far away from the set.

- Services must not be presented as fancy personal computer applications.

- Users spent more time on games rather than on obtaining information.

- Most people watched entertainment programs and used transactions, communications, and information.

- People established communities based on common interests rather than on common physical locations.

- No one reads instructions.

- The service needed constant updates to remain lively.

TCI   TCI found in trials in Littleton, Colorado, in 1993, that consumers appreciated near video on demand as much as video on demand.

British Telecom   In 1994, Ipswich, England, completed a video-on-demand trial in homes of 60 British Telecom employees. The trial used Oracle software and ran ADSL over copper wires. The employees were positive about the extremely friendly service. They reported that video on demand was far easier to use than operating a VCR or renting a videotape.

Southern New England Telephone Corporation   In 1994, Southern New England Telephone Corporation (SNET), in West Hartford, Connecticut, used VCRs and the existing cable infrastructure with 54 video-on-demand lines to test the preferences of 400 customers. Results showed that customers tended to stay with initial choices but that having a wide variety of choices was extremely important. SNET offered 1800 movies and videos on demand. Once a movie began, it could be paused, but not rewound or fast forwarded. The trial found that customers would pay $20 per month for basic service plus between $1 and $4 for each movie. SNET also found that customers preferred video on demand when offered both NVOD and VOD. They also found that subscribers selected older movies, travelogues, and how-to videos more than new releases. SNET has received FCC permission to expand video dial tone. They have selected Sybase, HP, and AT&T Network to help.

Time Warner   The Time Warner trial in Orlando, slated to begin early in 1994 and postponed until the end of the year, started with a small number of users. This is a very extensive trial of two-way switched-digital interactive television called the Full Service Network (FSN).

Bell Atlantic   Bell Atlantic sent a single compressed digital signal over fiber-optic cable to its central office, to a couple of close-by switches, and finally to a home television set in May 1995. This was a major milestone in its Dover Township, New Jersey, trial. Another milestone occurred one month later when Bell Atlantic assigned 304 channel numbers on Bell Atlantic's 384-channel video dial-tone (VDT) service. Bell Atlantic also received approval to offer an enhanced gateway service for other video information providers (VIPs) that includes interactive menus, search facilities, program guides, and navigation aids. In August, Bell Atlantic announced a slip in this trial because of complexities involving system administration and operations support software. Also in May 1995, Bell Atlantic accepted paying customers to its video-on-demand, 700-program, 42,000 minutes of choice, service designed for commercial deployment in Fairfax County, Virginia. Bell Atlantic officially began this Dover Township trial in late January 1996 with the first wave of 200 customers.

DIFFERENCES

Significant barriers stand between the state of the art—namely, that trials are expensive, risky, and prone to delays—and the vision—namely, that trials will answer enough questions to justify confident deployment. Some of the reasons follow.

Trials as Highly Complex Ventures   Distributed multimedia trials are more complex than testing a package design to see if shoppers will like the appearance or testing a movie to see whether audiences will like the title and the ending. The trials are more than trials of television entertainment, interactive television, pay-per-view video, or E-mail. Distributed multimedia trials involve all of these, more than these, and all combinations of these.

Distributed multimedia systems are difficult and expensive to install. They have large start-up costs that can include digitizing a critical mass of video and laying the last mile of fiber-optic cables.

Delivering distributed multimedia to large consumer markets requires responding to frequent problems. This is logistically demanding and costly.

Bandwidth is far from free in servers, delivery systems, and end-user devices. Economy demands that providers establish the smallest bandwidths that yield acceptable video quality in applications that range from high-resolution X-rays and fast-moving sports events to economy-driven industrial training.

Customers view a trial's service in terms of the end-user interface paradigm that the service presents. Both television people and computer people have difficulty providing end-user interfaces that are friendly without being dull. The line between excessive novelty and insufficient novelty is thin, unmarked, and variable. The Time Warner trial in Orlando attacks this problem with expensive end-user devices and two end-user interfaces, including a very sophisticated three-dimensional graphics interface called Carousel, which may or may not turn out to be worth what it costs.

Timing is everything. A trial that uses expensive set-top boxes' rotating three-dimensional objects answers questions about a different time frame from a trial that uses existing cable converter set-top boxes and voice telephone calls.

Consumer Involvement   Distributed multimedia trials involve many consumers. They are unlike other large-scale complex endeavors such as the NASA space program, which are very complex technically and logistically and which involve many suppliers but no consumers. Only a few experts need to be able to operate NASA's equipment. Any given paradigm or icon may affect different cultural groups in diametrically opposite ways. People's reactions may be sufficiently strong to outweigh the rest of the trial. It is necessary to overcome apathy, lack of trust, and worse, left over from bad experiences with Videotex in the United States. Customers may find a trial's version of interactive television insufficiently captivating after the novelty wears off. Highly interactive video may indeed have no appeal for couch potatoes who are strongly attached to their habits of partial listening and passive watching. Couch potatoes may be the rule, rather than the exception. Customers are suspicious about losing privacy and security and having too much accessible information in marketers' databases. Appearances may matter more to consumers than do technical explanations. Computer users felt that Prodigy was spying on them, when they found parts of their own documents in a file that Prodigy set up. This was even after Prodigy explained that the file was a cache and that the programs only gradually wrote over old data. Many trials suffer from being hard to explain. It is difficult for a company to tell customers what a trial's goals are and when the goals have been achieved. Major goals center around developing and improving operational aspects of delivery that should not concern customers. These goals can tend to be dull to report in the newspapers as well. A company may also have trouble explaining that a delay is natural and not a disaster.

TRENDS

The most significant trend is for major companies to combine forces and conduct highly publicized trials. Trials that involve Time Warner, Bell Atlantic, TCI, U S WEST, Microsoft, Oracle, AT&T, and Silicon Graphics seem to be particularly visible. Trials that involve other RBOCs, Cox Cable, Hewlett-Packard, and IBM, are important as well. Important trials are taking place in Europe and some in Asia. In fact, some people think that Europe is now ahead of the United States. Another trend, unfortunately highly publicized, is the to-be-expected scaling down of some trials and some expectations, particularly those involving expectations of miracle results or rapid deployment.

A less visible trend involves quiet progress. For example, Cablevision has been slowly upgrading their equipment and quietly testing upgraded services on a small scale. Cablevision says that, although it cannot afford a flamboyant trial, it can use an incremental add-on strategy to benefit itself and its customers. It relies on careful planning, using only one system integrator, AT&T, and using AT&T's and Silicon Graphics' joint venture, Interactive Digital Solutions.

Another less visible trend is that of trials involving tests of video conferencing, video digital libraries, and video training, inside businesses, particularly large corporations. Large corporations may even be willing to pay a premium for distributed multimedia applications and could end up being a major source of early revenue for providers.

Whether trials are large and flamboyant or small and little publicized, they involve a great deal of work and many decisions. Some examples follow. We strongly suggest that you track the progress of these trials, as their rightful place in this chapter moves from Trends to History.

Time Warner

Time Warner is the nation's second largest cable company. It serves 7.3 million customers in 34 states. The company's goal is to provide customers a fully interactive two-way digital multimedia service, or full-service network (FSN), starting with 4000 customers in a northern suburb of Orlando. Its service will offer homes and businesses a wide choice of information, entertainment, education, and communications. Northern Orlando is a high-growth market that contains many families interested in educating their children. It already represented a large Time Warner market of 0.5 million people. Time Warner wants to

- Track participants' usage patterns, to which participants must agree to submit.

- Test and tune different configurations, to verify they are stable, reliable, and desirable; for example, check that many users can access many services simultaneously from a switched network controlled by a cluster of Silicon Graphics servers.

- Put its high-speed delivery system into use by a couple of thousand demanding people rather than a few hundred sympathetic ones.

- Project how much revenue and cash flow will result from different charging algorithms.

- Provide an operational platform on which providers can develop additional offerings.

The trial's technical phase began on October 5, 1994, in two homes where company employees tested using the network's navigational software to retrieve digitized games and movies from a file server. By the end of 1994, after several postponements, the system was up and running in a few homes. Figure 7.2 shows the building where Time Warner has its office for coordinating some of the trial activities. An adjacent building houses the servers, switches, and related equipment. Time Warner found that its system, especially its software, requires extensive tuning. To investigate different options, it has prepared to deploy trial environments of 500 to 600 subscribers each. Time Warner says that it is designing its system to be somewhat flexible for accommodating different software and set-top boxes.

The trial's infrastructure involves several other major companies. Unique set-top boxes and remote controls come from Scientific-Atlanta, which is partnering with Silicon Graphics to provide the digital design and some of the hardware and software for the box. This set-top box contains a MIPS Technologies microprocessor that runs at 100 MHz. This set-top box provides a highly visual end-user interface. Silicon Graphics is providing the servers, hardware and software, which store many TeraBytes of data and use up to 36 similar MIPS processors in a distributed processing architecture. AT&T Network Systems is supplying an ATM switching system with a maximum throughput of 20 Gbps. Protocols and related standards include SONET, TCP/IP, and SNMP. Andersen Consulting is acting as system integrator.

**Figure 7.2   Time Warner's coordination office for the
Orlando FSN trial.**

Warner Brothers is encoding several hundred movies, compressed according
to MPEG-1 and eventually MPEG-2. Fiber runs from the head-end to each
neighborhood node. Existing coaxial cable runs from a neighborhood node
(see Fig. 7.3) to customers' homes.

A fact sheet provided by Time Warner Cable's Full Service Network, a division of Time Warner Entertainment Co., L.P., dated October 1994 describes
what happens when a user makes a request (reprinted with permission).

The movie request is first forwarded through the cable distribution system, through the demultiplexer to the ATM switch, and then to the media servers (Challenge XL series, we'll have 8 to 10 of these with an
Onyx administrator), which will access the movie requested from the
vaults which store the compressed, digital video on hard disks. The
servers will access the information, put the data into ATM packets (48
Bytes of data with a 5-Byte header or address for each packet), and send
the packets at OC3 bandwidth, 155 Mbps (3 to 6 Mbps per video
stream), to the ATM switch. The ATM switch automatically reads the
packets and routes them at DS3 rate of 45 Mbps. The video channels remain at DS3 rate of speed and are sent to the QAM modulator that puts

Figure 7.3   A neighborhood node in northern Orlando.

them into radio frequency signals. A few of the DS3s are control channel data for each individual node and are sent to the Hitachi mux,
which demultiplexes the DS3 signal to a DS1. Both the DS3 and DS1 signals are sent to a combiner that completes the spectrum by adding the
digital frequencies to the analog frequencies. They, then, are fed to the
laser and transmitted through fiber-optic cable to the neighborhood
node. There they are converted back to radio frequency signals that are
transmitted through coaxial cable to the user's home. The set-top box
retrieves the ATM data packets, reassembles them as a data stream, de-
compresses the video, and displays the movie. It takes less than one
second from the time a consumer makes a request to the time he/she
receives it.

TV Guide On Screen, from TV Guide, acts as an interactive on-screen guide
to services. Applications include entertainment, information, education,
communication, and video on demand. Applications also include home-
shopping services from Spiegel, Eddie Bauer, Warner Brothers Studio Stores,
the U.S. Postal Service, ShopperVision, and CUC International. Still others

will be added later. ABC News and NBC News will provide an interactive news-on-demand service called News Exchange. Viewers will be able to watch summary programs and background reports on selected subjects at selected times. Silicon Graphics and Atari Jaguar are going to provide games.

Current plans factor in prior analog trials' results in New York City, where Quantum System offers customers 150 analog channels.

Integrating the many complex pieces, coordinating the many suppliers, and making the complex system work are Time Warner's major challenges. Time Warner management denies a report that the initial cost of equipment for a customer's home is $7000, perhaps because they think that the price of a prototype is nobody else's business. Silicon Graphics and MIPS Technologies intend to reduce prices by integrating several graphics, ATM, and compression functions into a single chip in the set-top box. Time Warner is counting on such price cuts to become cost-effective for customers.

Time Warner has been experimenting in similar areas since the 1970s. Its partners include U S WEST, Toshiba Corporation, and ITOCHU Corporation. Time Warner intends to supply telephone service where and when regulations permit, including video telephone service and video conferences between classrooms and homes. It has permission to offer telephone service in Rochester, New York, but not in Orlando. In return for permitting access to its network, the local telephone provider, Rochester Telephone, will receive significant regulatory relief. Time Warner also has a trial, in Elmira, New York, testing setting up an on-line cable community for cable modem connected PCs described later in this chapter.

Microsoft and TCI

Tele-Communications, Inc. (TCI) and Microsoft Corporation have agreed to be equal partners in trials that develop cable networks. Servers are personal computer based. End-user devices are based on either personal computers or interactive television set-top boxes. These devices use Microsoft software. Initial trials in 200 employees' homes, and on the Microsoft campus in Redmond, Washington, are to test equipment, software, and the total system. The trials plan to use Microsoft interactive broadband network (IBN) software along with Microsoft's application guides and navigation aids in a fiber-to-the-node and ATM delivery environment.

Microsoft and TCI plan to expand the trials from company employees to 2000 TCI customers in the Seattle area. The goals of the trials are to investigate customer preferences and responses and to wring out Microsoft's software more thoroughly. An expanded trial will include more content, including movies from TCI, and additional services.

The trials use Microsoft's video-on-demand software, consisting of a distributed, microkernel-based operating system (Iceberg) and a continuous audio-video server (Tiger). Microsoft, General Instrument Corporation (GI), and Intel Corporation jointly developed Iceberg's previous version (Amazon) based on Microsoft's At Work kernel, but Microsoft developed Iceberg. Microsoft's video-on-demand software supports hybrid networks with fiber backbones and local coaxial connections. Part of the software runs on GI's set-top box.

Microsoft and TCI intend to extend a long trial process to involve other providers of set-top boxes and servers. Other providers include Hewlett-Packard Company and NEC for set-top boxes. Other providers of servers include Compaq Computer Corporation, Intel Corporation, and NEC.

TCI has several trials under way with other partners. One such trial includes AT&T and U S WEST for video-on-demand and enhanced pay-per-view services. Another trial in Denver to use IT Network's Interactive Channel was canceled. The significance of this trial was that its initial application was education.

Microsoft and SBC Communications

In a trial planned for Richardson, Texas, in 1996, Microsoft has Southwestern Bell Corporation (now SBC Communications) as its first RBOC partner. In addition to operating system software, Microsoft plans to provide SBC Communications with

- Video on demand

- A navigator that allows customers to move around the system easily

- An electronic guide to shows and other programming

- A network operator that will allow SBC Communications to communicate with customers on the network about billing and other matters

SBC Communications indicates that its video network will eventually serve 47,000 homes in the Richardson area. The plan is to test video services first with about 3500 customers beginning in the fourth quarter of 1995 and then roll out production commercial service in 1996 pending regulatory permission from the FCC. The goal is to provide movies on demand, home shopping, and enhanced telephone service. SBC views its goals as modest in comparison with those of some of the other RBOCs. Lockheed Martin is the systems integrator and is in charge of selecting equipment.

Microsoft and Others

Microsoft plans other trials of its end-to-end software solution with international partners including France Telecom, Alcatel, Andersen Consulting, Deutsche Telekom, Lockheed Martin, Nippon Telegraph and Telephone Corporation, Olivetti S.D.A., Rogers Cablesystems Ltd., SBC Communications, Telstra Corporation of Australia, and U S WEST Communications.

Microsoft has set up a collaborative program to provide prerelease information and software for others to conduct their own trials for early deployment and to evaluate options. Microsoft has involved systems integrators, network operators, set-top box providers, and server providers in trials of various combinations of Microsoft's software and others' hardware and delivery environments.

Neither bashful nor humble about this new arena, Microsoft spokespersons say they understand what they need to provide and they have a corresponding plan. However, this plan has undergone significant modification toward much stronger affinity to the Internet as a result of trial experience, customer reactions to their plans, and intense market pressure. Microsoft is investing heavily in distributed multimedia, appears to have a comprehensive plan of attack, and has lined up crucial participants. The firm is not as far along as a few of the others in trial deployment.

U S WEST

U S WEST has planned trials starting with 2500 homes in Omaha and continuing in Denver, Minneapolis, St. Paul, Portland (Oregon), and 10 to 15 other cities. It plans to scale up to more than 70,000 homes shortly after the first trials. The trials will use a hybrid fiber-optic and coaxial cable network and a Scientific-Atlanta set-top box containing a 3DO chip, with servers based on Digital's Alpha chip.

U S WEST's plan is to provide content including movies on demand, other pay-per-view programs, home shopping, interactive games, and access to information databases. U S WEST's subsidiary Interactive Video Enterprise is planning a service called U S Avenue. U S Avenue plans to provide one of the first interactive home-shopping services that customers can use to scan offerings at their own pace. U S WEST's subsidiary U S WEST Marketing Resources will provide GoTV. GoTV plans to provide movie listings, interviews with movie stars, and other movie-related information. U S WEST planned a navigational front end with music and snappy graphics.

In mid-1995, U S WEST asked the FCC to suspend consideration of its video dial-tone applications. It had submitted applications for Denver, Portland, Minneapolis, Salt Lake City, and Boise pending the conclusion of the Omaha trial. It stated that technological breakthroughs in broadband technology and deployment were taking place so fast that it made sense to modify their request.

One of this trial's goals is to check U S WEST's expectation that 15 percent of potential customers in Omaha will pay for the service. U S WEST bases its expectation on valuable early market research data that it got from smaller tests using VCRs and a tape library.

NYNEX

NYNEX has a multiphase trial plan. The first phase began in January 1994 with 25 customers in three apartment buildings in Manhattan. The trial provided analog service over an interactive hybrid fiber coax network. Content providers included Liberty, Advanced Research Technologies, and Urban Transport Corporation. Other partners include Zenith for set-top boxes and Digital for servers. The trial's purpose was to study usage patterns, subscriber demands, and ease-of-use features of a video-on-demand application.

NYNEX's second phase involves upgrading its network from analog to digital, adding capacity, supporting more content providers, and providing true video on demand. Customers will use a remote control to select movies and weather from menus on television screens.

NYNEX also plans trials of broadband networking services to carry multimedia to several thousand customers in New England, contingent on FCC approval. It believes it is moving deliberately and cautiously in its trial activity. It remains concerned about whether its business customers will actually commit dollars.

Bell Atlantic in Virginia

Bell Atlantic realizes that the complexity of its offerings and its uncertainty about customer demands mean that its sequence of trials and refinements may last through 2005. The firm's spokesperson predicts that it will deliver information, communications, and entertainment applications widely near the year 2000. They do not say which side of the year 2000. Bell Atlantic views its trials as production runs, rather than as mere tests of prototypes for only pioneers and early adopters. It does not expect to need to change its design in order to achieve significant cost reductions before it begins widespread commercial deployment. Bell Atlantic's trials are not limited to a single delivery method. In fact, Bell Atlantic is preparing to deliver content to a neighborhood in whichever of five methods is best for that neighborhood. Those methods are fiber to the curb or switched-digital video with fiber to a distribution point and with both coaxial cable and twisted pairs continuing to 20 to 30 homes, hybrid fiber coax with fiber going to a distribution point in the neighborhood of a few hundred homes and coax going the rest of the way to the homes, ADSL over twisted pairs where relatively few customers want video, wireless cable for suitable terrain, and direct broadcast satellites. In mid-1995, Bell Atlantic formally withdrew the plans for hybrid fiber coax that it had submitted to the FCC. This seemed to indicate that the switched-digital video method, which it planned for Dover Township, would be its preferred delivery method for the future.

Bell Atlantic points out that its technology trials have already verified MPEG encoding and decoding, video file server hardware and software, ADSL transportation of acceptable quality video over copper twisted-pair wires, and new video-switching techniques. Several of Bell Atlantic's early technology trials involved only small samples. They have moved methodically from an environment of employees, who are friendly testers, with a choice of only 40 to 70 programs, to larger groups. Next they moved to real customers and to many more titles, some of which change every month.

Bell Atlantic is expanding its customer trial from 1000 homes to 20,000 homes. Their video-on-demand trial in northern Virginia uses a system suitable for deployment in a commercial environment. They use a $300 set-top box. They say that a more desirable virtual mall interface metaphor would not be feasible without a $5000 set-top box. Their user interface presents four icons with which users can select movies, shopping, children's programming, or documentaries. A fifth icon is Stargazer, a sun face that smiles as a user makes a selection.

Their northern Virginia trial tests not only video delivery over ADSL, but also business support, operations support, and crucial customer services. Bell Atlantic has permission to provide content, as a result of filing a court case in 1990 to change the Cable Act of 1984 and winning the case in 1994. This trial involves experiments with different techniques of interactive shopping and advertising in an attempt to find synergy. More critically, the trial addresses the question of how much customers are willing to pay for various video-on-demand offerings. Bell Atlantic is trying out at least 30 pricing options, ranging from a flat rate per month to a different price for each movie.

In Fairfax, Virginia, Bell Atlantic plans a major trial in which over 100 major media companies are providing a wide variety of content. In addition to testing the marketability of the mix of content, the trial will test a variety of pricing algorithms. The on-demand service comes from the Bell Atlantic Video Services Company.

Bell Atlantic in New Jersey

Bell Atlantic received FCC approval to set up the nation's first video dial-tone service (see Focus 7.1) in Dover Township, New Jersey, becoming the first RBOC to compete directly with cable television companies. It is wiring Dover with fiber-optic cable to the curb and running coaxial cables into 38,000 homes. Phillips Consumer Electronics of Knoxville, Tennessee, will build the set-top boxes and lease the boxes to programmers who will in turn lease the boxes to customers. Microware's DAVID is important to the set-top boxes. Oracle is its major server software provider. Bell Atlantic expected the system to be in full operation by 1996. However, it recently announced a slip blamed on software complexity involving administration and operations. Its plan called for starting with 200 houses in 1995 and then quickly adding 2000 more homes, but the start slipped to January 1996.

Bell Atlantic will begin its service with 384 channels. Although FCC regulations generally prohibited telephone companies from providing programming at the time, Bell Atlantic won a court decision that specifically allows Bell Atlantic to be a programmer.

FutureVision, part of Digital Broadband Applications Corporation, a startup programming company in which Bell Atlantic holds a 5 percent interest, has contracted for 61 of the trial's 384 channels. FutureVision plans to offer 40 traditional cable channels, 10 pay-per-view channels, 10 two-way communications channels including home computer access, and a bulletin board channel called NeighborNet. Customers will access NeighborNet ini-

---

FOCUS 7.1 What does video dial tone mean?

What does video dial tone (VDT) mean? Consider the obvious analogy to POTS. An audio dial tone means that a telephone company is ready to connect your telephone line to some other telephone line. Although the company may be willing to connect you to a live person, a recording, a fax machine, or a computer-synthesized voice within the company, you usually request a connection outside the telephone company. In fact, past regulations prohibited telephone companies from supplying entertainment programs, or supplying information that is unrelated to the telephone service, in order to prevent companies from favoring requests for their own programming over requests for outside suppliers' programming. Moreover, regulations prohibited telephone companies from discriminating among potential customers and thereby restricting the connections that you can request. A video dial tone is a telephone company's offer to deliver anybody's video, as a common carrier, just as a trucking company offers to deliver anybody's cartons. ∎

tially through home computers and eventually through set-top boxes. All channels will provide an optional message box in which customers can record their opinions or request more information.

Cablevision Systems Corporation says that it wants at least as many channels as FutureVision. It already serves 5000 subscribers in the township and wants a gateway to 38,000 subscribers. Although Bell Atlantic and Cablevision are potential competitors, FCC regulations require Bell Atlantic to consider Cablevision's request for channels. Other potential content providers are the Community Medical Center and the Asbury Park Press, which want to run educational shows and advertising on FutureVision's channels.

Initial customer response has been that pricing is critical. Video dial-tone service should be cheaper than current services. Bell Atlantic predicts that 35 percent of potential customers will subscribe. Its initial roll out is at the rate of 2000 homes per month. Bell Atlantic's goal is to have their enhanced network ready to serve 8.75 million homes in the Mid-Atlantic service region by the year 2000.

IBM et al.

IBM wants to participate actively in trials, playing a variety of roles below the content level. They want to contribute basic architectures and both software and hardware for storage systems, networks, communications switches, servers, set-top boxes, consumer graphical interfaces, and content creation tools. IBM wants to be a system integrator. They have announced participation in trials in Hong Kong, Canada, Japan, and the United States.

IBM and Hong Kong Telecommunications Limited have announced plans to start a video-on-demand trial with 50 homes. IBM will provide a video server based on collections of RISC System/6000 processors. The trial's goal is to answer questions about what customers will actually watch and how much they will be willing to pay. The answers may become the crown jewels of companies' proprietary information portfolios.

IBM and Rogers Cable propose to test two-way multimedia services in 20 office buildings in Toronto, Canada, using a 1-Gbps network. In another Canadian trial, IBM is working with a consortium that is comprehensively titled Universality Bidirectionality Interactivity (UBI). The consortium consists of Hearst Corporation, Le Groupe Videotron, and the National Bank of Canada. This trial will provide movies on demand, home shopping, home banking, and other services to 34,000 homes, rising to one million homes over a five-year period. IBM will provide set-top boxes based on its PowerPC chip and provide servers based on RISC System/6000 or, if necessary, on Power Parallel high-end computers. Le Groupe Videotron has been working in this area for several years, as we noted in the History section. Its Videotron system allows viewers to choose their own camera angles and call up player statistics while watching games.

IBM is participating in still another Canadian trial with a consortium that the CulTech Collaborative Research Centre manages. Other members of the consortium are Bell Ontario and Northern Telecom. They propose to construct a hybrid fiber-optic broadband network to provide service to a community in New Market, Ontario. The community will consist of 1500 new $200,000 automated homes. Each home will have an outside box containing devices that separate television, voice, and data signals and bridge appropriate signals to coax, twisted-pair copper, and local area network wires inside the home. The consortium will conduct a pretrial in a student dormitory at York University, Ontario, Canada. It will connect the university, schools, businesses, and government services to New Market's fiber ATM broadband network.

In Japan, IBM and the Ministry of Post and Telecommunications will provide video-on-demand educational videos to several elementary and middle schools in Okazaki City.

IBM is also participating in a trial in Omaha, Nebraska. Services will include movies, music, and games on demand; interactive shopping; and educational information retrieval. IBM is providing the video servers based on its RISC System/6000 workstations, 3172 controllers, and software that includes network management. ICTV is providing the system software for the head-end unit. Its technology works with analog as well as digital set-top boxes. IBM holds an equity interest in ICTV.

GTE

GTE is offering its Main Street service to customers in and around Cerritos, California, and Newton, Massachusetts. Main Street is a premium cable channel that costs $9.95 per month. It uses a special set-top unit that connects to a telephone line as well as to a coaxial cable. A customer's input travels over the telephone line to GTE's computers, which send information back to the customer's television set by way of the cable company's coaxial lines. Main Street includes informational, educational, financial, travel, shopping, and entertainment services.

Cable Modems

Personal computer users, unlike television users, know what they want. They want faster connections to on-line services. Current 9.6-Kbps modems prevent users from enjoying using Mosaic and Netscape's Navigator and comparable browsers to access the Web from their homes. Cable modems promise home users better speed for approximately $300 and promise corporate customers 1.544 Mbps for a significantly higher price. Digital Equipment Corporation, General Instrument Corporation, Hewlett-Packard Company, Intel Corporation, and Scientific-Atlanta have indicated they will provide cable modems. Zenith's Home Works modems offer speeds from 500 Kbps to 4 Mbps. Intel says it will offer modems to consumers that will support up to an amazing 27 Mbps downstream, in the long term. In the near term, consumer cable modems usually offer an upstream return path of only about 16 Kbps.

Several trials of attaching computers to cables by high-speed modems are in plan or under way. Some examples follow.

- Microsoft Corporation and TCI plan trials of delivering interactive services over cable television lines to personal computer users as part of the Microsoft Network. Some of these trials will intersect with the interactive television trial in Seattle to determine the dynamics between the two types of service.

- Continental Teleport Communications Group and CompuServe Information Service have trials under way in New England that use high-speed Zenith Home Works modems. However, CompuServe has not yet announced that it will provide faster service to match the modems.

- Prodigy has announced an interactive trial with Cox Enterprises in San Diego, California, that also uses the Zenith cable modems.

- Time Warner, parent company for Paragon Cable, and Time Inc., have a trial in Elmira, New York, that provides on-line PC connections via cable to Time Inc.'s Pathfinder National News Service, Internet, CompuServe, America Online, Southern Tier Online Community, and the *Elmira Star-Gazette* On-line. They announced that this was, as far as they knew, the first attempt in the nation to create an on-line cable community. Five hundred users were involved in the trial by July 1995. The basic service cost $14.95 per month and an Internet connection cost $9.96 more in addition to the cable's monthly fee, so this was not a get-started-free service. Time Warner chose Elmira because various providers in Elmira were interested and enthusiastic and because this is a self-contained small community. For more information see Focus 7.2, an interview with Charles W. Nutt, editor of the *Star-Gazette* of Elmira.

FOCUS 7.2   Interview with:

Charles W. Nutt

Editor of the *Star-Gazette* in Elmira, New York

Why Elmira?

Paragon Cable Company, which is owned by Time Warner, recently replaced its coaxial cable with high-capacity fiber-optic cable. This allowed Time Warner to choose Elmira for testing a new high-speed electronic information service.

Why did you decide to participate?

We see this as another opportunity to deliver information to our customers. Many newspapers are experimenting with similar approaches.

What do you think your offering will look like in three years?

I have no idea, nor do I think anyone could really know at this point. It may be very different from what we are starting with. Our initial offerings involve news summaries, photos, and/or graphics posted each night of what will be in tomorrow's newspaper. We have no

intention of replacing our printed newspaper. This service is complementary.

What are some up and coming milestones?

We continue to experiment with new types of information and presentation. In the future we hope to provide classified advertising as well as news.

Has getting started been more difficult than you anticipated?

It has been difficult, but no more so than the launch of other major projects.

How will you know you are successful?

Time Warner has set a limit of 500 cable connections for this experiment. We expect to know how many people are using the *Star-Gazette*'s local news portion of the service, and we will gather feedback from the users. ∎

Printed with permission.

NYU Distance Learning

New York University (NYU) is teaching 25 students, located remotely from the campus, by means of a trial of Video Notes, an extension of Notes from Lotus Development Corporation. Having used Notes extensively, NYU is beginning by offering students a course on information technology for an $8000 fee, which includes the student's ISDN installation. The 1995 trial uses animation annotation rather than full-motion video. It uses two Pentium-based servers running Novell Netware 3.12, a Notes server running OS/2, and a video server running software from Starlight Networks, Inc.

Sprint

Sprint is funding a test bed that consists of an ATM and SONET network. The goal is to help potential providers test their service offerings in a real-world, open environment, without the expense and delay of setting up their own trial from scratch. The network includes a 150-mile backbone ring between San Jose and San Francisco, California, operating at 2.5 Gbps, and secondary rings operating at 622 Mbps. The network has ATM switches from several companies. It has a waiting list of companies, including several California computer companies, that need to test products such as computers and software applications.

Additional Trials Outside the United States

Trials continue or are about to begin in Europe in England, France, Switzerland, Sweden, Italy, and Germany as well as in Asia in Japan, Hong Kong, Korea, and Singapore.

World Wide Web Page Trials

WWW pages are growing exponentially, fueled by companies that cannot take the chance of being left out. The goals of the trials range from the setting up of effective home pages despite bandwidth limitations (causing many users to disable downloading images first) to constructing WWW environments to experiment with different models of making money. Here are some possibilities. Home pages may merely describe a company and its products and suggest that potential customers contact the company. Other home pages provide a service such as job referral with the home page provider collecting money from satisfied employers. Some home pages display merchandise and offer purchase options. Some companies' trials charge a fee even for accessing the pages. Another trial strategy is to offer some information free and then to charge for more detailed or specific information. Individual's http://www.newspage.com has adopted this strategy. A variation of this strategy is to offer the service free for a short interval and then charge for it. Other trials experiment with whether it is better to use mostly text for swift user access or to present something on the edge of the state of the art that is fancy but oh so slow. It is too early to know which alternatives are acceptable to users and providers or whether new possibilities will emerge.

CRITICAL SUCCESS FACTORS

The following factors are critical for successfully achieving the vision for distributed multimedia trials.

Expectations: Providers will need to manage customers' and potential customers' and stockholders' expectations. They will also need to keep venture capitalists' interest during inevitable trial tribulations.

Alliances: Companies will need to make the alliances work with synergy to produce successful results that allow the alliances to move beyond the trial stage. This includes executing excellently the various tasks involved in these complex trials.

Problem Solving: Successful firms will solve inevitable problems in a way that makes progress. One such problem is billing—what sort of charging algorithms, how much to charge, when to bill, and how to bill— as part of the various trials' process.

Flexible Financial Models: Providers need to build into the system enough flexibility to modify it if the financial models do not work as anticipated. This flexibility should include making sure that cost reduction takes place, which may require some cooperation and some standardization between diverse groups, such as to avoid having every trial digitize the top 500 movies.

Direction: Firms will need to find suitable directions for pursuing what customers want to buy from the trials and from other sources, for which surveys have not sufficed. They will need to build into the system's offerings enough flexibility to modify them as customer desires become more clearly understood and more refined.

Financial Responsibility: Companies will need to be financially responsible but not lose sight of the objective of providing fast two-way interactive connections upstream and downstream.

Spin-offs: They will need to generate some profit-making product spin-offs during the trials even if these do not meet the ultimate vision for the trials.

Corporate Cultures: Providers will need to overcome strong wills and culture gaps among the diverse providers that are necessary for success.

Paperwork: Regulators will need to eliminate the burden of filing a mountain of paper for each step of a trial.

SUMMARY

We have become accustomed to connecting twisted-pair telephone local loops to our telephones and computer modems and connecting coaxial cables to our television sets. Now, we may connect television cables to our personal computers with high-speed cable modems and display live television signals on our high-resolution computer displays. We may connect telephone local loops to our television sets and use set-top boxes that have more processing power than most personal computers. If we can no longer tell our computers from our television sets, how do we know where to plug in our telephones? If you find these combinations slightly mind-boggling, pity a poor consumer trying to answer survey questions about what distributed multimedia will mean to him. Valid answers come from trials rather than from quick, cheap surveys. Early indications conclude that moving to distributed multimedia will not be easy or quick. The complexity of the very undertaking, from laying fiber optics to managing the logistics of all the pieces, is enormous. Essential learning is taking place, ranging from concluding that customers do not seem to want video on demand without other applications and services to surmising that the WWW might be a killer application if its fanciest pages appeared quickly.

REFERENCES

Bourdon, Michele (communications contact). 1994. Microsoft Facts, information packets on Microsoft's Interactive Broadband-Network Technology. Waggener Edstrom International Public Relations Council, Bellevue, Washington, (206) 637-9097.

Ditlea, Steve. 1995. "Interactive Illusion." *Upside*, March, pp. 56–68 (San Mateo, CA: Upside Publishing Company).

Lindsay, Tammy L. (communications contact). 1993/1994. Time Warner Fact Sheets and Vision Statements. May 1993; March and October 1994. Time Warner Cable, (407) 660-5502.

Plumb, Larry (communications contact). 1994. *Bell Atlantic News Releases*, Fall, (703)-708-4360.

Rockefeller, Rob. 1994. "Putting Video Dial Tone to the Test in Manhattan." *Telephony*, June 13, pp. 40–46.

To keep up to date on trials, we suggest that you read periodicals such as the ones listed in Chapter 8's references.

Chapter 8

Skills

BACKGROUND

The multimedia wave is about to break on your beach. Depending on where you are standing, and depending on what steps you decide to take next, the wave may lap around your toes unheeded, may give you a good ride on your surfboard, or may drub your hair in the sand. The purpose of this chapter is to help you decide when and how to learn to deal with the wave.

In Chapter 1, we attempted to describe distributed multimedia in enough detail for you to recognize the wave when you saw it. In Chapters 2, 3, and 4, we discussed the hardware and software part of the wave, that is, the servers, the end-user devices, and the intervening delivery system. In Chapter 5, we discussed applications that make the wave potentially useful, and in Chapter 6 we discussed where parts of the wave come from. Chapter 7 concentrated on the parts of the wave that are already visible in the form of trials. These chapters should help guide you in judging how big the wave will be along your stretch of the shore, that is, how important multimedia will be to your job or to your life. This chapter discusses what you might want to do in response to what you have learned about multimedia.

Distributed multimedia is neither good nor evil. It has the potential to create remunerative jobs, improve lifestyles, improve education, and enable businesses to generate improved profits and revenues. It may also eliminate jobs, further separate haves from have-nots, encourage governments to spend tax money that might better be spent elsewhere, provide yet another time waster for employees, further exacerbate the plethora of information with which we must all deal, and further the physical and intellectual deterioration of children that has so worried adults for millennia.

Assume that you are impressed by the vision for an information industry built around distributed multimedia and are interested in at least some available or proposed products and services. What should you do to acquire appropriate skills and in what time frame should you acquire them?

Are you a technologist who naturally tries the newest the earliest? Are you a visionary selling massive change to your company or seeing change that distributed multimedia could bring as a pleasant possibility in your personal life that you would rather try sooner than later? Are you a pragmatist interested in incremental improvements or skeptical that any of this is for you? Do you see yourself as a novice or advanced customer, as an entrepreneur or concerned financial officer, or as a student or teacher wondering how to prepare for the future? Do you see yourself as playing a key role in bringing distributed multimedia to fruition, or are you happy and content with the way things are?

Let's get more concrete. Suppose your supervisor asks you to prepare a proposal to accomplish any of the following tasks.

- Revise a strategy for delivering your local newspaper's community section over an on-line network based on results of a six-month trial.

- Convert the custom-made multimedia database describing the life and times of Albert Einstein, of which a demonstration at a conference impressed the supervisor, to a multimedia database describing the company's esteemed founder. He wants the database to be modifiable. It must accommodate some of the company's information assets and include on-line updates from several partners. Paying customers need to be able to access the database.

- Create a home page for your company on the Internet at a time when your company is not even connected to the Internet. Your supervisor says that he wants a home page that is not slow, not dull, and not static.

- Specify a master architecture to hold your company's digitized assets so that they can be easily reused and repurposed into many applications on a variety of platforms.

- Create a home page for a local opera company whose management wants its page to have snippets of video and audio of the company's opera performances.

- Decide on the number of modems and phone lines required over the next two years to support your company's new on-line shopping service multimedia server.

- Develop a training program for retailers who will sell a new on-line service.

Where do you start identifying what you need to know and then how do you go about learning it? Suppose your professor asks you to prepare a multimedia presentation for the class on Bell Atlantic's trials, their technical and business purpose, and their current status in Virginia and New Jersey. He suggests using the Internet's resources as well as any other relevant resources as references. You have never used the Internet other than to send E-mail to your friends. Where do you start?

Suppose you want a career that involves you actively in this arena. How do you prepare? You are a computer science major. What and how many courses in other departments should you take? How about some in the business school or in fine arts? You haven't drawn a picture since fourth grade. Suppose you are a business major. Dare you take a course in computer science, and if so, which one?

Suppose that your local community has finally received a grant to fund multipoint video conferences among a local university, industry, and school. Your community needs qualified volunteers to serve as on-line subject experts and mentors for the school's students. Several people from the university, industry, and school district wonder if they have the skills or could get the skills. The grant funds provide equipment for the on-line subject experts' homes and even money for an ISDN connection. However, they admit they cannot provide much help in getting the equipment installed. Are you qualified? If not, how can you become qualified?

First, you should assess your skills. Next you must figure out a little about the beach that you are on and the size of the waves. You want to understand how your skills fit into your home and working environment. Where is your employer on this beach? We discuss some ways of thinking about you and your beach in the State of the Art section. In the History section, we look at basic literacy as a guide to the challenge of acquiring learning skills. Many visionaries say that digital media will be as significant as the printing press so it is somewhat appropriate to look at how long it took us to fully appreciate the words that the printing press brought us. In the Trends section, we discuss tactics for gradually incorporating multimedia technologies and applications into the lifestyle of an individual or into the individual's set of skills that can be brought to bear in working in business or in government. We discuss general and specific steps that people are starting to take as consumers and as providers in this industry. Finally, we discuss critical success factors that will turn out to be useful no matter what twists, turns, and rest stops distributed multimedia takes as it wends its way toward the vision.

Commercial providers must provide tools and total solutions that are very easy, effective, and fun for users to learn to use well. Users include a broad portion of the population. We believe strongly that most individuals will become providers of content of some sort (Gilder, 1995).

Those who learn new skills or increase their skills, even as consumers, will benefit more than those who do not. Consider a trivial example and one that is not so trivial. Knowing how to select icons with a mouse is not a born skill. It must be learned. Knowing how to call a Help number, being able to ask the right questions of a Help desk and then applying the recommendations, also, are not born skills. They must be learned. Those who know these skills are far ahead of those who do not know them. As a more advanced example, our graduate students studying broadband networking do better on their research papers and create them more efficiently if they have skills in using the Internet and most importantly if they can put information obtained from the Internet in proper perspective with that from more traditional sources. Those who can use multimedia tools to create multimedia research papers that document their understanding of basic concepts seem to perform better on traditional tests (Agnew et al., 1996). Table 8.1 is only a start at some basic competencies.

Table 8.1   Some new basic skills for using distributed multimedia.

- Know how to figure out navigational schemes of new products, on interactive television or personal computer, by having a good mental picture of navigation and experience in how several on-line multimedia databases offer navigation. Especially useful for all students is being able to apply these abilities to information sources such as encyclopedias and digital libraries. Products can range from a database of television reruns of the *Waltons* or research on what questions to ask in precedent-setting murder trials.

- Know the kinds of things you can be expected to be able to search for and the ways you can qualify searches.

- Know what you can do with the results of your searches and what these results mean.

- Know how or whether a product allows you to browse through video clips or audio clips, copy them, or add your own.

- Know what a home page is and what you do with it.

- Know who to call when a digital camera does not work with your new multimedia home computer.

- Know how to make certain you can download maintenance releases or other necessities.

- Know how to create multimedia documents on your desktop computer.

VISION FOR THE NEXT DECADE

Figure 8.1 presents some individuals' dreams of the promise of distributed multimedia.

The vision is to make dreams like those in Fig. 8.1 come true. The individual, no matter what role he or she is playing, has some responsibility in making this vision happen.

STATE OF THE ART

Individuals, companies, and governments are deciding what steps to take next in acquiring skills. An approach for people in their various roles is to conduct a self-audit on the present state of their skills, hardware, and software. You might find Tables 8.2 and 8.3 helpful in your assessment.

Recent newspaper help-wanted advertisements listed the skills shown in Table 8.2. You might like to see how many of these skills you can claim as your own. You might expand the self-audit of Table 8.3 to use it to determine how your company stands as a user or as a provider. If your company is a technology provider you might locate where it stands in Table 8.4 as well.

If your company is not currently a provider, you might become educated on possibilities that are relevant to you or your company. One approach is to attend a conference specific to your industry and listen to what others are doing or planning to do. In addition, you should find out from early providers what has worked and what has not. Finally you should develop a plan to become involved. A plan can include a wait-and-see step. However, part of this step should be an articulation of what to wait for and what to look for, and what to do next when it happens. Part of taking this approach is a rationalization that you will not miss a window of opportunity. For example, here is one person's rationalization: "I will wait until there is a local telephone access number for me to obtain high-speed 28.8-Kbps access to the World Wide Web from my home. When that happens, I will plan to attend the local university's seminar called Constructing a Home Page for Your Business. The time frame for this is the next six to eight months." This person might prepare to use the information in Focus 8.1.

Some elements of your plan could include the following tasks.

- Determine whether your company has problems for which distributed multimedia applications could and should be part of affordable, effective solutions. If so, what more do you need to learn to see if these solu-

Figure 8.1   Dreams?

Table 8.2 Wanted.

Checkmark the skills you possess.

Developing multimedia: all media, interactivity, and interfaces

Finding and organizing multimedia information in nonlinear ways on specific subjects

Writing and scripting for an interactive, hypermedia, distributed environment

Applying cognitive and pedagogical techniques to creating multimedia applications

Handling film, photographic, music, animation, and video preproduction, and postproduction

Knowing when to use what media for content and knowing when to use what storage device

Designing and developing distributed multimedia databases including program guides, navigation, and filters to use with the databases

Designing and developing networked multimedia applications and operating systems enhancements to support such applications using object-oriented design techniques

Knowing about network management protocols, data communications, and ATM/SONET

Installing and maintaining LANs and WANs

Planning for and implementing end-to-end usability

Planning distributed multimedia network operations

Repurposing or upgrading existing networks to support distributed multimedia

Providing for quality of service (QOS) offerings where a customer selects and pays for a specific QOS

Planning and implementing customer billing systems and other backroom services for distributed multimedia

Managing and participating in the construction of a distributed multimedia system from the ground up, from trial through commercial production

Planning multimedia distribution over hybrid broadband networks

Creating and using multiple client and server platforms for distributed multimedia

Creating and using Web servers and browsers

Performing business planning and developing marketing strategies for specific industries

Combining television experience with computer experience

Combining video game experience with computer and television experience

Combining cable television and computer experience

Planning and developing different amounts of interactivity and being able to measure effectiveness

Creating compelling and entertaining content for different markets

Combining telephone technology experience with computer and broadcast experience

Participating in new product development

Succeeding in start-ups involving "never been done before" products and services

Discussing, debating, and bringing to conclusion issues involving universal access, privacy, and copyright

Planning and participating in new product introductions

Planning and performing market research into new products; drawing conclusions especially regarding appropriate time frames

Successfully working with multiskilled teams that include creative artists, producers, writers, computer scientists, and cognitive psychologists

Table 8.3 Multimedia self-audit.

Checkmark as many items as apply to you.

My current knowledge about distributed multimedia:
I know nothing about it.   I know what it is and some of what it means.   I know a lot about it.

My feeling about new products and services:
I am an early adopter.   Keep them away from me.   I am interested in learning more.

My current equipment suitable for multimedia:
I have some literature.
I have some early equipment and software, know what to get next, and what price to pay.
I have some skills in using equipment and software and am building on these skills.
I have expert skills in using equipment and software.
I intend to add equipment and software soon.

My current status as a provider of multimedia:
I am actively working and assessing my progress.
I am actively improving my lifestyle as a result.
I am using my involvement to make money.
I am making measurable progress.
I have a plan for moving into interactive two-way broadband networking.
I feel I am at the state of the art.   I feel I am behind the state of the art.
I am actively participating as either a student or provider of education.

(cont.)

tions should be ones that your company pursues and perhaps even provides others? See Focus 8.2. You should find out whether your company has viable delivery systems for what you might propose to do with multimedia content.

- Determine whether within the company's core business, the company has any solutions that would be more attractive and have more added value if they were augmented with interactive multimedia. What do you have to learn to take the next step after this identification?

- See if there is any low-hanging fruit that, with only a little work and investment, you could pick and be successful quickly.

- Become part of a trial and be an astute observer to learn what might be valuable to you or your company in expanded contexts.

- Set up a small pilot test.

- Learn from past efforts in moving into products and services involving complex new ideas and technologies.

Table 8.3 Multimedia self-audit. (*cont.*)

I am waiting for the following to occur before I become involved:

When that does occur, I plan to do the following:

I am working to expand my business into the consumer market.
I am working to expand my business to use on-line services.
I am waiting for a government to do the following:

I am planning to participate in the following trials:

I have experienced a delay in a planned trial.
I have prepared some concept demonstrations.
I have seen some concept demonstrations.
I go to conferences and workshops.   I attend local workshops and seminars.
I am aware of where I could go to get additional information or training.
I have established an alliance or partnership to expand skills.
I am part of a new start-up that will provide parts or all of a distributed multimedia
    system.
I have expanded my use of on-line information services as part of my business.
I have expanded my use of on-line information services as part of my home life.
I have expanded my attention to networking options with growth toward the digital
    world.
I am part of a large statewide effort.
I am part of grants for preparatory work.
I see expanded interest in multimedia and plan to respond in the following way:

I am as aware as I want and need to be on early results of trials including those
    involving electronic commerce.
I am knowledgeable as I want to be about various sides of debates on universal access,
    ownership of electronic media, security, and privacy.

FOCUS 8.1 Getting on board the Web.

World Wide Web access, with a local fast phone number, is becoming readily available even in small communities. Some services even provide some form of help on constructing the optimal home pages for your business or personal life. Once you have created it, you can put up your home page on your local Internet service provider's server for some monthly fee or put the page on another remotely connected server. Optionally you might want to have your own World Wide Web server rather than putting up home pages on some service provider's server. Many books, consultants, seminars, and companies promise various forms of help that can have you up and running quickly. ■

Table 8.4 Stages of deployment for a provider.

1. Making predictions in visionary talks
2. Initiating research and development in corporate and university laboratories
3. Participating in discussions in research journals, trade conferences, or forums; developing laboratory prototypes; reporting interesting experimental results
4. Demonstrating prototypes to the public
5. Finding some technically oriented pioneers for early testing
6. Beginning with public testing trials using company employees and pioneers
7. Expanding from public trials to serving early visionaries
8. Starting early production and distribution of product spin-offs from trials
9. Deciding that efforts look promising for production, with moves into a mass market segment and licensing other providers to expand distribution
10. Deciding that efforts are suitable for use by professionals
11. Deciding that efforts are suitable for use by experienced end users in some niche areas
12. Deciding that efforts are suitable for use by typical consumers
13. Deciding that efforts are suitable for early introduction into specific market niches
14. Providing a widely accepted consumer product with several million sold
15. Providing a ubiquitous product or service with many millions sold

After figuring out where you stand and where your company stands or could stand, and starting to draft your plan, the next step is to figure out a little about your beach (where the new wave of distributed multimedia is likely to break). One way is by looking at surveys. In most cases, you will not be lucky enough to find a specific survey of your geographical area of interest. These surveys may be useful, however, for you to get some ideas about what

---

FOCUS 8.2 A problem identified and solved.
One company's problem consisted of having to continually educate new hires about the company's mission, technologies, and services. Their mission happened to be offering Web consulting and home-page implementation services for hire. After some analysis, they realized that they could package much of this education as just-in-time multimedia training and make it available not only for their employees internally but also for sale to others. ∎

others are thinking and doing and about how fast you can expect progress. As we have stated, there have been many numbers generated as parts of many surveys and there will be many more. We only include these as illustrative examples. We encourage you to find current surveys that might specifically interest you in learning about environments relevant to you. Eventually you may have to commission surveys to support your own marketing efforts.

Surveys

America's Research Group reported the following in the *Rocky Mountain News* on November 8, 1994. In a survey of 2000 consumers, a little over half had never heard the term *information highway*. After having the phrase explained, the same half did not think it was very important to them. Over half of the respondents felt they would never need a computer in their homes. An earlier Harris Poll got similar results.

In June 1994, *Broadcasting & Cable Magazine* reported on a survey of people in 1000 cable households. Of these people, 38 percent said that they had heard of interactive television. However, 40 percent indicated that they were aware of interactive games, on-line information services, interactive shopping, video on demand, and high-definition television. The survey found that 90 percent of television owners have remote controls and that many viewers channel surf, which is a primitive form of interactivity. That is, typical television viewers watch only parts of programs rather than entire programs. The average number of channels an average household watches for a significant interval, rather than just scans past, is 9 per week or 14 per month. It is unclear how these numbers would vary, depending on whether viewers could select from 8, 32, 102, or 500 different channels.

SIMBA Information reports that 17 million multimedia-capable personal computers with CD-ROM drives were in use by the end of 1995, up from 7 million in 1994.

Software Publishers Association reports that about 90 percent of the sales of CD-ROM titles in 1994 came from home products such as games, encyclopedias, dictionaries, and educational CD-ROMs.

Odyssey Homefront reports that 27 percent of homes have personal computers, although many home computers are old. Only 6 percent of working personal computers in homes have CD-ROM drives and 82 percent of personal computer owners who do not have such a drive say that they do not plan to buy one. The average owner of a home personal computer who does have a CD-ROM drive bought fewer than three titles in the summer of 1994. However, DataQuest found that half of these people plan to buy more titles, primarily games and references. Home users report that they want to use CD-ROMs primarily for educational purposes.

AST Research, in 1994, indicated that the typical owner of a home personal computer was a 42-year-old married man with children. The children used the computer an average of 8 hours per week. The owner used the computer an average of 13 hours per week.

Table 8.5 shows survey results from Computer Intelligence InfoCorp, located in La Jolla, California. More information is available on the company's World Wide Web home page (http://www.compint.com). The table was adapted from information released on Prodigy 08/23/95 15:56.

Investigations

We, the authors, live in a rural upstate New York community. This community has been included in no major detailed surveys as far as we know. We therefore assigned to our graduate students some investigations of local providers. It is not unreasonable for you, in your efforts to understand your environment, to call your local providers as well. In the fall semester of 1994, we asked our students to investigate steps that local businesses were taking, or planned to take in the next year, toward providing distributed multimedia

Table 8.5 On-line personal computer users.

Activity	People in the workplace using computers	Consumers using computers
% on-line use	33⅓%	33⅓%
Communicate	65% to larger computers or LANs	32% to larger computers or LANs Most to other users or to gateways to the Internet
Chat facilities	Less than 10%	33⅓%
Major activities	E-mail Browsing Downloading	E-mail Browsing
Internet usage	12%	10%
Major Internet application	E-mail	E-mail

applications. We suggested that the students contact some local television, telephone, cable, health services, and other industries.

Our students found that such companies were well aware of the information highway and were taking steps, however small, slow, and deliberate, to become knowledgeable and involved in multimedia. These companies realized the importance of a smooth transition to such a new technology that includes unresolved technical and regulatory issues and significant startup costs. The students' results follow.

WSKG   WSKG, the local Public Broadcasting station, offers use of its video conference room for $230 per hour. It also offers its video and production studio to local businesses.

NYNEX   NYNEX, the regional Bell operating company for this region, has found that, despite significant enthusiasm, business customers have not yet committed capital up front for multimedia applications. NYNEX sees one of its key technical problems as training personnel in digital installation and maintenance. It has been replacing copper with fiber-optic cable for the last decade. What is new to NYNEX is using hybrid local loops with fiber to a node in each neighborhood and with coaxial cable the rest of the way into homes and businesses. Federal regulations remain a major hurdle.

NYNEX plans to introduce *Interactive Yellow Pages* through Prodigy during 1995. It has elected a slow roll-out to have time to resolve the bugs and avoid potential bad initial reactions. Going on-line will allow NYNEX to provide business listings for all northeast states and will allow listed businesses to update their listings frequently with specials and new products and services.

Outside our neighborhood, in New York City, NYNEX is working on small trials of video on demand and video dial tone. Expanding these trials to our area will depend on having indications that customers here want what they can deliver and on their overcoming regulatory, technical, and financial hurdles. The highest hurdle is financial.

NYNEX provides ISDN services in some areas. It may make ISDN available in Binghamton.

NewChannels Corporation   NewChannels Corporation, a division of Newhouse Broadcasting Corporation, provides cable service to 60,000 subscribers in our area. It is in the process of laying fiber-optic cables to neighborhoods. It runs cable from the head-end or head node to boxes called *optical mainstream and return transmitters* (OMRTs). The signals on both parts of the network are analog.

NewChannels now provides interactivity by means of a special button on a user's remote control, which the user can press to order a pay-per-view event automatically over a telephone line. It is in the process of discontinuing this procedure, in favor of having people place a voice telephone call to place an order.

NewChannels is thinking about offering telephone service in our area. Details, such as how to charge for use, are still under discussion. NewChannels has a video conference service that runs to area schools. It rents fiber to each of several schools and also helps schools set up what they want. It offers a digital Primestar Satellite System consisting of a 36-inch satellite dish that feeds an MPEG-2 decoder in a set-top box.

NewChannels uses satellites, microwave, and videotape to bring cable programs to its head-end units. When the system goes digital, NewChannels does not plan to store any digital information.

United Health Services   United Health Services, a group of several hospitals in our area, has a strategic information plan for the year 2000. Its plan involves three forms of video conferences.

1. Telemed, to connect local patients with specialists in Syracuse for diagnostics

2. Distance-learning programs, to include several nearby educational organizations

3. Individual video conference systems, to be implemented incrementally

United Health Services expects the initial investment to be $10 million, with a $2.5 million annual expense. Work is underway on each of these forms.

Broome Community College   Broome Community College (part of the State University of New York) offers continuing education courses for the general public in elementary on-line information access and in how to buy a multimedia computer. These courses are overbooked.

Binghamton University   Binghamton University (another part of the State University of New York) offers graduate-level research and hands-on courses in distributed multimedia in its computer science department. Its Cinema and Theater departments offer courses in electronic art making and MIDI for theater.

Spectra.Net   Spectra.Net, a local service provider, supports incoming connections from 300 bps to 28,800 bps with no charges based on connection speed. PPP and SLIP accounts cost $19.95/month, with a $39.95 one-time connection charge. The company provides PPP and SLIP software to make a home computer into an Internet site. One million Bytes of disk space is free of charge and additional storage is available. The firm's primary revenue-generating activities are advertising for businesses in its virtual mall and its electronic classified pages. It offers a local access number but only in a rather small area surrounding Binghamton.

Newspaper Analyses

We also asked our students to check out help-wanted ads in a specific Sunday newspaper. Here and in Focus 8.3 are what they found. We changed the names of the respective parties somewhat. Common threads include the requirements for working well across different skills while having in-depth knowledge of one skill, being creative, being adept at developing new strategies, and being capable of resolving challenges.

Interactive Communication Design Professorship
Owego University is seeking an Assistant Professor in Interactive Communications, full time, tenure track. Salary and benefits commensurate with experience. MFA required. Teaching experience at college or university level preferred. Teach Interactive Multimedia, 3-D Computer Animation, Virtual Reality, Digital Audio. Include letter of application with teaching philosophy, CV, transcript, 20 slides of personal and 20 slides of student work, 3 letters of reference, and videotape, if appropriate.

Software Developers
A major on-line service provider seeks employee with experience in the C and C++ programming languages as well as UNIX and Windows NT. Require experience in user interface development, WAN communications software, and relevant environments. Must be able to work well in multidisciplinary groups.

Wanted: Interactive Television Producer
Department: Digital Production Studio. Summary: The Interactive Television Producer will produce interactive television applications for this full-service provider. Qualifications: Excellent communication skills, interacting with all levels of staff and clients. Responsibilities:

- Manage the entire production process of developing interactive television applications.

- Lead production teams to meet design requirements and supply deliverables, while meeting deadlines and budget requirements.

FOCUS 8.3 Some "help wanted" excerpts.

Help us redefine the way content is created and distributed in the information age. We need designers and system administrators familiar with publishing, electronic tools, and *creating virtual communities*.

We are staffing up to add an on-line newspaper to our already successful hardcopy edition. We need people who can set up information organizations, *establish connections* between information sets, and facilitate community participation in on-line conferences.

We need a manager of interactive marketing to help define appropriate strategies for interactive creation and participation. This person will also serve as *liaison* between marketing, computing, creative, and production resources to assure the successful outcome of the project. This person needs experience with CD-ROM, on-line services, design, production, and distribution and must have experience in consumer, direct, and advertising marketing. Experience in on-line transactions is highly desired.

Your background must include multimedia authoring with scripting, 2-D and 3-D graphics, C, C++, UNIX, and Windows.

We are looking for *explorers*, pilots, and crew on the trip through cyberspace. Knowledge of multimedia tools and programming languages helpful.

We are looking for negotiators who are familiar with working with alliances and in handling *regulatory logistics*.

Must have *excellent communications skills* and 7 years' experience in design and production of creative content.

You will be responsible for managing the integration of multimedia applications with the Internet and on-line services. *An MBA is helpful.*

You must be familiar with the Internet/HTML *design issues, especially as they relate to scalable delivery platforms and performance.*

Technical leader in an interactive television strategy and architecture group. Knowledge of cable networks and telephone networks. Be able to structure *total customer solutions.*

You must be a telecommunications and *information specialist.*

You will *liaison with our video server group* and address a variety of challenges in developing content. You need 10 years' project management experience of complex projects and multidisciplinary projects. ∎

- Provide and manage production schedules and budgets for each application.

- Work closely with clients to manage and meet their expectations.

Join a Hot New Interactive Cable Television Network

At the new Game Show Network, we're not just imagining all the possibilities. We're working on them, now, as we prepare to unveil America's first around-the-clock game show cable service utilizing the latest advancements in interactive technology. Viewers at home will watch, play, and win. And those who join our fast-paced team will meet the challenges and make their mark, as they get in on the most exciting game in town. For all positions, we seek detail-oriented and motivated self-starters who work well in a team environment.

Available for Hire

Hello, everybody. My name is Most-Compelling Smith, and I am a 23-year-old huge fan of Interactive Television who hopes to be an ITV producer someday, although I feel a little ahead of my time. My interests lie in the more consumer-oriented applications, such as interactive advertising, consumer targeting, children's programming, etc. I graduated Cecil College in Virginia recently with a B.S. of Communications and a Computer Science minor. I have interned for Jenson Interactive in Hollywood, CA, and have produced interactive applications for RBOCs on the east coast. I hope to soon gain employment in the interactive television field; however, we all know it is slim to none except at educational institutions. Private sector applications of ITV are mostly limited at this time to interactive trials in selected areas of the United States. I invite conversation pertaining to any of the above mentioned subjects (or anything else . . . I like skiing, golf, and banjo playing). I wish you all well in ITV as well as other pursuits. I'm Ready!

We asked our students to check with some local industries to see if they were working on providing any distributed multimedia products or services. Our students found companies working on technologies relating to set-top boxes, client-server networking, operating systems' multimedia extensions, multimedia servers, and real-time animation to be included in multimedia training delivered over high-speed networks. These projects were in addition to some local businesses that produced fancy presentations and home pages that use several media. The work was at stage 4 in Table 8.4's stages of technology deployment. The students were disappointed to learn that there currently were no local openings. However, the providers indicated that if they achieved some success in winning contracts, they would become interested in good applicants, so the students should keep in touch.

HISTORY

Education

As you can see from the dates and events in Table 8.6, it has taken humanity a very long time to learn to read. It is only within the last decade that various providers have established educational programs that address the integrated nature of distributed multimedia.

Adoption Rates

What can history tell us about how long the nation will require to adopt and thoroughly integrate distributed multimedia into its people's lifestyles and working environment? Depending on your assessment of yourself, from wait-and-see to pioneer, early adopter, and beyond, knowing the history and technology adoption cycles of such new technologies can help you plan a schedule for when to acquire skills yourself. Table 8.7 indicates that consumers have been adopting new technologies increasingly quickly. If you view multimedia as merely the next product in this sequence, you might add distributed multimedia at the bottom of the table and extrapolate the trend. You then might predict that half the nation's homes will have multimedia networks within a handful of years.

However, there is another way to read the table. Individual consumers could make relatively small investments in the last three products and see almost instantaneous benefits. The first product, cable television, required a large investment at the community level, in antennas, cables, amplifiers, and set-top boxes, before anyone could see a benefit. Many of the distributed multimedia applications discussed will require still greater investments, at the state level or even national level, before producing significant benefits. Reading the table this way, you would put distributed multimedia above cable television, extrapolate the trend, and predict that half the nation's households will have some distributed multimedia applications in a couple of generations.

Yet another way to estimate time frame would be to treat distributed multimedia as something comparable to the invention of the printing press in the fifteenth century. That is, we will require major changes in the ways we acquire and prepare information and go about operating our daily and working lives. In this case, if it is at all like the printing press, we may have to wait for several generations.

Does this mean that you can postpone acquiring skills? Well, it depends. Even if the build up of multimedia is very gradual, there may be good rea-

Table 8.6 Reading and media literacy history.

Date	Event
1636	Harvard opened.
1852	Massachusetts became first state to pass a compulsory school attendance law.
1918	Every state had a compulsory school attendance law.
1945	Several nations, which started the century at reading illiteracy rates of 70 percent or greater, virtually eliminated illiteracy.
1985	MIT started offering graduate degrees and undergraduate study in Media Arts and Sciences. They defined this as, "The study, invention, and creative use of enabling technologies for expression and learning by humans and machines." Research was an important component of the program. Students and faculty conducted research in the Media Laboratory.
1989	Florida State University's masters program in Interactive Communications, a unique learn-and-earn program involving authoring multimedia projects for FSU partners, began to award graduate degrees. Carnegie-Mellon University's graduate program in Information Networking began as a 14-month program integrating four major elements: communications, computers and information technology, business applications, and policy studies.
1993	Over one-third of Americans lacked functional literacy skills. That is, even if they could read, they could not interpret complex reading materials. Also, the functional literacy of college students declined.
1994	Thirty percent of homes had computers, indicating some level of computer literacy. Most K–12 schools had some computers but over 80 percent were out of date and some schools had too few computers to make any difference; 10 percent were sold with CD drives.
1995	Georgia Institute of Technology surveys showed that the ratio of men to women on the Internet was rising but still was about five men to one woman.

sons to start acquiring skills now. For instance, you may want to be an active participant with a well-paying, interesting job from the very early stages.

Stages in Marketing High-Technology Products

It might help you decide where you want to be to understand where various distributed multimedia applications are in a given point in this journey. We refer you to some of the tables in Chapter 6, specifically Table 6.11, which

Table 8.7 Penetration of consumer technologies.

Product	Year of introduction	Approximate number of years to penetrate half of U.S. homes
Telephone	1900	70
Car	1908	60
Cable television	1952	32
VCR	1975	15
Video game	1977	13
CD-DA audio player	1983	8
Personal computers	Early 80s	15+

stresses stages of marketing efforts for application categories. You may need to update these tables to reflect your current time frame. You may be dismayed to note where you are in relation to where your company, market segment, or friends are. Your analysis may turn up something like Table 8.8. While we do not want to infer that we encourage or in any way recommend blindly following, we do recommend that you consciously question whether this is where you want to be.

DIFFERENCES

In each of the earlier chapters, we have noted large differences between the vision and the state of the art for the chapter's part of distributed multimedia. The same large differences apply to an even greater extent in this chapter. Achieving the chapter's vision requires a step-by-step journey on what may seem to be a torturous road.

Any successful new technology, such as the telephone, passes through stages in which the technology appeals successively to researchers and pioneers, early adopters, the mass of society, and the laggards of society. Distributed multimedia is sufficiently diverse and sufficiently new to have portions that are at each of the earlier stages. This will continue to be true for many years.

The largest difference between vision and state of the art is in the difference between skills required and skills available for creating multimedia content. Relatively few people, even as a fraction of involved researchers, have

Table 8.8 Sample personal assessment.

Application categories Stages	1	2	3	4	5	6	7	8
Pioneers	I	I		I		I, C, G		I, C, G
Early adopters	C, G	C, G	My friends My company	C, G	My friends My company	*C, G*	I, C, G	*I, C, G*
Early mass market			I, C,G	My company	C, G			
Late mass market								
Laggard with respect to my company and friends			Me	Me	Me			

Key: Category: (1) desktop video conferences with collaboration; (2) multimedia store-and-forward mail; (3) consumer edutainment, infotainment, sociotainment; (4) shopping and advertising; (5) digital libraries; (6) video on demand; (7) educational and health applications; and (8) hybrid applications.

(I) for individuals; (C) for corporations as users; and (G) for the government as users of applications.

The italicized *I, C,* and *G* indicate current movement, whereas bold letters indicate the cells where the majority of each **I, C,** and **G** are located.

sufficient skills to create acceptable multimedia for entertainment, education, or social communication. Yet achieving the vision for multimedia will require the mass of society to develop some level of such skills. Please remember that these are not just skills at glitz and glitter, but skills of analysis, synthesis, and representation of information.

Quite independent of the time required to wire the nation with a suitable multimedia delivery system, history would lead us to believe that educating the nation to take advantage of this capability will require at least one generation. The extent to which yesterday's schools emphasized thinking linearly and expressing thoughts in linear text, seriously constrains today's adults. To the extent that tomorrow's schools emphasize creating multimedia to improve the efficiency and effectiveness of all education, the next generation of adults may be comfortable with using multimedia in their working and personal lives (Agnew et al., 1996).

TRENDS

This section discusses trends that individuals as consumers, employees of companies, and officials of governments are starting to follow to identify and acquire the skills they need.

Individuals

The trend has been to send people to many conferences that feature a few carefully nurtured, fragile demonstrations. However, as time progresses, there are better, more illustrative, more robust demonstrations that you can see up close and perhaps even try out. Here are two examples. (1) You can see futuristic demonstrations such as Oracle's Information Superhighway exhibit at Epcot in Disney World, Orlando, Florida. This exhibit includes

- The first working public display of interactive television using Oracle's server program, Oracle Media Objects. You can try out five different applications on four interactive television stations. Applications include HBO on demand, the Weather Channel, interactive shopping, and fine dining at world-famous restaurants.

- An educational program, "A Peek Behind the Information Superhighway," narrated by Ben Linder, a senior engineer at Oracle.

- A short film titled, *A Day in the Life of the Information Superhighway*, that depicts a family of four using new information technology to make life easier and more exciting.

(2) You can attend a demonstration of the Internet's World Wide Web, perhaps at a local college or your local computer users' society. Clearly, seeing some of the vision in a working form is beneficial. Even a demonstration can help you clarify what distributed multimedia is all about. Of course, you must remember that what you are seeing is only a demonstration. However, even better than watching a demo for the sake of learning is starting to use some early products and services. You can sign up for commercial on-line services or the Internet to get experience on the state of the art and to share information with peers. It is clear from the rapid growth in numbers of these services that this is an important learning trend.

Table 8.9 suggests some next steps for individuals. You should neither ignore nor laugh at the preschool entry. These folks may form the market that makes distributed multimedia take off in the next 15 to 20 years.

At some point you might decide that you need to move beyond conferences, beyond demos, and beyond initial experimentation. Formal courses, workshops, and seminars that cover theory, business aspects, and practical hands-on use rather than offering merely a sales pitch or one authoring language's syntax are becoming more available.

Some community colleges offer seminars on accessing and creating content for the information highway. Many conferences offer workshops on related topics. Here are some academic possibilities. It is not necessary to sign up for a graduate degree in most cases. You can take a couple of courses as a nonmatriculated student.

On the East Coast   The Interactive Telecommunications Program at New York University, chaired by Red Burns, is a unique program designed to give a master's degree in interactive multimedia technologies. Part of the Tisch School of the Arts, the program stresses experimentation. Its six required courses are Applications of Interactive Telecommunications, Communications Laboratory, Decision Analysis, Interactive Telecommunications Technology, Introduction to Computational Media, and one of Satellite Applications and Regulation, Domestic Telecommunications Policy, or Intellectual Property and the New Technologies. It also offers many electives.

The New School in New York City offers a distance-learning course titled *Multimedia and Society*. It also offers distance-learning courses in telecommunications and creating for the electronic digital world in cooperation with Connected Education run by Dr. Paul Levinson (PLevinson@cinti.com).

The State University of New York at Binghamton offers two graduate computer science courses specifically on the theory and practice of distributed multimedia as well as several others on related computer science subjects.

The MIT Media Lab has been a pioneer in digital media research. It offers courses leading to graduate degrees. Areas of research range from learning,

Table 8.9 Individuals' next steps.

Age range	Possible next steps
Preschool	Expand home computer skills, especially on-line service expertise with new mail systems for young people. Play some of the on-line information-hunting games. Expand home computer equipment to include a modem running at least 28.8 Kbps over cable or telephone lines. Obtain guidance from skilled caretakers and family.
Students, kindergarten through graduate school	Expand information access skills, particularly skills in articulating questions to obtain desired information. Acquire and practice provider skills. Be able to create a multimedia document. Become expert in some areas, but also learn multiple skills; learn how to communicate and work across the different cultures of television, broadcasting, publishing, telephone, and computer. Try some courses in different areas. Use your library to read to keep current (see Bibliography). Buy equipment and experiment with all the media. Take an opportunity to become an intern or apprentice.
Working adults	Know your company's strategic investment plan for distributed multimedia, or participate in creating such a plan. Have a plan for yourself. Participate in trials and pilot studies. Keep up with progress and news reports. Expand creator skills including on-line skills. Go to conferences, workshops, and seminars. Attend the right sessions. Subscribe to trade journals and professional journals (see Bibliography). Seek opportunities to use such skills.
Seniors	Buy equipment along with appropriate training and assistance. Seek out community-sponsored workshops or seminars. Consider turnkey systems. Participate in an on-line service, such as one that targets seniors.

common sense, and perceptual computing to information and entertainment such as interactive cinema and the television of tomorrow.

On the West Coast   The Association for Computing Machinery (ACM) and Institute of Electrical and Electronics Engineers (IEEE) hold specialized technical conferences on multimedia at least once a year, usually on the West Coast. Presentations focus primarily on research or prototype efforts in universities' and industries' research and development laboratories. A typical conference covers topics such as researchers' efforts in content-based retrieval, creating distributed multimedia applications, various algorithms for improving continuous media playback, and experiments in information caching for delivery of video programs.

The Center for Electronic Art (CEA) offers a 10-day intensive hands-on session of which the output is a running multimedia project. This workshop costs $2000 per attendee.

UCLA offers professional studies in the entertainment industry including several courses in multimedia creation on the desktop.

San Francisco State University College of Extended Learning has, over the past couple of years, extended its many offerings on stand-alone multimedia production and business practices to include some introductory courses in networked multimedia. It has been a pioneer in multimedia offerings and is now somewhat of a pioneer in offering short workshops at attractive prices for the serious general public on networking multimedia.

The American Film Institute in California, created by the National Endowment for the Arts in 1967, sees its mission as educating people in hands-on skills and techniques in "digital discovery."

Silicon Graphics' Silicon Studio in Los Angeles, with branches in Canada, New Mexico, England, and Germany, offers short courses at many skill levels on using authoring, editing, and animation tools that relate to its product line.

In the South   At Georgia Institute of Technology (Georgia Tech), Continuing Education and the School of Literature, Communications, and Culture offer several boiler-plate technique workshops as well as workshops on legal issues. The university has courses on the Internet. It is interesting to note the interdisciplinary nature of Georgia Tech's sponsors of the workshops.

A major benefit of attending a conference or workshop is mingling and exchanging information informally with the attendees and speakers. However, all is not lost if you cannot go to a conference. You may be able to buy conference proceedings or workshop materials at a fraction of the cost of attending in person.

The reality today is that despite the trend for more, there are still too few viable educational opportunities. Many are oversubscribed. Many are very expensive. Because there are too few, you usually have to travel to a distant, inconvenient, and expensive location. It can be beneficial to start formal learning with a formal course in multimedia creation for a stand-alone system. You may very well want, and in fact need, to move on into learning about multiple client-server platforms, networking multimedia, providing for different audiences and markets, and other business and legal subjects.

While in very early stages, the trend is for well-established educational providers to move in the direction of offering more along these lines.

Companies

Companies need employees who have skills in

- Selecting a part of the industry in which the company should become involved.
- Handling the marketing, financing, business, advertising, and legal aspects of converged environments and offerings, including working successfully with partnerships, alliances, and consultants.
- Managing the high cost of entry and making sure there is a payoff.
- Understanding relevant business models from the past.
- Remaining open-minded and quick in creating new business models that work for the digital future.

Multimedia projects tend to be complex to develop, install, and operate. Block-and-tackle skills of managing the whole project, from inception, through shipment, to end of useful life, become critical. These skills include managing budgets, schedules, tests, trials, and people's performance, while motivating diverse groups of people to produce their best. Interdisciplinary and intercultural skills are particularly important. For example, traditional computer programming people have to appreciate and understand television and movie people and vice versa. Table 8.10 illustrates jobs typical of these two groups.

The people skills involved in managing and participating in teams that create inspiring, imaginative, compelling, emotional, dramatic, engaging, and magical content that people will buy are not yet well defined. The trend is recognition of this diversity with considerable experimentation and groping for what will work best. People with the right mix of skills are hard to come by. Training is virtually nonexistent at this time. Focus 8.4 describes some multimedia development experiences.

Companies need skills in preparing and managing customer expectations. They may need to prepare customers to expect to see amateur video rather than professional-quality video and to expect to select from a simple row of buttons rather than from a three-dimensional virtual mall. A company may elect to participate in hype, for the public relations value of being perceived as

Table 8.10 Some different roles.

Television and movie roles	Programming development roles
Producer	Project manager
Director	Team leader
Scriptwriter	Architects and system designers
Production team	Programmers
Editors	Integration team
Music and costumes	Interface specialists

a leading-edge company, but must trade off this advantage against the potential disadvantage of disappointing customers with initial offerings. Many companies have had difficulty overcoming customers' poor initial impressions.

Partly to avoid premature investment of research and development dollars and to avoid creating poor initial impressions, companies need employees who have know-when as well as know-how. Some of the following expected events could signal that it is time to take a significant step.

- Microsoft, RBOCs such as Bell Atlantic and U S WEST, and cable companies such as Time Warner report generally successful test results.

- Legislation and regulations affecting telephone and cable companies evolve in a beneficial way.

- Numbers of users of on-line services, including shopping and advertising, and multimedia computers with CD-ROM drives increase significantly and increase for more than just a sign-up promotional trial period.

- On-line shopping malls report significant sales as well as significant numbers of visits.

- Availability in your area of high-speed two-way multimedia networks.

- Signs of adoption or product offerings rather than trials or concept demonstrations.

- Some early mass market penetration of some of the application categories even if this penetration is in some selected niches.

- Major companies move ahead to the next stage of technological evolution in the list of stages that Table 8.4 shows.

FOCUS 8.4 Experiences in managing diverse cultures.

The decision process of many multimedia developments involves group decisions. Everyone is in on the decision process.

Many battles among computer science programmers, producers, and designers occur. Producers and designers want flash and glitz, whereas programmers are concerned with people becoming lost in interface and navigation complexity. Developers say that the primary skill required is that skill that an overall project manager needs in facilitating excellent group dynamics. Battles must result in synergy that produces something better rather than the worst of the alternatives. Secondarily, the skill involved is appreciation and trust of each other's concerns. Third, it would be helpful if everyone had some base level knowledge about the overall objectives of project, the target market, and the capabilities and limitations of the underlying technologies.

One process for development is rapid prototyping followed by extensive user testing. One skill required to manage that test well involves picking a spectrum of users and instructing them, sometimes subtly. One development manager reported that to test how easily novice users could navigate through particular sections of content, he gave testers an alternative assignment that by its nature caused the testers to use the product intensively. Unfortunately, he found out that navigating was too complex. Fortunately, he had time to make changes. ■

Timing decisions can depend on noting when key delivery system providers move from left to right in Table 8.11 and incorporate more of the devices in Table 8.12. Alan G. Merten, the Anne and Elmer Lindseth Dean, S.C. Johnson Graduate School of Management, Cornell University, comments in Focus 8.5 on timing as well as trends in one of our nation's leading schools.

Finding the right market is as important as finding the right product and the right time. Even providing a product that is far down on a survey of consumers' interests can draw millions of customers and can be highly profitable. Products aimed toward children have high promise. Parents are willing to pay for educational interactivity. People who have skills to study the market, study the stage of technology, and proceed astutely are as scarce as hen's teeth and are incredibly valuable to a company.

Many companies' employees are far beyond initial steps toward distributed multimedia. Two examples are Boeing and Industrial Light and Magic. Boeing has decided that its very survival as a business depends on its employees' running a largely paperless operation and using the most advanced design tools. It has been investing hundreds of millions of dollars in an ad-

Table 8.11 Choice of providers' approaches.

Bandwidth downstream	High	Moderate	High
Bandwidth upstream	Low	Moderate	High
Cost to build	Relatively low	Low	High hundreds of billions of dollars
Key feature	Highly asymmetric	Switched connections for the masses	Unique video for each customer
Uses	Video on demand Gambling Shopping	Information Voting	Distance learning Two-way video communication Interactive television
Time frame	Soon	Possibly soon	Not soon
Fiber runs to	Neighborhood of 500 homes	Neighborhood of 500 homes	Curb near 6 homes
Approach	Improved CATV	Improved telephone ISDN	ATM

Table 8.12 Stage of use of end-user devices with delivery approach.

Bandwidth downstream	High	Moderate	High
Bandwidth upstream End-user device	Low	Moderate	High
Television and set-top box	Trials with pioneers and early adopters	—	Visionary talks
Personal computer	Cable modem trials downstream and telephone upstream for pioneers and early adopters	Pioneers and early adopters with top-of-the line modems and ISDN	Cable modem trials both ways for pioneers and early adopters
Other devices such as AT&T VideoPhone	?	Pioneers	Corporate video conferencing rooms

FOCUS 8.5   Interview with:

Alan Merten

Dean of Cornell University's Johnson Graduate School of Management

How will wide access to information expressed in all media, converged into the same digital form, affect management, education, and work?

The first effects of the new information technology will be to make it more convenient for people to get at information that already exists. Any successful new technology first makes it easier for people to do things they already do. It is a mistake to jump too quickly into using new technology to do completely new things. For example, you needed the Internet to set up this interview with me, because I am on vacation in Florida, but we are holding the interview by ordinary telephone. For another example, secretaries were happy when word processors replaced typewriters on their desks, but were bitterly unhappy when management introduced word processors simultaneously with forming large anonymous typing pools.

Even as the new information technology starts by helping us to perform existing functions, it will have revolutionary effects on us. It will redefine what work is as it enables us to interact with one another constantly, including evenings, weekends, and vacations. New rules for when and where work is appropriate will come into being, although we may not admit that the new rules exist. The nature of work is changing back from the industrial model, in which most workers go to an office, to a pre-industrial model, in which more work comes to the worker. This can be threatening and unsettling to many workers.

This technology is changing the whole experience and concept of education at the Johnson School. We are working hard to increase awareness of new information technology, on the parts of both faculty and MBA students. We are also working to improve skills in using the technology effectively and with innovation, both in education and in work environments. An increasingly large fraction of all workers will require such awareness and skills.

Information technology is changing the concept of a course, who teaches the course, where the teacher is, where the students are, and when the course is held. We have courses ranging from 0.1 credit to 15 credits. On Fridays and Saturdays, we teach short courses that last from one-half day to two days in which students earn credit toward their MBA degrees. One-third of these short courses deal with information technology. We use two-way videoconferences not only to accommodate teachers on campus in Ithaca, New York, and Executive Education students at the Cornell Club in New York City, but also to accommodate teachers in Washington, D.C., and full-time MBA students in Ithaca. Each side of the videoconference can control where the other side's video camera points. Long after a guest lecturer's class, students can contact the lecturer by way of the Internet.

The same technology will allow several business schools to collaborate, so that, for example, not all schools need faculty members who are wizards at derivatives. I recently exchanged guest lectures with another school using CU-SeeMe over the Internet. Although Cornell's vigorous tool development activities place us ahead of the pack in the area of tools, such tools will be common within five years. In courses on information technology skills, we teach how to use tools such as collaboration programs and databases. Courses in the standard curriculum, such as marketing and accounting, teach more detailed usage. After all these years of using information technology in organizations, we remain unsure of what common body of information systems skills and knowledge all MBA students need. We will need to work closer with the suppliers and innovative users of these technologies, and we will need to accommodate to constant change.

How quickly do you expect today's telephone, cable television, and computer industries to converge?

These industries have already converged, with significant effects on the environment of companies in these and other industries.

Do digital information technologies provide significantly new markets and industries to analyze for which MBA students need to learn new concepts and techniques?

The extremely rapid convergence of several previously completely separate

industries has already caused major problems for important companies. An early example was Wang's failure to recognize that general-purpose personal computers could replace special-purpose word processors. One or two such mistakes, such as attempting defense of an indefensible niche, can mean the end of a large company. Many medium-sized companies will not make it. Many medium-sized financial services companies and personal computer companies did not survive times of rapid technological change. Companies that develop products because technology makes the products possible, rather than because customers want the products, risk spectacular failures. People want familiar products that give easier and better lives; only early adopters want technology, per se. As in *Crossing the Chasm* (Moore, 1991), observing early adopters is a dangerous way to predict what masses of customers will pay for, because there is a wide chasm between what these two groups want. Customers will judge new video on demand against familiar television channels and video rental stores, as they judged new word processors against familiar typewriters.

This is not all downside, however. New information technologies are giving companies the opportunity to shorten a new product's time to market and tighten ties to customers.

(cont.)

FOCUS 8.5 (cont.)

What job skills are companies looking for in new hires?

There will be high demand for telecommunications consultants, for people trained to use technology to reengineer corporations, and for information systems specialists who can determine in advance of a proposed merger or acquisition whether the proposed partners' information systems will merge successfully.

What sources of information do you recommend to business people and computer people who want to keep up with each other's fields?

Forbes, Fortune, Business Week, the *Wall Street Journal,* and others are now doing a wonderful job on relevant articles, but are not reaching all the right people. Technologists often wrongly consider the articles too fluffy, and business people also tend to skip the article as being for the "expert." Similarly, many industry confer-

ences and functional conferences (such as on retailing) provide great sessions. We find that the people who need the sessions most are least likely to attend.

Every company needs a way to get its top 10 to 20 people knowledgeable in technology and needs a way to involve its top technologists in major business issues. No longer can people on either side make the case that they need not know about the other side.

What do you see as the most important issues in this area?

First, digital information technologies will significantly change the roles of individuals in their firms. Second, supply-driven products and services are risky. Third, all students must learn about new information technologies and their potential applications. Decades of experience prove that it does not suffice to train a few to understand technology. Such understanding must be widespread. ■

Printed with permission.

---

vanced fiber-optic network, so that its employees can transmit descriptions of parts of airplanes as three-dimensional objects. Industrial Light and Magic has decided that its designers will design digitally and then transmit advanced 3-D animation and digital video special effects among several locations in California. It deems the initial trial a success, despite investing at the peak of the technology's price curve.

Governments

It is especially critical for governments to learn the effects of new technologies and business models in order to regulate and legislate wisely. Typical governments are aware of this requirement and are taking large steps forward. We describe two examples.

The Human Resources Development Council is preparing a white paper on the federal government's use of learning technologies in training and educating its workforce. The report will go to the President's Working Group on Education, Training, and Reemployment Subgroup on Technology and Learning.

In a significant step that relates to governments, approximately 2500 citizens, in four pilot markets around the United States, learned to use the Voter On-line Information and Communications Exchange (VOICE) during its first two weeks of trial before the fall elections of 1994. VOICE offers candidate profiles, independent ratings of incumbents, voter activism guides, text of local ballot issues, and locations of local polling places. Access is provided. VOICE contains information from the League of Women Voters Education Fund and Project Vote Smart. Sprint, Inc., is providing the technology along with some grant funding. VOICE is available in local libraries and over the Internet's World Wide Web.

CRITICAL SUCCESS FACTORS

A critical success factor for taking any steps toward distributed multimedia's vision is acquiring the necessary skills. Everyone needs education about what questions to ask, what they can do and how, what they can expect, how they can participate, and what they can benefit from now.

It is important to work aggressively to lobby for more convenient and pervasive ways to obtain these skills.

Companies, as entities, need to step back and realize that while as providers they carry a strong burden of making the digital world easy and fun, their employees and their customers need skills to participate.

SUMMARY

Throughout this book, and particularly in this last chapter, we have discussed the vision of progressing toward widely available distributed multimedia. We are on a journey to an environment in which most people can receive, interact with, create, and transmit all five media. We noted that today's state of the art is such that taking this journey will require many significant steps. There will be many important milestones, rest stops, and even steps backward along the way. We also noted that history indicates that such steps can take a long time. We have provided a guide to help you understand how far you have progressed on this journey and what you might do to continue, as a user or provider of distributed multimedia. In this chapter, we emphasized that one requirement for opportunity and success is that individuals, companies, and governments must attain sufficient skills to make progress along the journey possible.

REFERENCES

Agnew, Palmer W.; Kellerman, Anne S.; and Meyer, Jeanine M. 1996. *Multimedia in the Classroom.* Needham, MA: Allyn & Bacon.

Auletta, Ken, and Gilder, George. 1995. "Focal Point on Convergence." *Educom Review.* Vol. 30, no. 2, March/April. (Washington, D.C.: Educom Interuniversity Communications Council.)

Moore, Geoffrey. 1995. *Crossing the Chasm.* New York: Harper Business.

Bibliography

PERIODICALS

We strongly suggest that you read several of the following publications to deepen and broaden your knowledge of distributed multimedia and to keep your knowledge and skills current.

Communications Industries Report. Fairfax, VA: International Communications Industries Association, monthly. (703) 273-7200. (ISSN 1070-4426).

Computer Video. Falls Church, VA: JRS Publishing, bimonthly. (703) 998-7600. (ISSN 1076-7959).

Educom Review. Washington, DC: Educom, bimonthly. (202) 872-4200. (ISSN 1045-9146).

Electronic Engineering Times. Manhasset, NY: CMP Publications, weekly. (708) 647-6834. (ISSN 0192-1541).

Fortune Magazine. New York: Time, Inc., biweekly. (ISSN 0015-8259).

Inter@ctive Week. Garden City, NY: InterActive Enterprises, L.L.C., biweekly. (609) 829-9313. (ISSN 1078-7259).

Interactive Age. Manhasset, NY: CMP Publications, monthly. (708) 647-6834. (ISSN pending).

Lightwave. Tulsa, OK: PennWell Publishing Company, monthly. (603) 891-0123. (ISSN 0741-5834). (This periodical is focused on fiber-optics technologies and applications throughout the world.)

TWICE — This Week in Consumer Electronics. Newton, MA: Cahners Publishing Company, biweekly. (ISSN 0892-7278).

Upside. San Mateo, CA: Upside Publishing Company, monthly. (415) 377-0950. (ISSN 1052-0341).

Wall Street Journal. 200 Liberty St., New York, daily. (ISSN 0099-9660).

BOOKS

Agnew, Palmer W.; Kellerman, Anne S.; and Meyer, Jeanine M. 1996. *Multimedia in the Classroom*. Needham, MA: Allyn & Bacon.

Blattner, Meera M., and Dannenberg, Roger B. (eds.). 1992. *Multimedia Interface Design*. New York: ACM Press.

IBM. *High-Speed Networking Technology: An Introductory Survey*. 1993. Document no. GG24-3816-01. Raleigh, NC: IBM International Support Center, June.

IBM. *Multimedia in a Network Environment*. 1993. Document no. GG24-3947-00. Boca Raton, FL: IBM International Support Center, March.

Keyes, Jessica. 1994. *The McGraw-Hill Multimedia Handbook*. New York: McGraw-Hill. (Contains a very useful annotated set of references and resources for multimedia technologies.)

Lynch, Daniel C., and Rose, Marshall T. 1993. *Internet System Handbook*. Reading MA: Addison-Wesley.

JOURNALS

Multimedia Systems. Secaucus, NJ: Springer-Verlag New York and ACM Press, 6 issues yearly. (201) 348-4033. (ISSN 0942-4962).

PROCEEDINGS

Proceedings of the International Conference on Multimedia Computing and Systems. 1994. Sponsored by IEEE Computer Society Task Force on Multimedia Computing, Los Alamitos, CA, May 14–19. IEEE Computer Society Press.

OTHER SOURCES

The Public Register's Annual Report Service. Woodstock Valley, CT: Bay Tact Corporation. (800) 426-6825.

Individual, Inc. FAX clipping service, 84 Sherman Street, Cambridge, MA 02140. (800) 414-1000.

Luther, Arch C. 1991. *Digital Video in the PC Environment.* 2nd ed. New York: McGraw-Hill.

Wodaski, Ron. 1992. *Multimedia Madness.* Carmel, IN: Sams Publishing.

"Interactive Video Data Services." 1991. Industry Perspectives, Bain and Company. April 15.

Index